Judicial Administration and Space Management

Copyright 2001 by F. Michael Wong. This work is licensed under a modified Creative Commons Attribution-Noncommercial-No Derivative Works 3.0 Unported License. To view a copy of this license, visit *http://creativecommons.org/licenses/by-nc-nd/3.0/*. You are free to electronically copy, distribute, and transmit this work if you attribute authorship. *However, all printing rights are reserved by the University Press of Florida (http://www.upf.com). Please contact UPF for information about how to obtain copies of the work for print distribution.* You must attribute the work in the manner specified by the author or licensor (but not in any way that suggests that they endorse you or your use of the work). For any reuse or distribution, you must make clear to others the license terms of this work. Any of the above conditions can be waived if you get permission from the University Press of Florida. Nothing in this license impairs or restricts the author's moral rights.

Florida A&M University, Tallahassee
Florida Atlantic University, Boca Raton
Florida Gulf Coast University, Ft. Myers
Florida International University, Miami
Florida State University, Tallahassee
University of Central Florida, Orlando
University of Florida, Gainesville
University of North Florida, Jacksonville
University of South Florida, Tampa
University of West Florida, Pensacola

Judicial Administration and Space Management

A Guide for Architects, Court Administrators, and Planners

Edited by F. Michael Wong

University Press of Florida
Gainesville · Tallahassee · Tampa · Boca Raton
Pensacola · Orlando · Miami · Jacksonville · Ft. Myers

Copyright 2001 by F. Michael Wong
Printed on acid-free paper
All rights reserved

06 05 04 03 02 01   6 5 4 3 2 1

Library of Congress Cataloging-in-Publication Data
Judicial administration and space management: a guide for architects, court administrators, and planners / edited by F. Michael Wong.
p. cm.
ISBN 978-1-61610-141-1
1. Court administration—United States. 2. Courthouses—Space utilization—United States. I. Wong, F. Michael.

KF8732 .J83 2001
347.73'13—dc21   00-053661

The University Press of Florida is the scholarly publishing agency for the State University System of Florida, comprising Florida A & M University, Florida Atlantic University, Florida Gulf Coast University, Florida International University, Florida State University, University of Central Florida, University of Florida, University of North Florida, University of South Florida, and University of West Florida.

University Press of Florida
15 Northwest 15th Street
Gainesville, FL 32611-2079
http://www.upf.com

This book is dedicated to my father, Andrew; to my late mother, Jean; and to my professor and mentor, Professor Emeritus Henry J. Cowan, of Sydney, Australia.

Contents

List of Figures and Tables xv
Preface xvii
Acknowledgments xxiii

Introduction 1
   Wednesday, June 22, 2020 1
   Space Management and Judicial Administration Integration 6
   Project Planning and Implementation 15

1. Caseflow and Space Management 17
   The Objective Is Justice 17
   A Complex Interdependent Process 17
   The Impact of Decentralization 22
   Specialization Impact 23
      Assignment of Judges to Specialized Areas 23
      Assignment of Cases to Judges and Departments 23
   Scheduling of Cases for Judicial Action 24
   Information Support 25
   Impact of Caseflow Management on Courtroom Assignment 26
   Changes in Caseflow Management 31
   Impact of Caseflow Management Changes on Trial Court Facilities 34
      Judicial Facilities—Courtrooms and Judges' Chambers 35
      Direct Judicial Support Facilities 39
      Indirect Judicial Support Facilities 43
      Law Library Facilities 48
      Shared Facilities 52
      Settlement Conference Areas 53
      Attorneys' Conference and Witness Rooms 53
      Shared Facilities for Support Agencies 54
      Attorneys' Lounge 55
      Bailiff's Facilities 56
      Law Enforcement Facilities 57
      Prisoner-Holding Facilities 58
      Transportation of Prisoners 60
      Videotape Recording Areas 61
      Public Facilities 61
      Courthouse Security 63

Accessibility Considerations 66
    Courtrooms 67
    Jury Assembly and Deliberation 67
    Courthouse Holding Facilities 67
    Restricted and Secure Entrances 68
    Security Screening 68
    Two-Way Communications Systems 68
    Outlets for Communications Systems 68
    Assistive Listening Systems 68
    Rationale for Accessible Courtrooms 68

2. Court Personnel, Structure, and Space Management 70

Personnel Systems 70
    Merit Systems 71
    Patronage 71
    Collective Bargaining 72
    Legal Framework Relating to Court Personnel 72
    Federal Requirements 72
    Court Rules 73
Basic Court Structure—Appellate Courts 73
    Personnel 73
    Appellate Court Facilities 76
    Facility Planning Considerations 79
Basic Court Structure—Trial Courts 81
    Personnel 82
    Trial Court Facilities 86
Personnel Management and Other Aspects of Court Administration 87
Trends Affecting Court Personnel 88
    An Overview 88
    Trial Court Consolidation 89
    Impact on Court Personnel 90
    Increase in Use of Hearing Officers (Parajudges) 91
Changes in Facility Configuration and Use and the Impact on Court Personnel 92
    Rural Trial Centers 92
    Branch Courts 93
    Neighborhood Courts and Dispute Resolution Centers 93
    Transcript Preparation 94
    Public Service Employees 95
The Prospect for Change 96
    Funding 96

3. **Jury and Space Management** 98
    Historical Perspectives 98
    Legal Requirements of Jury Use 100
    Component Areas of Jury Management 102
    Problem Areas of Jury Management 106
        Jury Selection and Clerk's Office 113
        Jury Assembly Facilities 115
        Entrance Lobby 117
        General Jury Assembly Area 117
        Jury Impaneling Rooms 118
        Jury Circulation within Courthouses 119
        Jury Facilities in Trial Courtrooms 120
        Jury Deliberation Suites 122
        Jury Sequestration Facilities 123

4. **Records Management and Space Management** 125
    Historical Perspective 125
    The Present Role of Records in Courts 126
    Factors Impacting Management 128
        External Influences 128
        Internal Influences 130
    The Record Continuum and the Application of Technology 131
        The Creation Stage 132
        The Active-Use Stage 134
        The Inactive-Storage Stage 142
        The Retention-Destruction Stage 143
    Impact of Records Management on Space Management 146
        Printing and Storage of Forms 146
        Active and Semiactive Case Records Storage 148
        Inactive-Records Storage 151
    The Records Study 152
        Study Products 154
        Facility Ramifications 155
    The Integrated Records Center 155
        Program 155
        Storage Space 155
        Storage Equipment 156
        Records Management Personnel 156
        Operating Expenses 158
    Designing the Courts Records Center 158
        Size and Type of Space 158

    Location   158
    Internal Design   159
    Equipment   160
    Security   161
  Exhibits Storage   162
    Receipt and Indexing   162
    Secure Storage   162
    Disposal   163
  Trends in Records Management   164
    Technological Application   164
    Centralized Management   164
    Facility Considerations   165

5. **Court Technology and Space Management   167**
  Introduction   167
  Characteristics of the Technology Environment   167
    The Rapidity of Change   167
    The Capability and Applicability of Technology   168
    The Affordability of Technology   168
    The Degree of Integration of Technology   168
  Technology Groupings and Their Impact on Space Management   169
    Core Data Configurations   169
    Data Exchange   171
    Data Retention   173
  Technologies in the Courthouse   174
    Automation   174
    Technologies   176
    Other Court Technologies   180
  Security Planning   182
    The Architectural Component   182
    The Technological Component   183
    The Operational Component   184
    Separation of Circulation   185
  Barrier-Free Access   185
  Conclusion   188

6. **Statewide Court Management Projects   189**
  Origin and Purposes of Comprehensive Statewide Court Studies   189
    Court Planning as an Impetus to Studies   189
    Court Reorganization as an Impetus to Studies   190
    State Agency Impetus for Court Studies   190
    Purposes of Comprehensive Court Studies   191

Scope of Comprehensive Court Studies   191
   Juvenile Justice   191
   Extrajudicial Components   192
   The Judiciary as a Special Component   192
   Auxiliary and Supporting Systems   192
   Law Reform and Rule-Making   193
   Vertical Scope   194
   Geographic Scope   194
   Time Frame   194
   Static/Dynamic Alternatives   195
   Subject-Matter Scope   195
   General Management Considerations   196
Involvement of Judiciary   197
   Importance of Involvement   197
   Method of Involvement   197
Data Collection   199
   Data Collectors   199
   Definition of Data Requirements   200
   Identification of Data Sources   200
   Development of Data-Collection Plan   201
   Development of Survey Instruments   201
   Development of Controls   203
   Conduct of Survey   204
   Editing and Follow-Up   204
   Storage   204
Transforming Data into Study Products   205
   The Raw Data   205
   Production Methodology   205
   The Basic Products   206
   Evaluation   208
Role of Space Management in Comprehensive Court Studies   208
   General Relationships   208
   Facility Financing   208
   Utilization of Court Facilities   209
   Adequacy of Facilities   210
   Relationship of Facilities to Study Design   210
Trends in Court Studies and Space Management   210
   Future Court Studies   210
   Unification Trends as a Factor in Space Management   211
   Capital Improvement Programs   212
   Dedicated Regional Facilities   212
   Statewide Judicial Management and Space Management Projects   213

7. **Statewide Space Management Projects** 214
   Goals and Objectives of Statewide Projects 217
   Methodology and Tasks 220
   Description of Tasks 221
      Project Planning and Data Compilation 221
      Judicial Facilities Information System 238
      Data Organization, Analysis, and Evaluation 239
      Judicial Facility Standards and Design Guidelines 240
      Projection of Future Needs 241
      Development of a Comprehensive Statewide Judicial Facilities Master Plan 242
      Recommending the Implementation Process 243
      Project Products 246
      Project Evaluation 248
      Court Participation 253
      Project Implementation 256
      Project Effort and Cost Considerations 258

8. **Changing Concepts and Trends in Judicial Space Management** 260
   Rehabilitation Potential of Existing Buildings 260
   Determining Building Adequacy 261
   Integration of Justice System Component Facilities 265
   Regionalization and Facility Consolidation 266
      Judicial Cost Considerations 270
      Facility Cost Considerations 276
      System Cost Considerations 276
      Local Autonomy Considerations 278
   Fair Rental Values of Judicial Facilities 279
      Analysis of Fair Rental Values in the Illinois Statewide Project 279
   Development of Branch Court Locations 280
      Criteria for Branch Court Development 284
      Functional Guidelines 285
      Branch Court Facility Standards and Design Guidelines 288
      Implementation Process 288
      Branch Courts—Conclusion 297

9. **Intergovernmental Relationships and Their Impact on Court Facility Development** 298
   The Judicial Branch—Its Role in Judicial Facility Development 298
      Separation of Powers—What Is It? 298
      How Is the Doctrine of Inherent Power Developed from the Separation of Powers? 299

Can the Inherent Power of the Court Be Used to Mandate Facility Renovation or Development? 301
Who Is Responsible for Articulating the Need for New or Improved Judicial Facilities? 305
How to Prove the Need for Improved or New Court Facilities? 305
The Impact of Court "Reform" on Court Facility Development 307
Cost-Effectiveness—A Critical Factor 307
The Executive Branch—Its Role in Judicial Facility Development 307
Executive Branch Responsibility Preceding the Appropriations Process 308
Executive Branch Responsibility after the Appropriations Process 308
The Legislative Branch—Its Role in Judicial Facility Development 310
The Importance of Understanding Legislative Composition 310
The Importance of Understanding Legislative Organization 311
Other Important Legislative Considerations 311
The Legislature as a Creature of Process 313
Timing of Legislative Contacts 314
The Legislature's Perception of the Judiciary 314
The Need for and Uses of In-House Staff and Consultants 315
Conclusion 317
Summary Checklist for More Effective Judicial-Legislative Relationships 318

10. The Financing, Funding, and Budgeting of Judicial Facility Projects 328
Philosophies and Concepts 329
Obtaining Funds for Facility Planning 329
Budgeting for the Facility 330
Obtaining Funds for Construction 331
Financing the Construction 332
Common Problems in Funding Court Facilities 333
Lack of Expertise 333
Lack of Facility Program and Standards 334
Lack of Planning 334
Lack of Continuity 334
Lack of Priorities 334
Confusion between Branches of Government 335
Lack of Coordination 335
Inadequate Information on Sources of Funding 335
Political Conflicts 336
Financing Techniques—Implementation and Constraints 336
Direct Appropriation 336

      Special Bond Issue for Courthouse Construction 337
      Federal Funds 342
      Public-Building Authorities 343
      Capital Development Authorities 344
      Using Bank Credit for Courthouse Construction 345
      Use of Fees and Fines Collected by the Court 346
      Investment of Surplus County Funds 347
      Borrowing from the State Employees' Retirement Pension Fund 347
      Appropriating or Borrowing from State Trust Funds 347
      Rental of Facilities by States 348
      Leaseback from Private Developers 349
      Regionalization and Consolidation 350
      Judicial Orders 351

11. Implementati6on of Judicial Facility Projects 352
   Adequate Funding for Project Implementation 353
   Cooperation between the Court System and Other Governmental Branches 356
      Conflicting Priorities within the Court System 361
   Management and Administrative Skills 362
   Construction Management Considerations 364
   Effective Site Selection 366
      Functional and Locational Relationships 367
      Locational Prominence of Courthouse 368
      Effect on Housing Supply and Private Businesses 369
      Proximity to Public Transportation Facilities 370
      Impact on Traffic and Parking 372
      Environmental and Site Conditions 373
      Urban Design Concepts 374
      Land and Project Costs 375
      Method of Applying Evaluation Criteria 376

12. Conclusion 380

Figures and Tables

Figures

3.1. Jury System, Facilities, and Circulation Pattern   114
4.1. Typical Personnel Organization, Integrated Records Center   157
4.2. Diagrammatic Plan of Typical Records Center   159
4.3. Records-Storage Container Arrangement   161
7.1. Statewide Judicial Facilities Project—Activities Sequence Chart   222
8.1. Courthouse Security Model of Circulation Patterns   262
8.2. Branch Court Function—Facility Used Daily   294
8.3. Branch Court Function—Facility Used Periodically   295

Tables

1.1. Court Participants and Caseflow for Criminal and Civil Case Process   19
6.1. Work Breakdown Structure—Comprehensive Courts Study   198
6.2. Identification of Data Sources   202
7.1. Project Work Plan and Time Schedule   232
8.1. Cost Comparison of an Existing Court System with Regionalization/Consolidation Concept   271
8.2. Costs to Court System between Existing and Regionalization/Consolidation   275
8.3. Analysis of Fair Rental Values for Court Facilities   281
8.4. Priorities for State Leasing of County Facilities   282
8.5. Functions, Spaces, and Users—Branch Court Function   287
8.6. Design Guidelines—Branch Court Function   289
8.7. Space Standards Summary—Branch Court Function   292
9.1. Methodology and Procedures to Improve Cooperation between Courts and Governmental Agencies in Implementing Judicial Facility Projects   323
10.1. Alternative Methods of Funding and Financing Judicial Facilities   338
11.1. Quantitative Measurement of Relative Significance between Alternative Sites   378
11.2. Quantitative Measurement of Relative Significance between Evaluation Criteria and Alternative Sites   379

Preface

Good courthouses do not happen by chance. They are the result of careful integration of space management and judicial administration—two relatively new professions. The main purpose of this book is to integrate the components of judicial administration with space management concepts, approaches, and principles and to evaluate the impact of changes in judicial administration on the planning, design, and utilization of space and facilities in judicial buildings. The relationships between space management and judicial-administration components are explored, with emphasis given to the realities of project implementation.

Judicial administration is the management of court systems. Reforms in judicial administration have been advocated by eminent jurists since the beginning of the twentieth century; improvements were not visible until the late sixties. While sophisticated administrative techniques and systems were developed and widely adopted in private industry, the judiciary continued to operate in obsolete facilities, using outdated equipment and antiquated systems. One reason for this situation was that the judicial system was not professionally managed by court administrators who had been trained in this specialized field of court management. In fact, court management did not become a profession until the late sixties and was not widely accepted by judicial systems until the late seventies and early eighties.

This situation was made still worse by the lack of communication and understanding between the judicial branch of government and the legislative and executive branches. The latter two knew very little about the judicial branch and assumed it was being managed efficiently. The annual budget of the state judiciary has always been a disproportionately small percentage of the total government budget. The judiciary's requests for improved facilities are often viewed with skepticism. Despite efforts by some judiciaries in some states to develop a better working relationship with the other two branches of government, many court systems continue to operate in substandard facilities with obsolete tools.

Space management is both the art and the science of providing adequate and suitable space and facilities to satisfy the short-, intermediate-, and long-term needs of the judicial system. It involves an interdisciplinary approach encompassing architecture, planning, operations research, financing, budgeting, and implementation. It is an art in the sense that renovation of existing court facilities has to be harmonious in materials, colors, and style with those used in adjacent existing buildings, and the design of new buildings involves considerations of function, aesthetics, site conditions, architectural materials, finishes, and other design elements. Space management is a science in the sense that projections of future needs; methods of financing, funding, and budgeting; project implementation and construction; environmental and security systems; and operational research require scientific methods and technical solutions. Space management is an integration of art and science. Not only does it define the quantity and quality of facility needs, but it also determines the most economical and most efficient methods of meeting those needs.

Most existing courthouses in this country were constructed toward the end of the nineteenth century and during the early part of the twentieth. They are invariably symmetrical in plan and constructed with masonry load-bearing walls. Structurally, these buildings will survive for centuries. Functionally and spatially, however, they have long been inefficient and inadequate to cope with the changing needs of the judicial system.

Prior to the past three decades, court systems had not changed significantly since the nineteenth century. In fact, even today, court systems in many states still cling to outdated administrative, operational, and technological methods and practices.

During the fifties and sixties, the postwar economic boom produced numerous new courthouses. Older and outdated courthouses were abandoned, demolished, or renovated for other government use. However, comprehensive facility planning within state judicial systems was practically nonexistent, and court and court-related facility needs were invariably accommodated by uncoordinated, piecemeal approaches. For example, facilities for related court functions would be assigned space several floors apart or in separate buildings; available vacant space would be assigned in willy-nilly fashion to a department whose major space might be several floors away; no priorities or procedures would be established for the assignment and planning of facilities that would benefit the entire judicial system.

The late sixties saw a trend toward stronger judicial administration. The creation of the Institute for Court Management introduced the philosophy of a judicial administration system that was more efficient and effective. The major goal of this organization was and is to train court executives capable of managing the court system with the most advanced management and technological tools available. The National Center for State Courts, a nonprofit organization dedicated to the modernization of court operation and the improvement of justice at state and local levels, was created in the early seventies. The master's degree program in legal administration at the University of Denver School of Law commenced in the early seventies and was the first and only law-school-based program created to train regular graduate students in the field of court administration and management. Other programs, notably at the University of Southern California, continue to offer professional training.

The improvement of court management was accompanied by an awareness among judges, lawyers, court personnel, architects, and planners that larger and better-designed facilities were needed to accommodate a more effective administration of justice. In 1968, through the joint effort of the American Bar Association and the American Institute of Architects, a substantial research grant was awarded to the University of Michigan by the Ford Foundation. The Judicial Facility Study, a two-year research program conducted jointly by the Department of Architecture and the School of Law at the University of Michigan, resulted in the publication of the first reference text in the unique field of courthouse architecture, titled *The American Courthouse* (ABA and AIA joint committee, 1973). The main purposes of this project were to establish minimum standards for the design of courthouses in the United States and to create a greater awareness among architects and planners of the complexity of courthouse design. A survey of historical and contemporary courthouses in this country was also made.

As part of the research work for this project, the project team traveled extensively throughout the United States to compile information on the administrative, functional, and operational aspects of state court systems. In particular, valuable information was obtained on the deficiencies of the court facilities visited. Minimum facility standards were established through a detailed analysis of functional and operational needs of judicial systems in more than thirty states.

Between 1970 and 1972, the United States Department of Justice, through its research arm, the Law Enforcement Assistance Administration (LEAA), funded a two-year program to solve critical facility problems in one of the largest court complexes in the country—Foley Square Courthouse Complex in New York City. This program, sponsored by the Appellate Division of the First and Second Judicial Departments of the State of New York, resulted in the publication of an eleven-volume report on solving facility problems peculiar to the New York Judicial System, a series of eight monographs on general planning, programming, and design of courthouses, and a reference text by F. Michael Wong published in 1973 by the United States Department of Justice, titled *Space Management and the Courts: Design Handbook*. The material presented in this handbook was compiled from several years of extensive research, with information and statistics gathered from more than thirty states. Many concepts, recommendations, standards, and guidelines contained in the handbook remain applicable to judicial-facility problems nationwide.

Both *The American Courthouse* and *Space Management and the Courts* have been widely distributed over the past three decades and are extensively used by architects and planners involved in court-facility projects, as well as by judges, court administrators, and others in the legal profession. The immediate impact of these publications has been a more acute awareness among judicial, architectural, and administrative personnel of the serious problems of our court facilities today, and the need for better and more functional planning and design, so that court operations could be adequately and suitably accommodated.

In 1975, the American Bar Association Commission on Standards of Judicial Administration published a supporting study titled *Courthouse Design: A Handbook for Judges and Court Administrators*. The report explores the process by which a new courthouse is created, and suggests general guidelines and procedures applicable to courthouse design. In 1976–77, the National Clearinghouse for Criminal Justice Planning and Architecture published a series of monographs titled *Guidelines for the Planning and Design of State Court Programs and Facilities*. These guidelines examine the existing judicial structure and its problem areas, particularly in the area of criminal courts. Major topics covered by these guidelines are system planning concepts, court planning concepts, prosecution planning concepts, defender planning concepts, courts of juvenile jurisdiction, and court-system computer applications. The concepts and information contained in these guidelines are compiled largely from previous reports and publications in this field. The project was funded by LEAA.

Over the past decade, there has been increasing awareness of the need for courthouses to be accessible to the elderly and the physically handicapped. The passage of the Americans with Disabilities Act (ADA) requires that all buildings be accessible to persons with physical, mental, and sensory disabilities. The 1991 conference conducted by the ABA Commissions on Legal Problems for the Elderly and on the Mentally Disabled resulted in the publication of its recommendations, titled *Towards a Barrier Free Courthouse: Equal Access to Justice for Persons with Physical Disabilities, Court-Related Needs of the Elderly and Persons with Disabilities*. Also in 1991, the National Center for State Courts published a monograph titled *The Courthouse: A Planning and Design Guide for Court Facilities*, which presents space standards and design guidelines of local trial courts. As part of the same project, *The American Courthouse,* published in 1973, was updated with a listing and photographic survey of courthouses built during the last two decades.

After more than three years of research, with funding provided by the Administrative Office of the United States Courts (AOUSC), a major revision of the *U.S. Courts Design Guide* was completed, approved, and adopted by the Judicial Conference of the U.S. Courts at its annual conference in March 1991. This guide provides all space standards and design guidelines for the planning, programming, and design of all federal court facilities nationwide. All federal court facilities planned and designed in new construction or renovation projects are required to comply with the guidelines and standards contained in this guide. The General Services Administration (GSA), the landlord of the federal government, has numerous other requirements that must be adhered to in the planning and design of all federal courthouse facilities.

Over the past two decades, more than a dozen states, and in particular those states that are responsible for the funding, construction, and maintenance of courthouses on a statewide basis, have developed judicial-facilities master plans, space standards, and design guidelines for the planning, programming, and design of court facilities in their respective states. This step was taken in an attempt to provide greater consistency and uniformity in the design quality of the various types of spaces normally provided in county courthouses statewide.

The main purpose of presenting the above list of publications is to familiarize architects and planners with the limited sources of planning and design information in this field; the complexities of the court systems in the United States; and the need for architects and planners to become knowledgeable in the operational and spatial requirements of the court systems prior to the planning and design of court buildings. Information contained in these publications was developed from an approach of developing architectural and planning requirements without equal consideration being given to changing judicial-administration requirements. The expanded purpose of this book, with contributing papers from practicing state court administrators and nationally recognized educators and consultants in judicial administration, is to explore the future limits of space management concepts, standards, guidelines, and requirements as they are applied to accommodate the changing needs of judicial administration and its many components.

Acknowledgments

The original manuscript of this book, titled *Space Management and Judicial Administration Integration,* was completed in 1981. That manuscript arose from the realization that courthouses in this country were being planned and designed by planners and architects without sufficient knowledge of court operations and judicial management. Similarly, judges and court administrators were not sufficiently knowledgeable of the complex issues involved in the planning, design, and construction of courthouses. It became apparent that the integration of space management and judicial-administration issues, concepts, and information would serve to bridge this communication gap.

The approach to producing the original manuscript was the personal involvement of nine of the most experienced and knowledgeable state court administrators and judicial educators and scholars in the preparation of position papers in various areas of judicial administration. The following are the contributors of the initial position papers: "Caseflow Management," Ernest L. Friesen, Former Dean, Whittier College School of Law, Los Angeles, California, and Former Executive Director, Institute for Court Management, Denver, Colorado; "Personnel Management," Harry O. Lawson, Director, Master of Science in Legal Administration, College of Law, University of Denver, and Former State Court Administrator for the State of Colorado; "Jury Management," Benjamin S. Mackoff, Former Circuit Court Judge, Cook County, Illinois, and Former Court Administrator, Circuit Court of Cook County; "Records Management," Robert C. Harrall, State Court Administrator for the State of Rhode Island; "Court Automation," Larry P. Polansky, Former Executive Officer, District of Columbia Courts, Washington, D.C.; "Communications Technologies," Ernest H. Short, President, Ernest H. Short and Associates, Inc., Sacramento, California; "Statewide Court Management Projects," Robert W. Tobin, National Center for State Courts, Washington, D.C.; "Intergovernmental Relations," Phillip B. Winberry, Former Administrator of the Courts for the State of Washington; "Financing, Funding, and Budgeting," William G. Bohn, Former State Court Administrator for the State of North Dakota.

All architectural and space management materials that were integrated with the judicial management component in each chapter of the original manuscript were prepared by Dr. F. Michael Wong, President of Space Management Consultants, Inc. (SMC), with invaluable assistance and support provided by SMC's professional, technical, and administrative staff. Dr.

Wong also contributed position papers that became chapters 7, 8, and 11 of this reference text.

Since the completion of the original manuscript in 1981, there has been considerable change in several areas of judicial administration, particularly in the area of court automation and communications technologies. Dr. Robert C. Harrall, State Court Administrator of Rhode Island and one of the original contributors, collaborated with Dr. Wong in the rewriting of chapter 5, "Court Technology and Space Management," which replaces two original chapters in the 1981 manuscript. Dr. Harrall also spent a considerable amount of his personal time to assist in editing the present work.

Introduction

Wednesday, June 22, 2020—Telenews Report—Philadelphia, Pennsylvania

An automobile, stolen in Rapid City, South Dakota, was located in Philadelphia last week through the use of one of the new vehicle observation devices (VODs) recently installed at all bridge and major highway connection points in the city. The VOD automatically identified the car and its license as corresponding to a stolen car description entered into the national auto file in South Dakota only two hours earlier; the device then notified Philadelphia police of the location, direction of movement, and speed of the vehicle. The car was stopped by police officers, who, through the use of sensing devices, determined that the car's two occupants were armed.

Since police officers no longer carry firearms, it was necessary for the officers to use their magnetic sealing equipment to protect themselves. In sealing the car, they also ensured that any evidence in it could not be removed or discarded.

The sealed suspects' car, with its occupants, was removed to the central investigation and arraignment facility, where, upon police officers' entering the vehicle and officially apprehending its occupants (all under the eyes of multichannel video and audio recording equipment), it was determined that contraband from an early-morning robbery in Philadelphia was inside the vehicle as well as the two weapons (pistols) indicated by the sensing equipment.

The two suspects were electronically fingerprinted and photographed, with the electronic images of both items being transmitted over communication lines directly to the National Central Identification Office in Kansas City, Missouri. Positive identification was returned to Philadelphia in less than five minutes over the communication device. The identification report contained an extensive criminal record for one suspect and no record for the other.

Meanwhile, the Philadelphia robbery victims were contacted by the Philadelphia District Attorney's Office and a videophone lineup was arranged to attempt to make a positive identification of the suspects. The public defender took part in the fair selection of three-dimensional photographs to be used for the videophone lineup, and the entire lineup procedure was videotaped in anticipation of possible challenge in court at some future date.

Concurrently, the arresting officers, back at their precinct station, were entering all of their report data into the computerized Police Arrest Reporting System (PARS). The data were simultaneously transmitted to the computerized court files, where a new case record was automatically initiated for each defendant.

At the same time, at the prosecutor's office, an experienced trial attorney was viewing the videotape of the apprehension, arrest, and lineup identification, as well as other video materials. He then activated a computer file in which he read the arresting officers' reports and reviewed the criminal record of the suspects. This trial attorney, who was also an assistant prosecutor, then entered into the computer, via his office terminal, the specific charges upon which he recommended the case proceed and provided the office recommendation regarding bail. If any question had arisen regarding the charges, he would have contacted the arresting officers and/or the victims, via videophone.

Meanwhile, the suspects, now fully identified and officially charged, had been brought to the arraignment complex, where they were interviewed by the pretrial release agency. This interview, designed to provide a basis for the arraignment judge's decision on the pretrial status of the suspects, also took place over the videophone. However, this video communication line was a private line, and the suspects were provided with a private, soundproof room in which to take part in the interview. The interviewer was physically located at the pretrial release agency office, where he had instantaneous access to the agency's files. These files were a combination of computer, microform, and CD ROM media and provided a complete record for everyone who had ever been previously serviced by the agency. Responses by the suspects to the questions posed by the interviewer were entered directly into a computer terminal, where those answers which were automatically verifiable, such as property ownership, driver's license, school affiliations, voter registration, previous criminal record, and so forth, were checked and a releasability score provided by the system. Other responses were verified through the files of the agency, which were stored on optical disks. Values were assigned to the responses based on a statistical evaluation of previous defendants' responses over a period of years and on the relationship of those responses to the incidence of delayed trial completion resulting from defendants' willful failure to appear. The computer arrived at a final score for each of the suspects and inserted this "recommendation value" into each suspect's computer record after verification and review by the pretrial release interviewer.

The suspects were also provided private videophone communication with their counsel or, if they could not afford private counsel, with the Public Defender's Office. Because of the recently enacted state rules for criminal discovery, their counsel was then entitled to, and provided with, access to all computer file data recorded to this point regarding their client and the case against their client. Copies of documents, when requested, were transmitted immediately over communication lines in accordance with security and privacy data regulations.

The arraignment proceedings began within one hour of the apprehension of the suspects. The judge, defense counsel (a public defender), prosecutor, arresting officers, and victims were in attendance via a closed-circuit television network. The arraignment courtroom was equipped with large screens for spectator and participant viewing as well as with a computer system terminal for the provision of entry of case information. This information, when requested or entered, was also projected onto another large-sized courtroom screen in order to assure everyone the opportunity to see all that was going on. Participants, who were connected via the closed-circuit network, were provided with multiscreen viewers, which enabled them to see all other participants, as well as the action and materials viewed in the arraignment room. All activities at all network locations were recorded on videotape for future review, if necessary.

The judge, who had been reached at his chambers in the city hall, reviewed the apprehension, police report, release interview, and prosecutor's charges at the remote TV arraignment complex in the city hall. He checked the computer, requesting the most suitable trial date for the felony involved, and was provided with three optional dates and times that the computer had recommended after it had analyzed the following data:

- the criminal procedural rules (must hold trial within five to ten days of arrest)
- the defense attorney's schedule
- the arresting officers' schedules
- the assistant prosecutor's schedule (a specific assistant had been assigned to this case by the prosecutor's office computer, based on work load, subject matter, etc.)
- the availability of courtroom facilities and staff
- witness availability
- the judicial workload and schedule

After consultation with all participants over the multiunit network, one of the dates was selected and recorded in the data system. A hard-copy notice was produced by the computer and provided to each of the participants as required by law.

The judge then called up the pretrial release actions on similar charges for defendants with comparable backgrounds and criminal history records. A decision was made, after discussion with counsel and others, to release the defendant with no previous record, subject to appearance at the trial. The second defendant, who had a rather long record and was also a fugitive from another jurisdiction, was fitted with a defendant locator bracelet (DLB) which would pinpoint the suspect's location at all times (until the DLB was removed at the court's order) and would emit an emergency signal if any attempt were made to leave the jurisdiction. Pretrial incarceration is reserved only for those few who evidence a present and apparent physical danger to others or to themselves.

In court (as required by court rule), the defense attorney formally requested a jury trial, whereupon the automated juror notification service immediately contacted the twelve-person panel required for the six-person jury utilized in criminal cases, and ordered the appearance of those twelve persons at 9 A.M. on the selected date in Courtroom No. 11 of the courthouse.

Courtroom No. 11, where the trial was held, is a compact room with a large, centrally located, three-sided overhead TV viewer screen; a desktop terminal device to one side of the judge; electronic recording media (for voice and video recording of the proceedings); only minimal staff; only a few seats for observers (a ceremonial courtroom is used for cases of high public interest); and space sufficient for only the jury, attorneys, defendants, and witnesses. Lighting and climate-control equipment maintain the area well within the limits of the standard human comfort levels.

On entering the courthouse, persons interested in viewing the trial are directed to the appropriate courtroom location by viewer devices which carry the title of all cases currently scheduled with room and time information. All other specific questions are answered by a central information office, which can be reached via house-phone connections available at all entrances and on all floors of the courthouse. This office is equipped with terminal devices which provide access to all public data on all cases currently active in the court system.

Sensing devices are also built into the courthouse security system, in conjunction with video systems, to detect the presence of weapons in the possession of visitors to the courthouse and to track the location of suspected weapon carriers.

The courtroom was sparsely inhabited at trial time. Few witnesses were required to appear in person. Most testimony, especially expert testimony, is presented over videophone in conjunction with the large multisided video screens. Where possible, testimony is prerecorded (with counsel in attendance) and is shown in court after the editing out of the testimony determined by the court to be inadmissible.

During the trial, defense counsel raised an objection to the sensing devices used in the discovery of the weapons. The judge then activated his legal research terminal and inquired into the latest status of state and federal statute and case law regarding the objection. Within minutes, the terminal response provided the Pennsylvania law (including a Pennsylvania Supreme Court decision of the previous day) and also a comparative analysis of the position of forty-six state courts of the United States where the issue had been litigated or where a statute was in effect.

After all testimony and argument was presented, the judge, with the support of specially prepared and easily understood visual aids, explained to the jurors the law to be utilized as well as the jury's responsibility to "find the facts."

During the deliberation, several questions were asked regarding specific testimony. After reaching the judge for approval and after judicial consultation with all counsel, the testimony was shown in the jury room (and on the courtroom screen) to refresh the jurors' memories.

The jury found each of the defendants guilty of three of the five charges after deliberation of several hours. (Five out of six jurors must agree on guilt in order to convict.)

After accepting the verdict from the jury, the judge activated his computer terminal requesting presentence investigation data as well as the range of acceptable sentences (consistent with the defendants' criminal records) for the crimes upon which they had been convicted. (Mandatory jail sentencing had been eliminated some years before as barbaric.)

Defendant No. 1 was placed on observed probation, and Defendant No. 2 (the one with the extensive criminal record) was sentenced to be banished to the moon colony for life. Imposition of both sentences was delayed for possible appeal. The defense counsel for both defendants were given the choice of immediate review of videotapes and voice translation printings in a soundproof viewing and/or listening area (the same facility was available to counsel during the trial, at any period of time that court was not in session) or a continuance of no more than seven days for a leisurely review of the record. Counsel for Defendant No. 1 elected immediate review and was provided a private room with access to the full trial record, the computer file on his client's case, the presentence investigation data and access to an automated legal research file. After an hour and a half of review and consultation with his defense counsel, Defendant No. 1 decided not to appeal the decision.

Defendant No. 2's counsel chose a seven-day continuance and was provided with a loan copy of the videotape as well as the official transcribed verbatim record of the trial, which was printed and available within thirty minutes of the conclusion of the trial.

The appeal of Defendant No. 2 would be heard on the seventh day, and if it is denied by the trial judge, sentence will be carried out. This defendant, who has been free subject to the wearing of the DLB, will be in court for the appeal effort. Since the sentence is banishment, the judge will give the defendant's family the opportunity to also be transported to the moon colony. If they decline, the defendant will be transported alone.

The defendant's attorney, at that point, will most likely appeal to the higher court, whereupon CD ROM copies of all documents and records as well as videotapes will be forwarded immediately to the appeals court. Computer file access will be provided to all pertinent records for the appeals court judges and their aides. If early analysis reveals no questions of first impression nor violation of procedural or legal rules, a per curium affirmation will be quickly rendered. The early analysis is partially supported by a computer review of the voice-translated record, with automated comparisons to standard procedures, changes to juries, and so forth.

If extensive review is necessary, the entire appellate procedure will take two weeks or less. The final opinion(s) of the court, formulated and finalized on word-processing equipment, will be immediately available electronically in the case decision files of the computer as soon as concurrence is achieved on the opinions, which have been carefully reviewed and edited simultaneously by the nine justices at their home office computer screens.

More than three-quarters of the technology described above is currently available, although some is still in experimental form. All the above should be technologically possible within the next ten years. Consequently, new court buildings should be designed to adequately and suitably house the changing needs of the judiciary and its complex operations.

Space Management and Judicial Administration Integration

The changing scene of judicial administration is what makes *Judicial Administration and Space Management* necessary. The decision to build a courthouse in a particular place literally sets in concrete a large number of decisions which, in the present state of the art, should be left undecided. The research is not complete on how best to allocate judicial resources within a state. The need for specialization of judges, specialized facilities, and special support personnel is yet to be decided. Buildings force premature decisions to be made.

In some respects, the examination of this material will be frustrating to the examiner. It will in turn force the examination of the biases of judges, government planners, lawyers, and the vested interests of the law in a way that sends these individuals back to the beginning rather than forward toward new monuments to justice. If these materials force the examiner to question basic premises, they will have served their purpose. If they challenge judicial administrators sufficiently to force more rational decisions, the judiciary, more than the space in which it operates, will benefit for years to come.

Decisions, of course, must be made. Court spaces must be provided. The uncertainty of modern judicial administration theory should not be allowed to impede the development of resources. The only appeal that can be made is to avoid building limited-purpose buildings. Structures should be designed and built which can be easily used for general office or meeting space if their abandonment as court facilities proves necessary. Temporary solutions should be sought for temporary problems, and each special area of potential utilization of space should be considered in developing the basic structure. Modern architecture is capable of such flexible design.

Courts serve many functions in society. They attempt to do justice, they provide a forum for dispute resolution, they record legal status, and they protect individuals from arbitrary applications of government power. Not all of these functions need to be in one location. The necessity in our scheme of government of maintaining the independence of these functions from executive and legislative interference is the unifying factor in their administration. The necessity for judicial independence is the basic reason for judicial administration being separate from public administration. Much of what follows assumes the reader is aware of and accepts this necessity. To the extent space allocation and design controls behavior, space management must be in the control of the judicial branch to make possible this independence. The integration of judicial administration with the management of spaces for the operation of the courts is thus a necessity.

The discourse that follows attempts to find and explain the interrelation of the judicial functions of American society to the spaces needed for their operations. Though these assertions may certainly be questioned, they are a substantial development beyond the conjecture of isolated efforts made in the past on the subject.

The consultant/architect team must understand the impact of space management on changing needs of judicial administration, and vice versa. Design flexibility can be prohibitively expensive when achieved without constraints. The degree of design flexibility should be determined by anticipated changes within the judicial system that impact on space management solutions.

With the influx of federal funds through the Law Enforcement Assistance Administration (LEAA) in the seventies and early eighties, experiments in implementing improvements in judicial administration were conducted. Unfortunately, many of these were attempted without the benefit of comprehensive planning and systematic evaluation. Early failures of such experimentation resulted in increased resistance from within the judicial system to administrative and technological changes. During that period, court buildings continued to be constructed or renovated without considering the complicated operational requirements and constantly changing needs of judicial system components.

Judicial administration and space management components are intertwined. Most decisions in judicial administration have direct impact on space management solutions. Similarly, space management decisions frequently dictate administrative and operational modes. Caseflow management, the central focus of judicial administration, requires different facilities for different management systems. Traditional caseflow controls have added complexity by dealing with symptoms rather than causes of problems. The master calendar, a mechanical solution to a human problem, requires space management solutions different from those designed for the individual calendar. Hybrid systems necessitate a combination, and frequently a duplication, of calendaring facilities. Future approaches, including the identification of decision points of the case-scheduling process and of information and technology needed, will require a more careful identification of facility needs and of limits in design flexibility.

Recent changes in jury management have significantly altered space management solutions. While the basic requirements of jury security and privacy remain inviolate, the variations in the size of juries for different types of cases, the changes in the processing of jurors, the length of jury service, and the selection of potential jurors by computers have changed the planning and design of jury facilities. Traditionally, jury facilities in major courthouses constitute one of the most serious misuses of space: single-purpose, oversized jury assembly spaces are grossly underutilized; each jury trial courtroom is provided with a jury deliberation suite, which, in many locations, is utilized for no more than a small fraction of regular court hours; and access to the jury deliberation room can only be gained through the courtroom. Anticipated systemic changes in notification, processing, impaneling, and sequestering of jurors, aimed at reducing operational inefficiency and waste in jurors' time, should result in more efficient design and shared utilization of jury facilities.

Court records storage invariably occupies large amounts of space in courthouses. In addition to basement and interior-building core storage spaces, prime office spaces suitable for personnel occupancy are frequently used for court records storage. In many situations, such misuse of prime office space is not the result of space shortage, but the insistence that all records should be conveniently located within the clerk's office for ready access. The lack of a coordinated system of records classification, storage, retention, and destruction is a major cause of space shortage in courthouses today. It is unpopular to take the responsibility of making decisions on which records are to be retained and which are to be destroyed. As a result, active, semiactive, and inactive records continue to accumulate and to occupy an increasing amount of valuable space that could otherwise be used more productively by other court functions. Anticipated changes in records management concepts, including a more coordinated system of managing the voluminous records generated within the courthouse, a more systematic method of storage and destruction of records, and the increased use of technological devices such as microforms, optical disks, and other forms of electronic media to record pertinent information in place of the traditional paper form, will have significant cost benefits on personnel utilization and records storage and retrieval.

Personnel management decisions have a direct impact on space management solutions, and vice versa. Traditionally, there has been an imbalance in personnel space utilization. Oversized chambers are provided for part-time judges, while clerks and probation officers share noisy cubicles in open offices. The prestige factor of position is given a higher space-allocation priority than functional requirements. This imbalance, representing a form of space misuse, frequently results in space shortage to the extent that certain departments cannot hire new personnel even though positions have been approved and funds appropriated. An even more serious problem is the indiscriminate and piecemeal allocation of available space to departmental personnel without considering the overall impact on the present and projected space utilization plan for the entire building. The lack of adherence to proper functional spatial relationships inevitably leads to serious operational and administrative inefficiencies. As court administrators gain in their awareness of space management concepts and of their impact on court management decisions, space in existing and new court buildings will be more efficiently planned and optimally utilized. Facilities developed in accordance with a comprehensive judicial facility master plan should minimize serious personnel space problems in the future.

Automated court information systems are still relatively recent innovations in judicial administration. Early applications of automated systems in the sixties by computer firms with inadequate knowledge of court operations and information management needs resulted in serious failures. Available systems include time sharing with other state and local governmental agencies, court-controlled maxicomputers in large metropolitan centers, court-controlled minicomputers, and recently introduced micro-minicomputers, personal computers, and distributive and network data-sharing systems. The impact of computer systems and equipment on space management is not as significant as the fluctuating programmers' and analysts' space requirements at various stages of software and hardware development. With the trend toward greater miniaturization of computer hardware, the computer-equipment-room size may remain constant, even with a substantial increase in capacity. On the other hand, as systems grow and become increasingly complicated, the number of programmers, analysts, database managers, and support staff is likely to increase, resulting in a corresponding increase in personnel and storage space. With the use of distributive data-sharing systems, electronic data transfer systems, and systems in which the main computer is remotely located outside of the court building, computer equipment space in future courthouses can be minimized.

Communications technology systems, including videotape recording, audio recording, closed-circuit television, security equipment, and telephone intercommunication, are becoming accepted as integral parts of courthouse planning and design. Telephone communication and audio-recording systems and equipment have been used in court buildings for many years. Security equipment and closed-circuit television were introduced into court buildings as a result of threats to judges and court personnel experienced in recent years. Videotape recordings of witness testimony can be introduced into evidence in many states. As witnesses will become less available owing to the increased mobility of people, the use of videotape recording as a valid means of presenting testimony during trials will increase. Televising of courtroom trials, with appropriate precautionary rules, adds other design factors. We are also seeing increased use of videoconferencing, particularly linking prisoner-holding facilities with courthouses, remote appellate judges' chambers with central appellate courts, and so forth. In the area of public information and communications systems, visual displays on electronically controlled boards or television monitors similar to those used in airports are already used to provide lawyers, litigants, witnesses, and the public with instant information about case status and pending actions at a central point near the building entrance. Receptionists are able to call up case information on computer terminals, similar to those used at ticket counters in airport terminals, upon request at the public information counter in public lobbies. Touch-screen monitors are installed in the public areas of clerks' offices to assist the public in accessing case-filing and case-processing information, such as in small claims and traffic cases, without the intervention of an information person. Computer terminals in public workstations or records viewing areas are also available to the public for accessing case information. Website and internet applications are expanding remote public access at a rapid rate. Anticipated increases in the application and use of communications technology systems and equipment will impact on the amount and location of equipment and personnel space in future court buildings.

The impact of changes in judicial administration on space management solutions is less significant in the planning and design of a single court building than in the development of a statewide judicial facilities master plan. The limited project scope of the former allows anticipated changes to be analyzed in greater detail within the influence of a limited geographic area. The significance of error is not as great, as it is relevant only to the particular building. In statewide judicial facilities projects, commonalities of problems and solutions within each range of courthouse size must be established in order to develop reliable facility standards and guidelines for statewide application. The adoption of these standards and guidelines has an immensely significant impact on the planning, programming, and design of all future court facilities throughout the state. For this reason, careful integration of space management and judicial administration is essential to the successful development and implementation of a statewide judicial facilities master plan. A detailed evaluation of the changing needs of each judicial administration component, and of its impact on the development of facility standards and space management solutions, may determine the short-term as well as the long-term adequacy and suitability of judicial facilities throughout the state.

Beyond statewide court projects completed over the past twenty years, the state of Alaska completed in 1978 the first and only statewide justice-facility-standards project, which integrated facility standards and design guidelines for the three major opponents of the justice system—courts, corrections, and public safety or law enforcement—were established on a statewide basis. If these standards and guidelines were incorporated into the administrative policies of the executive branch, the design of all justice-facilities improvements throughout the state would have to comply with them. The potential development of justice complexes involving all three components of the criminal justice system would significantly influence the future design of court facilities in relation to corrections and law enforcement facilities.

Changing concepts in judicial space management involve a more careful evaluation of the rehabilitation potential and true capacity of existing court buildings, and the development of more flexible new buildings to accommodate the anticipated changing needs of the total justice system. Changing concepts in judicial administration may involve system regionalization and facility consolidation, state assumption of facility costs, and development of branch courts. Cost comparison of an existing decentralized court system with a hypothetical system-regionalization and facility-consolidation model shows that, while the court system experiences some cost savings resulting from greater centralization of, and less traveling for, judges and support staff, the existing decentralized system is less costly for jurors, witnesses, attorneys, and litigants. In addition to costs involved in necessary constitutional and statutory changes, social costs and inconvenience costs to trial participants and the public are prohibitive in a system with a central trial-court location servicing several adjoining counties. The regionalization/consolidation concept requires careful experimentation, documentation, and evaluation within each state before any decision can be made for its broader application in the future.

The trend toward state assumption of court costs, including facility costs, involves an evaluation of whether the state should purchase or lease county courthouse facilities. Because age, condition, size, adequacy, and suitability of court facilities vary with each court building, a method of establishing fair rental value is needed for each state contemplating state assumption of court facility costs.

Many jurisdictions use branch courts to handle a wide range of judicial procedures in population centers outside the range of convenient distances from the main court facility. Branch courts relieve overcrowding and congestion at the courthouse and accommodate public and local police agencies by providing more conveniently located court services. In the future, branch courts are likely to be developed as alternative facility-growth solutions to courthouse space-shortage problems. Activities at branch courts could range from conducting weekly jury and nonjury trials for most types of cases to nonjury cases involving traffic and small-claims matters at infrequent intervals. For branch courts to be effective, facilities should be designed according to the specific needs of the court system and to space standards and design guidelines developed for that system.

Having developed the Statewide Judicial Facilities Master Plan or plans for individual court buildings, the obvious next step is to program, budget, fund, and finance the implementation of the master plan or the construction/ renovation of court buildings. Many problems and deficiencies exist in the present system of obtaining funds for court facility projects. The lack of facility project funding and financing expertise, of facility standards and design guidelines, of planning capabilities, of active involvement of judicial personnel in building planning and design processes, of funding priorities, of coordination between courts and related agencies, and of proper working relationships between the three branches of government are common problems and deficiencies facing administrators in their attempts to obtain adequate funds for capital improvement projects. Funding and financing methods evaluated include direct appropriation; bond issue approved by public referendum; public-buildings authorities; capital development authorities; court-generated funds; revenue-sharing funds; funding from various federal agencies; bank credit; borrowing from state-employee retirement pension funds and from other sources of state trust funds; leasing from or leaseback arrangement with private owner/developers; investment of any surplus funds;

and technical-assistance funds for minor projects. With the anticipated cutback in expenditure of public funds resulting from the recent trend in tax reduction, it will become increasingly difficult in most states to obtain sufficient funds for capital improvement projects at local or state levels. The judicial system will be forced to implement courthouse improvements through other funding methods within the limits allowed by law.

The separation-of-powers doctrine and its corollary, the doctrine of inherent power of the court, as well as the development of a strong base of intergovernmental relationships, can impact on the successful renovation of existing buildings or construction of new judicial facilities. On most issues, power rests with the party who controls the purse strings. Within this context, the judiciary's position is weak and vulnerable. The judiciary possesses no taxing power to coerce the funding of resources through the use of the veto, as can be done by the executive branch. The judiciary's real power, if such be a power, is the threat of litigation to compel, through its inherent power, the payment or appropriation of funds necessary to support its operations. This threat, to be successfully used, should be resorted to only in cases of extreme emergency. Even in such cases, the court will have to generate broad support if it hopes to be successful. Today, with escalating and/or increasingly complex caseloads facing courts at all levels and with government resources often shrinking, the court will either have to make a serious effort to collaborate with the legislative and executive branches of government in the development of an economically feasible courts-facility-improvement program, or to resort to use of the doctrine as an accepted means by which the judiciary can achieve its desired goals and objectives.

Successful implementation of any court facility project requires a combination of four essential ingredients: adequate funding and financing; effective cooperation between the court system and other involved agencies; proven management and administration skills; and an effective site-selection process. Communication gaps between the judiciary and architects/planners, a situation sometimes created by government agencies acting as owner/client, have frequently led to poorly designed and nonfunctional facilities. Experienced consultants are needed to bridge these gaps so that judicial needs can be fully and accurately translated into functional architectural solutions. A comprehensive design-team approach involving architects and space management consultants working closely with court administrators and user agencies is expected to gain broader acceptance in future major court facility projects.

Phased implementation of a facility master plan requires the integration of short-term improvements with long-term comprehensive solutions. Budgeting, funding, and financing approaches and techniques will become more sophisticated as direct funding sources become more restricted. Greater involvement of the judiciary in executive and legislative processes is essential to obtaining adequate capital appropriations. The judiciary, through its administrative arm, is likely to devote greater resources in the future to ensure its proper share of available funds. Management and administrative skills in handling large construction projects will become increasingly important criteria in the selection of court administrators in locations where major courthouse construction and renovation projects are anticipated. A competent project administrator will relieve the judiciary of heavy administrative responsibilities normally associated with such projects, and can effect greater cost efficiency to the owner/client.

Effective site selection is essential to project implementation. Site selection is seldom based on application of scientifically established evaluation criteria, unless those criteria are based on potential social and political considerations. Impacts on the neighborhood, on housing and commercial development, and on downtown rejuvenation programs are both social and political. Local interest groups can exert tremendous pressure, which frequently determines the site ultimately selected for the new court facility.

Most court buildings in the United States, even the more recent ones, have been designed without a precise appreciation of the complexities involved in the integration of judicial administration and space management concepts. Essential functional and spatial relationships have not been satisfied; separation of public, restrictive, and secured circulation patterns necessary for conducting serious criminal trials do not exist; unbalanced and piecemeal space allocation for a wide variety of occupants and users occurs; and facilities designed and planned for a single purpose go underutilized. If this discourse serves to bridge the information and communication gaps between space management and judicial administration in court facility projects, so that future buildings can be planned and designed to adequately and suitably accommodate anticipated, as well as unforeseen, changing needs of the judicial system, it will have served its purpose.

Buildings constructed today should have a life span of at least fifty years. Judicial administration as a profession did not gain recognition until the early seventies. Most state court systems have undergone substantial metamorphosis over the past twenty years. Major future changes are anticipated, as emphasis of the legal profession shifts, as judicial management continues to become a more effective profession, and as approaches to settle disputes and case determinations change. Facilities for accommodating these changes may be quite different from those we design today. Court buildings should be designed and constructed either to provide a much shorter life span so that they can be disposed of as they become obsolete, or to accommodate long-term functional and spatial changes. Facility technologies of the future may well provide such a choice. The cost of replacing disposable buildings should then be evaluated against the expenditure of funds necessary to remedy the operational problems and inefficiencies resulting from inflexibility and constraints of permanent structures.

One primary purpose of this book is to describe the elements of judicial administration components and to identify foreseeable changes. The potential impact of these changes on space management and architectural design is discussed. This book is not intended to cover the same material contained in *The American Courthouse, Space Management and the Courts,* and other available related publications; rather, it is intended to demonstrate a planning and design philosophy that court architecture should be created from an integration of operational requirements and architectural-planning solutions. The creation of architectural form without the application of a functional philosophy would be equivalent to designing an automobile that won't hold any passengers and doesn't go anywhere.

Project Planning and Implementation

Improvement of state court systems needs comprehensive planning and coordinated project implementation. Planning within court systems has often been piecemeal and haphazard—the result of providing immediate responses to urgent problems. Over the past decade, court administrators have become more appreciative of the advantages of comprehensive court administration and facility management planning. Short-term improvements are beginning to be implemented as integral parts of long-term master plans. Court administrators more and more are integrating improvements in judicial administration with emerging space management concepts. They realize now that most court management improvement projects, especially those involving jury, personnel, caseflow, records, data technology, and security systems, have a significant and influential space management component. Ignoring space requirements can create severe operational limitations on the implementation of court management programs. An understanding of the complex internal relationships between court administration elements has led to the preparation of comprehensive statewide court-improvement plans over the past two decades. Unfortunately, space management has often not been incorporated as an important component of such court management projects. Implementation of court improvements has been curtailed by the unavailability of essential facility information.

Significant changes in judicial administration and their impact on the court system can be most effectively accomplished at the state level. The sphere of influence of local changes is usually limited at the county or city level. Unless such local changes are developed as pilot projects or as models for statewide application, the advantages of such changes may not become widely known. For this reason, the responsibility of the state court administrator is important and far reaching. Where state court administrators are responsible for the management of the entire state court system—as is the case in the states of Alaska, Hawaii, Colorado, Washington, Rhode Island, among many others—their accomplishments in the various areas of judicial administration attain statewide impact and consequence. The cooperation and support of the state's highest appellate court, and of the chief justice in particular, make the implementation of administrative changes within the court system easier and more feasible. In states where the state court administrator is supported by district trial court administrators, cooperation and collaboration between state and trial court administrators is essential to the successful statewide implementation of court-improvement programs.

In the area of space management and facility improvement, procedures are needed for trial court administrators to communicate with the state court administrator on a regular basis with regard to the priority facility needs of local courts. A statewide judicial facilities project conducted with competent in-house personnel or by experienced space management consultants must be carefully coordinated with anticipated changes in court organization and judicial administration. If adequate funds are available, the statewide judicial facilities project should be conducted as an integral or at least a subsequent part of a statewide court management project. The data-compilation phase of the statewide facility project would be conducted simultaneously with the data compilation and analysis of the court management project. Once preliminary recommendations in various aspects of judicial administration have been developed, the process of integrating judicial administration with space management should begin. This relationship should continue until an integrated comprehensive statewide judicial administration and space management master plan has been evolved and refined. Such a plan would be very encompassing in scope, with recommendations and solutions developed to suit the specific short- and long-term needs of both judicial administration criteria and space management solutions.

Chapters 6 and 7 discuss in detail the concepts, methodologies, and results of statewide court management and space management projects. These are followed by a discussion of changing concepts and trends in judicial space management, and by chapters on intergovernmental relations; financing, funding, and budgeting of judicial facility projects; and judicial facility project implementation. A glimpse of future changes and their impact on judicial space management projects is included in the conclusion of this book.

Caseflow and Space Management

The basic work of any court is the orderly processing of disputes formally presented for resolution. All other work is ancillary to the process and, with a few exceptions, is designed to support it. The control of the flow of cases through the court system is the central focus of court administration, and is at best an art form far removed from scientific predictability. In its most advanced form, the management of the flow of cases is a game with slowly changing rules. In its worst form it is a free-for-all with little concern for justice.

The Objective Is Justice

The principle objective of a court system is to do justice in individual cases. The caseflow management process may be the most important device toward the accomplishment of this end. The adversary system of dispute resolution is a memory-dependent system. The hearing on an issue of fact presented to judge or to judge and jury is a forum for the presentation of witness recollection and the exploration of that recollection. To the extent memory survives with minimal distortion, justice can be done; the law can be applied to the fact. Since memory diminishes with time, any delay in the caseflow tends to reduce the ability to find the truth; justice is proportionately lost.

Though the judiciary performs other functions in society, its basic function is the just disposition of disputes. The manipulation of the caseflow to bring about delay in the disposition, or to serve other purposes of the lawyers or parties, makes the judicial process a sham and its agents hypocrites. Thus, caseflow control is more than a mechanical device to make effective use of court resources. It is the central device by which courts perform or fail to perform their proper function.

A Complex Interdependent Process

Students of management will acknowledge the complexity of the caseflow process. The large numbers of conflicting interdependencies in professional activities startle the person accustomed to orderly procedures. Instead of motivation for coordinated effort, the principal actors have motivation to disrupt their fellow processors. The fact that each of the processors is interested in an opposing product, a decision for his or her client, explains rather precisely the difference between normal workflow and caseflow. Impose upon this constraint a jury which is inadequately compensated for its time, clerks elected to administrative posts without direct responsibility to decision-makers, witnesses without motive to cooperate, and judges acting independently of any supervision, and it is a wonder that any decisions are made.

The workflow of a dispute, in fact, often originates in an office independent of the court, is recorded by an office independent of the court, is processed by at least three different independent governmental agencies, and is dependent upon the availability of persons (witnesses) not in the process for its ultimate purpose. It is difficult to imagine a system with more impediments to proper judicial activity.

Caseflow management is the art of pulling all of these diverse and sometimes opposed parties together. Thirty years ago, the basics of caseflow management had not been articulated. Fifteen years ago, they were not widely applied or accepted. Today, most major court systems have adopted some form of caseflow management, as the concept of court administration is commonly accepted and adopted in most states.

The management of the caseflow is the detailed, iterative process by which cases reach varying dispositions. No simple diagram is sufficient to model all of the possible steps of the process, and no diagram can accurately portray the interactions and adjustments which take place. Table 1.1, which lists events and their locations, illustrates this very complex interactive process.

Moreover, no two courts organize their work in the same way. Their operating procedures, however, do vary along several discernible lines which in combination make up the internal caseflow system within the courts. There are five components of each caseflow system:

- The assignment of judges to specialized tasks usually defined by divisions or departments of the court
- The assignment of cases to judges for necessary judicial action within the specialized areas
- Scheduling of the cases for judicial action
- The collection and maintenance of information necessary to support the scheduling and assignment
- The information reporting system, which reflects the performance of the court overall and in its various specialties

The variation of behavior within each of these components is substantial. Important to the operation of any caseflow system is the recognition that the

Table 1.1. Court Participants and Caseflow for Criminal and Civil Case Process

Criminal Cases

Actors	Organization (Usual)
Prosecutor	District or state's attorney's office
Defense attorney	Public defender or private office
Judge	Court
Witnesses	Independent
Courtroom deputy clerk	Clerk's office
Security officer	Sheriff's office
Process server	Sheriff's office
Secretary to the judge	Court
Case coordinator	Court
Court reporter	Court
Probation officer	Social service department
Information processor	Data-processing clerk's office
Record retriever-filer	Clerk's office
Jurors	Independent

Criminal Caseflow Ilustration

Location	Activity
Community	Crime is committed
Community	Police investigate
Community	Suspect is arrested (summoned)
Police station	Suspect is booked (jailed or bailed)
Police station	Suspect calls attorney (or friend)
Police station	Police prepare charge
Jail, office, or corridor	Suspect is interviewed by attorney
Court office	Charges are filed—clerk receives

Courtroom	Suspect appears before judge of limited-jurisdiction court:
	    to fix bail
	    to determine indigence (appoint counsel)
	    to be advised of charge
	    to be identified as the person charged

Courtroom	Suspect is scheduled for preliminary hearing
Jail, office, or corridor	Suspect is interviewed by attorney
Courtroom	Suspect attends preliminary hearing
Grand-jury room	Suspect is indicted
Jail, office, or corridor	Suspect is interviewed by attorney

Courtroom	Suspect appears before a judge of general jurisdiction court:
	    to review bail
	    to review appointment of counsel
	    to advise of indictment
	    to be identified as the person charged

(continued)

Table 1.1—*Continued*

Location	Activity
Clerk's office	Minute entries recorded
Office	Attorneys prepare motions
Clerk's office	Attorneys file motions—clerk receives
Courtroom	Attorneys appear before a judge to argue a motion
Chambers	Judge reviews brief on motion
Courtroom	Judge sets case for trial
Phone	Attorneys agree to continuance
Courtroom	Judge postpones trial on consent of attorney
Courtroom	Attorney moves for continuance
Courtroom	Judge grants continuance
Courtroom	Attorneys move for continuance
Courtroom	Judge denies continuance
Courtroom	Suspect pleads to reduced charges (in 10% to 15% of cases the suspect is tried)

*For illustration only—discovery can be accomplished by several methods less burdensome to the parties.

Civil Cases

Actors	Organization (Usual)
Plaintiff's attorney	Law office
Defendant's attorney	Law office
Judge	Court
Witnesses	Independent
Courtroom deputy clerk	Clerk's office
Secretary to the judge	Court
Court reporter	Court
Security officer	Sheriff's office
Process server	Sheriff's office
Information processor	Clerk's office
Record retriever-filer	Clerk's office
Jurors	Independent

Civil Caseflow Illustration

Location	Activity
Community	Events (accident, death, separation)
Office	Attorney-client discussion
Office	Attorney prepares papers
Clerk's office	Attorney files papers—clerk accepts papers
Community	Papers are served by officer—party receives papers (some cases end by default)
Office	Party consults attorney
Office	Attorney prepares papers (answer)
Clerk's office	Attorney files papers—clerk accepts papers

(continued)

Table 1.1—*Continued*

Community	Papers are served by officer or by mail—party receives papers
Office	Attorney consults client
Office	Attorney prepares for deposition
Community	Attorney serves notices of deposition*
Office	Attorneys, witnesses, and court reporter assemble*
Court office	Court reporter types deposition*
Mail	Court reporter is paid*
Mail	Court reporter furnishes transcript
Office	Attorney prepares a motion and brief
Clerk's office	Attorney files motion and brief
Clerk's office	Clerk schedules hearing on motion
Courtroom	Judge hears motion, reads brief (some cases settled)
Chambers	Judge studies papers and brief
Courtroom	Judge decides and announces decision
Courtroom	Judge sets a pretrial conference
Chambers	Judge holds a pretrial conference (some cases settled)
Office	Attorneys prepare a pretrial order
Clerk's office	Attorneys submit pretrial order to judge
Chambers	Judge approves and signs pretrial order
Chambers	Judge sets case for trial
Courtroom	Attorneys move for a delay (continuance)
Courtroom	Judge grants continuance and sets new trial date
Courtroom	Attorneys move for delay
Courtroom	Judge grants continuance and sets new trial date
Corridor	Parties assemble on trial date
Corridor	Parties confer and settle the case (in 10% to 15% of cases, case is tried)

* For illustration only—discovery can be accomplished by several methods less burdensome to the parties.

individual cases presented to a modern American court for adjudication are highly diverse. All cases are not equal in subject matter or complexity. All judges are not equal in experience or ability. Subject-matter labels are particularly deceiving. Some criminal cases are easily disposed of in a matter of minutes, while others can take months. Most divorce cases are disposed of without opposition, while a few involve long fights over child custody and property. The administration of caseflow must take these variables into account. No system has yet been designed that can eliminate the factor of human judgment in the assignment of cases to individual judges for disposition.

Some judges that are good at mediating a dispute are not particularly effective in controlling a complex trial. Other judges that are good in business disputes are not good in personal-injury cases. The allocation of judges for cases is an unexplored science. The future may see movement in this direction, but not without dispute. Though clearly not equal in all matters, judges are the last to acknowledge the inequalities.

In multijudge courts, the differences are usually accommodated by specialization both in subject matter and procedure. Special caseflow systems are set up for the courts operating in divisions. Classic divisions include civil jury, civil nonjury, criminal, juvenile, domestic relations, and equity. Large courts sometimes organize procedurally with motions being heard in one division, trials in another, and settlement conferences in another. The possible combinations in a large court are substantial. Most courts, including some with thirty or more judges, tend to restrict themselves to criminal, civil, domestic relations, and juvenile divisions. In most courts, cases are assigned to judges without regard to complexity or judicial experience, either on rotation or when a judge is available.

The Impact of Decentralization

The future development of specialization will turn on decisions with respect to centralization of judicial resources. Large metropolitan court centers may well yield to smaller subunits that serve local communities. Los Angeles, for instance, has chosen to decentralize the court structure by building and occupying courthouses throughout the county. As the control of court administration shifts to the state, small local courts may become consolidated into regional courts. Legislation will be needed to combine counties within the judicial region and to provide court facilities on a regional basis. Research as to the economy of scale which optimizes the use of judicial resources may suggest court complexes of twenty to thirty judges serving all judicial functions. Large, central courthouses will then tend to yield to more workable judicial units in which coordination of the available resources is more realistic. In effect, staff at the regionalized courts will be able to more effectively coordinate activities with local lawyers, local clerks, and so on, without the growing hierarchy, which becomes increasingly ineffective in controlling professionally prescribed individual behavior. As in most metropolitan centers, the location of major courthouses is determined primarily by political and geographical district lines. Funding for such facilities is also politically motivated in most situations. In reality, regionalization of judicial facilities is only implementable when it coincides with specific political agenda.

Crime is becoming more evenly spread across metropolitan areas. Business activity is widely dispersed. Tortious conduct basically follows the automobile and sale of products. If Los Angeles proves to be a viable model, local bar associations will emerge around the satellite courts. Local court facilities will catch up to the broad base of metropolitan activity, making it possible to rationalize the use of judicial manpower and control smaller caseloads with more personal attention.

Specialization Impact

In metropolitan areas which do not resort to branch court operations, specialization will have the same effect on calendaring operations as branch operation. Specialized scheduling to accommodate specialized bars will develop around subject-matter specializations. Clusters of lawyers, clerks, judges, and so forth will form to meet the specialty divisions. The practice of law in the courts will be uneconomic without this professional accommodation.

Assignment of Judges to Specialized Areas

For obvious reasons, smaller courts rarely divide into specialized departments or divisions. One or two judges in a particular locale with responsibility for all of the civil, criminal, probate, juvenile, and domestic work have to take it as it comes. In larger courts, specialization by subject matter is almost inevitable, though it is seldom accomplished along rational lines.

Rational specialization would distribute work to get it done most effectively. In the courts it is done to accommodate the desires of judges for an equitable distribution of the undesirable work.

Assignment of Cases to Judges and Departments

Beyond lawyer control of the cases by consent, conflicting theories of caseflow management have developed. The assignment of cases to individual judges when they first come into the court is referred to as an "individual assignment system." A natural outgrowth of a one-judge-per-county system, the judge has the case for all purposes from filing to disposition. Short of a change of venue or other movement by challenge to the bias of the judge, the court has the case for all purposes. There is little room for judge-shopping unless the point of initial assignment, usually the clerk's office, is corrupted.

The contrasting system of case assignment is through a "master calendar." Under such a system, the cases are held at a central point in the court until some judicial action is required, at which time the case is assigned to a particular judge for the judicial action and returned to the central point until further action is required. A case is often before several different judges under this system. Sometimes called the "central assignment system," it grew out of an efficiency theory of court operations, which was invoked to meet the shifting availability of judicial manpower.

In recent years a number of derivative or hybrid systems have been developed which are intended to accelerate, or at least bring more detailed order to, caseflow. Known by a variety of names, they all revolve around the principle of identifying particular types of cases or cases which share certain common characteristics and grouping them for selective and possibly different processing from that given the usual case in that court. Although used in courts of all sizes, they do tend to be more successful in courts in which the volume of such cases merits particular attention and where resources are available to devote to such specialization.

Beyond the success (or lack thereof) of such systems, they are significant for facility planning in that they may benefit from the reconfiguration of courthouse space (e.g., larger or smaller courtrooms, increased or decreased litigant waiting area, etc.) or the creation of specialty spaces (e.g., small conference or settlement facilities grouped around a central litigant/attorney waiting area).

Scheduling of Cases for Judicial Action

It is not surprising that case assignment principles should have developed slowly. They are the product of a conservative profession which resists change as a basic challenge to its principle of order. Caseflow control grew in a rural environment to meet the needs of itinerant judges who sat for fixed terms in different counties. The local clerk maintained the records, the local sheriff served the papers, the local lawyers waited for the judge to arrive. The lawyers, in cooperation with the local officials, developed the calendar system. They traded among themselves, accommodated each other's needs, and set the list of cases to be dealt with in the term of the visiting judge. They produced a lawyer's calendar with little regard for expeditious action.

Despite the fact that most metropolitan areas of the United States had permanent court facilities and resident judges by 1900, it was not until 1960 that any court thought it might run its calendar contrary to the wishes of the lawyers. A consent continuance of the case was the rule of administration, and few lawyers would refuse the request of a fellow lawyer, knowing full well that next time he might be the requester.

The work of the Joint Committee for Effective Justice in the early sixties saw a beginning of the end to this viewpoint. By 1966 a survey of judges reported a slight majority advocating judicial control of the caseflow process. By 1970 the majority was substantial. Today the lawyer ownership theory of case control is not dead, but judicial control in the caseflow process is dominant in most major court locations.

Evidence that one case assignment system works better than another has not laid the argument over the systems to rest. The battle between advocates of particular assignment systems can be found at any gathering of court administrators. The absence of science is conspicuous as the debate is waged between the ignorant of both camps.

To the extent data are available, one would have to conclude that the argument between assignment systems advocates is a specious exercise; proof exists as to the efficacy of all, which leads one to conclude that the truth must be in a different level of analysis which will explain the successes and failures on a different basis. As noted above, research indicates that the assignment system is not a critical variable. In fact, certain managerial approaches, properly applied, tend to reduce delay and thereby increase the justice in the system.

The descriptions of these approaches have been different forms but basically they acknowledge the following:

- The court must adopt standards for acceptable (tolerable) delay
- Courts must take control of the case at the earliest possible time (at filing of a civil case or arrest in a criminal case)
- A judicial officer with authority must monitor the explicitly defined delay limits
- Cases should always be set for a time and date certain for each step in the proceeding
- Expectations created by definite settings must be met with high probability
- Lawyer schedules must be accommodated within reasonable limits of their availability
- The system must have a mechanism to meet special problems so that cases are not permitted to remain undecided

These basic observations about caseflow management can easily become rigid with the spirit lost in the letter. The growing research and literature supports a flexible application of the basics to all kinds of caseflow systems. Each court should develop its own caseflow management system that fits its size, organizational structure, level of automation, and degree of operational efficiency.

Information Support

The heart of a modern, controlled caseflow management system is the information flow which supports it. The flow of cases must be controlled, based upon current information on all of the actors and the status of the cases. The complexity already noted makes this control difficult to achieve.

The presence of computer technicians in the courts has not been without benefit. The systems analysts necessary for computerization ask a lot of the right questions, such as: "What is the necessary information?" "Where are the important decisions being made?" "How can the necessary information be collected and made available to the decision-makers?" Where these questions have been asked and answered, appropriate hardware and software have been found and are in use, and assist the judgment of the case-coordinating persons. In larger and more complex systems, electronic data processing has provided the kind of quick entry and quick retrieval that gives the scheduler enough information to schedule effectively. However, in many courts simple, manually maintained card systems continue to work.

In a modern information monitoring and operating system, a combination of such technologies is used. However, a system which defines standards of performance and reports progress based on the standards noted above must come before the technology.

Impact of Caseflow Management on Courtroom Assignment

The type of case assignment system (individual, central, or hybrid) impacts directly on courtroom design and assignment. In a small single-judge and single-courtroom location, all types of cases are handled by the judge, and the courtroom must be adequately and suitably designed for handling all types of cases involving two or more parties. In certain rural counties, the use of a single-courtroom facility can be shared by several courts, such as the superior, state magistrate, the recorder's courts in the state of Georgia. In a two-judge, two-courtroom courthouse, two full-size jury trial courtrooms are necessary if both judges are assigned cases to their individual calendar so that each judge handles a full range of jury and nonjury matters. In a county with a relatively small, stable caseload and few jury trials, only one of the two courtrooms needs to be designed for jury trials, if the judges agree to share that courtroom for all jury trials. The second courtroom can then be a smaller, nonjury courtroom. If both courtrooms are planned as jury courtrooms, two jury deliberation rooms will also be needed. For small courthouses with fewer than four judges and courtrooms, it would be desirable for all courtrooms to be designed as jury courtrooms in order to provide the degree of flexibility in their future utilization as the court increases in size.

In a growing community, both courtrooms may be designed for jury trials, with a third nonjury courtroom planned in anticipation of caseload expansion or personnel increase. In courthouses with four to five courtrooms, an individual assignment system will require that all courtrooms be standardized for holding criminal jury trials. If a master or central assignment system is used, it is possible to provide a larger courtroom for calendar and motion calls (unless such calls are shared by more than one courtroom, in which case all trial courtrooms can be the same size) and for ceremonial functions, two to three regular jury trial courtrooms and one to two nonjury courtrooms or hearing rooms. By separating the judges' chambers from courtrooms by a private corridor, any one of the judges can be assigned to any one of the four or five courtrooms/hearing rooms, depending on the case assigned to that particular judge. With such an arrangement, no more than three juries would be active at any one time, and two or three jury deliberation rooms would be adequate to accommodate all jury deliberation activities of that court.

In larger metropolitan courts, regardless of the case assignment system adopted, judges can be assigned all types of cases, or they can be grouped into specialized courts (such as criminal, civil, juvenile, domestic relations, and probate courts), in which case they are assigned only those cases within that particular court division's jurisdiction. Since certain judges are more experienced and have greater interest in handling certain types of cases than other judges, specialized court divisions frequently occur in the larger metropolitan courts, such as those in New York, Chicago, and Houston.

In cities where grouping a large number of judges into divisions does not adversely affect the operational efficiency of the court system, it is not uncommon for each specialized court division to occupy a separate multistory court building. Sizes of courtrooms can vary for each specialized court division, as well as within each division, depending on the number of judges or judicial officers and the number of courtrooms.

In a unified court system, if trials are assigned to judges on a random basis, regardless of type of case (criminal, civil, domestic relations, etc.), then all trial courtrooms should be standardized at a larger size than if courtrooms were designated as specialized civil, criminal, domestic relations, juvenile, probate, or small-claims courtrooms. All-purpose trial courtrooms should be large enough to accommodate juries of 12 members (or 14 or 16 members in the case of 2 or 4 alternate jurors) for jury trials with multiple parties or defendants. All such courtrooms should be equipped for secure prisoner holding, interviewing, and access.

Prior to the insertion of very stringent Americans with Disabilities Act (ADA) requirements into the planning of court facilities, the standard size of these courtrooms, equipped for all-purpose court activities, would have been approximately 1,300 to 1,500 square feet of net usable courtroom area. Such a courtroom would be at least 30 feet in width, with a public seating capacity for around 50 spectators. With the newly adopted ADA requirements, the same courtroom would be approximately 1,500 to 1,700 net square feet, and a minimum width of 35 feet in order to accommodate long ramps in the courtroom for wheelchair access to the judge's bench, witness box, clerk's station, and so on.

On the other hand, if certain types of cases are assigned to specific judges, then courtrooms can be standardized by case types. For example, criminal courtrooms to conduct 12-member-jury trials should be larger than civil courtrooms for 6-member-jury trials; nonjury juvenile, uncontested domestic relations, and probate cases can be heard in significantly smaller hearing rooms. In jurisdictions with specialized criminal, civil, and family courts, courtrooms and support facilities for each court can be designed specifically to satisfy the spatial, functional, and environmental needs of that court. Consequently, criminal courtrooms can be different in size from civil and family courtrooms. Within each court, however, most trial courtrooms should remain similar in size and layout.

In jurisdictions where judges are assigned to courtrooms according to the type of trials conducted, a judge may be assigned a criminal jury trial followed by a civil nonjury trial, and subsequently by an uncontested divorce case. The judge would be assigned first to a large, 12-member-criminal-jury trial courtroom equipped to try multiple-defendant criminal cases. Such a case may take several days to several weeks. At the completion of this case, the same judge may be assigned to a small nonjury courtroom to try the civil case and the uncontested divorce case. Because the judge does not know in advance the courtroom to which he or she is scheduled to try a specific case, locating his or her chamber near a specific courtroom is no longer a necessary design criterion. In the Garrahy Judicial Complex in Providence, Rhode Island, judges' chambers are located on a floor separated from the courtroom floors. A small judge's conference room is provided adjacent to each courtroom for the judge assigned to that courtroom to confer with attorneys during the course of the trial, thus eliminating the need to travel during short recesses to the judge's chamber located at a different area of the courthouse. Private judges' elevators connect this chamber floor with the courtroom floors, as well as with the floor where judges park their cars.

The advantages of this arrangement are better security and a higher level of privacy for the judges and support staff, and cost savings in utilizing shared facilities such as law library, conference rooms, lounge facilities, and stenographic (secretarial) support spaces. By providing three major types of judicial spaces, small hearing rooms (600 to 800 square feet of net space), regular trial courtrooms (approximately 1,200 to 1,400 square feet), a small number of major trial courtrooms (approximately 1,600 to 1,800 square feet), and courtrooms with and without direct secured prisoner access, judges may be assigned to any one of many courtrooms in accordance with the special needs of a specific case or a group of similar cases.

Another very significant advantage in a major multistory court building is the ability to fully utilize all courtrooms on one floor (providing there is a mix of courtroom types and sizes on each floor) before assigning judges to courtrooms on an adjacent floor. This provides the opportunity to conserve energy when courtrooms are not in use. In jurisdictions where judges travel on circuit, and during the summer months, when judges normally take their vacations, several courtrooms may be left unused for extended periods of time. If these courtrooms are scattered on all courtroom floors, energy conservation is seldom possible. However, if occupied courtrooms can be grouped on entire floors by their assignment so that HVAC and lighting systems on floors of unused courtrooms can be switched off, substantial savings in annual operation and maintenance costs can be realized.

On the other hand, the disadvantages of this arrangement include inconvenience to judges when they have to travel regularly between judges' chambers and courtrooms on different floors, and inconvenience to attorneys, litigants, witnesses, and the public in locating the appropriate judge on a specific day. Inconvenience to judges can be alleviated by providing a judges' conference room across a private corridor from each trial courtroom so that while the court is in session, and during short recesses, the judge can confer with attorneys and staff in that room. While this space can be regarded as a duplication of the judge's chamber on another floor, the amortized cost of providing such a space over the life span of the building is small when compared with the savings in annual operating and maintenance costs, the lower wear and tear on courtrooms, and the lower cost of providing adequate security and privacy to judges and their support staff. Furthermore, these conference rooms can also be used for settlement conferences and plea-bargaining sessions, with or without the presence of the judge.

A variation of this arrangement, without the need for judges' conference rooms, is the provision of a larger number of judges' chambers than the number of trial courtrooms on each floor. For example, in the Circuit Court Building in Salt Lake City, six judges' chambers are provided behind four courtrooms, separated by a private corridor. By locating the judges' chambers on the same floor as courtrooms, there is no need for the separate judges' conference rooms. However, this arrangement would continue to permit the assignment of each judge to a specific courtroom on the same floor; and if there is a mix of courtrooms of varying sizes, the more senior judge would probably be assigned the courtroom of his or her choice while the two judges without courtrooms would be assigned to two courtrooms on an adjacent floor. Consequently, the concept of assigning judges to courtrooms would not work as efficiently when judges' chambers are located on the same floor as courtrooms, unless court rules specify master assignment of judges to courtrooms by case type.

Whether all courtrooms should be standardized or of mixed sizes, based on varying functional requirements, requires examination. Common objections raised in response to standard trial courtrooms include the following:

- Inadequacy for calendaring and motions session when a large number of attorneys, witnesses, and litigants assemble in the courtroom for a short period of time to respond to the call of the daily or weekly case calendar or to hear brief motions on cases
- Inadequacy to handle multiple-defendant cases, as standardized courtrooms tend to be too small
- Inadequacy to handle sensational public-interest trials

Standardizing all courtrooms to one size would probably be excessively restrictive on their use to dispose of cases with different legal, personnel, security, and spectator requirements. By providing three or four different types and sizes of courtrooms and hearing rooms, and by assigning various types of cases to courtrooms according to their respective spatial needs, courtroom facilities can be optimally utilized. At the same time, it is important for the court system to examine its internal operating procedures to ascertain, for instance, whether trial and motions calendars could be handled in different courtrooms instead of being centralized in one courtroom or with staggered sessions such as morning and afternoon calls.

With an individual calendar system, each judge knows in advance the number and type of cases on his or her calendar. If the judge is responsible for only civil cases, a trial courtroom without adjoining prisoner facilities should be assigned. The judge would be responsible for his or her calendar, and be held accountable for his or her caseload. In terms of facilities, since there is no external control over case assignment, the judge basically controls his or her own time, and the availability of the courtroom and chambers largely depends on the judge's individual approach to hearing and trying cases. In any case, by knowing in advance the judge's vacation and work schedule, the courtroom and ancillary facilities can be assigned to visiting or other judges when they are not being used by the regular judge.

In a hybrid individual-central case assignment system, with all actions prior to trials handled by an individual judge but all trials assigned from a central trial calendar to judges as they become available, a more effective use of available courtrooms can be achieved. From the initiation of a case to its being ready for trial, a single judge handles all motions, hearings, and other necessary legal proceedings. This provides the continuity and control over the early stages of a case, which may lead to settlement or plea bargaining. Once a case is ready for trial, and the attorneys, parties, and witnesses have been summoned to the courthouse for calendar call, the trial of the case is assigned to any available judge upon the conclusion of his or her previous case. This eliminates judge shopping to a great extent, and injects some degree of control over the allocation and use of the judge's time in the courthouse.

Thus, assignment systems dictate to a large degree whether each judge needs a courtroom. Conversely, the design of facilities may significantly influence the type of assignment system that can be suitably accommodated. In a unified court system with judges handling all types of cases and with their chambers remote from the trial courtrooms, a central control trial calendar with judges assigned to courtrooms that are specially designed to accommodate specific case types would provide an efficient use of courtroom facilities. It is also possible to use a separate central control trial calendar for civil or criminal cases while others would be assigned civil cases over a period of time after which their assignment may be changed. With this system, judges can be assigned on a regular basis to specific courtrooms over the period of time that they are assigned civil or criminal cases. This would tend to avoid the situation in which the judge moves on a daily or case basis to a new and unfamiliar courtroom. During slack periods, such as when many judges are on vacation or on a traveling schedule, courtrooms used would then be grouped for full utilization in order to conserve energy. This consideration will become increasingly significant, as the cost or providing energy for buildings continues to increase at an accelerated rate.

Spatial relationships between courtrooms and judges' chambers also dictate whether the courtroom should be assigned to a specific judge. For example, in many older courthouses, the only way to reach the judge's chamber is through the courtroom. With this arrangement, there is no alternative other than to assign the courtroom to a judge. The courtroom becomes the waiting room to the judge's chamber when it is not used for hearing court matters. The court clerk or bailiff in the courtroom usually serves as the judge's receptionist. In newer court buildings, judges' chambers are separated from courtrooms by a private corridor so that visitors are screened at a reception area by a secretary or receptionist before being allowed into the private corridor leading to the judges' chambers. Further screening by the judge's secretary is necessary before the visitor is allowed to enter the judge's chamber. With this arrangement, each judge can be assigned, if necessary, to any one of several courtrooms on the floor.

Changes in Caseflow Management

The behavior of litigants within the court system is predictable from the past. The cycle of change is largely dependent on the conservatism of the legal profession and the process by which each generation passes its values on to the next. No structure as complex as the judicial system can be changed rapidly without substantial dysfunctional consequences.

As a consequence of this cultural stability, it is safe to predict that settlements or pleas will continue to account for 80 to 95 percent of all cases. Pressures for speedier dispositions involve the judiciary, through its officers, in the settlement process. Judicially supervised conferences contribute to the appearance of justice and in some instances help to reach settlement through mediation techniques. The need for suitable facilities for settlement conferences in the courthouse is increasing.

In both white-collar crimes and class-action litigation, the tendency toward longer trials is developing into a significant part of court workload.

Criminal case settlement comes under close court supervision, as plea bargaining becomes more exposed to the control of the courts. Facilities which were once thought complete when they included a courtroom, judges' chambers, lockup, and jury deliberation rooms will not be complete without multiple secure conference rooms where persons in or out of custody may be brought to participate in an open discussion of proper charges and disposition. Criminal court settlements will become a more open process if proper facilities are designed and made available.

Trials by jury in civil cases will continue to diminish in number, and six-member juries will become widely accepted. The selection of judges is changing to an emphasis on merit at all levels. As a result, lawyer confidence in the ability of judges is rising. The pressure on judicial leaders to move away from civil jury trials is having its effect, and the effect will be a lasting one, since there appears to be little economic incentive favoring jury trials.

The complexity of the issues presented to juries requiring long trials and therefore long absences from regular pursuits will lead jurors to resist service. Though the jury will continue to be a part of the judicial structure for many years, its role as the controlling variable in caseflow management is likely to decrease. Jurors will become increasingly less patient with delays and inefficiencies in the system. Improved jury management will become a necessity, as citizens resist the waste of time now demanded of them (see chapter 3: Jury and Space Management).

The increasing mobility of the modern population will tend to make witness availability an increasing problem. Speedier hearings will be necessary to ensure the presence of key witnesses. Electronic and video recording of testimony is becoming common, as a new generation of younger lawyers and judges becomes comfortable with its possibilities. The public is accustomed to learning from television and accepts videotape as a sufficient live witness under appropriate safeguards.

To provide the necessary safeguards, the tape recordings must be court-supervised. Present court reporters may well find a new vocation in operating recording studios for courts under controlled conditions. Recording the proceedings in courthouses may make it possible to get quick rulings from judges on doubtful evidentiary questions. Real-time reporting, with the court reporter using a stenographic machine linked to a computer which instantaneously translates the proceedings into an unedited English script on video monitors at various locations in the courtroom, is being installed in many newer courthouses. A scopist in an adjoining office would be editing the proceedings so that a complete transcript of the day's proceedings would be ready for distribution or purchase as early as the following day. This system also complies with the ADA requirements for the hearing impaired. Deaf trial participants, including judges, attorneys, witnesses, and others, are able to follow the proceedings by viewing the monitor screen.

Litigation will continue to increase in direct proportion to the concentration of population around urban centers. The past increase has been a product of increasing friction brought about by the close contact of people in urban centers. The trend appears to continue. Criminal cases are a product of the size of prosecutorial staffs, which will not be reduced if crime falls off. In fact, prosecutors continue to reject large numbers of cases presented to them by the police because of the lack of adequate resources to prosecute them.

The high number of persons graduating from law schools will increase the amount of litigation in civil areas where people are not now represented. The growth of group legal services for middle-income persons and the development of paralegal personnel to support litigating lawyers will increase the number of lawsuits. Since these cases will often be of marginal economic value, the settlement rate will increase as the "corporate" lawyer of group practice settles the cases that are of less economic importance.

The public's need for information in a modern courthouse is not now being met. With the more complicated procedures of the future, the public will not be able to find their way without the use of a modern information display. A visual display system, using updatable destination-oriented monitors similar to those used in airports, will assist the public to get to their courtroom or other destinations in the courthouse without necessary and excessive use of information personnel at the main public entrance lobby. Touch-screen monitors in public areas can also be used for this purpose as well as for the public to learn about the processing of traffic and small-claims cases, the filing of documents, and the payment of fees and fines, and so forth. Such information should be made generally available to all persons coming into and going from the courthouse.

Developing technologies in record keeping and file storage will make special booths and equipment necessary. New book storage and retrieval systems and equipment will reduce the amount of bookstack space and will introduce more efficient methods of searching for and retrieving books and documents in law libraries. Advanced electronic technologies will further reduce the space needs in law libraries and in court clerks' offices as paper documents are replaced by alternative electronic media, such as film, optical disk, and web and internet driven technologies.

Shared offices, interview rooms, and conference rooms will be necessary in courthouses to accommodate specialists who travel to regional facilities. These rooms will also be shared by representatives of court-related departments such as the public defender's office, the probation department, and the social and welfare departments, whose main offices are housed in other buildings. They would use these shared facilities on an as-needed basis when they are conducting court business in the courthouse. Judges' chambers and support offices will be designed to accommodate differences in skill and approach in various court divisions. Greater design considerations will be given to ancillary and related facilities as their importance to the efficiency and effectiveness of caseflow management becomes more apparent.

The message to the modern court facility designer must be multiform. The future may see a gradual adoption of new litigation caseflow patterns involving more specialization of facilities. At the same time, these changing patterns of caseflow will not be static. The modern courthouse must not lock the system into past patterns. It must be designed with the flexibility of a modern office building while bowing to the tradition of stability which must characterize a legal institution.

The ritual court building must be a thing of the past. Buildings must be built to do justice, not be a monument to it. The flow of cases through the courts must be designed and redesigned in the coming decades with the stricture of ritual courtrooms and preconceived notions about the order of the caseflow. A limited number of ritual high benches and high ceilings will be necessary but by no means in direct proportion to the number of judges.

Impact of Caseflow Management Changes on Trial Court Facilities

From the previous discussion, it is apparent that caseflow management changes will have significant impact on the planning and design of trial court facilities. Anticipated increase in dispute settlement conferences, coupled with projected decrease in civil jury trials, will influence the type and amount of judicial facilities to be provided for the future. Wider application of technologies to court information and communication systems, balanced by a somber awareness of the potential capability of people to shape their working environment according to the changing needs of the judicial system, will produce a strong effect on the effectiveness of future judicial administration as well as on the adaptability of future court buildings. The following section discusses emerging trends and concepts in the planning and design of trial court facilities as they relate to changes in caseflow and court operations.

Judicial Facilities—Courtrooms and Judges' Chambers

Courtrooms are designed to try cases. They should adequately accommodate the needs of trial participants and spectators during hearings or trials. All things being equal, the larger the courtroom, the more expensive the cost of construction and the higher the cost of operation and maintenance. The functional, spatial, symbolic, and aesthetic considerations of trial courtrooms require that they be different from regular office space. Construction costs of county courthouses are presently in the vicinity of $160 to $180 per square foot of gross building area, compared with around $100 to $120 per square foot for regular office space in a multistory office building.

A question often asked is, What constitutes an adequate courtroom? An adequate courtroom for one type of court may be inadequate for another. Courtroom components vary somewhat with different types of courts. The sizes of courtrooms may be different. On the other hand, the trend is toward greater standardization of trial courtrooms, judges' chambers, and ancillary facilities. Standard courtrooms are suited to the disciplined structural solutions of modern architecture. Regular spacing of beams, girders, and columns facilitates modular ceiling grid design with standardized lighting, heating, air conditioning, and ventilating fixtures. Regular structural spacings determine the size and dimensions of standard courtrooms, and vice versa. A major advantage of standard courtrooms is the possible elimination of the procedure involving the senior judge moving to a larger courtroom when the previous senior judge retires or is defeated in an election. The availability of a large courtroom normally triggers a chain of moves of several judges. This "musical chair" approach to courtroom and chamber assignment is both costly and unnecessary.

Trial courtrooms should be designed to adequately accommodate judicial and public seating capacity for around 90 percent of their use. Courtrooms large enough to accommodate the maximum number of spectators or attorneys and parties would be oversized and underutilized for 90 percent of the time. For example, trial courtrooms should be designed to accommodate the number of attorneys and defendants, as well as public spectators, for 90 percent of all trials. During a motions call, the number of people present may be more than the capacity of that courtroom, and the people in excess of that capacity may have to stand in the public area for a short period of time at the beginning of the court session. As the number of people decreases and cases are assigned for trial in other courtrooms, there would be adequate seating for all persons in the motions or calendar courtroom. It is not anticipated that the public seating capacity of a regular trial courtroom needs to be more than 60 people. The capacity of public seating in a trial courtroom is largely determined by the size of the jury panel brought into the courtroom. For a 12-member jury, a regular panel of 30 to 40 potential jurors is brought into the courtroom from the jury assembly area. For a 6-member jury, a panel of 15 to 20 potential jurors is used. As the jury panel is seated in the public area of the courtroom, the judge briefly explains the facts of the case and the panelists' duties as jurors. Twelve potential jurors are selected by the clerk to sit at the jury box as the voir dire procedure begins, at which time the public area would have a spectator seating capacity of around 30 on one side of the courtroom. Once the jury is impaneled and the remaining jurors have returned to the jury assembly facilities, the entire seating capacity would be available to the public. Since there are usually very few spectators in the public seating area during most trials, the public seating areas in most trial courtrooms are underutilized.

Civil cases are becoming increasingly complex, and frequently involve multiple parties. Not only does this situation require more seating for attorneys and litigants in the judicial area, the larger number of preemptory challenges and challenges with cause of potential jurors means that more jurors are required in the jury panel for multiple-party jury cases. Consequently, either courtrooms of different sizes should be provided, with regular trial courtrooms of approximately 1,600 square feet and larger courtrooms of over 2,000 square feet for multiple-party jury cases, or the standard trial courtroom should be sufficiently flexible in space utilization so that the attorneys' and litigants' spaces in the judicial area of the courtroom can be easily expanded by reducing the number of public seating areas once the jury has been impaneled. To accomplish this, the low railing normally separating the public and judicial areas of the courtroom should either be movable, so that it can be relocated further into the public spectator area, or it should be eliminated, so that the judicial and the public areas can expand or contract as the occasion demands.

In this age of government fiscal austerity, courthouses are designed largely for their functional efficiency rather than for excessive space allocation or aesthetic value. Economic and cost-saving approaches are being developed to eliminate nonessential personnel and facility utilization. In a multistory court building with both criminal and civil court courtrooms and ancillary facilities, and with judges designated as criminal or civil judges, criminal courtrooms can be stacked and grouped around secure prisoner-holding and interviewing facilities. In-custody defendants would be escorted into and out of the judicial area of criminal trial courtrooms without mixing with either public or private circulation patterns. Civil courtrooms, on the other hand, can be stacked together without adjacent prisoner facilities. By separating civil from criminal courtrooms on different parts of courtroom floors or on different floors, security precautions can be more effectively planned. It should be noted, however, that it is possible to use criminal courtrooms to handle civil trials, but not vice versa if in-custody defendants are involved.

If it is possible to separate judges' chambers from courtroom floors, or if judges are conditioned to being assigned to courtrooms of varying sizes regardless of where chambers are located, then the most efficient solution would be to provide a large number of standardized trial courtrooms, a small number of larger courtrooms for special case assignment (most with secure prisoner access), and a small number of small hearing rooms for uncontested civil and domestic relations, juvenile, and probate matters handled by referees, masters, and/or commissioners. An appropriate mix of courtrooms and hearing rooms (say, one large and six to eight regular trial courtrooms, and two small hearing rooms) should be provided on each floor for maximum courtroom/hearing-room space utilization. During low caseload and high judges' vacation periods, one or two of these floors may provide adequate space for the proper mix of case types, enabling other court floors to be closed. For public interest, sensational, and heinous felony cases, the regular trial courtroom, and even the larger courtrooms, may not be adequate to accommodate the number of spectators trying to gain entry into the courtroom. While it is possible to provide a specially designed large courtroom to which all such cases could be assigned, there is a distinct disadvantage in providing such a space. It is well known that security risk in a courtroom increases with the number of persons in the courtroom. A large crowd in the spectator area of the trial courtroom could present a major security and disruption problem during the trial process. A large number of security personnel would be needed to ensure the security of the in-custody defendant, the safety of the judge, jurors, and court staff, and the behavior of spectators. With the admission of television news cameras into courtrooms in an increasing number of states, an added dimension of media exposure further increases the amount of movement within the judicial area of the courtroom.

Public interest, domestic relations, and felony cases should be tried in regular trial courtrooms equipped with adequate security precautions. Overflow public spectators can be directed to a large training or conference center equipped with audio-visual equipment (closed-circuit television system) so that the trial can be viewed and heard by the large number of spectators remote from the courtroom. This would guarantee the rights of the defendant(s) to a public trial, and at the same time minimize the security risks.

In a major multicourtroom courthouse, it is reasonable to provide one very large multipurpose, special-proceedings or ceremonial courtroom of 2,500 to 3,000 net square feet in size. This courtroom would have direct prisoner access from holding and interviewing facilities so that a serious criminal jury trial can be conducted. The judicial area of this courtroom would have sufficient space for four to six litigants tables to accommodate multiple-party or multiple-defendant trials, and the judicial area could also be cleared of all tables and replaced by additional seating during ceremonial occasions.

Hearing rooms for confidential cases, such as juvenile and adoption matters, should be provided with large enclosed waiting rooms for parties, attorneys, relatives, and friends. These waiting rooms serve basically as public areas of courtrooms. They are outside of courtroom or hearing room because of the confidentiality of cases being conducted. Procedures should be developed for calling parties and attorneys from the waiting room to the hearing room. Perhaps attorneys' names or case numbers, instead of juveniles' names, could be called.

A public-address system with ceiling speakers above public waiting areas outside of courtrooms or hearing rooms is usually available for summoning parties and witnesses into the courtroom/hearing room. For family and juvenile court facilities, separate public waiting areas or alcoves are desirable for isolation of disputing parties and their witnesses. Such separation is essential to avoid undesirable confrontation and arguments, which could lead to violence and destruction.

Questions are frequently raised as to whether each judge needs a separate courtroom. On the one hand, judges need the necessary resources to perform their duties effectively. On the other hand, judges essentially work in two separate spaces—chambers and courtrooms. Since a judge cannot be in two places at the same time, managers frequently question the need for a full courtroom for each judge. At the appellate court level, where set terms of court are established, such as the court hearing oral arguments in the courtrooms one week each month, it is possible to schedule the courtrooms for other uses during the other three weeks of each month that the court is not in session. In fact, barring unforeseen additional court sessions, the courtroom schedule of the appellate court can be set up for the entire year or court session.

Unfortunately, most trial courts do not, and cannot, operate in this manner. With a central case control calendar system, ready trial cases are assigned to the first available judge for trial. With this system, the judge occupies a courtroom full time, and the courtroom must be adequately equipped to handle all types of cases that are regularly assigned by the calendaring control manager or presiding or administrative judge. Within such a system, the only time when the courtroom is not in use should be when the judge is ill, on vacation, or when he or she hears cases at other court locations within the judicial circuit. By knowing the judges' vacation schedules, which the judges should be required to submit early each year, it is possible to schedule the use of each courtroom and ancillary facilities by a visiting judge. Unless visiting judges are used on a regular basis, visiting judges on brief visits should be assigned regular courtrooms which are not being used by the regular judges. In large courthouses, several courtrooms may not be used each day or week throughout the year. Part-time assignment to visiting judges would improve the utilization of such courtrooms.

In the state of Florida, civil judges are each provided with a private hearing room adjacent to his or her chambers. Most uncontested hearings, settlement conferences, and so forth are conducted in this hearing room. Courtrooms for conducting trials are provided on a ratio of one for each two judges. On the other hand, criminal judges tend to conduct most of their hearings and trials in open court. Consequently, each criminal judge is provided a regular trial courtroom with direct but separate in-custody defendant access from holding facilities adjacent to each courtroom.

Direct Judicial Support Facilities

Regardless of whether judges' chambers are located adjacent to or remote from trial courtrooms, the offices for secretaries, court reporters, and law clerks are usually grouped and located near the judges' chambers. Conversely, the bailiff's and the courtroom clerk's stations are usually located in the courtroom. Unless the bailiff and court clerk are part of the judge's personal staff, they do not normally have office space within the judge's suite of offices. In many locations, the courtroom clerk belongs to the clerk's office and the bailiff is part of the sheriff's staff. When the court is not in session, the courtroom clerk usually returns to the clerk's office while the bailiff returns to the sheriff's office for other assignments. In certain jurisdictions, court reporters are the responsibility of the court administrator or court clerk. They are centrally pooled and assigned to various courtrooms on a regular or case trial basis.

Frequently, the judge's chamber and offices for the secretary, judicial assistant, court reporter, and law clerk are designed inefficiently. In the judge's chamber, the traditional executive desk and credenza consume a significant amount of space at the center of the chamber. With the large desk placed at the center of the room and the credenza behind the judge's armchair, there is very little space left for other related functions, even in a reasonably large judge's chamber. There are several different activities normally performed in the judge's chamber: research, formal conferences, and informal meetings. The research activity is performed at the judge's desk. This activity involves legal research, correspondence, telephone communication, dictation, and so forth. Formal conferences are conducted either at the desk, with several armchairs surrounding it, or at a conference table with six to eight chairs. Formal conferences usually involve staff or attorneys. Informal meetings with friends and visitors can be conducted around a group of lounge furniture (sofa, lounge chairs, low table, and lamps).

In many chambers, the room size is not adequate to house all three functions. In many instances, however, an improved layout of the chamber may provide a more efficient use of the existing space. For example, perhaps the most inefficient use of space is to have the desk and credenza in a room; the desk provides a limited work surface and the credenza is nonfunctional. Instead, a thirty-inch-deep work surface could be built along the end wall to replace the bulky desk. Two-drawer lateral or vertical file cabinets can be placed under the work surface to increase filing space; the credenza can simply be eliminated. The research and work activities of the judge, and of other staff members in their offices, would then be provided with the maximum amount of work surface at minimum expense of floor space. With ample work surface located at one end of the room, the remainder of the chamber can then be designed to accommodate a conference table and chairs along one side and lounge chairs along the other side. The separation of research and work activities from the conference and informal meeting activities produces other benefits: the judge's visitors would be restricted to the portion of the chamber opposite the work surface, and the judge would not have to put confidential files and papers away in drawers or file cabinets when visiting or conferring with attorneys and staff. When the secretary announces the arrival of visitors, the judge would simply move away from the private research and work surface to the conference and meeting areas, and return to the work area once the visitors have left.

This concept of separating work area from conference and meeting areas within the same space applies equally well to the offices of secretaries, judicial assistants, court reporters, and law clerks. The judge's secretary usually requires a large work surface to spread out and collate papers and to type and write. The desk surface alone is grossly inadequate to accommodate the large variety of secretarial and clerical duties. An additional work surface along one wall behind the secretary's workstation would significantly improve the efficiency of the secretary's office. This work surface should be approximately 26 inches above floor level if it is to be used for typing, or 29 inches for regular clerical work. If a typewriter or computer terminal is used on this surface, a part of the work surface could be lowered by 3 inches to compensate for the height of the keyboard, while the other part could be built high enough to provide sufficiently clear height to slide two-drawer vertical or lateral file cabinets under the work surface. With a 29-inch work surface, the keyboard could slide under the work surface at the appropriate height while the monitor would be mounted on the work surface at suitable eye level.

In addition to the work surface, the judge's secretary's workstation should be near file cabinets containing the judge's work files and to storage closets for supplies. A coffee-preparation galley should be provided either on each floor or on each side of each floor, for the preparation of coffee and refreshments. This space would be equipped with a small refrigerator, a sink, and storage cabinets for supplies. A small galley could also be provided within each judge's chamber suite.

Court reporters' offices can be significantly reduced in size if adequate work surface can be provided along one wall and special provisions are made to store both used and unused recording media. Storage is frequently a major problem in court reporters' offices. Cardboard boxes filled with such media are frequently strewn on the floor. Built-in storage closets along one wall should be provided. Completed cases should be stored in boxes and placed in records storage spaces in the basement or central building service core areas.

If the court reporter is part of the judge's personal staff, an office should be located directly behind the judicial area of the courtroom so that convenient access exists between that office and courtroom. Since there is some contact between attorneys and court reporters regarding preparation of trial transcripts, the location of the court reporter's office between the courtroom and the private corridor would avoid excessive attorney traffic into the private corridor. If court reporters are assigned from a central pool, as is the practice in certain courts, then the court reporters would return to the central pool, and any business transactions with attorneys would be conducted there. Court reporters in a central pool share storage facilities provided in close proximity to all court reporters' workstations or offices. Only current trial records would be stored at the court reporters' workstations. If the court reporter is responsible for trial exhibits, a secure shared exhibits room should be located adjacent to the central tapes storage room or a separate storage room provided within the judge's suite of offices. (Exhibits storage facilities will be discussed in the next section of this chapter.)

Law clerks are responsible for conducting legal research for judges. Most of their time is spent either in the law library or in their offices. Because they have few visitors, their space requirements are not the same as those for court reporters, and more than one law clerk can be housed in an office, thereby conserving space. A recommended layout would be to provide built-in work surfaces (with bookshelves on the wall above the work surface and two-drawer file cabinets below) along the walls for two or more law clerks in an office. A shared conference table and chairs at the center of the office would be used for meeting with visitors, attorneys, and with each other. If there are four law clerks in the office, each person would have a private workstation. The workstations could be partly enclosed and would share the central conference space, which could also serve as a discussion and lunch area.

If the bailiff and court clerk were also part of the judge's personal staff, workstations should be provided for them outside the courtroom. Since the bailiff is responsible for the security and safety of court personnel and jurors, an appropriate location for that workstation would be near or adjacent to both the judge's chamber (perhaps as part of the secretary's office) and the jury deliberation room across or along the private corridor from the judge's chamber. The bailiff would need no more than a small work surface and a file drawer to hold personal belongings. From this workstation, the bailiff should have visual contact with the door leading into the jury deliberation suite as well as the door leading into the judge's chamber. A light and buzzer communication system should be installed between the jury deliberation suite and the bailiff's station. Upon reaching a verdict, the foreman of the jury would press a button that activates a light and buzzer at the bailiff's station. The bailiff would then escort the jurors from the jury room to the courtroom to render their verdict.

The court clerk is primarily responsible for the swearing in of jurors and witnesses, for recording judgments and actions rendered by the court, and for the safety of case files used by the court during hearings and trials. In most court jurisdictions, court clerks return case files to the central clerk's office at the completion of each court session, and these files are centrally stored and supervised. In certain civil courts, pending case files assigned to the court are kept by the court clerk assigned to that court. In several courtrooms, case files are stored in filing cabinets along the side wall of the courtroom. This produces an unsightly environment and is not recommended. However, case file storage in an office shared by the court clerk, process server, and bailiff would be appropriate. There is a strong functional relationship between the clerk and the process server, whose main responsibility is the service of civil papers, and the bailiff could then be responsible for the safety and security of court records housed in this office. Such an office could adjoin the court reporter's office between the courtroom and the private corridor. Proximity of these personnel to the courtroom is a significant design consideration.

Courts also often have a court coordinator, who is responsible for the coordination of cases scheduled for that particular court. Since the court coordinator should be easily accessible to attorneys and litigants, his or her office should be the closest, among the judges' offices, to the reception area where visitors are screened.

If the judges' chambers and direct judicial support offices are grouped behind courtrooms on each floor, there should be a reception area located between the public elevator lobby or circulation area and the court personnel's private corridor. This reception area should be supervised by one of the judges' bailiffs, perhaps assigned on a rotating basis. All persons entering the reception area would be screened by the receptionist before entering the private corridor leading to the judges' support offices and their chambers. If judges' chambers and support offices are located on a separate floor, the number of reception areas can be reduced to the number of floors on which these chambers and offices are located. In Providence, Rhode Island, the Garrahy Judicial Complex has one floor of judges and magistrates, together with their support staff, from three separate court divisions. A receptionist or bailiff is located directly off the public elevator lobby to control visitor access to private areas. In addition to improved security to court personnel and cost savings in minimizing duplication of shared facilities, the personnel cost in providing this degree of privacy and security is minimal when compared with having a reception area on each of several courtroom floors.

Indirect Judicial Support Facilities

Most court clerks today are an integral part of the court system. In most metropolitan courts, each specialized court has its own clerk's office—for example, a county civil clerk's office, a county criminal clerk's office, a probate clerk's office, and so on. The clerk's office frequently experiences space shortages. In many situations, space problems experienced by the clerk's office are not truly a space shortage problem, but a space mismanagement or misuse problem. Many clerks' offices waste too much prime office space for storage of inactive records or bulk supplies, and available office spaces are not optimally planned or fully utilized by the staff.

Clerks' offices are frequently inappropriately located within the court building. Attorneys and members of the public who are transacting court business at the clerk's office do not necessarily attend court sessions as well. People go to the clerk's office to file papers, pay fees or fines, check on records, get certified copies of legal documents, make inquiries of procedures and trial schedule, and so on. The clerk's office usually has the highest volume of public traffic on a continuing basis, with peak volume occurring at approximately the same time as that of courtrooms—early mornings and afternoons. In a multistory court building, the location of the clerk's office on an upper floor would result in the need for a larger number of public elevators to accommodate the high peak volume during early-morning court hours. The most effective solution is to separate the high-volume public traffic to the clerk's office from that of the courtroom floors, by locating it at the main public entrance level. This would minimize the amount of peak public traffic load on the elevators, thus decreasing the number of public elevators needed for the building. The clerk's office, together with other public-oriented high-traffic-volume spaces, such as jury assembly and law library facilities, may need more than the available space on the main public entrance floor, and the adjoining upper floor or basement could also be used. These floors can be connected by escalators, which have a much higher passenger capacity than elevators, and/or by an open staircase.

In specialized trial courts such as family, domestic relations, and juvenile courts, as well as certain criminal courts, there can be a large number of support departments, including intake, probation, youth diversionary units, public defender and appointed counsel, and clerical units such as child-support enforcement, Uniform Reciprocal Enforcement and Support Act (URESA), and others. Several of these departments may require after-hours access. Their location at or adjacent to the main public entrance level would also ensure their accessibility after regular court hours without the use of elevators.

In many multistory court buildings which house more than a single-level court, clerks' offices are sometimes located on different floors, in close proximity to the courts which they serve. In the planning and design of a new court building, the fragmentation of space occupied by clerks' offices frequently results in inefficient operation and poor personnel utilization. With few exceptions, there is no compelling reason for any clerk's office to be located on an upper floor. A court of limited jurisdiction handling traffic cases involving payment of fees on an upper floor may require a cashier's station directly outside the judicial area of the courtroom so that offenders sentenced to pay a fine are required to pass through the cashier's station before being allowed to leave the restrictive area of the courtroom. This may require a clerk-cashier being assigned to this station when the traffic court is in session. Such a personnel assignment does not warrant the location of the entire clerk's office on an upper floor, to the inconvenience of litigants, and creating a high traffic load on the public elevators. A better solution would be to locate the trial court clerk's office on the first floor, with the traffic courtroom located either directly adjoining the clerk's office on the same floor or on an adjacent floor. Facilities for traffic, small claims, or other courts involving payment of fines should be designed to require sentenced offenders to move directly from the judge's bench area to a cashier's station either adjoining or a floor below the courtroom, where the fine is paid before the offender is allowed into the public area.

Another problem in locating several court clerks' offices on different floors is the confusion created for visitors, witnesses, and jurors. In addition to overloading the public elevators, visitors find out after reaching one of the clerks' offices that their destinations are on different floors. Consequently, they have to get back into the elevators in order to reach other clerks' offices. This places heavy demands on an already overloaded elevator system, further eroding its efficiency during peak traffic periods.

By locating clerks' offices contiguous to one another on the main public entrance floor, designers can allow visitors, witnesses, jurors, and the general public to transact all court business at a central clerks' location. If a visitor should inquire at the wrong counter, he or she could easily be redirected to the correct counter on the same floor. Courtroom clerks located in the clerk's office would travel either on public or private elevators or stairs to the courtrooms on the higher floors. Since such inter-floor travel normally occurs outside of the peak morning and afternoon traffic load, it does not significantly affect the operation of the elevator system. Transportation of files to and from courtrooms is a regular routine that courtroom clerks and judges' staff can accommodate and schedule to avoid the peak traffic load periods. In large judicial buildings, a separate staff or service elevator should be provided for such uses.

In a court system with fragmented courts and clerks' offices, their central location on a single floor would allow their possible consolidation with few physical constraints. By being contiguous to each other, the dividing walls can be removed when clerks' offices are functionally and organizationally combined. This would not be possible if the clerks' offices are fragmented on different floors.

Certain probate clerks' offices are functionally integrated with the probate court. There is usually a constant flow of papers between the court and the clerk's office, and the relocation of the probate clerk's office to a consolidated clerk's office on a lower floor may not be feasible unless the court is also relocated to the same floor. The appellate court clerk's office may also be separated from the trial court clerk's office. Since the appellate court reviews decisions made by the trial courts, the combination of the appellate court clerk's office with the trial court clerk's office could present an undesirable functional and spatial integration. According to the U.S. Constitution, a person charged with an offense has the right to one trial and one appeal. Since the trial and appellate processes are quite different, their clerical functions should also be separate. Since the only link between the two clerks' offices is the transfer of transcripts and briefs of cases, the separation of these offices should not present an operational problem. Also, the appellate court usually has a single courtroom, and the public traffic to this clerk's office is minimal when compared to that for the trial clerk's office. The appellate court clerk's office can be located in close proximity to the appellate courtroom and ancillary facilities so that they can function effectively as a separate judicial unit.

The clerk's office can be designed as several distinct groups of spaces: public counter and records examination, general clerical, private offices, records, supplies and exhibits storage, and systems and equipment facilities. In general, adequate public counter space is directly accessible from the public lobby or circulation area. The records examination area is adjacent to the public counter so that it can be visually supervised by the counter clerks. The general clerical area is usually behind the counter clerks, separated, if necessary, by records in file cabinets, index card equipment, office furniture and equipment, or partitions. Private offices occupied by the clerk, administrative, and secretarial staff are usually located to the side of the counter and general clerical area so that the clerk can have visual contact with both areas, and visitors may have convenient access to the clerk's private offices. Active records areas in the clerk's office should be centrally located and easily accessible to counter clerks and general case processing clerks. Supplies storage should be in close proximity to the general clerical area and to the private offices. Exhibits storage should adjoin the workstation of the clerk who is responsible for its security and accessibility. Duplication equipment may be needed at two locations: one in the records examination room for use by attorneys and public; and the other in the general work area of the clerk's office.

With proper design, it is possible to combine public counter space with adjoining public lobby or circulation space in order to maximize the use of such spaces usually provided at the main public entry floor. Security of clerks' offices can be provided by means of shutters over the public counter. To provide an effective separation between the public area and the counter clerks' area, the public counter should be 42 to 48 inches high. The public at the counter should be in a standing position. Counter clerks can either stand up at the counter while serving customers (which would be the case if many clerks have counter duties), or sit at workstations arranged perpendicular to the counter on a raised platform (if specific clerks are assigned as counter clerks). Provision must be made to accommodate wheelchair access to public counters.

General clerical offices are open areas with clerical workstations arranged according to the functional and spatial relationships between clerical units, including criminal, civil, domestic relations, small claims, and so on. Because of the frequent shift in personnel throughout the clerical work area, and the increase in the number of full-time, part-time, and sometimes night clerks, the general clerical area should be planned to be as flexible as possible to accommodate continually changing needs. The adoption of computer-based information systems in the court system over the past few years has resulted in substantial changes in the layout of clerks' offices. The use of terminals for data entry, inquiry, and retrieval has become commonplace in most major court centers. Because of the need for accessibility by data-processing clerks, these terminals are conveniently located at clerical workstations in the general clerical area. When data entry is a primary function of the clerk's office, equipment should be located in a separate enclosed area in close proximity to the counter clerk's and active records storage areas. Clerks in the general clerical area who also serve as relief counter clerks should be located in close proximity to the counter clerk's area.

In general, specific clerical units assigned to handling different types of cases (criminal, civil, small claims, etc.) should occupy space surrounding centralized shared units, such as imaging, records and supply storage, staff conference, and restrooms. Imaging activities may require special light treatment around sensitive equipment, and a central location with some low-light internal area should be planned. Active records storage facilities must be centrally located in relation to the counter clerks and to the clerks within the various court units in the general work area. Case files should be color coded and stored in lateral shelves that can be locked up at the end of a regular workday. Only currently active records (no more than one or two years) should be stored in prime office space of the clerk's office. Older and less referenced records should be housed in basement or building service core storage spaces. This subject is discussed in greater detail in a subsequent chapter on records and space management.

Private offices for the clerk, deputy clerks, and their support staff should be easily accessible to counter clerks, visitors, and clerks in the general clerical area and records and exhibits storage areas. Since the clerk or the chief deputy may meet with senior staff on a regular basis, the use of a built-in work surface along one wall of the office, leaving the remaining space for a conference table and chairs, would be equally applicable to these offices as to judges' and support staff's private offices. In addition, a conference room should be provided in large clerks' offices for the clerk to meet with a large number of visitors, to confer with a large number of staff, or for conducting seminars and in-house training programs. The clerk's office should also be equipped with a safe or vault so that monies collected from fees and fines, and any sensitive trial exhibits, could be locked up after regular working hours.

Staff lounge, lunch room, and coffee/tea preparation areas are important design elements in any large clerk's office. Procedures should be established and enforced to prevent indiscriminate proliferation of coffee machines throughout the clerk's office units. At the same time, it is not effective to have clerks leaving the office en mass to a central cafeteria or coffee shop several floors away from the clerk's office. A large staff lounge and lunchroom should be provided in each court building, preferably on each floor or on the first floor (main public entrance level) or in the basement, for use by clerks and other court employees in the building. Vending machines for sandwiches, coffee, and refreshments should be provided in this room, which should be separated from similar facilities provided for the public. However, smaller coffee/tea preparation and staff lounge rooms should be provided on each floor for staff to take their coffee breaks without using the elevators to go to another floor.

A constant complaint from clerks is too little room for storing office supplies and forms. It is possible to store the supplies of several clerical units (say, criminal, civil, domestic relations, and small-claims) in the same room on separate shelves, provided the room is large enough. Frequently used forms should be housed under public counters or in storage facilities close to the public counter.

Law Library Facilities

The law library is a major space in most courthouses except those that are very small, and these latter may or may not have a space designated as the law library. Adequacy of the law library in a court building depends on the number, frequency, and type of users of its facilities. Where an adequate law library exists in a nearby law school or state capital, there may not be the need for a duplicated law library in the local courthouse. However, if the law library in the courthouse is the only one within reasonable distance, then adequate and suitable facilities should be provided to accommodate both the court and the legal community needs.

Law libraries should be located where they are most needed. If the law library is intended to be used by both the court and practicing attorneys, it should be located on either the main public entrance level or in the basement, where a separate entrance into the library could be provided. This separate entrance would provide access only into the law library and other spaces which require accessibility outside regular court hours (e.g., public defender, probation, or social agencies, if they are located in the courthouse). When several departments must be accessible at night and during weekends, their entrances should be centralized at one location in order to maximize accessibility control and to minimize security personnel needs. All interior doors leading from the law library or other accessible spaces at night or during weekends must be locked so that no unauthorized person can accidentally or intentionally gain access to other spaces within the court building. If possible, all departments requiring after-hours access should be located on the main public entrance level so that all upper floors can be closed to the public after regular work hours.

If the law library is used exclusively by judges and law clerks, and is not open to practicing attorneys unless special permission is granted (as is the case in some appellate court facilities), then the law library could be located near the court, the law clerks, and those personnel who must have convenient access to it. In the main courthouse in Anchorage, Alaska, the supreme court library is located on the fifth floor, where the supreme court facilities are also housed. The main law library used by the trial courts and practicing attorneys is located on the main public entrance level, equipped with separate exterior entrances for use outside of regular court hours.

Bookstacks usually require the largest portion of total law library space. Books that are frequently referenced by users should be provided in multiple sets and located near the reading and study areas. State reports and digests are among the most frequently used volumes. Such books should be housed in regular seven-shelf bookcase units, 30 to 40 inches in width and approximately 8 to 10 inches in depth. These bookcase units can be easily reached by users of average height. If additional shelves are provided to the ceiling, less frequently used volumes should be housed above the seventh shelf. Frequently referenced volumes should not be housed in "Conserv-a-File" or mechanized moving units because of the difficulties these systems cause, namely, in making books harder to find, in making it hard for more than one person at a time to use the bookstacks, and in the likelihood of mechanical problems that result in books being inaccessible when needed. High-density storage equipment should be used in areas where books are infrequently referenced, and where space-saving by closer stacking of books becomes crucial to the overall space use of the court building.

Bookstacks do not have to be located on one floor. In larger law libraries, if the main reading area and bookstacks with frequently referenced volumes are housed at the main public entrance level, maximum storage space should be provided in the basement directly below the main library space. By connecting these two or more levels with internal stairs, dumbwaiters, or booklifts, the infrequently used books can be stacked closer together in the basement than those frequently used volumes on the first floor. "Conserv-a-File" and other high-density storage equipment, including mechanically or electrically operated moving units, can be used in the basement with benefits to the court system, if their high initial costs can be justified through savings in building costs.

Law libraries are extremely expensive to maintain and they are especially costly to duplicate. Updating of sets (reports and digests, etc.) involves annual recurring costs. Duplication of such sets can be minimized if the law librarian carefully evaluates the number of sets required in the law library. In most states, each trial court judge is provided with a set of reports and digests for that state. By designing judges' chambers in such a manner that several judges can share an adequate private library, the cost involved could be substantially reduced. Regardless of whether there are one or more courts in a court building or building complex, the provision of more than one fully equipped law library cannot be justified. Judges, law clerks, and attorneys can share the law library. The fact that an appellate court and trial court are located in the same building does not justify the cost of equipping and maintaining separate law libraries.

Although recent technologies are not likely to eliminate the use of hard-copy text in law libraries, they do present an opportunity for law librarians to address two of their major problems: cost of materials and space constraints.

Large numbers of state and federal reporter series and other material are available on various photographic and electronic media. Although giving way to electronic media, various microforms, particularly microfiche technology, are extremely effective space savers at a cost below hard copy. CD-ROM systems, which have of course been developed more recently, allow even more flexible research capabilities and amazing space savings at a cost now within the reach of virtually all court systems. Most recently, the dramatic growth of Internet technology provides access to legal materials on a worldwide basis. It is a bit early to say whether such access is adequate to allow libraries to reduce their own holdings, but it is clearly a development which bears watching in terms of its impact on library design.

All of these developments have major potential for the rethinking of law library space. Beyond the certainty that the space required for material storage can be markedly reduced, it is possible to create more extensive legal collections in distributed or remote locations at relatively low cost either by physically housing photo and/or electronic-based collections in multiple locations or by connecting remote locations electronically to centralized data bases.

Although these developments should reduce the average cost of library space, they are not without other related costs. Space may have to be configured to allow the effective use of photographic media, and other expenses, notably those relating to the installation of appropriate wiring (fiber optic, twisted pair, etc.), will be increased.

Despite the adoption of the technologies noted above, it is not yet realistic to assume that law libraries will totally abandon their more traditional configuration.

As the number of volumes increases within the fixed space of an existing law library, the reading and study area tends to decrease proportionately. This has resulted in an overcrowded condition in many of the law libraries throughout the country. The lack of trained library personnel leaves the small library disorganized and dilapidated. Reading and study areas are drab, cramped, and poorly lit.

Three types of reading and study spaces should be provided in most larger law libraries. There should be a general reading area surrounded by books, publications, and periodicals that are frequently used. This area should be near the administrative, entry control, and catalog areas, and be supervised by library personnel at the control counter. It should be furnished with a combination of study and lounge furniture. Work tables for one to four persons, including some carrels designed for legal research (42 to 48 inches wide and 30 inches deep), should be provided in a well-lit (70 to 100 foot-candles at work surface), glare-free, and temperature-and-humidity-controlled space. Adjoining this area, and perhaps separated by shelving for journals and periodicals, should be a space furnished with comfortable lounge furniture for casual reading. This space can be near the noisier control counter, reference book, and catalog area, and can serve as a noise buffer between the counter area and the quiet reading area of the library.

The second type of reading and study area involves small special study and research alcoves with a table for two researchers, or two carrels, surrounded by bookstacks containing volumes on special legal subjects such as civil rights, legal treatises from foreign countries, oceanographic laws, military laws, and so on. A series of such study and research alcoves can be created throughout the bookstack areas on the main library as well as in the high-density stack area located in the basement. These study alcoves should also be well lit and environmentally comfortable for concentrated legal research over a lengthy time period.

The third type of reading and study space consists of small individual rooms for the single researcher involved in long-term legal-research projects. Each of these rooms should be equipped with a built-in work surface along one end wall, with one or two armchairs for the researcher and for an occasional collaborator or visitor. A phone jack should be provided to allow the plugging in of a telephone or a laptop computer unit, when needed. The environmental condition of these rooms should be the same as the other reading and study areas, except they are quieter and are usually located along more remote parts of the law library. These rooms should also be appropriate for dictation and transcription when the need arises.

Whether one or more of these types of reading and study spaces are used depends on the size and configuration of available law library space and on the philosophy of the law librarian, court, or court administrator. The design of the law library, especially the relationship between the reading and study areas and the book storage areas, requires the expertise of a consultant experienced in this field.

Perhaps the most deficient spaces in any law library are the offices for the law librarian and support staff, and the related library facilities such as control counter, duplication facilities, and workroom. In small libraries in rural county courthouses, such areas are combined into one space, together with reading, study, and bookstack areas. In larger law libraries, there could be several private offices for the librarians and support staff, a separate control counter adjacent to the entry area, and a separate duplication room that contains—besides duplication equipment—work surfaces, storage shelves or cabinets for supplies, and postage and other equipment.

Whether the administrative offices need to be near the control counter and the entrance area depends on the size of the law library and on the need for the law librarian to be accessible to the library users. In a small library, the only person responsible for the operation of the library might be a part-time law clerk or law student. This person would have to be located at the control counter or desk and be easily accessible to all library users. In a larger law library with a full-time librarian and no other support staff, the librarian's location would also be at the control counter. In large law libraries with a number of library staff, only the reference librarian needs to be at the control counter; the law librarian and other support staff can have their offices either adjacent to the control counter or on another floor connected to the main library entrance area by means of an interior staircase or elevator. This would relieve the law librarian from the routine operation of the law library, and permit him or her to concentrate on library development and on facilities in outlying branch law libraries, if such exist.

Workrooms, catalog areas, and storage facilities, on the other hand, should be located near the service entrance and loading dock of the building on the ground floor. This would facilitate the movement of books and supplies from the loading dock to these work and storage facilities. If possible, the administrative offices should also have convenient access to these facilities.

Shared Facilities

Beyond considerations given to the major court and related facilities, there are a number of shared support facilities that are frequently neglected in court building projects. Attorneys' conference and witness waiting rooms are frequently inadequate and sometimes completely ignored in the design process. Little consideration is usually given to conference rooms, offices, and interview rooms that are needed by agencies located outside of the courthouse but whose representatives appear in court on a regular basis. These agencies, including the public defender, probation, and family-related social and welfare departments, do not require permanent offices in the courthouse, but they do need facilities for temporary use when their representatives are in the courthouse. Adequate space is seldom provided for prisoner-holding facilities, attorneys' lounge, police waiting rooms (in criminal court facilities), bailiffs and court process servers' locker and restrooms, general building janitorial supplies storage spaces, nursery for small children to be cared for in family court buildings while parents appear in court, and so on. While it is possible for the court system to operate without these facilities, collectively they contribute significantly to improved operational efficiency, which differentiates between a poorly functional and an effectively functional court building.

Settlement Conference Areas

As litigation shifts away from jury trial orientation to more sophisticated negotiation and settlement mediation, less area in a courthouse will be dedicated to courtrooms and more to the ancillary needs of processing litigation. At present, modern caseflow techniques are in part restricted by traditional courthouse design. Either space is not available in the immediate area of the pretrial conference to permit meetings, or the space is poorly accessed for this purpose. In some cases, telephones needed to consummate a settlement are not conveniently or privately located. In many cases separate conference rooms are needed for lawyers to confer independently with their clients. The purpose served by having such facilities available in the courthouse is to avoid losing the momentum of consideration established by the conference with the judge. Private and deliberate conferences between attorney and client must be possible to make settlements fair. The caseflow can be enhanced by careful provision for this need.

Attorneys' Conference and Witness Rooms

Justice is compromised when trial participants have to use inadequate facilities. In many courthouses, attorneys and litigants discuss their cases in busy public lobbies and hallways simply because no attorneys' conference rooms are available. Witnesses are seen waiting in public lobbies in full view of litigants, attorneys, and the public because no witness waiting rooms are provided. Conversations between attorneys and litigants, and between attorneys and witnesses, can be overheard by other people in the public lobbies and hallways. Where appropriate, it is recommended that each trial courtroom be equipped with a conference room and a witness room, the use of which is interchangeable.

Because attorneys' conference rooms are usually directly accessible from the public lobby, they have been known, together with public toilets, to be the main targets of bomb planting in major court buildings. In the Criminal Courts Building in New York City during the seventies, a bomb was planted in the suspended ceiling of a public toilet adjacent to a trial courtroom. It blasted the toilet and the adjoining courtroom at three o'clock the following morning. Fortunately, no one was hurt. Attorneys' conference rooms and witness rooms, if freely accessible from public lobbies, should not directly adjoin courtrooms, but should be separated from them by a public lobby or corridor. If these rooms have to adjoin courtrooms, it is recommended that entrances to them be provided from the courtroom vestibule or soundlock instead of directly from the public lobby or corridor. When the courtroom is not in use, the vestibule or soundlock should be locked and the conference and witness rooms would not be accessible to the general public. A number of conference rooms can be provided across the public lobby from the courtrooms. These can be opened directly from the public lobby and their use can be controlled, if necessary, by the clerk's office or the court administrator's office.

Attorneys' conference rooms do not need to be large; they are used by attorneys to confer with their clients or with witnesses for brief periods of time. However, they should not appear or feel cramped or drab. This can be accomplished in a small room by a built-in work surface along one wall, with two or three armchairs, and by using bright accent colors on one or two walls. In larger conference or witness rooms, a round conference or low coffee table can be centrally placed, surrounded by several comfortable conference or lounge armchairs.

The more preparation a lawyer can accomplish while she or he is in the courthouse, the more economic is her or his necessary waiting time. It has been observed that lawyers cannot make a living at trying cases. The main reason for this statement is not the time in trial, but the wasted time waiting. Areas of privacy for witness and client discussion will make the lawyers' waiting time more effective.

One or more witness rooms should be accessible from the private corridor behind the judicial area of trial courtrooms. These rooms should be somewhat larger than attorneys' conference rooms; witnesses may wait for hours in these rooms to testify before the court. They should be furnished with informal lounge furniture, and colors and surface treatments should present a pleasant atmosphere. These rooms can also be used as judges' conference or robing rooms if necessary.

Shared Facilities for Support Agencies

Certain judicial support agencies are located outside the courthouse either because of space shortages in the courthouse or because the agencies prefer to appear not to be associated with the court system. These include the public defender's office, probation department, and certain social and welfare agencies that deal with indigent defendants, probationers, and parents and children involved in the judicial process. These agencies do not wish to appear to their clients that they are integral parts of the prosecutorial process within the court system. They are located near the court building in either leased commercial office space or state or county buildings.

Since these agencies are housed outside the court building, only shared facilities are needed for their use while their representatives appear in court on case matters. Shared facilities normally include office, conference, and interview rooms. Not all agencies have personnel in the courthouse at the same time, and such shared facilities strategically located on each floor or every second or third floor could be used by any one agency or a combination of several agencies on an as-needed basis. It would be preferable for these facilities to adjoin the clerk's office or the office of the person responsible for the control and assignment of their shared use. If one of these agencies assigns a secretary or clerk to these shared facilities, it should be possible for the court to arrange for this person to monitor the use of shared facilities and to make sure that they are not abused.

Shared offices should be small and suitably equipped for a variety of activities: work, research, interview, and conference. A built-in work surface along one wall, together with armchairs, lockable two-drawer file cabinets located under work surfaces, and adjustable work lamps are standard furniture in these offices. All shared facilities should be carpeted and walls should be finished with appropriate colors to reflect a cheerful environment. Shared conference rooms adjoining reception and work areas should be equipped with a conference table, several conference armchairs, a fixed chalk or magnetic board, and provision for future videotape and closed-circuit television systems and equipment. Shared interview rooms are essential for probation and social or welfare personnel to interview their clients before or after court appearances. These rooms can be grouped around a central reception or work area.

Attorneys' Lounge

Attorneys use this lounge to wait for their cases to be heard, to hang their coats, and to meet with clients and other attorneys. Since most attorneys spend only what time they absolutely have to in the courthouse, the strategic location of this lounge is crucial to its availability and use. Based on present court operations, the attorneys' lounge needs to be near trial courtrooms. Attorneys can arrange to meet with their clients at a specified time at the lounge, where they can discuss their cases prior to their court appearance. For this purpose, small conference rooms adjacent to and accessible from the lounge are recommended. These conference rooms offer the degree of privacy needed for client conference, witness instruction, and attorneys' case preparation. Telephones or payphones should be provided in these rooms.

The attorneys' lounge should be furnished in an informal manner with lounge chairs, low tables, table lamps, worktables, and bookcases. Tables and chairs should be grouped and arranged for small group discussion. A private toilet and a coffee preparation and vending machine area should be provided for attorneys' convenience. Frequently, if such a facility is planned, the local bar association is willing to equip, furnish, and operate the facility without cost to the court system. However, few courthouses have such a facility. Even when an attorneys' lounge is provided, it is often, owing to a shortage or a misuse of space, poorly located and, as a result, poorly utilized. For such a facility to function efficiently, the bar association should be informed early in the building planning process, and an agreement should be established for its design, furnishing, and operation. Design input from local practicing attorneys is usually helpful to the location and design of the attorneys' lounge and its ancillary facilities.

With the use of more sophisticated communications systems, such as closed-circuit television and videotape recording, the location of the attorneys' lounge will become less significant. It is possible for this lounge to be equipped with television monitors that simultaneously depict docket and case trial information for several courtrooms. Updated activity information in each court can be shown on a television screen by means of switches. One screen would provide a continuous update of case status in all courtrooms. This information will enable attorneys to remain in the lounge and work in the conference rooms until their cases are shown on the television monitors to be ready for trial or hearing in specific courtrooms. Attorneys and clients would then proceed to their respective courtrooms without undue time delay or confusion. When such a communications system is installed in the attorneys' lounge, a larger lounge will be needed to accommodate the equipment which can be appropriately installed in an adjoining space separated from the lounge by a glass wall, and to house the greater centralization of attorneys and their clients waiting for their cases to be called. With such a system, the attorneys' lounge can be located near the courtrooms, the clerk's office, or the main entrance area of the court building.

Bailiff's Facilities

A facility frequently neglected in courthouse design is the bailiff's locker room and restroom. This facility should be centrally located among courtrooms or courtroom floors so that summoned bailiffs can reach those courtrooms without undue delay. In the future, with the installation of sophisticated security and communication systems and equipment and the provision of a central security and control room within the courthouse, the bailiff's locker room and restroom facility should be located next to such a control room (assuming such a room is located near courtrooms) so that any emergency situations can be immediately relayed to the bailiffs on duty. In multistory court buildings, bailiff's locker room and restroom facilities can be located on each floor or on every second floor, depending on the size of the building and the most efficient means of providing bailiff service to the court during emergency situations.

Law Enforcement Facilities

In criminal and traffic courts, law enforcement officers are frequently in the courthouse either as arresting officers or as witnesses to criminal cases. As arresting officers, police officers are not particularly well liked by defendants and their relatives and friends waiting in the public lobbies or waiting area for their cases to be heard. These officers should not have to wait in the same area as the defendants or their relatives and friends. Such a situation could only create unnecessary emotional tension and potentially dangerous security risks. Similar situations are created when the judge's chamber is on a floor different from the courtroom and he or she has to walk through the public corridor with the defendant's relatives and friends after a trial in which the defendant has been sentenced. Such situations can be avoided by careful separation of public and private circulation patterns. By providing the law enforcement officers with suitable facilities in the courthouse, with a separate means of entrance into and egress from the courtroom, potentially explosive situations can be avoided.

Law enforcement officers need a space, preferably located near the courtrooms, in which to wait for their cases to be called by the court, to prepare and complete reports while waiting, to lock up their firearms upon entering the courthouse, and to meet with attorneys regarding their appearance as witnesses. Law enforcement facilities should only be accessible from the private circulation system. Work surfaces and chairs should be located in an adequate room. A gun lock unit with small lockers for firearms should be built into one of the walls near the entrance into this facility. Small work booths could be provided at the end of the room for report preparation, and one or two small conference rooms could be provided to enable police officers to meet with assistant district attorneys or other court-related personnel.

Such law enforcement facilities may be equipped with closed-circuit television monitors which would allow officers to follow the status of their cases in each courtroom, and to proceed to their respective courtrooms when they are called. A paging system should be installed to summon the police officer to the courtroom when it is time to testify. Police officers would proceed to courtrooms and return to this central facility by means of private staff circulation, thus avoiding mixing with the public.

Prisoner-Holding Facilities

In a small, single-courtroom courthouse, the separation of public, private, and secure circulation patterns can be accomplished by providing three separate entrances in the appropriate facilities on the ground level. For example, the public enters from the front of the building and has direct access to the public counter area of the clerk's office, attorneys' conference rooms, shared offices, law library (if used by practicing attorneys in the community), and the public spectator area of the courtroom. The private entrance into the building for judges and court staff is located at the opposite end of the building, with direct private access to the judges' support offices and chambers, jury deliberation room (which can be designed as a multipurpose space), law library, and the judicial area of the courtroom. A third entrance along one side of the building, with adequate provision for prisoner loading and unloading, leads into the secured prisoner-holding facilities adjoining the judicial area of the courtroom. Prisoner-holding cells, secured interview room, and supervision areas are provided. A soundlock is provided where necessary between prisoner-holding cells and the courtroom. Prisoners are brought into the courtroom at a point closest to the defendant's seat adjacent to the defense counsel in the judicial area of the courtroom. The distance between prisoner-holding facilities and the defendant's seat in the courtroom is minimized for security reasons.

In large multistory court buildings, prisoners have to be transferred from the jail or central prisoner-holding facilities by means of secured prisoner elevators. The inclusion of a third circulation system for secured prisoner transfer in a multistory court building can only be accomplished successfully in one of two ways. With the public entry into the courtroom from the public end, and the private judges' and court staff's entrance from the opposite end of the courtroom, the prisoners can only be brought vertically by means of a secured prisoner elevator located between courtrooms. Prisoners taken to a specific floor would be housed in satellite prisoner-holding cells which, together with secured prisoner interviewing and supervision facilities, are located between courtrooms. From these facilities, prisoners can be taken directly into adjoining criminal courtrooms. The limitation of this design is the number of courtrooms on each floor that can be provided with secured prisoner access by one prisoner elevator. By stacking criminal courtrooms on one side of the building, the number of criminal courtrooms with separate secure prisoner access increases with the increase in the number of courtroom floors. In most situations, a prisoner elevator can service two criminal courtrooms on each floor.

The other alternative would be to provide a secure mezzanine corridor above each courtroom floor so that personnel escorting prisoners brought by means of the prisoner elevator to the mezzanine level of a particular courtroom floor would have the flexibility of moving through a corridor system to any of the trial courtrooms located on that floor. This solution is particularly applicable to a court system in which all judges housed in the building are criminal court judges or are assigned both criminal and civil cases. The requirement of both alternatives is that all courtrooms be provided with secured prisoner access entirely separated from public and private circulation system. However, it is worth noting that the provision of a secured prisoner circulation system on a mezzanine level at each courtroom floor increases the initial construction cost of the project, and may result in an overall floor-to-floor height that is greater than can be justified.

From the mezzanine level, prisoners are escorted to courtrooms through the use of internal staircases or elevators which lead to satellite prisoner-holding cells, interview rooms, and supervision areas between courtrooms. It is possible to design this mezzanine-level circulation corridor so that staircases connect both the floor above and the floor below. This means that two floors of courtrooms can be serviced by a secured corridor system sandwiched between them. This design would be less costly than that with a mezzanine level for each courtroom floor.

Satellite prisoner-holding facilities between courtrooms house prisoners waiting for their cases to be called. Such facilities adjacent to arraignment courtrooms need to be considerably larger than those adjoining trial courtrooms. It is preferable to locate arraignment courtrooms on the same floor as the central prisoner-holding facilities in the courthouse (the ground floor or basement) so that such facilities are not duplicated (at great expense) on an upper floor. The large number of prisoners held for arraignments can then be brought directly from the central prisoner-holding facilities into the adjoining arraignment courtrooms. For the trial courtrooms handling felony trials on the upper floors, the number of prisoners required at each courtroom each day is usually very few, and the number of prisoner-holding cells adjoining courtrooms on each floor does not need to be more than one multidefendant cell and one or two individual cells for defendants that may have to be segregated. One of these individual cells should be equipped with a one-way sound system so that a disruptive defendant removed from his trial may continue to hear the trial proceedings. In the future, it is possible that federal or state laws may require that the defendant be able to see as well as hear his trial proceedings, in which case a closed-circuit television monitor can be installed in this cell and cameras in the courtroom.

At least one secured interview room should be provided in each secured prisoner area adjoining courtrooms. This room should be designed and located so that attorneys from courtrooms can enter it from one side while the prisoner enters from the other. In high-security situations, the attorney's area of the interview room is separated from the prisoner's area by means of bulletproof or thick tempered glass, with conversation conducted either through telephone receivers or specially designed metal grills that do not impede sound transmission but would prevent anything from passing through them. In low-security situations, the interview room can simply be equipped with a fixed table and several fixed seats. A soundlock should be provided between the prisoner-holding cells and the judicial area of the courtroom to minimize distracting noise transmission from the cells into the courtroom. No eating facilities are necessary at these satellite prisoner-holding facilities. If necessary, sandwiches can be brought up to these areas during the lunch recess, or prisoners can be returned to the central prisoner-holding facilities, where they are provided with sandwiches or other types of lunches.

If the county or city jail is located within or adjoining the courthouse, the central prisoner-holding facilities in the courthouse may not be necessary. When the jail is located in the courthouse, it serves as the central prisoner-holding facility. When it is adjacent and connected to the courthouse by means of a bridge or tunnel, the need for a central prisoner-holding facility will be determined by the size of the courthouse and the number of trial courtrooms handling criminal trials involving detained defendants. For a small courthouse, the jail may serve adequately as the central prisoner-holding facility, and prisoners would be transferred to the courthouse via the tunnel or bridge when they are needed by the courts. In a multistory court building, the large number of prisoners transferred each day between the jail and the courthouse may necessitate the provision of a central prisoner-holding, interviewing, and supervision facility in the basement or on an upper floor of the courthouse. When the jail is remotely located from the courthouse, and prisoners have to be transported in secured prisoner vans, a central prisoner-holding facility, equipped with secured vehicular and prisoner sallyports and other related processing and control facilities, is definitely needed in a major courthouse.

Transportation of Prisoners

Transfer of prisoners between a remotely located jail and the main criminal court building is a costly process. Personnel, vehicular and operating costs incurred from transporting prisoners between the jail and the courthouse may run into millions of dollars each year in a moderately large city. Where possible, local county or city jails should be located near the courthouse. They should not be in the same building, but can be visually and functionally connected, by means of underground tunnels or overhead bridges, so that prisoners can be transferred securely between the two buildings. In the development of major court and jail facilities in downtown locations, a multilevel parking structure is usually involved. Should this parking structure be an integral part of the downtown judiciary complex, a double-level bridge or a split tunnel may be needed in order to separate the prisoner circulation pattern from the public and court staff moving between the courthouse and the parking structure.

In metropolitan centers with an efficient public subway or railway transportation system, it may be possible in the future to incorporate such systems as a viable means of transporting prisoners between jail and courthouse. Planning of subway or railway locations to link the jail with the criminal courthouse, special design of prisoner-holding compartments, and the scheduling of arrival and departure times so as not to present a routine schedule have to be carefully implemented before such a system becomes functionally and economically viable. In New York City, the subway system, with stations located near the jail and criminal court buildings, could be adapted for transporting prisoners at a reasonable cost. Special prisoner security precautions would have to be taken to ensure that prisoners do not come into contact with the general public. A special subway train with one or more compartments could be designed exclusively for transportation of prisoners. This train would use the express line and would not stop at stations between the jail and the courthouse. Such a system would minimize security risk in prisoner transportation when compared with the regular method of transporting prisoners in vans through busy city streets.

Videotape Recording Areas

The modern trial will require more and more the videotape recording of testimony. These systems have failed in the past because they have not been convenient or are unfamiliar to the litigant. Their availability in court complexes would greatly facilitate the growth of this capacity. Video arraignment between jail and courthouses is becoming a common application in courthouses. Videotaping of trial proceedings has passed the experimental stages and is being planned for all newer judicial buildings. Video-teleconferencing between remotely located witnesses and attorneys' offices or courtrooms is also becoming more acceptable, and is predicted to be widely used as costs continue to decrease.

Public Facilities

Public facilities in courthouses are important because they generate the public image of the judicial system. Impressive entrance lobbies with soaring heights may present the same impression as a large international hotel. Regular office ceiling heights, on the other hand, can result in an oppressive and uncomfortable feeling when used to enclose large entrance lobbies of major courthouses. Public spaces provide the first impression of the judicial system to the public, and should be sensitively and creatively designed to achieve a balanced and dignified appearance. Excessively high ceilings represent waste of space and expenditure, oppressively low ceilings imply poor design solution. Use of colors and materials in public lobbies may generate positive or negative emotional reactions to court spaces, and may affect the amount of building maintenance necessary over its life span. Public spaces do not need to be excessively large, yet they do need to be designed for an intensified sequential spatial experience as people move from one space to another. There is a need for architectural harmony and order, which should be reflected in the spatial and functional design of the complex components of the judicial system. The seating arrangements in public lobbies should reflect both the formality of the judicial process and the informality and flexibility of many of its procedures.

A well-designed public information center is essential in the main public lobby. This center can vary from a public counter manned by an information officer or receptionist to a complex center equipped with sophisticated computerized equipment showing currently updated case docket and status information. Case calendaring information involving the cases being heard in all courtrooms and their status can either be shown on television screens or on computerized information display boards similar in principle to those used in commercial airport terminals for displaying flight arrival and departure information. For such display boards to be used in the courthouse, their size will have to be substantially reduced and they'll have to be placed closer to eye level so that they can be accommodated within the available ceiling height of the public lobby. The public information center can also be manned by regular clerical employees or by volunteers trained in the computer applications. By means of one or more terminals, these information offices will be able to answer all inquiries regarding case status, location of defendant, judge and courtroom assigned to the case, location of courtrooms and clerk's office, and so on. A coordinated information and sign system is crucial to the movement of the public to their various destinations in the courthouse.

In most court buildings separate public and staff vending and lunch areas should be provided, preferably in the main entrance lobby area. These areas should be enclosed so that eating activities are contained within those areas and not extended into other spaces in the building. For provision of food, a vending machine operation may be adequate for most court buildings. The public should be encouraged to patronize the local restaurants and eating places in the community close to the courthouse. But when such eating establishments are lacking, and when the court building houses a large number of court employees, then a full-scale cafeteria operation can be justified. Separate rooms or partitioned spaces should be planned for feeding impaneled and sequestered jurors.

Public elevator lobbies require careful consideration. A width between public elevator banks of more than fifteen feet is not desirable, as the distance of travel between one side of the lobby and the elevator on the other side is excessive for the time allowed between opening and closing of elevator doors. Public circulation and waiting areas on courtroom floors should be designed sensitively. People tend to congregate around the entrance doors leading into the courtroom. Consequently, public waiting and seating areas should be provided either opposite the courtroom across the public circulation corridor, or adjacent to the courtroom entrance between conference rooms, which are accessible from the soundlock or vestibule of the courtroom. Seating in public waiting areas should be durable and easily maintained. Seating can be the built-in upholstered bench type or individual seats sufficiently large that they cannot be picked up and used as weapons. Movable items should be avoided; they should be fixed, built in, or too heavy to be moved by even a strong person.

Conference rooms and public toilets that are directly accessible from the public waiting areas should be separated from the courtrooms by means of public circulation and waiting areas. This would minimize the extent of damage should a bomb explode in those publicly accessible spaces. Public waiting areas should be designed to provide a sense of openness and visual relief. Colors and materials in these spaces should evoke elegance and quiet dignity.

Courts have recognized the requirement to accommodate the litigant who, either by necessity or choice, brings the small child to court. Such visitors can be extremely disruptive to proceedings, often aggravating an already tense and difficult situation.

Assuming that questions of insurance, staffing, security, and so forth can be satisfied in a particular jurisdiction, it is possible to create a satisfactory facility for child care at a separate, yet convenient, location within the courthouse. The prime consideration is obviously child safety and comfort, which are addressed through space size, design, materials, and equipment used.

Beyond reflecting a legitimate concern for the children using such a facility, its existence will go far to remove a potential irritant from court proceedings and remove a source of concern for parents in litigation, many of whom are troubled and preoccupied.

Courthouse Security

Optimal courthouse security involves a balance between architectural planning, technology and equipment, and security personnel assignment. The most cost-effective approach to providing an appropriate level of security in courthouses is through the separation of various circulation systems—public, restricted (staff and judges), secure (prisoners), and service. Arriving at the optimal security planning solution at the conceptual phase of courthouse design would be the least costly solution to security problems. Technology and equipment—including closed-circuit television (CCTV) systems; video cameras in courtrooms linked to security monitors in the central control room; key-card access systems connected to a monitoring computer system; bulletproof material protecting the judge's bench, witness box, and clerk's station in courtrooms; adequate physical separation between counter clerks' or receptionists' workstations and public in the clerk's office and court-support agencies; and a coordinated duress alarm system throughout the courthouse—are common security systems in today's courthouses. The most costly solution to security problems is to employ large numbers of security personnel, yet this is typically the only solution available for courthouses that were not functionally or architecturally designed to provide optimal security. Security screening at more than one primary public entrance to the courthouse multiplies the number of security personnel for security screening. Personnel-based solutions are expensive because they are recurring and escalating, compared to the one-time construction cost of the building and the initial costs of security technological systems and equipment, which have annual operating and maintenance costs but not major recurring and escalating costs. Consequently, having a single public entry into the courthouse, minimizing the amount of prisoner transfer between a remotely located jail and the courthouse, and a cost-effective design solution to minimize security personnel monitoring and escorting of prisoners would have a major impact on the long-term operating cost of security in courthouses.

Courthouse security issues and solutions have already been adequately covered in several definitive texts in courthouse planning and design, notably *The American Courthouse: Planning and Design for the Judicial Process* (see chapter 21 therein), *Space Management and the Courts—Design Handbook* (see chapter 5 therein), and *U.S. Courts Design Guide* (see chapters 10 and 14 therein), among others. It is not the intent of this book to provide details on courthouse security but to recognize it as an essential component of effective courthouse planning and design.

The following is a summary of essential courthouse security considerations that should be incorporated in all courthouse projects:

Exterior and Perimeter Security
- Sufficient setback of building from street or driveway
- Security barriers between street or driveway and building to keep vehicles from approaching closely

- Safety zones around building for restrictive or secured uses
- Adequate lighting of surrounding areas, particularly open parking lots
- Landscaping that makes the grounds open and visible and does not create places in which individuals can conceal themselves
- Minimal number of public and staff approaches to the building
- Central monitoring of perimeter security systems and entrances
- Use of impact-resistant glazing, where necessary, on the ground or first floor
- Avoidance of creating large open areas under the building

Interior Building Security

- Minimal number of public and staff entrances requiring security screening
- Appropriate separation of circulation systems, both vertical and horizontal
- Limiting and controlling after-hours access into the building
- CCTV surveillance and central monitoring of all restricted and secure circulation spaces
- Adequate central and satellite (adjacent to courtrooms) prisoner-holding facilities
- Secure vehicular sallyport for transfer of prisoners
- Control of reception access to judges' chambers, prosecuting attorney, public defender, probation, pretrial, and clerks' offices, and so forth
- Key-card readers to monitor and restrict staff access to restrictive and secure areas
- Alarmed emergency exits that pass through restricted areas, with delayed existing features
- Installation of public address system to facilitate orderly building evacuation during emergencies

Security in Courtrooms and Ancillary Facilities

- Duress alarms connected to central security control and bailiff station
- CCTV surveillance connected to central security control and bailiff's station
- Controlled access between courtroom and prisoner-holding and interview facilities
- Secured jury access between courtrooms and jury deliberation suites
- Bailiff or security personnel control stations on each court floor, if necessary

- Monitored and controlled file-viewing areas and glazed cashier stations in clerk's office

Accessibility Considerations

Court buildings, like other state and local government buildings, are required by Title II of the Americans with Disabilities Act (ADA) to have their services, programs, and activities accessible to persons with disabilities. The following areas must be in compliance, and many of them are common to all building types:

- Parking
- Passenger loading zones
- Exterior accessible routes, curb ramps
- Entrances and exits (and areas of rescue assistance)
- Building lobbies and corridors
- Ramps, stairs, and elevators
- Doors and gates
- Toilet rooms and drinking fountains
- Signage
- Alarms
- Detectable warnings
- Service counters, ATMs

On June 20, 1994, in the *Federal Register,* the Access Board issued an interim final rule for state and local government facility guidelines that more clearly addresses the specialized spaces in judicial facilities. The Departments of Justice (DOJ) and Transportation (DOT) have issued notices of proposed rulemaking to adopt these guidelines; however, until the two departments publish a final rule, these guidelines are not officially considered requirements.

In practical terms, however, these interim guidelines should be followed (insofar as they do not conflict with local codes) for all new and altered judicial facilities. It would be costly to incorporate these guidelines later in the design and construction process; thus, they should be regarded as requirements until the final rule is issued.

The interim final rule addresses accessibility guidelines for elements in the courtroom, jury assembly and deliberation spaces, courthouse holding facilities, restricted and secured entrances, security screening, two-way communications, outlets for communication systems, and assistive listening systems.

Courtrooms

The following courtroom elements must be *accessible:*
- Gate into the courtroom well (if applicable)
- Jury box (one position, minimum)
- Witness stand
- Fixed seating areas (where greater than fifty seats, in more than one row)
- Fixed stations for bailiffs, court reporters, litigants and counsel
- Fixed lecterns

These elements must be on an accessible path of travel that would coincide with the same path used by all users of that station, whether disabled or able-bodied.

The following courtroom elements must be *accessible or adaptable:*
- Judge's bench
- Clerk's station

The stations must be constructed so that full accessibility can be easily provided in the future.

Jury Assembly and Deliberation

The areas which must be accessible include refreshment areas, fixed seating or tables, and drinking fountains.

Courthouse Holding Facilities

Where central or satellite holding cells are separated into groups for different categories of detainees, for example, male, female, and juvenile, at least one of each type should be accessible. Where cells are not separated, at least one should be accessible.

Accessible cells should provide accessibility to the following elements:
- Doors, except where controlled by security personnel
- Toilet facilities
- Drinking fountains
- Fixed seating and tables
- Fixed benches

Five percent or a minimum of one of the interview booths should be accessible on both sides, which includes:
- Accessible counters
- A method to facilitate voice communication (where airtight partitioning exists) with volume control

Restricted and Secure Entrances

At least one restricted entrance and one secure entrance are required to be accessible, connecting to the transit, parking, and passenger-loading areas as appropriate.

Security Screening

Security screening equipment is required to be accessible, or an alternative adjacent path is to be provided.

Two-Way Communications Systems

Security intercom systems to gain admittance to restricted areas are required to comply with the general ADA requirements for controls and must provide both visible and audible signals.

Outlets for Communication Systems

Additional outlets and wiring, conduits, or raceways are to be provided at all courtroom stations (including that for spectators) and in meeting rooms used by the public. These would be used to support communications equipment for persons with disabilities.

Assistive Listening Systems

Permanently installed listening devices are required in 50 percent of each type of courtroom, plus 50 percent of hearing rooms, jury deliberation rooms, and jury orientation (assembly) rooms, with a minimum of one for each type. The number of receivers should be 4 percent of the room occupant load or a minimum of two for each space. Signage is required to indicate the availability of the communication equipment.

Although there are other national accessibility codes now in effect, such as the Uniform Federal Accessibility Standards and ANSI A117.1, it is expected that the American with Disabilities Act Accessibility Guidelines will eventually be the single national standard for publicly accessible facilities.

Rationale for Accessible Courtrooms

Since the passage of the Americans with Disabilities Act, accessibility requirements have become a major factor in the design of courthouses. Recent rulings require that every courtroom in the courthouse, regardless of the number of courtrooms in the building, be accessible. A jury trial courtroom designed for ADA compliance could be 10 to 15 percent larger in net area than one not designed to meet ADA requirements. For example, what would otherwise be a 1,500-square-foot courtroom for a 12-person jury panel and public seating for approximately 70 people would need to be between 1,650 and 1,700 square feet, depending on the need to install ramps and/or lifts for handicap access. In terms of construction costs, each square foot of a courtroom interior space with higher ceilings averages around $200 per square foot, compared with the average of $125 per square foot for other courthouse spaces. The additional 100 to 150 square feet would represent an extra $20,000 to $30,000 for each courtroom, exclusive of the cost of the lift equipment. Consequently, for a large courthouse with twenty trial courtrooms, the additional construction cost of courtrooms alone would be around $500,000. This same analogy can be applied to jury deliberation suites, public and staff toilets, training conference rooms, and so forth.

In parking lots throughout the country, a percentage of parking spaces is assigned to certified handicapped drivers; and these specially designed spaces, with curb cuts and/or ramps, are located as close as possible to the entrances into the building. While it is crucial that adequate consideration be given to ADA compliance in the planning and design of court facilities, it is recommended that a more rational approach, such as the example of providing a small percentage of parking spaces for the handicapped, be applied to court facilities. There should be handicap-accessible facilities such as courtrooms and auxiliary facilities, public and staff restrooms, and so forth on each floor of a courthouse. For a four-courtroom floor, at least one courtroom should be designed for full ADA compliance. For a six-or eight-courtroom floor, there should be at least two accessible courtrooms, depending on how courtrooms and judges' chambers are organized in the building.

Assignment of judges to courtrooms also has a significant impact on the number of accessible courtrooms needed. If judges are assigned to specific courtrooms of similar sizes for a period of time, a handicapped judge could be assigned to a set of chambers and a courtroom that are designed to be accessible. However, if judges are assigned to different courtrooms of different sizes to hear different types of cases, then there should be at least one accessible courtroom for each size and type of courtroom (e.g., large and regular jury trial courtroom, nonjury trial courtroom, small juvenile or domestic relations hearing room, etc.). This scenario is particularly applicable to a building housing multiple courts, courtrooms and hearing rooms of different sizes and configurations, and judges' chambers that are housed on floors separated from courtroom floors. High-volume courtrooms for handling arraignment or preliminary hearings or traffic and small-claims cases, large major trial courtrooms involving multiple defendants, and ceremonial courtrooms should all be accessible.

The adoption of a reasonable rationale to provide adequate and suitable facilities for the handicapped in courthouses will be beneficial both to handicapped staff and visitors, as well as to government entities that are responsible for the funding and construction of courthouses in the United States.

2

Court Personnel, Structure, and Space Management

State and local court personnel in the United States include judges, referees, and hearing officers, as well as administrators, court reporters, clerks, law clerks, and other personnel. Personnel employed by ancillary agencies include, but are not limited to, prosecutors' offices, public defenders and legal aid, social service agencies, probation services, mental health services, and detention facilities. The variety and composition of courts' personnel vary from jurisdiction to jurisdiction.

Persons employed by courts work in myriad occupations covering professional, technical, and clerical positions in a variety of court settings. They are recruited, hired, retained, promoted, demoted, or removed in a number of different ways, ranging from union contracts and fairly sophisticated personnel merit systems to no system at all and patronage employment.

While there are considerable similarities in the organization, operation, and functions of the fifty state judicial systems, there is also great variety. No two systems are organized, administered, or funded in exactly the same way. Court structure varies from state to state, as do court nomenclature and jurisdiction. There are differences in the way judges are selected and retained, as well as in their length of term. More significant is the variation among state and local jurisdictions in personnel practices and procedures.

It is also important to emphasize that court officials and employees perform similar functions, regardless of how the judicial system is organized and administered and how employees are selected and paid.

Personnel Systems

Despite the large number of people employed by state and local courts, state judicial systems and their components have lagged behind other public employees in personnel administration. All fifty states and most counties and municipalities have some sort of civil service or personnel merit system and an established compensation plan for executive branch employees.

Merit Systems

A separate statewide merit system for judicial employees is found only in a handful of states. Statewide judicial employee merit systems usually go hand in hand with state funding and with administrative integration and unification of the judicial system. In state court systems in which the trial court is funded locally, personnel merit systems are found in many trial courts in urban or more populous areas, either as a separate plan or as part of the system used by the local unit of government for employees of the executive branch.

However, an increasing number of state judicial systems and individual courts have adopted and implemented formalized personnel systems.

The basic components of a personnel system for court employees are set forth in the *American Bar Association Standards Relating to Court Organization*.

Patronage

Many court employees in a number of states are still hired and hold their jobs under some form of patronage. Patronage systems survive primarily in small or rural courts and in large courts closely linked to the partisan political process. They are also found in many states where the clerk of court is elected and selects his or her staff on a patronage basis.

Patronage systems basically operate through a network of relationships formed on a personal, professional, or political basis. Whatever the contact points may be, the ultimate authority tends to reside in the presiding or senior judge for positions that serve the whole court and with an individual judge for courtroom positions, such as division clerk or bailiff.

While inherently less selective than more formalized systems, patronage systems tend to create or reinforce trust and loyalty, if for no other reason than the employee has no safeguards against removal or demotion, and usually there is no formalized salary scale paying the same rate or rates for the same work, regardless of who the employee is.

Obviously, this system is the antithesis of the one described in the *ABA Standards Relating to Court Organization*. Patronage systems have tended to be nonselective in recruitment and hiring and have provided employment for very few individuals who belong to racial or ethnic minorities. They have also tended to perpetuate incompetent or mediocre employees who have maintained outmoded methods, procedures, and techniques. As a consequence of all these and other shortcomings, patronage systems are slowly giving way in the wake of demand and concern for employee rights and the loss of competent, qualified personnel to more progressive personnel systems, both public and private. The continuing shift away from election of judges in favor of some form of judicial merit selection and tenure has also weakened the hold of patronage selection of employees.

Collective Bargaining

Unionization of and collective bargaining by public employees has been on the scene for many years, and many states have legislated in this area, although the legislation is by no means uniform from state to state in its application either to state or local employees.

Judicial systems and individual trial courts have had limited experience with collective bargaining, although employee organizations have represented court employees in grievances and other matters in a number of jurisdictions with formalized personnel systems. However, unionization of judicial employees continues to increase, giving employees added influence in the general management of courts, including facility conditions.

Legal Framework Relating to Court Personnel

The previous discussion illustrates the vast differences in court personnel systems, practices, and management. The way the system is organized and administered may be determined by a variety or combination of constitutional provisions, statutory requirements, and court rules. The content and mix of these provisions, requirements, and rules differ from jurisdiction to jurisdiction, and in some states, no formal requirements or guidelines exist.

Where there are no judicial systems or formal court requirements or guidelines, court personnel are usually administered in one of two ways. First, court personnel may be hired, retained, promoted, or terminated under traditional unwritten practices—usually found in patronage systems. Second, an agency outside the judicial system may step into fill the vacuum—an executive branch personnel system at the state level or a county or municipal personnel system at the local level.

Federal Requirements

Court personnel administration is subject to very few federal statutory requirements or rules. A United States Supreme Court decision, *National League of Cities v. Ussery,* determined that state and local employees are not subject to the provisions of the Fair Labor Standards Act.

The Equal Employment Act of 1972 does apply to court personnel and states that state and local governments are subject to the provisions concerning discrimination in the employment process as outlined in the 1964 Civil Rights Act. The courts are ordered to correct discrimination practices and may order back pay for two years preceding the filing of a charge.

Although judicial systems and individual courts have been sued under the provisions of this act by persons alleging discrimination in hiring or other personnel practices, the main impact on courts has come through federal grant requirements, one of which is an Affirmative Action/Equal Opportunity Employment Program, for a system that has more than fifty employees, or the population to be served has more than 3 percent minority representation.

Court Rules

Statewide personnel rules have been adopted in a number of jurisdictions where the court system has been state funded. In Colorado, these rules were adopted by the supreme court pursuant to the court's general rule-making authority and specific statutory provisions. In South Dakota, it was done under the supreme court's general constitutional superintending authority. This pattern has been followed in most of the states which have statewide personnel rules.

In those states where local courts have established separate judicial system personnel and plans, it has usually been accomplished by local court rules.

Basic Court Structure—Appellate Courts

Personnel

More than five thousand judges and other court personnel are required for the operation of state appellate courts, including courts of last resort and intermediate appellate courts in those states which have them.

States vary considerably in the number of justices on the court of last resort, usually known as the supreme court; 6 states have 9 justices—Iowa, Washington, Texas (civil), Oklahoma (civil), Alabama, and Mississippi; 18 states have 5 justices; and the other 26 states have 7 justices. Two states (Oklahoma and Texas) have separate courts of last resort for civil and criminal cases.

The number of justices is only one indicator of the volume of appellate work, that is, the number of employees and the facilities needed. Other factors include the presence or absence of an intermediate appellate court; the use of commissioners to assist the court in opinion preparation; the use of staff attorneys for screening and research; the frequency of oral argument, and whether it is mandatory; and the nature of the appellate process itself, such as whether an appeal is a matter of right, and in what cases and under what circumstances it is a matter of right.

Intermediate appellate courts differ from state to state in the number of judges, in jurisdiction, in whether the court or panels thereof sit centrally or in districts or regions, in opinion publication rules, and in general operating procedures.

Aside from judges, appellate court personnel may be divided into the following categories: (1) administration, (2) direct judicial support, (3) indirect judicial support or case processing, (4) law library maintenance, and (5) ancillary or auxiliary agencies or services. Each of these categories covers several different kinds of positions and functions:

Administration

This category includes personnel involved in the overall administration of the court, with responsibility for budget and fiscal management, purchasing, personnel, space management, and so forth. An appellate court may have a separate administrator or administrative staff for these functions, or it may be included in the duties of the clerk.

Direct Judicial Support

This category includes all personnel who assist the justices or judges in appellate review and the termination of appellate cases. These are commissioners (if used to assist in writing opinions), staff attorneys, law clerks, justices' and judges' private secretaries, reporter of decisions, editor of opinions, and any assistants and bailiffs (although bailiffs might be considered under a separate category, that of security).

Usually, law clerks and private secretaries are personal or confidential employees of the justices or judges. This is true even in those judicial systems or appellate courts with a formalized personnel plan. Where this is the case, confidential employees are likely to receive fringe benefits and work under salary scales and other conditions established in the personnel rules, but they are hired by and serve at the pleasure of the justice or judge. The number of law clerks and secretaries may be set by statute or determined by court rule. It may be subject to negotiation with the appropriate funding bodies. In the smaller states, the usual practice is for each judge to have one law clerk and one secretary. In larger states, two or more may be provided, especially for the chief justice.

The other employees who fall in this category—commissioners, staff attorneys, and reporter of decisions—are usually hired by the court as a whole (or by a division of an intermediate appellate court if it sits in a separate location). The selection, compensation, retention, and so forth of these employees generally are subject to formalized personnel rules, if there are any.

Indirect Judicial Support

The personnel in this category are the clerk of court and other personnel of his or her office. They are responsible for the filing of cases and all related papers and transcripts; the handling of pertinent exhibits; records management, including the handling of completed case files; and all related activities, such as notification of attorneys, referring appropriate matters and documents to the justices or judges, and so on.

In some states, for example, Kansas, Indiana, Oregon and Minnesota, the clerical offices and functions of the court of last resort and the intermediate appellate court may be combined. The usual practice is for these offices to be separate, especially in those states where each division of the intermediate appellate court covers a separate area of the state, such as in Washington, Illinois, and New York.

The clerk of court may be an exempt employee, even if there is a formalized personnel system. The trend is in the direction of including the clerk and his or her employees under the personnel system, if one exists.

Law Library Maintenance

In some jurisdictions, maintenance of the law library is the responsibility of another agency, usually in the executive branch. In most, the law library is staffed by personnel selected by and responsible to the court of last resort or the intermediate appellate court. Where the court of last resort and the intermediate appellate court, or a division thereof, are housed in the same building, one law library serves both courts. Divisions of intermediate appellate courts which are geographically dispersed may either have separate law libraries or share them with the trial court in the same location, if it is convenient to do so.

Appellate court law librarians are usually professionals having both a law degree and a degree in library science. The number of assistants, of course, depends on the size of the library. They may include professionals, paraprofessionals, and clerical workers. The library staff is likely to be under a formalized personnel system, if one exists.

Ancillary or Auxiliary Agencies and Services

In most jurisdictions, there are several activities that are carried out under the supervision of the court of last resort or with its participation. These are the discipline of judges and attorneys; admittance to the bar, including conduct and grading of the state bar examination; and attorney registration.

Generally, discipline of judges and attorneys is carried out by separate bodies. Discipline of the former is usually the responsibility of a commission consisting of judges (one of whom may be a supreme court justice), attorneys, and nonlawyers. In larger states, the commission may have a full-time executive secretary, one or more investigator-examiners, and a secretarial-clerical staff. In smaller states, the executive secretary may be the state court administrator (or someone else) serving part-time, with investigators and examiners hired under contract as needed. There is usually a constitutional requirement that matters before the commission are confidential, becoming public only when referred to the court of last resort for appropriate action.

A separate body, composed primarily of attorneys, is responsible for investigating and recommending action on attorney grievance matters. This group has personnel needs similar to those of the judicial discipline commissions. A growing practice is to have the activities of the lawyer discipline body financed by annual attorney registration fees. Fee collection, administration, and record keeping may require the service of one or more employees, depending on the size of the bar and the extent to which the record-keeping system may be automated.

Administration of the bar examination and admittance to the bar usually requires an executive secretary and one or more supporting employees, depending on the size of the bar and the number taking the examination.

Employees of these ancillary agencies and services are likely to be selected by those responsible for their operation and may be exempt employees because of the officials to whom they are responsible.

Appellate Court Facilities

Appellate court facilities are different from trial court facilities. While trial courts conduct truly adversary proceedings, which frequently involve jurors and witnesses, the appellate court (supreme court or intermediate court of appeals) is a court of review, which involves only judges, court staff, and attorneys. No jurors or witnesses are involved in its proceedings. The atmosphere of most appellate courtrooms is solemn and dignified, and the proceedings of oral arguments are formal. Attorneys presenting oral argument are given a set amount of time, usually thirty minutes for each side, with a short time period of rebuttal. Electronic timing and lighting devices notify attorneys and justices of the amount of time remaining during oral argument. A yellow light comes on at the attorney's podium and at the justice's bench when oral argument reaches the final three or four minutes, followed by a red light at the end of the designated period. Outbursts from the public viewing area are infrequent, and when prisoners, defendants, and witnesses are not active participants during appellate proceedings, courtroom security is seldom a major problem.

The formality of the courtroom is accentuated by its furniture layout. The justices' bench is centrally located to accommodate three to nine justices. At each end, or in front of the justice's bench, and at a lower level, are workstations for the clerk of court and the court reporter. The attorneys' tables are also symmetrically located in the judicial area, separated from each other by a specially designed podium at which each attorney presents an oral argument before the justices. The design of the justices' bench and the attorneys' tables can complement one another, with a curved surface of the justices' bench to facilitate the justices' seeing each other reciprocated by a reverse curve of the attorneys' table and center podium. The distance between the justices' bench and the podium should be governed by the cone of vision of the attorney to see all justices at the bench without moving his or her head while addressing the court. The attorney's podium should be centrally located in relation to the justices' bench (directly in front of the chief justice). Bailiffs' stations are usually symmetrically located on each side of the attorneys' tables. Public seating is also formally arranged, with public entry through a public foyer and a soundlock or vestibule area. In contrast to most trial courtrooms, the design of an appellate courtroom is usually approached from a unique direction. A well-defined public foyer usually precedes and at the same time provides a more formal entry into the courtroom.

Major Appellate Court Components

The major design components of an appellate court include the courtrooms, the justices' robing room, and the justices' conference room. Especially during court oral argument procedures, justices' circulation involves moving from the justices' chambers, through private corridors or secretarial offices, to the justices' conference room, which is absolutely off-limits to everyone, including court staff, when the justices confer on cases. From their conference room, the justices move into the robing room, where they robe prior to entering the courtroom. Justices' toilets, lockers, and a shower are usually provided within this area. Justices' entry into the appellate courtroom can be either dramatic or restrained. In Providence, Rhode Island, a central curtain parts, revealing the justices who then move to their respective seats on the justices' bench. In Anchorage, Alaska, the justices enter the bench area from one side. In Des Moines, Iowa, justices appear individually on the bench through a central doorway behind the bench.

After an oral argument session, the justices retire to the robing room, where they remove their robes. They then proceed into the justices' conference room, where they may confer about the cases heard and where they vote on the resolution of each case. One of the justices on the majority side is assigned to draft the opinion. After their conference the justices return to their chambers, which are usually separated from the conference room by a private corridor. The traditional appellate court operation requires the level of privacy that is provided by the close grouping of the justices' conference room, the robing room, and the courtroom. In jurisdictions where justices confer on cases at a set time each week, the conference room can be separated from the courtroom and robing room by a private corridor, if the design is improved by such an arrangement.

Appellate Courtroom and Meeting Rooms

The size of the appellate court courtroom should be adequate to accommodate all courtroom procedures, such as oral arguments. A courtroom designed to accommodate hundreds of people during admission-to-the-bar ceremonies twice a year would mean that for the rest of the year the courtroom is grossly underutilized. Where such large courtrooms exist in historical courthouses, they should be maintained. However, the cost of constructing oversized and ornately furnished courtrooms cannot be justified in an austere economy. On the other hand, since the supreme court courtroom is singly symbolic of the judicial branch of our state government, an impressive designed ceremonial courtroom, to be used for multiple purposes, and at the same time representing the highest court of the state, is an essential element of the state judicial building. The recently completed Supreme Court Courtroom in the Alabama Judicial Building in Montgomery is an excellent example of this approach.

An area of space inadequacy frequently experienced in existing appellate court facilities is the lack of meeting rooms for use by commissions and committees and by the local bar association. Since these meeting rooms should be accessible from public or semipublic circulation spaces, it is suggested they be located contiguous to the public spectator seating area of the courtroom, and separated from it by movable full-height partitions (manually or electrically operated) when a larger public seating area is required for occasional ceremonial functions. These meeting rooms would normally be used as multipurpose spaces. When the courtroom is scheduled for a bar admission or a judge's investiture ceremony, these adjoining meeting rooms can be combined with the public area of the courtroom to increase the public seating capacity of the courtroom. However, it would be important to make sure that sight lines from these additional public seating areas are not obstructed by other walls or by structural columns. It may be desirable to arrange these meeting rooms symmetrically along the sides and rear walls of the courtroom so that the enlarged public space would wrap around three sides of the public area. This would minimize the distance between the furthest spectator in the public area and the justices' bench and attorney's podium in the judicial area, and enable the proceedings to be seen and heard clearly.

The architectural design of these meeting rooms must be consistent with the design quality of the courtroom so that, when combined as a single space, the adjacent rooms are viewed as integral and seamless parts of the courtroom design, furnishings, and finishes.

Justices' Chambers and Support Offices

Justices' chambers and offices for law clerks, secretaries, court reporters, and staff attorneys (if any) should be accessible from private circulation corridors. The general public has access to the clerk's office, attorneys' lounge, law library, and the courtroom when the court is in session. In some appellate court facilities, the attorneys' lounge is locked when the court is not in session, and the use of the law library is restricted to court staff and attorneys with special permission.

At the supreme court level, secretaries and law clerks are usually assigned to individual justices. Separate offices for secretaries and law clerks should be grouped with the justices' chambers to form a suite of offices for each justice. At the intermediate court of appeals level, not all justices have secretaries assigned to them. Consequently, the pooling of secretaries in a central secretarial area shared by all justices of that court, or the provision of a secretarial space between two justices' chambers, should be considered. Law clerks should be provided with separate offices in close proximity to the justices' chambers as well as to the law library, the latter being a more significant spatial relationship. In states where a supreme court justice has two law clerks, it is proper for them to share a private office.

Facility Planning Considerations

Courts

Appellate court justices within each state may sit in panels of three or five. With simple scheduling, one appellate courtroom can be used by up to four court panels to hear oral arguments. There are usually set court days within each month for each court panel to hear scheduled cases. Each panel usually hears oral arguments and uses the courtroom no more than one week each month. In states with a supreme court as the sole appellate court, or with appellate courts sitting at different locations, the appellate courtrooms are usually grossly underutilized. In a city with more than one appellate court and each court with more than one panel of judges, an appellate courtroom can be efficiently utilized by careful scheduling.

When one courtroom is shared by several panels of appellate justices, the grouping of justices' chambers and their support offices in reasonably close proximity to the courtroom can be accomplished most effectively by having them surround the courtroom–robing room–conference room component on two or more levels. Where both the supreme court and an intermediate court of appeals exist, then the chambers and offices of one court can be on one level while those of the other can be on a second level. As this courtroom symbolically represents the highest court of the state, it should be the most impressive and uniquely designed courtroom. Each appellate court may require its own justices' conference room and robing room. By means of an internal elevator and/or staircase, it is possible for the court of appeals judges to gain access to the courtroom from their conference room and robing room located on a different level. The chambers and support offices of one court would be grouped around the courtroom–robing room–conference room at the entry level while those of another appellate court would surround the justices' conference room–robing room on the second level. In the State Judiciary Building in Denver, Colorado, both the supreme court and court of appeals are located on the same floor. Each court has a separate courtroom, justices' conference room, robing room, chambers, and support offices.

The housing of appellate courts within a single building has many advantages. They can share common facilities, such as the law library, attorneys' lounge, and the courtroom, which would otherwise be duplicated if the courts were located in different buildings. Duplication of the law library is extremely costly and is unnecessary when both appellate courts are located in the same city. The law library should be conveniently accessible to the justices and especially to the law clerks, who spend considerable time conducting legal research for the preparation of case memoranda and draft opinions. Appellate court justices usually have their own set of reference books within their chambers. If these books are supplied by the state or county, substantial cost savings can be achieved by locating a justices' library between two or more justices' chambers so that one set of reference books (reporters, digests, and certain treatises) can be shared. Adequate bookshelves are needed in each justice's chamber for the storage of the justices' personal books.

Clerk's Office

Appellate court clerks' offices should be conveniently accessible from the public lobby. If both the supreme court and court of appeals are housed in the same building, the respective clerks' offices of the courts can be located either on separate floors or contiguous to one another on one floor in order to ensure better communication and greater convenience in the transfer of case transcripts and briefs between the two offices. While each court can have a separate public entrance at opposite ends of the building, such an arrangement may create confusion to the public and visitors. In Alaska, the creation of an intermediate appellate court resulted in a consolidated clerk's office that serves both the supreme court and the intermediate appellate court. The advantages of this consolidation include more efficient use of clerical personnel; greater convenience in the handling of all appellate documents from trial courts and from attorneys; convenient accessibility to the public and visitors at a single location within the court building; and potential cost savings in operation and in space and equipment duplication. If each appellate court has its own clerks, they can be separated from other clerks by furniture, file cabinets, and movable partitions within the shared space and be equipped with a separate public counter. Their being in a single location provides a high degree of flexibility in space use. In a consolidated office, clerks can be cross-trained to handle all clerical duties of both courts. While there might be an appearance of collusion if the appellate clerk's office is combined with the trial court clerk's office (the appellate court being responsible for the review of cases decided by the trial courts), the consolidation of the clerk's office of appellate courts should not present a similar problem.

In most states, the supreme court is located at the state's capital. In several states, including Alaska and New York, it also sits at the larger population centers. To duplicate justices' chambers and courtroom facilities solely for supreme court use at these centers would not be a prudent expenditure of public funds. Instead, one of the trial courtrooms could be converted for use as an appellate court when the supreme court is scheduled to hear oral arguments in that city. If an intermediate court of appeals sits permanently in a city, the supreme court session can be scheduled for the same courtroom when it is not being used by the court of appeals. In the design of a new court building, provision should be made for several offices to be located near the judicial area of the courtroom assigned for use by the supreme court justices when they are in the city to hear oral arguments. When these rooms are not used for this purpose, they can be used for other court functions.

Basic Court Structure—Trial Courts

Each state has a trial court of general jurisdiction. Both the nomenclature and the jurisdiction vary from state to state. In most states, trial courts of general jurisdiction are referred to as the superior court, circuit court, or district court. There may be a separate trial court of general jurisdiction in each county, as in California and Arizona, or the court may be organized in districts or circuits encompassing one or more counties, with judges traveling among the locations. Some trial courts of general jurisdiction located in only one county may have branch courts situated throughout the county, as does the Superior Court in Los Angeles County, California, and the Circuit Court in Cook County, Illinois.

In the broadest sense, a trial court of general jurisdiction means that the court has jurisdiction over any and all matters arising at the trial level. These include all civil, domestic relations, criminal, juvenile, mental health, and probate cases. In most states, many of these matters, such as civil cases under a certain amount, misdemeanors, and juvenile, mental health, and probate cases are heard in courts of limited or special jurisdiction, which also may have jurisdiction over traffic cases, small claims, and municipal or county ordinance violations. There may be one or more courts of special or limited jurisdiction and their jurisdiction may overlap with each other and with the trial court of general jurisdiction.

Personnel

The trend in the United States is to reduce the number of trial courts to one level, as is found in the District of Columbia, Connecticut, Illinois, South Dakota, Idaho, Iowa, Kansas, Missouri, Oklahoma, and Wisconsin, although in some jurisdictions there is more than one level of the judges, with the second level designated as associate judges.

The usual pattern is a two-tier trial court arrangement, such as is found in Hawaii, Colorado, Maryland, Kentucky, Washington, New Mexico, and a number of other states. The two trial courts may be under the same administration, such as in Colorado, where the chief judge of the court of general jurisdiction is also the chief judge of the limited-jurisdiction court. However, it is more likely that they are administered separately, as in Maryland and New Mexico. The pattern in the New England states, other than Connecticut, is for the trial courts to be organized separately statewide, with a statewide presiding judge. It is also common for municipal courts to be excluded from the state court system scheme, especially if their jurisdiction is limited to municipal ordinance violations.

In any discussion of trial court personnel and personnel systems, it is important to be aware of differences in court organization and jurisdiction, because these differences have a pronounced effect on the number and category of personnel needed, how they are trained, how their work is organized, the working area required, and to whom they are responsible. Even so, many tasks and the job skills required to perform them are quite similar, regardless of the court environment. For certain kinds of analyses it is possible to place trial court personnel into several broad categories related to functions that are required in all trial courts: (1) administration, (2) case disposition, (3) direct judicial support, (4) indirect judicial support, (5) jury administration, (6) law library maintenance, and (7) ancillary auxiliary and miscellaneous services and functions. These categories are quite similar to those applied to appellate courts above, but are more detailed and specific as required to describe trial court personnel activities. A number of positions and functions are included in each of these categories.

Administration

This category includes personnel involved in the overall administration of the court, including budget and fiscal management, personnel administration, facility maintenance, and purchasing. Typically, the court administrator, his or her secretary, and any other assistants would fall into this category. In a small court, probably only a portion of the time of one or two employees could be ascribed to these functions.

Case Disposition

This category includes masters, referees, and hearing officers—personnel other than judges who hear and dispose of cases. These parajudges usually hear certain kinds of juvenile matters, noncontested domestic relations cases and temporary orders, minor civil and traffic cases, or small claims, depending on the court and its jurisdiction. Parajudges are paid less than judges and require hearing rooms considerably smaller than regular trial courtrooms. Usually a parajudge requires only one support employee, who serves as secretary, clerk, and operator of the electronic equipment used to record the proceedings.

The method of selecting these officials varies from state to state. In some states, their qualifications, salary, and term of office are prescribed by statute. In others, they may be selected under a formalized personnel system or by court rule.

Direct Judicial Support

Supporting staff for judges and parajudges are in this category, including court reporters, division or courtroom clerks, private secretaries, bailiffs, law clerks, and any other personnel whose duties are generally confined to serving one judge or parajudge.

Court reporters are found primarily in courts of general jurisdiction. If courts of limited jurisdiction are courts of record, the record is usually made by using electronic equipment. A reporter may be a confidential employee of the judge who hires him or her, even in states with judicial systems or trial courts with a formalized personnel plan. In a growing number of trial courts, reporters are pooled and assigned to courtrooms as needed under a rotation scheme by the reporter in charge of the pool. Pooled reporters are more likely to be under a formalized personnel plan than reporters who work for individual judges.

Some states set reporters' qualifications and salary by statute. A number of states have a Certified Shorthand Reporters' Act, which requires reporters to pass a proficiency test to become certified. In some states without this statutory requirement, the state court administrative office is assigned this responsibility. Most reporters use stenographic machines to record proceedings, but there are still a few "pen" writers who use Gregg or Pitman shorthand. Other reporting methods include closed microphone recording (stenomask) and single- and multiple-track audio recording equipment. Computer-aided transcription and the expanded use of electronic and video recording are systems provided in many court jurisdictions.

Law clerks are usually found only in the larger trial courts of general jurisdiction. In some places this function is combined with that of bailiff, and second- or third-year law students are employed. Usually, law clerks, bailiffs, courtroom or division clerks, and secretaries are considered confidential employees of the judges. The personnel rules may specify qualifications for the job, the salary scale, and fringe benefits, but individual judges select the employees, who serve at their pleasure.

In many jurisdictions bailiffs are employees of the sheriff's office or another law enforcement agency, as in New Jersey, Florida, or Utah. Consequently, the court has little or no control over their recruitment, compensation, or work assignments.

Indirect Judicial Support

The clerk of court and his or her staff make up the major portion of this category. These employees are responsible for all case files and records; issuance of process; collection and disbursement of fines, fees, and court registry funds; recording of judgments; issuing copies of documents; and so forth. In courts with probate jurisdiction, their functions may include estate auditing and examination. Employees involved in the calendaring process also fall in this category.

In most states, clerks of the court of general jurisdiction are elected. A number of clerks of court of special or limited jurisdiction are also elected. Where clerks are elected, the court has little, if any, formal control over the clerks' offices, despite its importance in court operations. The employees of elected clerks are likely to be selected under some form of patronage, although one notable exception is North Carolina, where elected clerks appoint their employees in conformance with the state judicial personnel system, which sets requirements for classification, pay, and staffing patterns. If the employees of an elected clerk are under a formalized personnel system, it is more likely to be the one used by the county government for executive branch employees.

Many elected clerks of court have other duties besides serving as court clerk, such as recorder of deeds and election registration, and some are paid—as are their employees—from the fees of the office.

In courts where the clerk is not elected, clerical employees are likely to be under an existing formalized personnel plan. In some jurisdictions, clerical functions of the court of general jurisdiction and the court of limited jurisdiction may be combined.

Jury Administration

The jury commissioner and any related employees are in this category. The number of employees will depend on the size of the court, the number of jurors summoned, and the extent to which the process is automated. Management of the jury lounge or assembly area is also a responsibility of jury administration, along with summoning, assigning, and paying jurors.

In some jurisdictions, especially in smaller courts, the jury commissioner may also be the clerk of court or an employee designated by the clerk. It is also possible that the jury commissioner could be someone other than a direct court employee who is selected by the county governing body.

Law Library Maintenance

The size of trial court libraries will depend on the size of the court and the practicing bar and the proximity to state or university law libraries. In a large trial court library, the law librarian may be a professional with a degree in library science and one or two library assistants. Paraprofessionals or clerical employees (some on a part-time basis) usually provide minimal staff services in smaller law libraries. Courts of limited or special jurisdiction are not likely to have libraries and may share in the use of the one in the court of general jurisdiction.

Ancillary, Auxiliary, and Miscellaneous Services and Functions

This group includes all court personnel and activities that cannot be otherwise categorized.

a. Many courts employ marriage counselors, who provide marriage counseling upon order of the court in domestic relations matters. These counselors are professionally trained, usually with graduate degrees in social work and/or psychology, and are assisted by secretarial-clerical personnel.

b. It is not unusual for courts, especially those exercising juvenile jurisdiction, to have court-employed psychologists and psychiatric social workers to conduct evaluations and even take part in court-ordered treatment programs. Part-time psychiatric services are usually purchased under contract. Secretarial and clerical support is required for professional staff providing these services.

c. Bail bonding should be recognized as a distinct activity to the extent that employees are either assigned exclusively to this function or a special night and weekend staff is required. In most medium-sized and small courts, employees handling bail bonding may do so as part of their regular clerical activities, but in large courts, a separate unit may be required, although the employees' qualifications and skills are comparable to those of clerk's office personnel.

In many jurisdictions, the personal recognizance release program is also a judicial responsibility rather than that of the district attorney or probation department (assuming the latter is part of the executive

branch rather than under the judiciary). This activity involves investigations and interviews to provide reports and recommendations to the court. Personnel engaged in this activity may have the same professional training and qualifications as probation officers, or they may be paraprofessionals. In either case, clerical support is required.
d. Probation services in some jurisdictions are under the judicial branch, as in Colorado and Hawaii. In some states, the judiciary has the responsibility for probation and related services for juveniles, while adult probation services are provided by the executive branch. Sometimes probation services for misdemeanors are a judicial responsibility, while similar services for felons are under the executive branch. In some jurisdictions, where probation services are not in the judicial branch, the courts have staffs of investigators to conduct presentence investigations and may even have counselors to supervise offenders released under deferred sentence or deferred prosecution programs. Whenever these activities are a judicial responsibility, court personnel requirements usually call for trained professionals, usually with graduate degrees and with varying degrees of skills and experience. Probation staffs also require sufficient clerical and secretarial support.
e. Community corrections now involve the judiciary to a greater degree than ever before. A community corrections program may involve only an individual court or two in a state, as in Des Moines, Iowa, and Salt Lake City, Utah, or it may be a coordinated statewide effort, as in Colorado. In either case, the courts need professionals with a corrections and sociological background to serve as their liaison and advisors with other community agencies participating in the program.
f. Juvenile detention facilities in several states are the responsibility of the court exercising juvenile jurisdiction, whether it is a separate court or a division of the trial court of general jurisdiction. This responsibility extends judicial system personnel requirements even further to encompass cooks, maintenance staff, unit counselors, nurses, and, perhaps, teachers.

Trial Court Facilities

A detailed discussion of trial court facilities and process is contained in chapter 1, "Caseflow and Space Management."

Personnel Management and Other Aspects of Court Administration

Personnel expenditures account for 75 to 80 percent of the operating costs of a court or judicial system, including furniture and equipment, but excluding building, maintaining, and remodeling facilities. If for no other reason, the magnitude of personnel costs necessitates that good personnel management be closely related to other facets of court administration. Good personnel management involves more than the recruitment, compensation, retention, promotion, and discipline of employees on an equitable basis relating to job content and employee performance. It is also concerned with employee orientation, morale, and motivation, and is directed toward providing an adequate number of qualified employees, properly allocated and supervised to carry out required functions as effectively and efficiently as possible.

Accomplishing the goals and objectives of personnel management requires

- understanding and determining employee skills required, which in turn requires an understanding of all facets of court processes and those of related agencies
- gaining knowledge of the labor market and its various components
- developing and implementing training programs, both for new employees and those already on the job, designed to meet the special needs of the court or judicial system, including the development of supervisory skills and the adaptation of technological change
- understanding budgetary needs and constraints
- forecasting personnel needs
- determining and improving adequacy of work space and equipment
- developing and implementing sound career ladder and promotional policies and opportunities
- developing and implementing adequate fringe benefit programs to attract, retain, and maintain the morale of qualified and motivated employees

These are not easy goals, and their successful achievement requires the integration of personnel management with the other management skills and functions needed to efficiently operate the court system and its many related components. Significant relationships exist between personnel management and budget and fiscal administration. Projecting personnel needs is an integral part of the budgetary process. Budgetary constraints have a direct impact on improvements in fringe benefits and revisions in the compensation plan. These limitations can be offset to some extent by improvement in employee efficiency and better deployment of personnel. Both of these are affected by training programs and the introduction of cost-effective technological change.

Decisions on filling vacant positions are affected by expenditure patterns and fiscal controls, as well as by personnel needs. This is another reason for good communication between the two disciplines and the development of a system of shared management decisions.

Trends Affecting Court Personnel

An Overview

The accuracy of projecting personnel needs decreases as one tries to project farther and farther ahead. Court personnel projections are based on population and caseload trends as they relate to the increase in the number of judges. The number of support staff is proportional to the number of judges; once the number of judges is projected, the number of support staff can also be determined. In projecting court personnel, it should be realized that administrative, legislative, political, and economic factors exert significant impact on the increase or decline of the number of court personnel.

Courts are invariably underfunded, especially to meet the needs of continuing caseload increases. This situation is not likely to improve appreciably if the state assumes funding of the court system. While state governments may have greater fiscal resources than most cities and counties, some states are experiencing serious fiscal problems. Even in financially healthy states, present attitudes requiring government spending to be held in check are likely to prevail for some time. This means that locally funded judicial systems and individual courts will have to allocate and manage their resources very carefully by operating as efficiently as possible.

The impact of changing political attitudes on court personnel should be clear. Judicial systems and courts cannot expect to add personnel at the same rate as in the past to cope with increasing caseloads. By necessity, courts will be required to examine, adopt, and adapt efficient technological innovations. Manual procedures should be streamlined to increase employee productivity. These changes will require greater emphasis on employee training.

Appropriating agencies will require courts to justify expenditures for new systems and equipment by demonstrating cost savings through a reduction in new or existing personnel, despite caseload increases. It will probably be necessary for courts and appropriation bodies to agree on productivity or workload formulae as an acceptable basis for determining savings through greater productivity and elimination of employees. Such negotiation efforts, already occurring in some jurisdictions, place even greater emphasis on the need for professional management in courts and related agencies. More and better-trained court administrators, management analysts, and budget analysts will be required. Other occupations that are likely to increase within the court environment include planners, systems analysts, computer specialists, and those with technological competency in video, electronics, and related fields.

It is predicted that professionals with these skills will not necessarily be added to existing court administrative and clerical staffs, but that some kind of cost trade-off will be expected. The possibility of further efficiency and employee reduction will be prime considerations of those advocating court system consolidation and unification.

Although such changes have occurred in some locations, their acceptance is slow, especially in jurisdictions where a patronage system of employment not only prevails but is necessary for sustaining the judiciary or the clerk of court at election time. Nevertheless, it is likely that most judicial systems and courts will continue to be involved in these systemic changes and related budget struggles. There will no doubt be exceptions, primarily in rural areas, which account for a relatively small proportion of judicial activity and court employees.

Despite technological innovations and attempts to reduce the number of court employees, it is unlikely that employment levels in state and local courts will decrease during the next two decades, but will probably increase slightly, given the relative inertia of governmental institutions and an expected steady rise in the amount of litigation and resultant workload. Increases in judicial and parajudicial positions and support staff are to be expected, unless greater attention continues to be focused on removing certain substantive matters from the judicial system, and efforts are directed at finding simpler, faster, and less expensive ways of dealing with some forms of litigation. In this regard, it is likely that matters such as traffic offenses will be removed from the judicial system by creating administrative remedies. This could be counterproductive if it results in the creation of administrative operation complete with administrative judges, employees, and procedures that become more cumbersome and expensive than those in the courts, in addition to creating a parallel and potentially duplicative system.

Trial Court Consolidation

A number of states reorganized and consolidated their trial courts in the late fifties and early sixties. Since that time many states have followed suit, with some currently in the process of implementation or considering consolidation. This trend is expected to continue, but probably at a slower pace, for several reasons:

- It is difficult politically to accomplish substantial consolidation in highly populated states where judges are elected.

- It is difficult to mount or sustain an effort for further consolidation in states where partial consolidation has already taken place.
- It is difficult to gain support for elimination of all courts, especially those with municipal jurisdiction, even when consolidation of all other jurisdictions in one or two tiers is likely to be adopted.

Impact on Court Personnel

Trial court consolidation will continue to have a significant impact on the number of court personnel, work assignments, and employee efficiency. It should foster the creation of formalized personnel systems, the unionization of court employees, or both, especially in urban areas.

If clerical and case-processing functions are consolidated in one or two court levels, the number of employees needed would be less, assuming a constant workload. Experience in Colorado and Illinois, for example, shows that court employees in larger courts are more efficient, that is, can handle more work than employees in smaller courts. Economics of scale come into play, making labor-saving equipment such as word processing, microfilming, or automated data processing cost-effective, resulting in increased employee output. Personnel become more aware of the benefits of minimizing and eliminating duplication.

A possible reduction in the number of employees can also be expected in rural areas. Consolidation usually reduces the number of rural or branch court locations. Combination of clerical and other case-processing functions, even on a small rural scale, can lead to more efficient standardized procedures.

There are many impediments to court consolidation. First, if elected clerks are retained, it may not be possible to consolidate clerical functions or reduce the number of employees. Second, as a price of consolidation, all employees may be grandfathered in, postponing potential personnel savings until it can be accomplished by attrition. Third, if the judicial system is not management-oriented, consolidation may have little impact other than to shift employees who operate in the same manner at new locations. Fourth, consolidation may not necessarily result in fewer court locations. In rural areas, the number of court locations may be reduced; but in urban areas, branch or neighborhood courts may be established as part of the reorganization effort to keep court and court services available and convenient.

Trial court consolidation is usually part of a broader court reform effort which may include judicial merit selection and judicial discipline. It will invariably embrace, either specifically or by implication, administrative improvements and better management of the system and its components. There will probably be more central administrative authority in the system, and phasing of state funding may also be included. Even if nonjudicial court personnel are not addressed directly, emphasis on management and funding will have an impact on all aspects of their employment.

Good management practice dictates that compensation and fringe benefits offered by the courts be competitive with other employers in both the public and the private sectors, so that the courts can recruit and retain qualified personnel. Fringe benefits, including good working conditions and environment, are very important in labor market competition. The recruitment and retention of qualified personnel takes on added emphasis in a court consolidation setting because of the impetus and possibilities of technological innovation. The workforce must also be rationally organized with like compensation for like work. Further, there should be procedures and guidelines for making the transition to a consolidated court system as smooth as possible. Trial court consolidation provides a catalyst for the development and implementation of an organized personnel system if none existed before. The inclusion of an elected clerk's office in such a system may not be possible, but the clerk may create a parallel system in response to employee and other pressures.

Unionization may also be fostered because court consolidation provides potentially larger bargaining units. Seniority, job security, and working conditions become very important to employees uprooted from a familiar system with familiar pecking orders and work environments.

Increase in Use of Hearing Officers (Parajudges)

Referees, hearing officers, magistrates, or parajudges hear a large variety of matters. The use of these judicial officers in lieu of judges will no doubt increase. This is based on simple economics: the cost of providing a parajudge, supporting staff, recording equipment, and other capital outlay is only 50 to 60 percent of the cost of creating a new judgeship, including supporting staff and capital outlay.

The cost differential becomes even greater when facilities are considered. A parajudge needs a small hearing room, a small office, and office space for his or her secretary-clerk. In contrast, a judge would require chambers, office space for two or more employees, a courtroom, and perhaps a hearing room or conference room as well.

The anticipated increase in branch and neighborhood courts for the convenience of litigants involved in minor disputes should also lead to an increase in the number of parajudges, who can hear small claims, noncontested domestic relations cases, and minor juvenile and criminal matters. If neighborhood or branch courts are set up solely or primarily for these matters, only hearing rooms, parajudges' offices, and other support spaces would be required to handle litigation, reducing facility costs considerably.

Changes in Facility Configuration and Use and the Impact on Court Personnel

Rural Trial Centers

There is a slow but perceptible trend toward the creation of trial centers in rural areas. In some places this has come about by design. In others it is a result of habits and practice over a considerable period. In a multicounty rural judicial district or circuit, lawyers tend to congregate in the population centers, which are also the marketing and commercial centers for the area. One result is that this community (or communities) has the most court business and court employees in the district or circuit, thus requiring the largest court facilities. Ancillary services tend to be centered in these communities as well.

The practice is to move most trials and protracted litigation to these one or two court locations where the judges and lawyers are located. The court of general jurisdiction still sits in the other counties from time to time, but not for any extended period, unless there is a serious criminal case. The court of lesser or limited jurisdiction still sits in all locations and handles minor matters.

These patterns have evolved haphazardly and may vary among and within jurisdictions. Some jurisdictions are planning for the creation of trial court service centers to be served by satellite courts in surrounding areas, much in the same way that public health, mental health, and social services are being organized. Implicit in this approach is the dual recognition that modern transportation and communication systems have made distances less important for court accessibility, and also that relatively minor matters can be heard and disposed of more efficiently and with less cost closer to the source.

Ideally, satellite courts would be staffed by a judge of limited jurisdiction or a parajudge and one or two supporting staff. Large or elaborate court facilities would not be needed, and those in existence could be closed down or remodeled. Satellite courts may have limited space for prosecution and defense counsel, and for ancillary services like probation, on an as-needed basis. Filing space could be minimal, with files of all but the most active cases maintained at the trial court center. Jury-pooling facilities would also be housed at the trial court services center, as most jury trials would be conducted there. Circuit or district administrative activities would also be centered and conducted from this location. Satellite courts invariably duplicate facilities and personnel already available in the trial court services center.

Branch Courts

Branch courts can be differentiated from neighborhood courts or neighborhood dispute resolution centers by the type of cases filed and litigated. Branch courts are usually located in urban counties with extensive urban areas. They are designed to minimize travel distance to court for litigants and lawyers which, in counties such as Los Angeles or San Diego, may be fifty to one hundred miles away.

Branch courts offer a possible solution to growth patterns in some suburban areas. Urban growth may be in areas located away from the county seat and could be serviced by branch courts. However, branch courts bring with them a number of problems. While they provide greater convenience to lawyers and litigants, the benefits should be carefully scrutinized in light of the cost of additional personnel, facilities, and potential duplication of services.

In determining the number of judges, judicial officers, and other personnel, a number of questions need to be answered: Should jury trials be conducted at branch court locations? Should branch courts be limited only to civil filings in the broadest sense, including domestic relations cases, probate and mental health cases, and juvenile cases? If there is more than one trial judge in a branch court, should both share the same courtroom facilities and clerical support? If possible, should judges of different trial courts in a branch location sit interchangeably? What is the best way to administer a branch court structure? To what extent should the main court location be the central record repository? How much record storage capacity should be located in the branches? What is the best communication network to establish between the branch courts and the central court location?

Despite all of the possible problems, branch courts are likely to increase in number in the future. The expense of travel will provide greater impetus to place branch courts where people will have easy access to bus and rapid transit systems. Branch courts are also adaptable to technology, such as automated information systems, which could help (1) transmit and maintain court records and to coordinate calendars among courts, including branches; (2) select and administer juries; and (3) facilitate legal research, reducing branch court library needs considerably.

Neighborhood Courts and Dispute Resolution Centers

Neighborhood courts and dispute resolution centers will be located primarily in the inner city. Jurisdiction of the former is likely to be limited to small claims, minor traffic violations, and petty misdemeanors. Each court will need a small hearing room, a large public waiting area, and a small clerical office where small-claims and other matters may be filed. They are staffed by one or two clerks, a hearing officer, and a transcriber-division clerk. The clerks will be trained paralegals who can help people fill out forms and help them understand the process. Neighborhood courts may have staggered hours, opening on some evenings and perhaps on Saturday. If open during regular court hours, as well as some evenings and weekends, additional staff will be required to handle the extra hours.

Neighborhood dispute resolutions centers for some procedures and actions may need even less formal facilities than neighborhood courts. Other activities may take place more appropriately in a neighborhood court setting, and would require an additional conference room and more public waiting space.

Transcript Preparation

Technical advances in the preparation of trial transcripts can eliminate the transcript delays which have plagued most appellate courts. Two procedures in particular have considerable potential for general application in the courts. One is computer-aided transcription (CAT), and the other is the videotaping of trials. Videotaping of trials may have less significant application because of the traditional method in which appellate judges generally review the record on appeal.

CAT is a system in which a specially modified stenotype machine is used by a trained court reporter to record proceedings simultaneously on both paper and magnetic tape. A code dictionary, containing all or most of the words and terms likely to be used during the recording process, is stored in a computer along with the translation key and the individual reporter's idiosyncrasies. Before the magnetic tape is fed into the computer, the reporter reviews the printed notes to determine words, terms, abbreviations, and so forth that may not be in the computer's dictionary. This information, along with the magnetic tape, is fed into the computer, which in turn generates an unedited transcription of the proceedings. This transcription is then edited, proofread, and resubmitted to the computer, which produces the final copy. While court reporters are still required in the application of CAT, transcript preparation time is greatly reduced.

Videotaping of trials is in use in a growing number of court locations. This procedure involves videotaping trial proceedings using multiple voice-activated cameras to capture gestures and expressions along with a word-for-word recording of actual statements. When needed after trial, a duplicate tape can be created from the original and reviewed at the parties' leisure. The format and the television screen can be split to allow the simultaneous viewing of the entire proceedings by using a split-screen approach. Obviously, a court reporter is unnecessary when using this method.

While videotaping and subsequent playback of trials may offer the most accurate recording of proceedings, the storage and retrieval of tapes can be a major problem. Purchasing the necessary equipment requires a capital outlay, and the maintenance and operation of the equipment may require additional personnel and costs which must be taken into account.

Public Service Employees

The previous discussion suggests that court system operation in the future will be governed to even a greater extent by public needs and convenience. This can be seen by the predicted increase in branch courts and neighborhood facilities, by the anticipated development of less expensive and speedier methods of handling certain types of disputes and alleged criminal actions, and through technological adaptations to improve efficiency and achieve greater cost-effectiveness. All these changes will affect space needs and use.

Court facilities will have more convenient central public receiving and waiting areas staffed by court employees who have special training in public relations and in using computer terminals and TV monitors to answer public questions concerning case status, alimony and support, and the court calendar, whether asked in person or by phone.

Eventually courts will take advantage of the electronic fund exchange for payment of fines and fees. In the meantime, it is probable that new or remodeled court buildings will include drive-in facilities for the convenience of attorneys and the public in paying fines and fees and in filing papers. This facility would be reasonably near the clerk's office, much in the same way that many banks arrange interior and drive-in services, so that the same clerical personnel can be better used.

More attention will be paid to jury management, including the space provided for assembling jurors. Large, open, attractive rooms are required with comfortable furniture, a variety of reading material, television sets, and a display screen to show films about how juries function and their significance.

Anticipated changes in space requirements and utilization suggest more flexible wall and partition designs in court buildings for easier adaption to changing needs. This degree of flexibility is needed also in court personnel space, in view of the anticipated technological changes that may impose different space configurations and requirements, and the possible reassignment and reduction of personnel. Modular workstation furniture and equipment, with power communication and data wiring incorporated into the modular wall panels, are widely used in courthouses today.

The anticipated reduction or elimination of manual files, because of automation, expanded microfilm use, or both, will have significant impact on both personnel requirements and space needs. Public convenience will be improved through easier document access. Fewer employees and less file space will be needed. Court managers should anticipate this change when planning for remodeling or alteration. Good personnel management dictates that excess employees be retained and reassigned to more appropriate duties.

The Prospect for Change

The changes in administration and the application of innovative technology for courts will not be realized easily or uniformly, even when their validity has been established. In addition to political impediments, the conservative nature of the judicial process with its emphasis on tradition and *stare decisis* presents a more serious problem. Unless judicial leadership actively supports change, it is not likely to take place. Often, administration may take a back seat to concerns over judicial salaries, retirement, and facilities. Funding bodies do not normally consider the needs of the judicial system to be a high priority.

Court personnel frequently resist change, especially if job security is seen to be threatened or an established procedure is changed. Collective bargaining may well become a significant factor in determining changes in internal operations in the use of court personnel.

A major requirement for change to take place is agreement both within and outside of the judicial system as to who has the ultimate responsibility for court system planning, operation, personnel, and funding. As long as that responsibility is fragmented, and the major participants do not understand and appreciate their respective roles, change will come slowly and with considerable friction.

Funding

Resolution of the question of how the judicial system and its components are to be funded is basic to effective personnel management and proper judicial administration and planning. This issue may not be resolved on the principle of good administration, but on local governmental units' (especially core cities and declining rural areas) lacking sufficient resources to support adequate levels of service. The trend is to shift the financial burden to the state level. This shift in financial burden to state funding of judicial functions, as well as the standards of judicial administration, have been major political considerations advocated by those primarily concerned with the improvement in the organization and administration of the judicial branch. These advocates take the position that state funding provides the framework (when accompanied with other changes, such as in court structure) for the provision of equal justice throughout a state, including adequate qualified personnel and facilities. It facilitates comprehensive statewide planning and proper resource allocation.

Opponents of state funding feel that local courts can best determine their own needs and that funding should remain local, thus keeping the courts close to the people. This position is based on local rather than systemwide considerations. It would not be possible to continue local courts and to have at the same time a systemwide personnel management, although some would argue that systemwide personnel plan is not needed. Local units may be willing to give up the expense of operating the system, but are reluctant to part with the revenue generated, especially by courts of limited jurisdiction.

Another facet of the controversy is the determination of who is responsible for facilities. If this responsibility remains at the local level, while all operations and personnel become a state responsibility, planning for change, additions in personnel, and relocation of functions become more difficult and subject to considerable negotiation between state and local officials. It can be worked out, as experience has shown in some jurisdictions, but not as easily as in states such as Alaska and Hawaii, where total responsibility for all facilities and operations has been at the state level since statehood.

The willingness of the judiciary to manage its own affairs must be accompanied by a willingness on the part of the other two branches of government, not only to let the judiciary carry out this responsibility, but also to support it in its efforts. The legislature, in the final analysis, controls expenditures, but the courts must have the authority for personnel and resource management. This problem of comity among the branches will not be easily resolved in many jurisdictions.

3

Jury and Space Management

The right to trial by jury is a basic constitutional guarantee which distinguishes the American system of justice from more authoritarian systems. The wronged and wrongly accused are grateful for the opportunity to present their case to an impartial jury. Increasingly, however, jury trials have become so expensive and cumbersome that disputes formerly resolved by a jury are being handled more expeditiously by other means. Witnesses are appalled at the formalism and delay in the jury process. Prospective jurors are dismayed at the prospect of lengthy jury duty. Court administrators wince at the escalating costs of jury trials. An unmistakable duality exists between constitutional decree and actual practice, which questions the basic values of the jury system. Is it part of the American character to simultaneously venerate and criticize tradition? Or is there legitimate uncertainty about the continued value of a seemingly medieval forum for finding truth in a Computer Age society?

Whether justified or not, criticisms of the jury system often find their way to the court administrator's desk. Can administrators afford to simply "cope" with an inefficient system or can they be permitted to imagine, for instance, an entire community turning thumbs up or down at an accused at the push of a button; jurors summoned by computer and screened by videophone to serve in the comfort of their homes while watching the trial on closed-circuit television; jury trials taking place only a few days after the crime took place or the claim arose; rerunning sequences on a video playback; voting guilty or innocent by home computer and feeling secure that the appeal will be decided by bedtime.

Historical Perspectives

The jury trial in America, like its historical antecedents, stands as the ultimate expression of the social conscience. Its credibility as an institution lies in its acceptance by the whole community. That acceptance has depended upon both the degree of public participation and the basic fairness of the procedures employed in reaching a verdict.

A jury has been defined as "a body of men taken from the community at large, summoned to find the truth of disputed facts, who are quite distinct from the judges or court." While many primitive societies and early civilizations had councils of elders or other groups of men designated to decide matters of importance to the community, their members acted as both judges and jurors. Almost four thousand years ago the early Egyptians employed an eight-man *kenbet*, which tried minor charges against workmen. In the sixth century B.C., the great Athenian lawgiver Solon instituted the *dikastera*, which voted, in secret, on both law and fact. Its verdict was not subject to appeal. The oligarchy abolished the *dikastera* when they seized power (411–404 B.C.), but it was restored upon the return of a more democratic form of government. The Athenian jury found its way to Rome in about 451–450 B.C.

Roman jurors were chosen once a year to try criminal cases. Resolving both questions of fact and law, the *Judices* determined the guilt or innocence of the accused and could acquit or condemn without regard to the evidence. It is believed that the *Inquisitio* of the Franks, an ancestor of the modern jury, was influenced by Roman jury procedures.

After Charlemagne became king of the Franks (A.D. 768), he established the *Inquisitio* to determine facts in civil cases. The process was accusatory in form and allowed a judge "to summon at his discretion a number of men from the neighborhood in whom he could assume a knowledge of the matter in question and demand from them a promise to declare the truth upon the question to be submitted by him." If the *Inquisitio* was unable to reach a decision, another panel might be ordered, while retaining those jurors who had definite knowledge. If the second panel was unable to reach a verdict, the parties were compelled to submit formal proof.

The *Inquisitio* greatly influenced William the Conqueror, who imposed a similar system on England after 1066. His royal successors permitted the jurors to declare guilt or innocence in addition to determining fact in civil cases. By the time of Henry II's reign (1154–1189), twelve jurors were generally required.

The Magna Carta (1215) codified many previous jury practices and provided that a jury "shall be granted *gratis* and shall not be denied." King John revoked the "Great Charter" almost immediately, but Henry III reinstated it in 1225. Prior to 1367, jurors could return a majority verdict, but thereafter, only a unanimous verdict was accepted. By the seventeenth century, the jury trial was refined to the extent that its procedures appear just and reasonable even by contemporary standards. Its impartial verdict theoretically stood as a bulwark against the excesses of government.

English colonists brought the jury trial to the shores of North America. By the time of the American Revolution, each of the colonies had provided guarantees of the right to trial by jury. Abuse of this right by the British became a source of complaint. The Declaration of Independence referred to the abuse of the right as one of the reasons necessitating the separation of the colonies from England—"for depriving us in many cases of the benefits of trial by jury."

From the early Egyptian *kenbet* to the colonial jury trial, the device of a trusted representative body determining the true facts, weighing the applicable law, and rendering an impartial verdict has provided Western civilization with a just mode of trial. When the framers of the Constitution considered a charter for the United States of America, no fewer than three of the first ten amendments guaranteed aspects of trial by jury. The Fourteenth Amendment provided for "the application of due process of law and equal protection of the laws" to all citizens of the United States and prevents any state from "making or enforcing any law" to abridge these guarantees. Today, the constitutions of all fifty states include references to the right of jury trial.

Legal Requirements of Jury Use

The Fifth, Sixth, Seventh, and Fourteenth Amendments provide the constitutional basis for the right to trial by jury in both civil and criminal cases. Case law interpreting these constitutional guarantees has, in turn, provided the basis for legislation and court rules which determine the availability, nature, and procedures of the jury trial.

The Fifth Amendment protects persons accused of a crime from unwarranted federal prosecution by guaranteeing that no person shall be tried for certain crimes except after a grand jury indictment. This provision does not apply to state proceedings. While the original purpose of the grand jury was to initiate formal criminal proceedings against the accused, present-day grand juries not only return criminal indictments, but may also investigate suspected criminal activities.

The Sixth Amendment requires speedy, public, and impartial jury trials for all criminal prosecutions to further protect the accused from the overzealous prosecutor and the biased judge. Originally limited to the federal government, the Sixth Amendment right to jury trial applies to state prosecutions in which the penalty may exceed six months.

The Seventh Amendment reserves the right to jury trial "in suits at common law where the value in controversy shall exceed $20." Matters considered "at common law" at the time of the framing of the Seventh Amendment were guaranteed trial by jury in federal courts. The term is used traditionally in contradistinction to those equitable matters which were triable only before a judge. Today, a jury is not required in cases which did not exist "at common law: within the meaning of the amendment." Further, parties may agree to forgo the right to jury trial. Failure to assert the right in a timely fashion constitutes a waiver. The Seventh Amendment guarantee does not apply to civil matters tried in state courts.

The rights protected against state action by the due process clause of the Fourth Amendment were initially quite limited and did not include all the guarantees of the Bill of Rights. Recognizing that the nature of due process depends on the circumstances of each case, the Supreme Court has held due process of law to require only such procedures as are appropriate to the matter to be decided and just to the parties affected. A state is free to regulate the procedure of its courts in accordance with its own conceptions of policy and fairness unless in so doing it offends some principle of justice so rooted in the traditions and conscience of our people as to be ranked as fundamental.

Since the right to trial by jury has not been deemed an essential element of due process in civil proceedings, the states are free to retain or abolish civil juries and to change their form. The same is true in minor criminal cases. Nor are the states required to provide grand juries. However, any jury provided must be fair and impartial and must represent a cross section of the whole community.

The provisions of the Bill of Rights that have been held applicable to the states through the Fourteenth Amendment include the basic guarantees of a fair trial, the right to counsel, and the right to a speedy and public trial. The Sixth Amendment right to a jury trial is imposed upon the states only in criminal cases where the penalty may exceed six months. Traditionally, jurors are required for the trial of criminal cases. However, the Supreme Court reversed itself and held that the twelve-member jury was "an historical accident" and not a necessary ingredient of trial by one's peers. In allowing a state to provide a six-member panel to try noncapital criminal cases, the court did not set a minimum permissible jury size but recognized the appropriateness of basing jury size on the severity of the penalty that could be imposed. The court has also stated that neither the Sixth Amendment nor the Fourteenth Amendment requires agreement by all jurors in a state criminal prosecution. While unanimity is still required in a federal court jury, state courts are free to accept verdicts in which not all jurors agree. Verdicts agreed upon by ten out of twelve jurors have been accepted in some state courts.

While the Equal Protection Clause of the Fourteenth Amendment guarantees equality of treatment to all, it is rare that a law affects all persons equally. Inequalities that do occur, however, must be reasonably related to a valid governmental purpose to survive judicial scrutiny. It has been held that exclusion of specific ethnic or racial groups by law from grand and petit juries bears no reasonable relationship to any valid state goal and violates the constitution. Such exclusion removes from the jury room the varieties of human experience and opinion that make up the community and ensure impartiality. Any defendant, regardless of his own group identification, may complain of the partiality of a jury from which any large and identifiable segment of the community has been systematically excluded.

The "new equal protection analysis" goes beyond directly discriminatory classifications by states (*de jure*) and seeks to overturn laws that are valid on their face but discriminatory in effect (*de facto*). The scope of this extension has been limited to rights which are deemed fundamental and to classifications which are inherently suspect, such as sex, race, religion, and economic class. Distinctions based upon the ability to pay for basic legal advantages have been held to violate the Equal Protection Clause.

State constitutional provisions for the right to jury trials in both criminal and civil cases conform substantially to the federal model but may be refined and modified by statute. Statutory provisions usually relate to the manner and mode of jury qualification and selection; authorized summonses; the number of jurors required and their alternates; the number and nature of peremptory and "cause" challenges; the method and means of trial; and the forms of verdict and compensation for jury service. Statutes further provide for the use of the grand jury and for the selection and service of the grand jurors.

While the legislature has authority to confer substantial rights, the courts have the inherent power to determine by rule how those rights are to be exercised. Such rules may establish procedures by which jurors are summoned, means by which challenges may be exercised, methods by which the right to jury trial is demanded or waived, and the process of selecting and screening jurors themselves. Court rules may determine the sequence of trial and jury instructions. They may even provide for the care and management of jurors during their term of service.

The jury trial, as guaranteed by the Constitution, structured by statute, and refined by court rule, is an elaborate and revered institution in its own right. Its usefulness today, however, is dependent on its ability to meet the needs of those it serves in an efficient and impartial manner. As a mechanism for decision, its working parts must function smoothly.

Component Areas of Jury Management

The first step in selecting jurors is the creation of a jury pool. The federal government and most states use voting lists from a geographical area which is ordinarily defined by the jurisdiction of the particular trial court. The pool consists of persons who are at least eighteen years old, citizens of the United States, and residents who satisfy voting requirements. Some jurisdictions supplement the poll drawn from the polling lists with lists of licensed drivers, state taxpayers, public utility and telephone subscribers, and so on.

Once the initial lists have been prepared, they must be culled to ensure that statutory requisites are met, primarily dealing with minimum and maximum age and being able to understand the English language. Good character may also be required in some jurisdictions, even though little effort is made to define the term.

After screening for qualifications and exemptions, potential jurors are available for summons to service. Most jurisdictions require that jurors be notified personally in sufficient time to allow them to make arrangements for the term of service. In metropolitan areas, however, the cost of such personal service upon the large number of jurors required has made service by registered or certified mail a likely alternative. The summons served upon the potential jurors usually states a time and place to appear, the length of service required, and the court in which they are to serve. It may also list a person or office to contact for further information or explanation. Jurors seeking deferrals of service are usually required to contact this office within a specified time prior to the commencement of service. Deferral may be granted by phone or the potential juror may be requested to appear personally to state the reasons for such request. Most jurisdictions have provisions allowing emergency service by the sheriff of any suitable citizen who can be found if the pool is insufficient to meet court needs.

Most jurisdictions expedite the induction process by preparing all the documents necessary to record the jurors' term of service. These include records as to qualifications, possible exempt status, personal history, daily attendance logs, notations of assignments and selection, and tabulation of fees earned. In some jurisdictions, this information is recorded for the first time when the juror arrives at the courthouse.

The potential juror must be registered upon arrival at the courthouse or other assembly area. Once assembled, most courts provide potential jurors with some form of orientation regarding jury service and its importance in the trial process. The methods used range from an informal introduction by the presiding judge or his or her designate to a more formal presentation in the form of videotapes, printed pamphlets, or jury handbooks.

Once properly oriented, the jurors are ready to be assigned for service. This assignment may come at any time, in response to immediate need or by prior scheduling. Whenever the call is made, however, a sufficient number of jurors must respond within a reasonable time. This last requirement may present a problem if jurors are housed remotely from the courthouse and must be transported to their destination. Also, the jurors chosen to respond to each request must be designated in a random fashion.

The process of selecting a jury from among the potential jurors is determined by the lawyers for the parties involved and controlled, to some degree, by the trial judge. Judges usually introduce the parties and their lawyers, indicate the potential witnesses, and give a brief statement about the case. They may also acquaint the jurors with the fundamental legal principles applicable to the case and indicate that this discussion will be supplemented at the end of the case in jury instructions.

The jurors are then questioned to allow the court and counsel to determine their qualifications to act in the particular case. This examination is called the *voir dire;* it may be conducted by the judge, the parties' counsel, or all three in turn. Jurors may be questioned either as a whole while seated in the courtroom or individually; or as whole jurors or portions of juries (panels) seated in the jury box. The individual juror may be questioned alone or in the presence of the other jurors.

During the *voir dire,* lawyers note the jurors' answers and determine whether they wish to excuse the juror from service in that particular jury. Jurors are excused for cause, peremptorily, or on some other basis. Jurors may be excused for cause when they do not meet the legal requirements for jury service, fall within a mandatory exemption (e.g., is a party to a suit pending in the court or has served as a juror just prior to the present service), or when their answers indicate that they cannot be fair and impartial. A lawyer may excuse a juror peremptorily, that is, without stated cause. These challenges are limited in number by law. Jurors may be excused for other reasons, such as hardship or inconvenience, but only with the concurrence of the court. The order of questioning and challenging is usually established by statute or court rule. Most jurisdictions favor allowing the party with the burden of proof to proceed first. When neither side has any further challenges to assert against an individual juror or portion or full panel of the jury, such juror or jurors are deemed selected. When the full complement of jurors, plus any alternates, have been selected, the jury is sworn to try the issues in the case.

At this point, the jurors should be treated as a single jury unit. That unit must be kept together at all times during the trial. The court may sequester or insulate the jury from public contact during the entire proceeding. This may be required by statute in certain types of cases, such as murder, where pretrial publicity has been considerable or a great deal of publicity during trial is expected. Sequestration requires the court to provide secure quarters for the jurors during their term of service.

The progress of a jury trial follows a definite pattern in all cases. Each side is allowed to make an opening statement to tell the jury what the case is about. Usually, the party that made the complaint will proceed first. After opening statements, the complaining party is required to produce evidence to support its claim. This is done through witnesses, who are called and interrogated to demonstrate their knowledge of the relevant facts. Cross-examination, conducted by the opposing party, is aimed at undermining the witnesses' credibility and hence the weight to be given their testimony. Documents and other physical evidence may be introduced upon meeting certain legal requirements. Charts, maps, and other demonstrative evidence may be used to assist the jury in understanding the matters testified to.

When the complaining party has offered its evidence and has stated that it "rests," the defending party may allege lack of sufficient evidence and move that the court direct a verdict in its favor. If that motion is overruled, the defense may present its own evidence in a similar manner to that employed by the plaintiff. The plaintiff may then rebut any issue raised for the first time in the defense portion of the case. After both sides have "rested," each lawyer is permitted to argue to the jury what he or she believes the evidence has proven and to ask the jury for its verdict. The attorney for the complaining party proceeds first, to be answered by the defendant. Arguments end with the plaintiff's rebuttal. The judge then instructs the jury in the applicable law, usually by reading from written instructions submitted by the parties or prepared by the court.

When the court has finished its instruction, the jurors are directed to deliberate in secret and, when they have agreed, to return their verdict in open court. The lawyers may agree to a sealed verdict, which entails the jurors placing their decision in a sealed envelope and then dispersing, returning to the court later for publication of their verdict. Upon publication, the lawyers are usually given the opportunity to inquire as to whether or not the jurors still abide by their verdict. Where a juror refuses to abide by the verdict, the panel will be returned to continue their deliberations.

When the verdict has been returned and duly recorded, the jurors' service in that particular jury is over. If a verdict is returned within the period of service, the individual juror may be required to return to the jury assembly facility for another assignment. In jurisdictions where jurors are called for a single case or when their service has extended beyond the required period, the jurors are excused. After the jurors have completed their service, records must be completed and the juror must be suitably compensated for his or her service. This may be done immediately upon completion of the term or shortly thereafter.

Grand jury procedures are similar to those of petit juries, but there are certain striking differences. Although drawn from the same lists as petit jurors, grand jurors are subject to stricter standards of qualification and exemption. Culling is normally done by personal interview. Availability for an extended term of service requires the court to allow grand jurors greater preparation time prior to service. Those selected are randomly designated as regulars or alternates on the summons. Grand jurors must also be assembled, oriented, and sworn. While all those chosen constitute one jury unit, only a quorum need be present at any proceeding. The minimum number for a quorum varies.

Grand jury operations are conducted in secret and are closed to all but the jurors, the prosecuting official, witnesses, and the clerk, who swears the witnesses in and records who is called and what action is taken.

The grand jury serves two basic purposes: the determination of probable cause in felony cases and the investigation of matters and conditions of public concern. A determination of probable cause is based upon the reasonable belief by the grand jury that a crime has been committed and that the person indicated by the prosecuting official has committed it. The person may already be in custody or may be under investigation. The proceedings are usually conducted by the state's attorney, district attorney, or other prosecuting official with the participation of the foreman and jurors. The grand jury acts on evidence given through testimony or documents presented by the prosecuting official, although the grand jurors themselves may subpoena witnesses and physical evidence. Witnesses summoned may be compelled to testify and produce evidence without benefit of counsel and without being informed of the purpose of the investigation. The accused generally has no right to be present at grand jury hearings, to offer testimony, or to have counsel present. If the grand jurors find probable cause, they return a "true bill." If they do not, they return a "no bill." Penalties are prescribed for making grand jury deliberations public before they are officially published. Transcripts are not available except through court order.

The second basic function of the grand jury is investigation. It is empowered to subpoena even if no one has been accused of a crime. Grand jury service may be extended to allow completion of any matter of public concern under investigation. Several grand juries may be in operation at any one time. Grand jurors are released at the end of their service terms or at the completion of their investigations.

Problem Areas of Jury Management

Problems will arise at any stage of the selection process or trial. The most frequent criticism of the initial jury pool is that juries do not reflect an accurate cross section of the general population. While exclusive reliance on voting lists yields jurors who feel positively about their role in government and the elective process, large segments of the population are thereby excluded. Polling lists are not generally updated between elections, thus they are not always current. Moreover, if the pool is extremely large and the number of jurors summoned is relatively small, the names from a particular polling list are used for a long period of time. In metropolitan areas with a large proportion of renters and transients, many of those summoned cannot be located—a wasteful and costly procedure.

Culling presents additional problems. Some question whether qualifications for jury service are related to tasks performed or whether they are overly restrictive. Others complain that they are not restrictive enough, implying that stricter requirements would provide jurors with a more positive attitude toward jury service. These complaints result primarily from a lack of public awareness of what is required of the juror, from reports of negative experiences from former jurors, and public indifference to jury service in general. The culling process also suffers from the failure of questionnaires to provide a rational basis upon which to separate the qualified jurors from the unqualified and exempt. If an informal examination lacks objective standards for qualification or rejection, arbitrary choices may result.

Exemptions and excused service can be problem areas. It is generally agreed that an overly liberal exemption policy excludes persons whose experience or occupation might add perspective to the panel. Too much discretion in excusing prospective jurors may result in the loss of governmental workers, professional people, and community leaders, as well as the very rich and very poor, women, and minorities. Potential jurors often seek excuses to avoid loss of wages during their term of service. Many large corporations pay employees their regular paycheck during jury service, but require that they pay back any remuneration received for such service. Employees of companies which allow the juror to keep both regular salary and jury paycheck encourage jury service. It is not surprising that employees of small businesses, which cannot afford to pay their employees during their absence, are frequent applicants for excusal.

The advantage of personal service of summons is the certainty of notification of the prospective juror. This allows for the assessment of penalties upon failure to appear. The disadvantage is its cost, particularly when lists are not current or where people have moved within or from the jurisdiction. The "yield" is that percentage of designated prospective jurors served who respond; it can be used as a measure of efficiency of the service and summons system. Service by mail is less costly, more haphazard, and usually results in a lower yield. It affords no follow-up on persons who have not received their mail or who have moved. Service by telephone is probably the most efficient method, but it requires double service—original verified service together with the agreement of the prospective juror to stand by for telephone service when needed.

After notification, prospective jurors often request excusal for time conflicts, important emergency matters, hardship, lack of transportation, and so forth. The procedure set up to handle these requests must take into account the important public relations aspect of compulsory jury service. Too unyielding an attitude may cause real hardships and result in persons who will prejudice other prospective jurors and make their displeasure known at the polls. Too liberal an excusal policy will result in a low yield and the need to call more jurors. Such a policy may also give rise to charges of discrimination through skewing the process of random selection. Clearly, the balanced approach requires service in all but the real hardship cases and allows one deferral to a time in the immediate future when no conflicts are expected. Public education should inculcate the importance of jury service and an understanding of its requirements.

One of the better methods of encouraging jury duty is the recent "one-day, one-trial" system. Jurors are summoned for one day only; if they are not selected on the day they are on call, they are excused from further service. If they are selected, they serve to the end of the particular case. Service under this plan is definitely prescribed in length and is usually short. It also allows a greater number of persons to be summoned. Depending on how the system is structured and how jurors are compensated, it may be more costly to the jury system. Some jurisdictions that have not adopted the "one-day, one-trial" system have shortened the time period for jury duty to reduce the hardship on those willing to serve.

Once the jurors are assembled at the courthouse, the physical appearance of jury facilities may affect their attitudes as jurors. Surroundings should be designed to make jurors comfortable. There should be adequate lighting, heating, ventilation, and air conditioning, and toilet facilities should be provided and suitably designed. Jurors should be able to contact their family and friends to arrange for transportation or emergency domestic matters. If required to wait for long periods, steps should be taken to relieve their boredom.

The human dimension is also important. Those in charge of jury supervision and assignment should be sensitive to problems of the jury system. If too many jurors are summoned, many may not be used at all. If too few are summoned, they may be hustled from courtroom to courtroom in order to provide sufficient numbers for trials to commence. Poor utilization of jurors, together with the confusion and dissatisfaction that causes, can be avoided by improved estimates of supply and demand as well as by improved operational efficiency. Effective orientation emphasizes civic pride rather than the juror's own personal sacrifice. An understanding of the jury process and what will be required of jurors will mollify the anxiety of unfamiliar circumstances. Jurors who are required in different locations should not have to stand idly by waiting to assemble and proceed. Transportation arrangements should be as pleasant and comfortable as possible. The juror must not be left stranded and unable to return home. Court personnel should assemble jury panels large enough to survive challenges but not so large as to clog courtrooms with jurors needed elsewhere. The time from when a juror is summoned to when he or she is to appear should be minimized, especially where the jurors must be transported to their destination elsewhere.

The greatest delays occur during actual trial. The longer the trials, the fewer the trials that can be accommodated in any given time frame. Jury trials are more costly and tie up more personnel than nonjury trials. They use facilities that are unnecessary in nonjury trials, such as impaneling and deliberation rooms. They are subject to more errors, reversals, and retrials, which result in additional costs of time, space, and personnel. Community attitudes and amount of publicity directly affect the pace at which jury trials proceed. Delay is increased by the tendency of lawyers to prolong the selection process by questioning and challenging jurors. This may be limited by local rules, by the attitude of the judge, by narrowing the bases for excusal, and by restricting the number of peremptory challenges. Picking alternate jurors in trials expected to last long periods of time further lengthens the process. These delays are reduced where six-member panels are permitted. Poor control by the court allows the lawyers to "romance" the jurors and make lengthy speeches to them in an attempt to indoctrinate them. This is prevented by restricting their questions and eliciting only necessary information for peremptory challenges. Jury screening may be hindered by a certain reluctance on the part of jurors who feel the questions asked are too personal or are needlessly embarrassing. They may also suspect that they are being analyzed through the use of psychological profiles or investigations of their personal lives, as has recently occurred in some well-publicized cases.

After they are sworn in, jurors should be able to hear and see clearly the evidence presented. The room jurors retire to during court recesses should be comfortable, physically attractive, and have adequate toilet and rest facilities.

Sequestration provides more problems. Keeping juries incommunicado from family and friends and insulated from any publicity surrounding the trial are difficult tasks at best and require court personnel who are firm but considerate. There must be adequate facilities to house the jurors during the sequestration period of the trial. These facilities must be comfortable and attractive, inasmuch as the jurors will be away from familiar surroundings. If the jurors do not have individual rooms, arrangements must be made to provide some sense of privacy. Adequate bathroom facilities must be available, and, to the extent possible, the jurors must not feel as if they are imprisoned. Sufficient recreational facilities should be provided where possible. Trips away from the confines of the courthouse may be scheduled to break the monotony. Food should be adequate and well-prepared, but caution must be exercised to prevent liquor or other intoxicants from impairing the jurors' ability to serve. Those having responsibility for jurors' care and housing must also minimize the opportunity for improper conduct between jurors and for the personality conflicts that may occur over long periods of time. The hardships of "lockup" jury service are well known; the sacrifices made by sequestered jurors are real. Every effort should be made to consider the problems and alleviate the conditions causing them. In extremely lengthy cases, sufficient alternate jurors should be provided to accommodate any incapacity which may be expected from the regular jurors. Agreement might also be obtained from the lawyers to proceed with fewer than the required number of jurors so that the case need not be retried.

Responsibility for the proper conduct and management of the jury during the trial process rests primarily with the trial judge. Once the lawyers have selected a jury that they believe is fair and impartial, it is up to the trial judge to see that the jury has an opportunity to see and hear clearly the witnesses and to consider any physical evidence that may be allowed. It is also the role of the trial judge to conduct the trial as expeditiously as possible and to instill into the jurors a feeling that they are indeed a significant part of the adjudicatory process. Above all, it is the duty of the trial judge to prevent any prejudicial matters from being placed before the jury which may adversely affect their deliberations and which may require a reversal and retrial. However, other factors outside the control of the trial judge may militate against his or her effective management.

The physical layout of the courtroom itself may obscure the jury's view. Lack of sound-amplification equipment and poor acoustical design may prevent the jurors from hearing vital testimony. Steps should be taken to avoid unnecessary distraction. The activities of other court personnel and the public may prove distracting to the jurors. During the summer, a lack of air conditioning may require that the windows of the courtroom be opened to a cacophony of sounds from the street below. If those windows overlook a busy public area, there is an additional source of distraction. Lack of adequate lighting may contribute to eyestrain on the part of the jurors and hamper vision at a crucial point. Lack of electrical outlets, projector screens, blackboards, or equipment for the presentation of demonstrative evidence may inhibit the jurors' understanding. The spatial relationships between the witnesses, lawyers, judge, and jury may also affect their attitude toward the case. Long, uninterrupted sessions at trial may adversely affect juror attention. This is particularly true if the testimony extends beyond the normal span of attention, if the jurors must sit in uncomfortable chairs, and if there are too few breaks. The judge also sets the tone of the jurors' participation by allowing them to take notes or to propound questions during the trial.

While each litigant is entitled to a trial free from substantial prejudice, no one is entitled to a perfect trial. The fear of prejudicial error usually hampers efficient jury management. The resulting mistrial and retrial requires both parties to begin again; the time previously expended is wasted. It is the task of trial judges to see that error does not creep into the proceedings. They must anticipate prejudicial occurrences and avert them. They must allay the jurors' curiosity about matters which have been withheld from them. Where such matters are inadvertently presented in court, the judge must instruct the jurors to seek honestly and earnestly to disregard them, and must also take precaution to prevent recurrences, which may cumulatively cause a mistrial.

In addition to excluding evidence that may be prejudicial, the judge must police the conduct of the attorneys to eliminate any reference to matters which are not relevant to the litigation or that are not in evidence. This breach most often occurs in opening statements or closing arguments.

Another area where error is likely to occur is in the submission of legal instructions. Because the instructions must precisely inform the jury of the law of the jurisdiction and be appropriate to the facts of the case, there is much room for error, particularly where uniform jury instructions are not used. Here again it is the obligation of the able and experienced trial judge to reduce the chance of error.

Once the jury has been instructed as to the law and directed to deliberate, every effort should be made to see that their deliberations are conducted in absolute secrecy. The jury deliberation room should be comfortable without being too informal. There should be adequate toilet facilities and sufficient equipment (such as screens and blackboards) to display the evidence and allow the jurors to illustrate or demonstrate their own points of view. The room should be soundproof, with no chance for their conversations being heard outside. Equipment should be available for the replay of evidence as allowed, and provisions should be made for responding quickly to questions as they may arise. When deliberations become lengthy and the need arises to lodge the jurors overnight, the same considerations confront the court which were discussed in the problems of sequestration. Every effort should be made to encourage the jurors to arrive at a decision allowed by law in order to avoid hung juries and the necessity of retrial. Jurors find most difficulty reaching a verdict in complex cases with multiple parties, in cases in which there are multiple charges or claims, and in cases which require the jurors to answer special interrogatories with regard to certain aspects of the case. There are additional time delays where a jury is required to set the punishment after a finding of guilty or to set the amount of damages after a finding of liability. The suggested use of bifurcated trials, in which a jury would determine liability and then fix damages or punishment, does not alleviate the time delay but rather contributes to it. Inconsistent verdicts or improper verdicts will give rise to further delay, appeals, and retrial. Delays may also occur where one or more jurors, after polling, change their verdict and the jurors must return to continue their deliberations.

Once the trial is over, the court must then decide whether the juror should serve on additional cases. While the experience gained during his or her jury service makes the juror more knowledgeable and sophisticated with regard to the jury process, lawyers tend to regard prior experience with suspicion and may excuse such jurors in future cases, thereby reducing the efficiency afforded by the use of experienced jurors. When the juror's service is complete, the court must be prepared for official release and compensation. Here again, we must recognize the fact that throughout the country, remuneration for jury service is notoriously inadequate and that many of the problems of jury response, attitude, and public relations would be vastly improved by a reasonably adequate fee.

Supervision and management of the grand jury must be guided by its unique history and current status. To fulfill its role as a buffer between the state and the individual, the grand jury must be composed of persons selected at random and drawn from a representative pool of the general public. Grand jury proceedings must be substantially free of prejudice, and their operation and development must be superintended. The grand jury has been considered an adjunct of the executive, specifically the prosecutorial, branch of government. Most jurisdictions, however, treat it as more closely associated with the judicial branch, which ultimately supervises and has the responsibility for its conduct. Many courts now impose the safeguards of procedural due process upon grand jury proceedings and practices to ensure fairness both to the interests of the community in protecting against general criminal activities and official corruption and to the interest of the potential accused. Some states have enacted laws which provide the right of counsel for witnesses and potential defendants and even allow their lawyers to be present in the grand jury room to advise them.

Other areas of difficulty lie in the construction and maintenance of the grand jury facilities themselves. The deleterious effects of poor light, drab and uncomfortable surroundings, and inadequate protection from interference and distraction are all heightened in grand jury service, since it is generally longer than that of the petit jury. Public access to the grand jury entrance or waiting room will allow publicity that may compromise the secrecy of the proceedings. Heat and ventilation shafts often carry the sounds of proceedings to areas where they can be overheard. Grand jury service in the evening hours has been permitted in some jurisdictions and allows the grand jury to work at a relaxed pace. Working in off-hours, however, has the drawback of reduced access to witnesses, documents, and other court materials. Too relaxed an atmosphere is counterproductive if case volume is large. Grand jury service also requires ancillary facilities for the typing of reports, indictments, "no bills," and for the usual record keeping of grand jury proceedings.

Jury Selection and Clerk's Office

The jury clerk's or commissioner's office should be designed as an integral part of jury assembly facilities. If possible, it should also be adjacent to the clerk's office if jury operation is part of the clerk's responsibilities. Since the clerk's office should be conveniently accessible to the public, attorneys, and staff for the filing of legal documents and payment of fines and fees, and so forth, it is preferable for the clerk's office to be located as close as possible to the main public entrance level of the courthouse. It may be desirable for the jury clerk's office and the jury assembly facilities to adjoin the clerk's office along the side that is less accessible to the general public (fig. 3.1).

With a manual jury selection process, the jury clerk's office generally consists of clerical office furniture such as desks, chairs, and filing cabinets; equipment such as typewriters and calculators; and a lottery box from which jurors' names or numbers are drawn to select the jury panel for the impaneling process. In older courthouses, jury clerks' offices are often poorly lit, inadequately furnished, and inappropriately located. Technology has brought sophisticated data-processing systems and equipment into the process of jury selection and the impaneling process. Jury lists derived from voter registration, motor vehicle registration, and other existing registration lists are fed into computers; jury notices and checks for payment of jury services are processed through computers; time records of jury service and number of jurors called and used can all be automated with CRT monitors used for input and retrieval of data and information. Automation of the jury system has also brought visual changes to the jury clerk's office. In addition to workstations for jury clerks, it is common for the jury clerk's office to be equipped with terminals on work surfaces with which to input, update, or retrieve information from either a remotely located central county or state computer, or from a minicomputer or PC network located within or near the jury clerk's office.

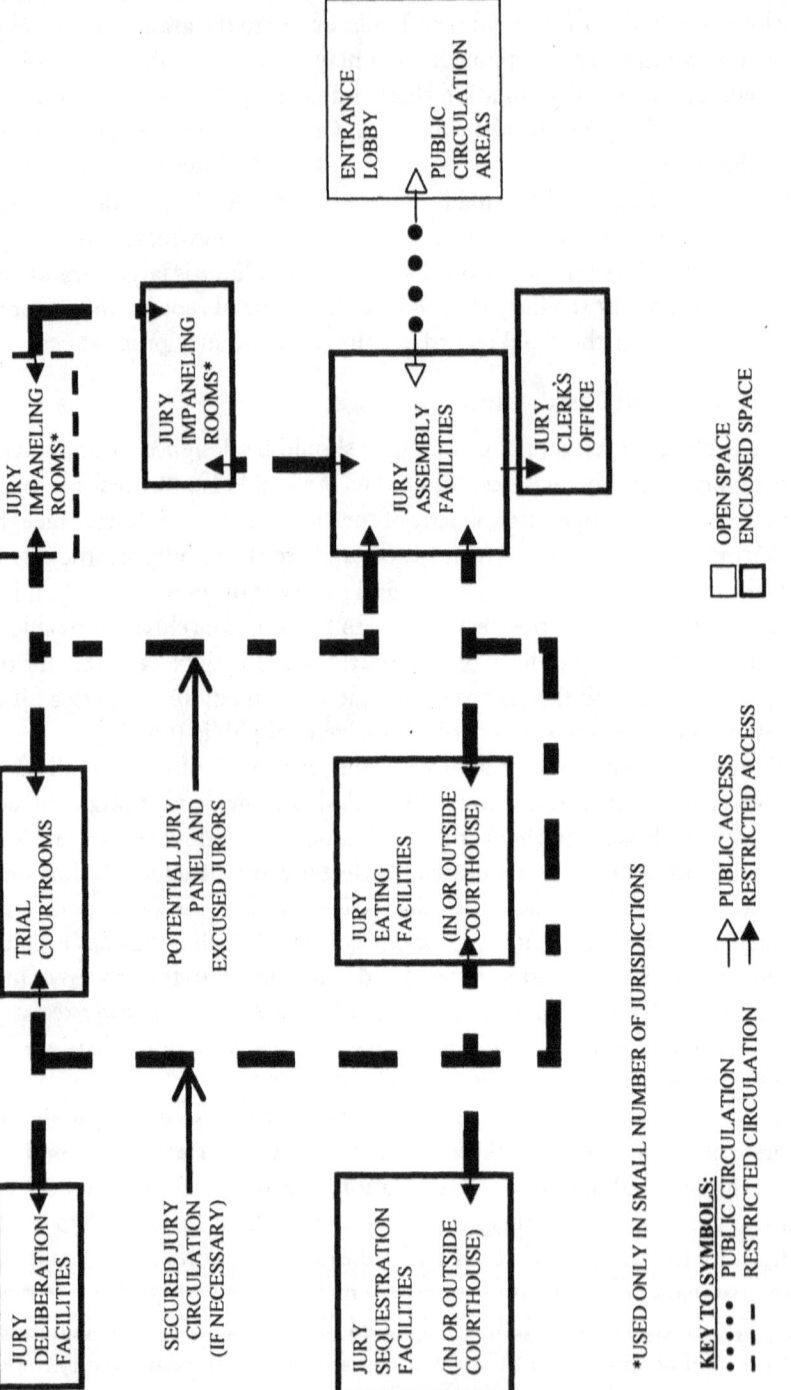

Figure 3.1. Jury System, Facilities, and Circulation Pattern

When designing jury clerks' offices in a new building, adequate power should be provided at appropriate locations in anticipation of wall stations, laser printers, and other data-processing equipment. The jury clerks' workstations should be near the jurors' entry into the jury assembly area, and a reception–waiting room area should be provided. On the other hand, computer wall stations should be located at the rear and sides of the office, out of easy reach of jurors or visitors. If a computer wall station is provided for each jury clerk, it should be incorporated within the clerk's workstation, preferably along the side or rear of the station.

Jury Assembly Facilities

Possible combinations of the following spaces should be considered in planning of jury assembly facilities:

- Entrance lobby into the jury assembly area, with access to vending machines and toilets for jurors
- Public counter area
- General jurors' assembly area, with provision for juror orientation and panel selection
- Quiet reading and study area
- Noisy activity area, such as for television viewing, game tables, and so forth

Because jury assembly is not a public function, jury assembly facilities should not be too readily accessible to the general public. Potential jurors should not mix with the general public, nor should opportunities be created which would encourage communication between them. Jurors should be clearly identified by wearing badges or identification cards so that other people in the building will not make contact with them to discuss cases. On the other hand, potential jurors reporting for jury duty at the courthouse should not have great difficulty in locating jury assembly facilities. This situation can be resolved by locating jury assembly facilities either at the less public side of the clerk's office, or on the adjacent floor connected by both elevators and escalators or stairs. By locating the jury assembly facilities directly above or below the clerk's office, an internal private staircase can be constructed to connect the jury clerk's office with the court clerk's office. The jury assembly facilities, while remaining reasonably accessible to potential jurors, are removed from the primary traffic flow pattern of the public at the entrance level.

Many jury assembly spaces are overdesigned and underutilized. During a regular jury trial day, the maximum number of jurors congregate at the jury assembly space at the beginning of the trial day (usually between 8:00 and

9:00 A.M.) and after the lunch recess. The number of jurors after the lunch recess is considerably fewer than in the early morning, as some jurors are excused or impaneled during the morning court sessions. Many jury assembly spaces are overdesigned to accommodate the projected peak load of jurors and potential jurors, and are underutilized because this peak period of jury assembly usually lasts for no more than an hour or two early in the morning. An efficient jury system should reduce the peak load to the minimum load as quickly as possible. This means that jury panels should be scheduled and transported to courtrooms as efficiently as possible.

The size of jury assembly space should therefore be based on an estimation of the number of jurors and potential jurors using the space at regular time intervals each day over a predetermined time period, and the method of use. There are two criteria in determining the size of jury assembly spaces: seating area and comfortable lounge area. The space should be large enough to accommodate the regular seating area for the projected peak load, but would need only to house the comfortable lounge area for the average off-peak load. For example, if the projected peak load between 8:00 and 9:00 A.M. is 200 while the average off-peak load throughout the day is 50, then it is recommended that adequate space be provided to minimally accommodate the 200 potential jurors, even if they are uncomfortable during that one-hour period. On the other hand, the space should also be large enough to comfortably house the 50 jurors during the average off-peak.

To resolve this architecturally, it is possible to subdivide the jury assembly space into two connected spaces: one equipped with a lounge chair configuration, the other with predominately bench or stack chairs. These two spaces could be separated by a movable or double-folding partition with a rated sound attenuation of forty-five decibels. During the jurors' orientation period, both rooms would combine to form one large jury assembly space. After the morning peak load, the partition could be closed and the assembly space would consist of comfortable lounge furniture to accommodate the average off-peak load. The other partitioned space could then be used as a staff room, a meeting or conference room, or a hearing room if acoustical treatment permits.

Another approach would be to group multipurpose and similar-use facilities that complement each other. For example, we may locate the large staff conference or training room adjacent to the main jury assembly space, and connect them by a pair of double doors so that both spaces can be jointly used for jury assembly during peak periods. The jury assembly facilities can be used in conjunction with staff conferencing and training sessions outside of regular work hours. The large jury assembly space can also be used for meetings, alternative dispute resolution (ADR) conferences, mediation and arbitration activities, and so forth outside of peak jury periods.

Entrance Lobby

The entrance lobby that leads directly into the main jury assembly space should be accessible from a public corridor or lobby space. In major court complexes, it is advantageous to provide a private jurors' access to elevators for jury and staff to transfer jurors to trial courtrooms. A large service elevator accessible from a private corridor can also be used for this purpose. Entrance and exit points should be controlled visually from the jury clerk's counter and work space. Potential jurors reporting for jury service, as well as paneling of potential jurors for transfer to trial courtrooms, center around the jury clerk's counter and assembly space. The entrance lobby may also provide access to vending machines and to a jurors' coatroom and private toilets, which should be located near the general jury assembly space.

Coin-operated vending machines, where possible, should be grouped in an alcove adjoining either the entrance lobby or the assembly space. Since this space tends to be used often, the selection of easily maintained floor finishes is especially important. From a design viewpoint, vending machines should be snugly fitted between built-in bases and headboards whose width should be similar to that of vending machines. This eliminates spaces below or above the vending machines which otherwise would collect dirt, dust, and trash. Adequate trash containers should be provided in the vending area and in the various jury assembly spaces. Careful design integration of these containers into the overall design of furniture and equipment would enhance the environmental quality of these spaces.

General Jury Assembly Area

The general jury assembly area should be designed in an efficient and comfortable manner. Furniture should not be bulky; rather it should be easily movable so that its arrangement can be altered whenever necessary. It is not necessary to use partitions to subdivide the various functional areas. This can be accomplished by applying office landscaping concepts involving the grouping of furniture according to its use, the use of bookshelves, plants, and low, movable acoustical panels to delineate these functional spaces within the general jury assembly area. Seating should be grouped for small group conversation. Visually attractive stacking chairs should be used in open areas when needed during jury orientation sessions.

The space for television watching does not have to be partitioned off if it can be combined with the area for games and other more noisy activities. By separating noisy areas from quiet reading areas, and by locating television areas as far removed as possible from the quiet areas, it is possible to accomplish more functions within the general jury assembly area, with proper office landscaping. It is also desirable to be able to dim the light level in the television area to enhance television viewing. To minimize sound transmission into adjoining areas, the television area should be surrounded with sound absorptive finishes. If a juror orientation videotape is used, provision should be made either for large-screen projection or for an adequate number of television locations so that all jurors may view the tape at the same time.

Quiet study and work alcoves can be created for potential jurors who wish to work while waiting to be called. These alcoves, which should have the least amount of noise and disruption, could be incorporated into the design of the quiet reading area without resorting to closed study booths. Since many courthouses have been designated as nonsmoking buildings, jury assembly facilities are often planned for nonsmokers. However, because some jurors will be smokers, an adjacent exterior balcony or patio that is accessible only to jurors may be provided to accommodate them.

In planning jury assembly facilities for a future jury system that does not presently exist, it would be economically desirable to be able to use these facilities for other functions during the interim period. In most major court facilities, one area that is frequently neglected is staff training and conference facilities. Over the past decade, judicial education and training programs in all aspects of judicial administration have proliferated. Where no specialized training and meeting space is provided, ill-equipped courtrooms and hearing rooms are used on an as-needed basis. Each major courthouse building in a metropolitan center should provide an adequate staff training and meeting room, appropriately equipped with audio-visual and media equipment, to accommodate ongoing training programs for judges, clerks, court administrators, and various levels of professional and technical staff. The provision of an entrance lobby and toilets, vending machines, and other support facilities makes the jury assembly space an ideal training and conference center for the judicial system.

Jury Impaneling Rooms

In some states, impaneling of jurors for civil cases, including the *voir dire* procedure, can be conducted in jury impaneling rooms located outside of trial courtrooms. Impaneling of jurors for criminal cases is invariably conducted in open court. Jury impaneling rooms can be located within the jury assembly facilities or near trial courtrooms. The former arrangement requires attorneys to meet at the jury assembly area to conduct the *voir dire* in the jury impaneling room. In order to minimize attorney traffic into the jury assembly spaces, jury impaneling rooms should be accessible from the entrance lobby, under the visual control of the jury clerk's station. With this arrangement, potential jurors can be summoned by the jury clerk from jury assembly space on an as-needed basis. If jury impaneling rooms are located in close proximity to courtrooms on another floor, the appropriate jury panel (for a six- or twelve-member jury) has to be transported from the jury assembly area to one of those rooms. This means that the size of jury impaneling rooms has to be larger in order to house entire jury panels. Centralization of jury impaneling rooms within or adjacent to jury assembly facilities also has the advantage of maximizing the use of these rooms for other jury-related facilities. Jury impaneling rooms that are grouped behind trial courtrooms on each floor tend to be underutilized, unless courtrooms are centrally assigned to handle jury cases. For this reason, jury impaneling rooms should be planned as multipurpose rooms that are accessible from both private and public circulation systems.

Jury Circulation within Courthouses

Potential jurors reporting for jury service do not require separate entrances or circulation patterns. Upon being selected to serve on a jury panel, it would be preferable for jurors to travel between the jury assembly area and the trial courtroom by means of private corridors and elevators, particularly for a jury panel selected to hear a public-interest or sensational trial involving celebrities or notorious criminals. In most major courthouses, jurors are escorted by bailiffs to courtrooms. In some cases, private judges' or staff elevators are used to transport jury panels. In some instances, large freight or service elevators with capacities of up to thirty people are used to transport an entire jury panel to the courtroom floor without mixing with the public. Use of these elevators to move jurors is usually controlled by bailiffs.

After a jury of six or twelve members, together with alternate jurors, has been impaneled from the original panel of potential jurors, the level of security required by the jury increases with the level of notoriety of defendants and the sensationalism of cases. In most civil and criminal cases, public attendance and security risk are low. The occasional sensational criminal trial may require juries being sequestered, in which case provision should be made in courthouse design to transfer sequestered jurors by means of private corridors and elevators. In most courthouses, the number of times that juries are sequestered does not justify a separate circulation pattern for jurors. Jurors should be able to share the same private circulation spaces as court staff, under the supervision of court-assigned bailiffs.

Jurors' circulation between the jury box in the courtroom and the jury deliberation suite behind the courtroom should be by means of a private corridor.

Jury Facilities in Trial Courtrooms

The two areas used by the jurors in the courtroom are the public seating area and the jury box. A panel of potential jurors can either be summoned directly to appear at a specified courtroom (usually in a small court facility) or be escorted to the courtroom from a central jury assembly facility within or in close proximity to the courthouse. The size and the amount of seating in the public seating area are largely determined by the size of the jury panel and the estimated number of spectators expected during the jury impaneling process. For example, for a regular trial courtroom, the panel of potential jurors for a twelve-member jury brought from the jury assembly facilities to the courtroom varies from 24 to 40, depending on the number of peremptory challenges allowed by law for each party. Since there are, or should be, at least 14 seats in the jury box (12 regular and 2 alternate jurors), the required number of seats in the public seating area needed to accommodate the remaining jurors is between 10 and 26. If 12 additional seats are provided for the spectators during the jury impaneling process, the total seating capacity of the public seating area in the courtroom would not need to be more than 24 to 40. After the jury has been impaneled, the remaining jurors would be either excused from jury duty for that day or returned to the jury assembly area, leaving the entire public seating capacity of 24 to 40 for spectator seating. For 95 percent of regular civil and criminal trials, a courtroom with such a public seating capacity should be adequate. Where the panel of potential jurors is seated initially in the public seating area while the judge and/or attorneys make certain statements regarding the facts of the case, the minimum seating capacity in the public area of the courtroom should be around 50.

For 6-member-jury trials, the size of the jury panel brought into the courtroom varies from 14 to 20 potential jurors. If the case is heard in a trial courtroom with a 14-member-jury box, most, if not all, potential jurors can be accommodated in the jury box. Seating capacity of 30 should be adequate for 95 percent of all trials, with some potential jurors seated in the public area. In most 6-member-jury trials, the jury impaneling process is not normally a time-consuming process, and the brief period that a smaller courtroom is overcrowded during this process, in view of the increasing budgeting limitations imposed on judicial facility projects, should not be considered an undue hardship. In a large, multicourtroom facility, cost savings in the economic design of courtrooms can be substantial, and can result in funds for other high-priority facilities that otherwise might not be affordable within the available budget for the project.

For public-interest trials and trials with extensive pretrial publicity, a much larger jury panel is needed from which to select a twelve-member jury.

In these cases, either one of the few larger trial courtrooms should be used, even just for the jury impaneling process, or a second or even a third jury panel can be brought into the regular trial courtroom after the first jury panel has been exhausted but the full panel has not been accomplished. The jury *voir dire* and impaneling process in the large courtroom would require that the panel of potential jurors be instructed at one time by the judge regarding the fundamental legal principle applicable to the case. The use of the regular trial courtroom may require that the judge discuss these principles each time a new jury panel is brought in. A small number of large courtrooms, designed to adequately accommodate major jury trials and large spectator attendance, should be provided in all multicourtroom court buildings. These courtrooms should be grouped around secured prisoner-holding, interviewing, and access facilities so that all major civil, criminal, domestic relations, and other types of trials requiring larger panels of potential jurors may be assigned with maximum flexibility and convenience to them. An earlier reference to the use of regular trial courtrooms for high-public-interest criminal cases involving potentially disruptive defendants or possible escape attempts, accompanied by the use of a larger remote spectator area, remains applicable for reasons of the need for a high level of security and safety.

Design criteria for the jury box have already been established in *Space Management and the Courts* and in other publications. However, the following considerations should be stressed:

- Because the jury box is used only during jury trials, it is not used for much of the time. For this reason, jury boxes should be designed for multiple uses. It is suggested that the front row of the jury box be located at the same floor level as the judicial area of the courtroom, and be provided with a visible 15- to 18-inch-wide work surface (instead of the regular modesty rail) so that the front row of the jury box can be used by attorneys and litigants in a multiparty nonjury trial when the regular attorneys' and litigants' tables provided are not adequate. Jury boxes have also been designed to seat witnesses or prisoners in situations where a separate prisoner-holding facility adjacent to the courtroom is not available. For these functions, the use of durable and low-maintenance materials or jurors' chairs would be of paramount importance.
- All jurors in the jury box must be able to see and hear the witness, attorneys, judge, clerk, and court reporter during a trial. Proximity to the witness, who may be nervous and speak softly, is especially important. Jurors should be clearly seen by all trial participants. For this reason, it is not desirable to have windows behind the jury box that

require jurors to be seen in silhouette. If appropriate, the light level at the jury box can be lower than the high light intensity at work surfaces within the judicial area of the courtroom.
- The jury box should be close to the door leading into the private corridor which in turn leads to one of several suites for jury deliberation. Jurors should not have to traverse the width of the judicial area in order to exit from the courtroom.
- When a jury deliberation suite is accessible directly from the courtroom, or when it opens directly into a public or private corridor, a soundlock should be provided to minimize sound transmission between the jury deliberation room proper and the access corridor or courtroom space.

Jury Deliberation Suites

Jury deliberation suites can constitute a major space item in a courthouse project. The proper ratio of jury deliberation suites to courtrooms in courthouse design can result in significant cost savings. An efficiently designed twelve-member-jury deliberation room unit, including soundlock which serves also as an entry area to jurors' toilets, coat closet, coffee preparation area, and jurors' rest area, requires approximately 500 square feet of net space, or around 800 square feet of gross building area. Using a conservative unit construction cost figure of $125 per square foot of gross area, the cost of a jury deliberation suite unit would be about $100,000. In a 20-courtroom courthouse, a ratio of 1 jury deliberation suite to 1 courtroom would require a construction budget of approximately $2 million for the 20 jury deliberation suite units. The use of a ratio of 1 jury deliberation suite to every 2 trial courtrooms would result in savings of approximately $1 million.

With few exceptions, the provision of 1 jury deliberation suite for every 2 trial courtrooms is an optimum ratio for the design of trial court facilities for courthouses with more than 4 courtrooms. In small courthouses, the ratios of 1 jury deliberation suite to 1 courtroom or of 2 jury deliberation suites for 3 trial courtrooms can be used. In large courthouses, it is highly unlikely that all trial courtrooms are used simultaneously for trials, let alone for jury trials. If half of the courtrooms are used simultaneously to try jury cases, the provision of 1 jury deliberation suite for every 2 trial courtrooms assumes that all the juries would deliberate simultaneously, or if not all the juries deliberate simultaneously, that certain trial courtrooms require more than 1 jury deliberation suite. The latter applies to those courtrooms in which a second jury trial may commence while the jury of the first trial is still deliberating in the jury deliberation suite.

The ratio of providing fewer jury deliberation suites than trial courtrooms is feasible only when the former are not physically attached to the latter, meaning that the only way of entering the jury deliberation suite is through the courtroom. When the situation occurs in an existing courthouse, the high ratio of one jury deliberation suite to one courtroom becomes inevitable. The optimum locations and design of jury deliberation suites is to group them together and separate them from the row of courtrooms by a private access corridor. The jury from any one of several courtrooms can then use any of several jury deliberation suites for deliberation. By grouping and centrally locating them in relation to the courtrooms, plumbing stacks for jurors' toilets can be shared (if adequate soundproofing is provided) and the jury deliberation suites are conveniently accessible from all courtrooms. If there are six courtrooms along one side of a major court facility, the provision of three jury deliberation suites assumes that three of the courtrooms have simultaneous jury deliberation. Except for minor cases involving six-member juries, this would not be a common occurrence.

Jury Sequestration Facilities

Jury sequestration facilities, including bedrooms, kitchen, and eating facilities, are provided in a small number of courthouses. These facilities are used by impaneled jurors in high-publicity and high-security trials in which the jurors might be unduly influenced with media publicity or exposed to potential jury tampering or personal threats. In a large court facility with more than ten jury trial courtrooms and where jury sequestration is a frequent occurrence, the cost of providing jury sequestration facilities within or near the courthouse may possibly be justified. However, the maintenance cost of such facilities, especially if kitchen and eating facilities are provided, would be substantial, and the court system may not wish to become involved in this kind of specialized operation.

In the courthouse in Anchorage, jury sequestration facilities, including bedrooms and toilet facilities, were provided for two panels of jurors and their bailiffs. Each panel was provided with six double rooms, and two central bedrooms were provided directly outside the secured jurors' area for bailiffs. No kitchen or eating facilities are provided. While one set of jury sequestration facilities was used quite frequently, the second set was used only once in the first five years after the courthouse was occupied. Consequently the bedrooms were converted into private offices for much-needed support facilities. In jurisdictions in which jurors are seldom sequestered, it is less expensive to use available hotel facilities in the community on an as-needed basis than to construct jury sequestration facilities that are infrequently used.

In locations where bedrooms and toilets are provided, kitchen and eating facilities are not usually installed for this purpose in the courthouse. The cost and inconvenience of maintaining such facilities cannot be justified, especially when restaurants are readily available within the community. While jurors' security and privacy is a main concern during sequestration, it is possible to arrange with restaurant owners to provide a private room for jurors to take their meals. Where no jury sequestration facilities are provided in the courthouse, a continuous row of interior hotel rooms at the end of a building wing can be reserved on an as-needed basis for sequestered jurors. Bailiffs assigned to escort sequestered jurors must be trained and experienced in all aspects of jury security and safety.

4

Records Management and Space Management

The scope of the term "record" in the court context varies widely from one jurisdiction to the next. Some systems restrict it to the case papers proper, which are filed relating to the case. Others include book entries and supporting documents, such as depositions. For purposes of facility planning, this chapter assumes that court records are a collection of material that enables a neutral person to reconstruct the essential aspects of the matter under consideration.

A record, according to this definition, is a transitory element. It is not permanent in a management context. Material of great importance at one stage of a legal proceeding may have little or no significance at a later stage. The effective records system views all material in relation to its point in time and the degree of its necessity to the legal process. Decisions on what should be preserved must be based on the need to reconstruct the necessary aspects of the matter.

Records system design should enable a neutral person to obtain clear answers to questions concerning matters in which he or she has legitimate interest. This clarity should be available either by providing adequate staff with the time and training to deal with such inquiry or by so structuring the records system that basic information can be obtained with a minimum of assistance. Most systems develop a mix of these approaches, based on the resources and demands of their system. Systems design will also affect the type of equipment and facility design.

Historical Perspective

Throughout our history, courts have traditionally been one of the custodians of the essential records of society. From the earliest days of records keeping, the collective memory of society in such areas as property rights, genealogical relationships, and financial agreements was preserved by the joint effort of the courts and the institutional church. This role has changed only slightly for courts in today's society. The types of records kept today and, in too many cases, the technology with which they are kept, do not differ substantially from the earliest records. A case recently taken from the files of a northeastern trial court had all the characteristics (document file fold, multiple copies, warrant and subpoena issuance, clerks' notations, appellate procedures, etc.) which we find in such case records across the country. The interesting thing is that this case was dated in the fall of 1732 and bore the seal of George II, by the grace of God, King of England.

The significance of that is twofold:

First, it illustrates that legal process really has not changed very much in 268 years.

Second, it shows that the generation and initial handling of court records has seen little change in many courts throughout the centuries.

The role of the courts as a records keeper continues to grow both in sheer volume and in sophistication in terms of the types of records which must be kept and the manner in which they must be kept and referenced. Even the smallest courts are faced with a need to recall and reference records for users such as the local police, title search companies, credit bureaus, and genealogical researchers. Virtually every court in the country must handle records at least one hundred years old, and many of the older systems have in their custody records from the colonial period. Common records management problems include physical deterioration, excessively high volumes of paper, and inconvenient and time-consuming reference. Efficient retrieval and cross-reference capabilities are emerging as problems in the increasingly sophisticated criminal case records. Computers are usually required, with the attendant problems of security and privacy.

The Present Role of Records in Courts

It is only a slight exaggeration to say that "a court is its records." If courts are to remain an essential recorder and a stabilizing factor in society, they must be able to reference their records efficiently and accurately. Courts exist for two basic purposes. The first and most specific is dispensing justice in individual cases. The second, and more abstract, is the development of a "just society." The role of records in both these purposes is immediate and essential. Records help ensure individual justice by recording title to property or land, or dispositions under probate matters. They ensure the validity of contracts, grant citizenship, maintain vital statistics, and record for all time the activities of criminal offenders. In the broader sense, courts have a clear state-society role. They protect the state against unjust claims, enforce statutes, rules, and regulations, and establish or support judicial rules or interpretations that become effective guiding principles. The concept of *stare decisis* is entirely dependent upon the effectiveness of the court record system.

Court records serve three basic functions within the court system: they have a litigatory role, a managerial role, and an archival-historical role.

- *Litigatory Role*—The primary function of court records is in the litigation of cases. Records management systems must be designed to satisfy the needs of parties to litigation, their counsel, and the court. This role imposes certain restrictions upon any records system. The ease of reference, the rate at which relevant records may be retrieved, control systems, and security questions are central to records management. It is during this stage that records get their heaviest use in terms of reference, adding of information, and travel from different locations within the court system.
- *Managerial Role*—The managerial role of court records may occur at the same time that records are involved in the litigatory process. Statistics, case scheduling needs, workload measurement, and a number of other managerial concerns impact record use. A major concern in records management is the accommodation of these concurrent but sometimes conflicting needs.
- *Archival-Historical Role*—The third major role that courts play in records management is the conservator of records for archival-historical purposes. Courts have traditionally been the repository of vital records. These include vital statistics, land records, and such personal information as adoptions and name changes. All such information must be preserved over long periods of time and be accessible to legitimate inquiries. However, it must not conflict with the more immediate litigatory and management needs. In most jurisdictions, this archival-historical role receives the least attention, yet these materials constitute the vast bulk of the records maintained by the court.

The significance of these roles is that they cause unique problems for court managers. Most organizations do not maintain records which cover such a wide range of use, are of such importance, or must be maintained for such a long period of time. The variety of decisions to be made by court records managers, often with inadequate resources, compounds the seriousness of records management problems.

The court that must accommodate its records program within an existing facility may find problems in attempting to accommodate the unique needs of one of these roles. Conversely, the court designing new facilities will find its design affected by the distinct roles throughout the life of court records. This transitional facility impact phenomenon is probably greater in the records area than any other aspect of court management. Records management is virtually the only aspect of court management which reaches from the initiation of the case until long after the case is disposed. Because it has this long life, and because the use of records changes within that life, it has a pervasive impact on facility design.

Factors Impacting Management

The amount and type of space allocated to specific records functions and the design of that space are both direct results of management decisions made in response to internal and external system demands.

External Influences

A basic problem in court records management is that court managers are usually not complete masters of their record-keeping house. Courts are subject to a number of pressures, controls, and other inhibiting outside factors which make the effective management of records even more difficult than it is by its very nature. These external influences differ in origin and nature, but they all affect, in varying degrees, records management considerations of most court systems.

The following is a rather generic summary of the most common external influences on court records management. There may be others in individual jurisdictions. The primary need is that they be identified in each jurisdiction and accommodated in a specific records system design. Their identification and analysis is particularly important as a manager plans new or renovated facilities to accommodate court records.

Constitutional and Statutory Provisions

In some areas, the responsibility for records management is placed by constitution with an elected state official, often a secretary of state. This is commonly a general provision dealing with state records, but in many jurisdictions, court records have traditionally fallen within that responsibility, usually by default. In other jurisdictions, statutory provision is made for court records management, particularly relating to access and security-privacy questions. Beyond the obvious question of the separation of powers of the branches of government, this intermingling of supervisory authority often raises serious practical management problems.

Funding and Facilities

A second problem area central to facilities design and management is the question of the provision of resources. Effective record-keeping systems need not be expensive. However, there must be adequate funding for the essential storage and retrieval systems and for qualified personnel. Court systems in many jurisdictions are notoriously underfunded and poorly equipped, forcing court administrators to set priorities. Records management solutions, which are invariably low on the list of priorities, are often among the first to be shelved. This may happen even if the court administrator or manager chooses to appeal to his or her funding agency for adequate records management money. Records management lacks political appeal. It has no constituency, save an occasional frustrated searcher, and affects no group of voters directly. Even in the best of financial times, it often comes out on the short end of resource allocation. The net result is that many court records are relegated to second-rate equipment in inadequate storage space and are supervised by no one, or at best by untrained clerical staff.

Fiscal Controls

Very few judicial systems enjoy fiscal independence. Even those which may have formal or informal influence in the appropriation process are usually subject to the general accounting and fiscal controls of the jurisdiction from which they receive their funding. This is important to records management in that it often structures a significant percentage of the records maintained by court personnel. Fines and costs, filing fees, escrow accounts of various types, bonds, and the like are usually all subject to accounting by a governmental agency outside the judiciary and often by an agency whose overcommitted workforce audits a given agency at lengthy intervals. Not only does this type of control condition the way in which court records must be kept, but it often dictates the length of time for which many records must be held subject to ready examination.

Archival Commissions and Historical Societies

A fourth external factor affecting court records management involves archival commissions and historical societies. Many court administrators have the opportunity or obligation to relate to governmental and nongovernmental groups that have a general interest in the archival aspects of court records. These groups may be official state or county archival bodies with statutory responsibilities, or they may be groups of interested citizens. It is not suggested here that a comprehensive archival program should be included within a judicial records management system. Archival concerns are extraordinary and could overtax the limited records resources of most judicial systems. However, any adequate court records program must provide for the proper storage of archival materials. Liaison should be maintained with available archival groups. Statutory responsibilities which relate to court records should be accommodated. Archival groups often contain a pool of trained and interested people who can prove very helpful in the establishment of a complete records management program.

Internal Influences

Court Rules and Precedent Cases

In many jurisdictions, court rules define records management. These rules range from general mandates to administrative personnel for the responsibility of managing records to very specific provisions on a record-by-record basis concerning creation, access, retention, and disposition of records. Appellate cases usually deal less specifically with individual records but may well affect system design by establishing guidelines for access and retention of records, particularly in the criminal area. With the growth of security-privacy litigation, case law may be expected to play an ever increasing role in records considerations.

Judges

Judges may play a creative or destructive role in the design of court records systems. It should be understood that many of the records created by a court are the product, to some degree, of the judge. At one time or another, the judge handles many of the papers filed in a given case, even if the case itself never comes to issue. Some of the records are actually judge-created. Faced with such association, and at times authorship, and having neither the time nor often the inclination to analyze records systems, it is a small wonder that judges as a group suffer from "packratism." As a general rule, it is always easier to save everything than to throw anything away. If it weren't for the problem of index and retrieval, this would be an acceptable alternative, assuming that adequate and appropriate storage space is available. There are jurisdictions which have decided against purchasing high-maintenance-cost microform or optical-disk systems or making basic decisions regarding records dispositions because sufficient storage space is economically available. However, in most jurisdictions such space is not available, or what is available will be overtaxed so quickly that is not a realistic alternative.

The Aura of Legal Paper

Complicating the packrat syndrome is the aura that often surrounds what may generally be described as "legal paper." Any capable records manager is well aware that certain records are essential to what may be called the "legal integrity" of a matter before the court, and a sound records program must have the ability to preserve and reference this material. However, a certain amount of material attaches itself to the typical legal proceeding which has value for a very short time or is duplicated elsewhere and need not be preserved. The fact that this material has some connection with a legal proceeding does not hallow it. The most feasible solution is a records evaluation and destruction system. The impact of this on facilities design and management is obvious.

The establishment of a successful records system is dependent upon the understanding and cooperation of the judges within the system, and their concern for legal integrity must be satisfied. However, system design must not hesitate to question all aspects of the material in question. Managers who do not do this will find themselves either overrun with paper or forced to move to a relatively expensive alternative storage mode (e.g., microform, optical disk) long before it might otherwise be necessary.

Attorneys

The bar makes a variety of demands on a record system, most legitimate, but some open to question. The court must assume the responsibility for maintaining an accurate, official record that is readily available to the practicing attorney. However, the demands of attorneys sometimes structure records management systems beyond what might be considered a reasonable degree. Suffice it to say that attorneys often become concerned when a court attempts to attack records problems by standardizing paper sizes, charging for photocopies, requiring certain forms of filing, centralizing file access, converting paper documents to image, or refusing to allow file personnel to find cases with well-drawn filings of a certain type for attorneys with similar questions to file. A records system planner must be aware of the needs of the bar, but also of the needs of the system as it attempts to meet a variety of demands.

The Record Continuum and Application of Technology

The only way to successfully address a records problem is by viewing a records system as a continuum stretching from filing to destruction and systematically dealing with each stage. The system which allows haphazard forms design and disorganized filing systems at the beginning of the process will have to live with those problems months or years later in the retention stage. Without a total approach to the continuum, the application of technology and personnel will have only limited effectiveness. Any records continuum can be considered to have four stages: creation, active use, inactive storage, and retention-destruction. The facilities considerations vary for each stage, and a manager must evaluate the relationships between all stages before making records system decisions.

Courts have been slow to adapt existing technology for the management of records. This is partially due to inadequate resources and a lack of incentive, as their needs have not reached crisis proportions. Further, when they have adapted existing technology, some managers have chosen inappropriate applications. This often leads to disillusionment and withdrawal from the use of further technology.

The Creation Stage

In order to develop a comprehensive and effective records program, the manager must gain control of as much of the system input as possible. The creation of the records requiring management has a direct impact upon subsequent questions regarding volume, variety, and use. The manager should develop as much influence as possible in the areas of forms and design, as well as in the manner in which cases enter the system and generate records. The difficult aspect of this state is that most of these factors are beyond the court's control. This is particularly true if the court is unwilling to deal with attorneys on the court's own terms.

Forms Program

Despite the continuing advances in technology which permit electronic filing of cases and subsequent information, the vast majority of court systems continue to use paper forms as their basic record. Because this has major facility consequences, we must consider the factors which make up a forms program.

In order to develop an effective forms program, the records manager must have the authority to mandate design and enforce a comprehensive forms program. That authority is usually given by rule of court. The development of a design program is central to the establishment of effective forms management. Ideally, a central management program should standardize all court forms, including those filed by attorneys and litigants and those used within the court. Ideally, this should be done by in-house personnel operating under authority established by the court. However, there are several alternatives. In some jurisdictions, standard form designs are developed and included in a practice book for use by attorneys. In jurisdictions using legal printing houses to produce the forms sold to attorneys, the court maintains certain standard forms. In either situation, the key is a policy that only those forms which the court approves are admissible in a specific case. The techniques of forms design are not difficult to learn. A number of private vendors will provide training assistance to the staff. A number of government jurisdictions also offer training in forms design. The United States National Archives and Records Service offers an excellent course on a national basis. The options open to a forms designer in terms of materials have greatly increased in recent years. More printers now have the capability of producing multipart carbonless and snap-out carbon forms. This increased availability has decreased costs in relative terms for those kinds of forms.

Forms fall into three basic categories:

- *Flat Printed*—The simplest and least expensive form is the one-part flat-printed, one- or two-sided form. It is widely used in court systems where the need for multiple copies is minimal. This type of form can usually be produced in-house and meets a number of needs very well.
- *Multipart*—Although multipart forms come in a wide variety, they are usually either carbonless paper or interleaved carbon paper. They are most appropriate where a number of individuals require the same information at the initial completion of the form. They may be developed in a number of color combinations and paper stocks to serve varied purposes. The disadvantages to such forms are printing costs and a tendency to develop superfluous copies.
- *Miscellaneous Exotic*—There are a number of design techniques available for specific purposes. Many jurisdictions utilize turnaround forms, window envelopes, and so on for specific applications, particularly notice procedures. Other jurisdictions have adapted machine-printed forms for a variety of uses. The problem here is that a relatively expensive custom design may be substituted for an application which could be performed more simply.

Beyond a design program, it is important that a jurisdiction gain as much control as possible over forms printing and distribution. Two techniques have already been mentioned: working with legal printers or prescribing forms content. However, the preferred situation is one in which the court contracts for or prints in-house all forms, which are centrally stored and distributed. In most jurisdictions, this is not possible on a statewide basis. However, many courts could develop a local program for their county or municipality. Beyond the obvious advantages of uniformity and control, this system has economies of scale in terms of printing cost and storage. Buying printing services is a complex business. It is safe to say that any deviation from "the usual" costs money. Custom paper sizes, multicolor printing, unusual paper stock, and so forth all increase cost and production time. As in so many other services, the largest single factor in the procurement of printing is labor costs. Any aspect of form design which affects labor intensity in the production process has a direct influence upon the cost of the form.

The best approach is for the jurisdiction to work closely with the printer on forms development. If an administrator goes to competitive bid, there must be detailed form specifications.

All jurisdictions should evaluate the cost of "in-house" printing. This is particularly applicable if the bulk of court forms is relatively unsophisticated flat printing.

The final aspect of a successful forms program is control. It is impossible to successfully implement a comprehensive forms program if the administrator cannot ensure that courts within that jurisdiction will follow the program as designed. This calls for constant monitoring of the program by administrative personnel. There is nothing to be gained from the establishment of a sophisticated program if revised forms are not substituted for existing ones. The use of obsolete forms often creates problems for systems which rely on the revised forms for such related functions as statistics and scheduling functions. Someone must be charged with the responsibility of enforcing the forms program. This includes on-site visits to subsidiary offices to review the extent to which the forms program is being observed.

Facility Consequences

The "creation" phase of a records program has a multitude of facility consequences. A comprehensive design program will enable a manager to control factors which have a direct bearing on facility design. Control of forms proliferation reduces volume, affecting both stock storage (if the system buys and distributes centrally) and active records storage. Control of such variables as format (e.g., books versus cards), paper size, weight, colors, and number of copies affects equipment type and size and on related questions such as microform facility needs, long-term-storage facility capacities, and copy machine usage. Printing and distribution policies determine the extent of need for central and on-site storage facilities.

The Active-Use Stage

The active-use phase is when records must be most accessible and when the most frequent changes or additions occur. This stage extends from the time the first record is created in the manager's office to the time the case is disposed. It is during this time period that most of the litigatory and management functions take place with records. This may be the most difficult stage in some courts, particularly those with high-volume activities, but in other courts it may be the easiest stage, particularly in those courts with low volume but with ineffective long-term storage and management facilities.

Storage Modes

There are three basic media within which active records may be maintained: hard copy, photographic, and electronic.

Hard Copy. Hard copy, the preservation of original papers, is still the most commonly used storage mode for active use records. The reasons for this are twofold. Generally, this is the most economical method of active file maintenance. There is also frequent resistance to the other two modes (photographic and electronic) from judges, other court personnel, attorneys, and researchers. The advantages to this mode are obvious: it maintains the basic records in their original and most familiar form and utilizes readily available equipment for storage. Hard copy may be readily referenced without special equipment and can be reproduced on any standard copy machine. The disadvantages are that it is the most space-consuming of any of the three modes, as well as the most difficult to preserve in long-term storage.

Photographic. An alternative which is becoming more commonly used, even in the active use stage of records, is some form of photographic process. Several jurisdictions have developed systems under which active court records are maintained in a microform format. The state of the art is now such that earlier problems of indexing and reference have been largely eliminated. This has fostered the widespread use of such systems. The obvious advantage of microphotographic storage is the tremendous savings in storage space. There are two drawbacks to the maintenance of current records in this manner. The first, and most obvious, is expense. Although some economies are realized in space savings, the operation of a micrographic system is relatively expensive, particularly in the area of personnel costs. The maintenance of current records in a microform mode requires constant update. This update problem was eased somewhat by the introduction of "updatable fiche" systems. However, such systems are still relatively expensive to purchase and labor-intensive to maintain. The second problem is that many users of active records are not comfortable using photographic media. This either means that hard copy must be produced from the film for courtroom and other uses, or that a large number of microform readers must be provided and detailed orientation given to users.

The majority of well-designed records management systems use some form of microform technology. Regardless of the retention schedule, it is unlikely that any system will be able to either retain all material in the original hard-copy form or destroy all material after a specified time period. Therefore, an appropriate mix of filming and hard-copy retention is probably the most appropriate system for most records managers.

Obviously, there are two essential components of a successful and appropriate microform program: application of the proper technology and orientation and training of users. Technology systems are as follows:

- *Roll Film*—Roll film in either 16-millimeter or 35-millimeter is the most economical type of microform. However, it has limitations for court applications, as it may not be updated without cutting and splicing, which destroys the legal integrity of the record. It may be used most successfully for the filming of records which are completely disposed and to which additions or changes are not anticipated.

- *Microfiche*—The microfiche format is essentially a card format in which a series of microphotographic images are aligned in rows and reproduced on a film card. This has some court application in that all documents in a particular case can be photographed and arranged on one card or series of cards. Initially, microfiche could not be changed or updated without adding the document and producing an entirely new microfiche. Later developments made available an updatable microfiche with greater applicability to court use. As microfiche is more economical than microthin jackets, records managers should explore this alternative carefully.
- *Microthin Jackets*—For some time, microthin jackets were the only possibility for court records with any level of activity. The microthin jacket is a clear plastic envelope divided into sections. Each of those sections, or tracks, contains a certain number of microphotographic images. Images may be added to the jacket as the case progresses. Although this has the necessary high level of flexibility, it is also among the most expensive of the microform systems, particularly in the cost of personnel needed to maintain the jackets. Managers should weigh this system carefully against more recent microform developments when surveying technological alternatives.
- *Computer Out-Put Microfilm (COM)*—For specialized, high-volume applications, computer out-put microfilm (COM) may be useful. Records and reports which a court system normally receives in a hard-copy computer printout can be produced on COM. Most large computer operations have COM capacity. Courts may also procure COM from service bureaus. To be economically feasible, COM production, storage, and use cost should be equal to or less than the cost of the production of hard copy and the storage of that hard copy. When this economic parameter is met, records managers should explore receiving reports in a COM format.

Any records manager considering the use of microform systems should realize that there are related equipment costs and very specific space needs which accompany such system development. If records are to be maintained on a film format, the manager must provide adequate readers and reader-printers, appropriate storage equipment, and space for utilizing the technology. Such equipment is readily available and economical. The key is the selection of the appropriate equipment for the task involved. In addition to procuring the equipment, the manager must see that adequate and appropriate space is provided for proper utilization.

Beyond the selection of appropriate technology, the records manager seeking to utilize microforms must realize the problems in the development of such a system. The widespread application of microform technology requires some reorientation on the part of records users, notably clerical personnel and judges who are accustomed to working with hard-copy records. A change to a microform system requires that they must cope with the new technology. There are various ways a manager may orient court staff to this change. The following is a list of guidelines which should be considered by the court manager interested in installing microform technology:

- The change should not be introduced without extensive prior consultation with and explanation to personnel who are affected by it.
- Prior to actual system conversion, affected personnel should have complete training in terms of technical requirements. This includes users such as judges and attorneys, as well as system operators.
- Court managers may have to provide for the generation of hard copy from the film format for certain applications, notably for the use of judges on the bench.
- The new system must be at least as convenient as the system it replaces in terms of access, speed, and accuracy. These are the criteria by which users measure a system. Cost benefits may accrue to the administrator in terms of space saving; however, system users in general have little or no interest in those factors.

Optical Disk Systems. The third medium of records storage, computer-based optical-disk imaging systems, is increasingly with us. Although these systems remain relatively expensive both to purchase and maintain, they are becoming more cost-effective. They do offer impressively high levels of data compaction and, when properly designed, notably in the indexing area, effective recall capabilities. Their utility and cost-effectiveness, if installed solely as a records storage technology in lieu of the retention of hard copy or film-based technologies, is not yet proven. However, if courts are utilizing such systems for broader purposes earlier in their records creation process, they will benefit from considerably reduced requirements for storage space as records in this medium replace older, hard-copy material.

Indexing Systems

Indexing systems are essential to effective records management. All indexes are either alpha or numeric, although there are a number of variations within those categories. Most alpha systems are straightforward letter systems, varying only in the detail of breakdown within the alphabet. However, there are some exotic systems with alpha basis, notably such systems as the "Russell Soundex" system, which assigns numeric values to certain letters, ignores certain letters, and thus enables the user to find any name which sounds the same regardless of how it is spelled (e.g., Smith, Smythe). Numeric systems have more variations. One commonly finds prefixes to numbers designating year of filing, case type, and so on. Some systems also employ terminal digit filing, notably in situations where large volumes of records are being kept in one location and a high rate of reference to a given year would create problems if all cases of that year were filed together. Terminal digit filing automatically combines cases of several years in one file. This has the obvious disadvantage of distributing cases from the same year to a number of locations. However, it offers certain advantages of spreading active files throughout a storage area and avoiding "backshifting" of records when some years are transferred to other storage from that area. From a records management perspective, the indexes are among the most permanent records created and should be designed for operation over a long period of time.

Filing Systems

Filing systems are structured to correspond with indexes. The medium to be used to hold the case material is the primary consideration for hard-copy systems, and this will invariably be some type of jacket.

Jacketing styles have changed greatly over the years. In most courts, the earliest form was a three-or four-way fold of the case documents. These were usually placed in some form of jacket or "wrapper," numbered on the exterior, and stored upright in specially designed "document folder" drawers. This system is still used in some jurisdictions and still has limited appropriate applications. This is particularly true in courts which handle a high volume of cases, each containing very few documents. It lends itself well to courts where cases are disposed rapidly, thus eliminating extensive handling or posting of extensive information on each case. (Traffic courts are probably the best example.)

The most common storage medium today for records is the "flat file." This is a generic term which applies to a wide variety of file folders. Flat-folder systems may vary in size, folder design, and materials. The most common is probably the 9-by-11¾-inch folder or envelope, but there is tremendous variety even within that design.

Of the photographic filing systems, the most common for active use is the microthin jacket. This is essentially a card divided into a number of compartments, each of which holds a microphotographic image. Each image constitutes one document in the case. Some systems also employ roll film. This is appropriate for long-term inactive-records storage, but not in an active mode, as it is extremely difficult to update, and loses its legal integrity once cut and spliced.

Computer-based system storage media are electronic, usually with magnetic tape or compact disk.

There are many techniques to increase the ease of reference within filing systems. One of the most popular in courts is color coding. There are a number of other techniques: notches, hole punching, and so on, which exist in file systems technology but which are less appropriate for court use. Color coding has been improved recently by a number of equipment manufacturers. The basic principle is that by grouping certain records within a particular color or combination of colors, the likelihood of misfiling is greatly lessened. For high-volume applications, some manufacturers have developed rather elaborate systems for categorizing files within a color combination.

In low-volume situations, the same result may be achieved at lower cost by using adhesive color dots attached to a case jacket to designate year, case type, particular judge, and so on, or by the use of colored file folders.

There are other variations within filing systems which may be applicable to certain courts. Chronological files and other time- or date-based variations in which all cases filed on a certain date are placed in a common file, sometimes work in specific situations or for specific management applications. However, they are seldom satisfactory for a general filing system.

Filing Equipment. Filing equipment is either manual, mechanical, or in a very few cases, electronic. Variations within each of these categories are extensive. The majority of hard-copy records material is kept in either a manual or a mechanical file. Manual files come in a variety of sizes, configurations, and materials. Virtually all manual files are some type of filing cabinet that has been adapted to a particular use.

Drawer Filing Cabinets. These come in a variety of heights and drawer sizes but are most commonly either "letter" or "legal" in size. A number of variations exist, such as trays and tub files, but these are actually drawers on wheels. Drawer filing cabinets are still widely used, and probably remain the most common method.

Lateral Filing. These are simply file drawers turned sideways. They come in varying configurations and are particularly useful in office spaces which have a reasonable amount of wall space but which are restricted in the distance that file drawers can be opened. They also come most commonly in "legal" and "letter" size but are available in custom-made configurations.

Shelf Filing. Shelf filing is very much in evidence today. It usually offers the highest ratio of records per square foot of floor space of any of the manual or mechanical files. It consists of shelving, usually with dividers, on which flat files are placed horizontally. There are many variations of design in these units. They are usually modular and come in varying heights. In active records areas, care should be taken to limit shelf height, since use of the upper shelves declines markedly if file managers have difficulty retrieving records. Vendors also place shelf units on tracks so that they may be moved within a room. Although this movement sometimes restricts access to a particular shelving unit, it has the great advantage of allowing a higher file density in a given floor area. These tracked units are particularly appropriate for semi-active or inactive storage.

Mechanical Files. Mechanical files are commonly misunderstood and their effectiveness often highly overrated. They are often mislabeled as "automated files," which they are not. Essentially, mechanical files are conventional file drawers or trays placed on a power-driven belt within a cabinet. They may be designed so that the drawers revolve vertically or horizontally, dependent on the needs of the space and material to be stored.

Records may be arranged within the file in any usual indexing system (alpha, numeric, etc.). Mechanical files are usually referenced by an operator at a keyboard who rotates the belt to the proper drawer. The operator then removes the record from or replaces the record in the drawer.

Mechanical files have application in specific situations. They are often efficient in facilities with limited floor space and high ceilings (the case in many older court facilities), since they allow greater file density than conventional files. However, mechanical files are more expensive than the same capacity in nonmechanical drawers, have restricted access in that only one drawer may be referenced by an operator at one time, and may not always provide the most capacity for the available floor space. They also require regular maintenance to avoid breakdown and can create floor load problems in some buildings. Mechanical files can represent a technological advance but should be evaluated closely in the context of the specific application for which they are intended.

Electronic Media Files. Equipment for the storage of electronically maintained records is specialized such as tape and disk cabinets, computer printout folders, binders and racks, and so on. A large portion of electronic storage equipment would normally be located off-site, or at least in a data-processing center where it does not directly affect court facilities. However, a clerk's office dealing with electronically maintained records would assume a need for shelving for bound computer printouts, film cabinets, reference stations for computer files, and electronic disk storage.

Physical Security and Data Security

One of the prime facility considerations for records management is the type and degree of security that a records manager requires. Courts are responsible for maintaining records that have a high level of public significance. In contrast to a private firm maintaining records which are relevant to its own internal uses, the court system maintains records that authenticate basic facts in a society, such as title to land, births, deaths, marriages, adoptions, criminal records, and so on. This raises unique records problems in that at the same time that courts must maintain records with a high degree of significance and long-term use, requiring a high level of security, the nature of those records demands a high degree of public access.

Physical Security. Court records should be kept as physically secure as possible from such threats as fire, flood, and theft. This can be accomplished in part by physical equipment specifications and space design. The procedures established by the court and the records manager also affect physical security. All storage equipment comes with a "fire rating." The fire rating of storage equipment is usually directly related to the cost of the equipment. The manager concerned with protection against fire must weigh such factors as the type of records to be stored and their location against the cost of storage equipment.

Security against theft is a function of equipment and facility design. The records manager must weigh the potential for theft against the cost of developing a theftproof system. The potential for theft is greatly reduced in a system in which records are kept in secure cabinets in restricted access space. However, such a design greatly increases the need for employee involvement in records retrieval for litigants, attorneys, and so forth. The records manager attempting a theftproof system will be faced with high costs in both development and maintenance.

Data Security. A more abstract consideration in terms of security is the security of information. Data security is a function of system and facility design. The threat to many court records today is not solely the physical destruction of these records. An equal threat is the dissemination of information to unauthorized people. Such dissemination can occur either because file systems are poorly designed and unauthorized persons have access to them or because employees make available unauthorized information. Such security problems are not restricted to the criminal area, although they are more common there. Credit bureaus, banks, and other financial institutions have an interest in much of the information which is found in civil files on individual law suits. "Freedom of information" legislation in a number of jurisdictions and "security-privacy" statutes have compounded this problem. For example, a file of criminal cases left in a public place to serve as an index may well legally constitute a "cumulative criminal history" and thus should be restricted.

The records manager must make similar but more difficult choices to those made regarding physical security. The manager can design the physical facility and the file structure so that public access is greatly limited. This will lead to an "employee intensive" system and to space configuration that may require more expensive design and construction, such as restricted access areas and vault construction. The key difference is attempting to establish security over a commodity which may be taken from the building mentally by an employee—information.

The impact of computer technology on records security is the proverbial "two-edged sword." Records kept in a well-designed computer system (or other computer-driven files such as optical-disk systems) have the obvious advantage of accessibility only by individuals with the requisite operating capabilities and authorizations. The threat of the unsophisticated or casual intruder is thus greatly reduced. However, once access is gained to such a system, large quantities of data are often readily and rapidly accessible. In addition, the ability to extract large amounts of data by transfer to small and easily concealable media such as disks makes the theft of such records relatively easy for the sophisticated thief.

The Inactive-Storage Stage

This is a stage which occurs in every court system but which goes unrecognized in many. This stage may be characterized as the time period between case disposition and the making of a final decision regarding destruction or long-term permanent retention. Very few records management systems consciously address this phase. In many systems inactive storage is simply left interfiled with pending cases. In others, it may be separated on the basis of having been disposed but receives no particular management beyond being left in storage.

One of the records management decisions which has the most impact on facilities utilization is the method adopted for the storage of these inactive records. Ideally, records which are considered to be inactive should be removed from files which occupy prime space in any court office. However, a practical problem arises when making this determination: the definition of "inactive" varies widely from court to court. In some jurisdictions, "inactive" applies only to those cases which have been disposed. In others, it applies to cases which have had no activity within a specified period of time. The court must decide what will be placed in the inactive category and then adopt filing techniques to handle that material.

Some courts leave inactive material interfiled with active cases. This simplifies reference and creates fewer problems for long-term storage file integrity, as all cases in a given category remain in the same location with number sequences, and so on, undisturbed. This may be acceptable in facilities that have adequate space for this practice. However, some jurisdictions may be so short of storage facilities in the immediate clerk's office that they must remove inactive cases to remote storage. If this is done, care must be taken that indexing and filing systems identical to those used in active storage are maintained and that all material in the particular category is eventually interfiled. Only in this manner can consistency of file reference be assured.

In deciding to remove material to remote storage, the degree of the storage location's remoteness should also be considered. A remote storage area physically adjacent to the main clerk's office may hold material with a higher reference rate. Conversely, remote storage in an adjacent building or in another part of the city should only hold material with a very low reference rate.

Security considerations are just as important, if slightly different, for inactive material as for active. Protection from physical threats, such as fire, flooding, insects, rodents, and so on, is probably more important at remote sites, as they are less subject to human supervision than active-storage areas. Questions of information security are probably less relevant in that this material is less current than active records and may simply be of less interest to potential violators. If full-time supervision is not possible, inactive-storage areas should be inspected regularly to ensure that they are being properly maintained.

The Retention-Destruction Stage

Court managers are usually the least effective in the establishment of retention-destruction programs. They have often neglected this area because they have not been forced to make decisions, and they find it the most difficult area in which to get agreement on policy. However, it is probably the area that has the most overall impact on court facilities, particularly in high-volume courts.

A comprehensive retention-destruction schedule is the most overlooked aspect of court management programs. Even if a court has access to a high level of technology, it must utilize that technology within the framework of an established and enforced retention-destruction schedule.

The design of such a schedule is delineated in detail under "The Records Study" later in this chapter. However, there are certain fundamentals that must underlie any such program. The first is the authority to develop and enforce. This authority can normally be granted by the court in question, and is most logically done by rule of court. The retention-destruction schedule should be clearly delineated, and all employees involved in court records should be familiar with it. As retention-destruction schedules must be designed specifically for the jurisdiction in question, they must realistically reflect the legal and management requirements of that court and must assist the court in dealing with its records problems. Enforcement includes regular inspections of the storage locations that should adhere to the schedule. They must also establish a clear system for recording whatever disposition has taken place, whether it be filming-destruction or simple destruction.

There are three basic alternatives in the design of a retention-destruction schedule: complete retention, total filming, and filming-destruction.

Complete Retention

Some systems, either by choice or through inaction, choose to retain all records in their original form. Unless this is a conscious decision based on a unique set of circumstances (such as unlimited cheap storage space) this is generally an unsatisfactory plan. Even if large amounts of storage space are available, problems will eventually develop. Index systems become unwieldy. Material begins to physically deteriorate. Costs increase in terms of personnel to manage such retention, even if the space itself does not require direct payment. There is no such thing as "free" space. Unless the area has no other use, the jurisdiction which fills such space with essentially useless records is paying a cost for that space. A system which retains all records indefinitely may find itself restricting appropriate use of records by parties with a legitimate interest such as archivists, genealogists, and researchers simply because the inventory has become too unwieldy.

Total Filming

The second alternative is the filming of all records which are to be placed in long-term storage. This would be the most satisfactory method if conservation of long-term storage facility space is the only factor under consideration. However, there are several very obvious problems with this approach. The first and most obvious is expense. The major cost in a microform program is personnel. The system that plans to maintain all records is committing itself to a high initial filming cost and a correspondingly high maintenance cost. The second problem is that reference within a system which films everything can become very difficult. Although indexing in microform systems has become much more effective in recent years, there are still problems in finding individual records within a large collection of material. The system which films everything may be defeating one of the prime purposes of records management: ready and convenient reference.

Filming-Destruction

Probably the most satisfactory system is that which develops a mix of filming and retention of hard copy. There is no such thing as a "standard mix," and each system must develop its own. Factors affecting information to be filmed include the type of material a court is handling, the period of retention which is placed on specific types of material, and the type and amount of long-term storage space available. Many jurisdictions choose to film the material that must be retained permanently and to leave in hard copy that material which has a definite life and can be physically destroyed at the end of that life. This works well if the hard copy of the permanent material is destroyed after filming and if there is adequate storage space available to efficiently retain the limited-life material prior to destruction. Systems that cannot meet one or both of these criteria sometimes opt for filming the limited-life material (which in a well-designed schedule always represents the great majority of the physical paper) and retaining the permanent material in original form unless it starts to physically deteriorate. The film of the limited-life material is then destroyed when the time period has run out.

Filming of any material is ineffective if the filmed material is not then destroyed. To film material and then retain the hard copy benefits neither the records system nor facility design.

The type of retention-filming mix that is adopted has great impact on facility planning. A court system involved in high-volume filming needs space designed to contain adequate film-processing and storage facilities. A system doing high-volume filming will almost always find it cost-effective to do its own processing. The records retention area design should reflect the configuration of the retention-filming mix in terms of total space, equipment selection, and staffing. Conversely, the system that chooses a mix including a high level of hard-copy retention, even for limited time periods, must design its space to accommodate both hard copy and microfilm.

Storage Areas

Regardless of the storage mix chosen, a court must designate an appropriate storage area. Such an area generally falls into one of three categories.

If a court is the sole occupant of a records storage area, the optimum design may be implemented. However, this kind of space is not usually available. A second alternative is to share storage space with other governmental agencies. This may not be particularly desirable, however, as access by several agencies to the same storage space often destroys most of the security considerations mentioned earlier, unless the space can be so subdivided as to retain some internal court integrity. A third alternative is to rent commercial space. Many warehousing companies provide records storage facilities at an annual cost per square foot. This is a realistic alternative assuming that the cost is reasonable, the space can be properly secured, and the records to be placed in that facility are properly selected to avoid the need for constant reference.

There are also increasing numbers of private commercial records storage and management companies. If well run, they can be an effective option. However, they tend to be expensive, and all changes must be carefully analyzed to see if they are cost-effective.

Destruction

Careful supervision is required if a system adopts schedules that include destruction. There must be clear destruction guidelines as to time schedules, method of destruction, and certification of that destruction. Most destruction schedules operate on an annual basis under which the material that has become eligible for destruction that year is disposed of at a designated time. Destruction should be effective (normally by shredding or burning) and should be carried out under the supervision of appropriate authorities. A certificate of destruction should be completed for each category of records so destroyed. Those certificates should be kept on file on a permanent basis so that the manager will know what documents have been destroyed, when they were destroyed, and by whom.

Court systems should not overlook the possibility of the scrap value of records. Paper which has been shredded can be chemically treated and bailed for resale. Since much court paper is of high quality, this can be a surprisingly lucrative practice. That money can often be returned to the records management program for the purchase of equipment and other related expenditures.

Impact of Records Management on Space Management

Printing and Storage of Forms

Printing of court forms represents a major court expenditure item. The decision on whether to print forms in-house or to contract with commercial firms requires careful evaluation. In general, small court jurisdictions do not require, and cannot afford, setting up their own printshops to do offset printing of court forms, and it would be less costly to use commercial firms to print the small amount of forms that are needed. However, in larger jurisdictions with high-volume printing requirements, or in states with unified court systems, centralization of printing activities within a single printshop operated by court printers could result in major cost savings in form printing and distribution. With the need for high-volume form printing for all courts throughout a state, county, or even in a major metropolitan center, a central printshop equipped with up-to-date offset and high-speed duplication equipment, operated and maintained by experienced printers, would provide the entire court system with high-quality standardized forms at considerably lower cost than contracting with commercial printing companies.

Offset printing and duplication equipment for medium- and high-volume copying, with collators, are commonly used. In addition to printing and duplication equipment, consideration should be given to providing adequate work surfaces for report- and book-binding equipment, preparation and collation, and clerical work. An ample supplies storage area is essential to all printshops. The supplies storage area should be adjacent to the printshop and readily accessible either to the loading dock of the building or to the freight elevators if the printshop is located on an upper floor. Printshops in large court jurisdictions usually handle high-volume form and other printing requirements. Paper and printing supplies are delivered in bulk and must be stored either within the printshop area or, preferably, in a storage room adjacent to the printing area. Open and adjustable metal shelving along walls and at the center of the storage area has been found to be the most appropriate method of printing supplies storage. Adequate facilities should also be provided for the storage of printed standardized forms to be distributed on a regular basis to other court locations.

Because of their functional relationship, the printshop and the mail room can either be parts of a large open space or separate spaces adjacent to each other. In a state court system, because forms and other printed matters are regularly distributed by mail or parcel delivery to outlying court locations, it is desirable for mail and postage equipment to be located near the printshop. Packaging, wrapping, and taping of bulk forms for mailing and distribution require extensive work surfaces both at desk height (29 inches) and at counter height (42 inches approximately).

The close proximity of the printshop and mail room to the freight elevator in a multistory court building would also expedite the delivery of forms and other printed matters to the various court and court-related departments housed within the building. To be located closely to the loading dock, the printshop, mail room, and related storage facilities would have to be on the ground floor or basement level. In view of the weight of printing equipment and of heavy paper and supplies storage, a ground or basement location for these facilities is desirable.

With the printshop and ample supplies storage areas located within the court building, the clerk's office would not require oversized forms-storage rooms within its work area. On the other hand, a busy outlying court location would require adequate forms-storage space. There are several types of storage facilities for printed court forms depending on the size of the clerk's public counter, which, of necessity, must be easily accessible to counter clerks while transacting court business with attorneys, litigants, and the general public. In most clerks' offices, forms are stored in shelves or drawers under the counter surfaces, within easy reach of counter clerks. Depending on the size of the clerk's office and the volume of forms to be stored, if the public counter is not able to accommodate all the different forms, a separate forms-storage cabinet can be located behind the counter clerks. This cabinet can also serve as the visual divide between the counter clerks and the other clerks working in the general clerical work space.

In jurisdictions where clerks assist the public in completing certain forms (for example, small-claims forms and so on), a forms cabinet can be designed as an integral part of each counter clerk's workstation.

Beyond the storage of frequently used forms at or near the public counter, the clerk's office without a printshop in the same building should have an area designed specifically for the storage of forms. If a storage room is provided, forms storage can be combined with general supplies storage. This room should be located near both the private work area of the public counter and the general clerical work area behind the counter area. In clerks' offices, the volume of forms required on a regular basis can be stored either in storage cabinets or in specially designed forms cabinets with shallow sliding shelves. The cabinets should be conveniently located in relation to the clerks.

Active and Semiactive Case Records Storage

Frequently referenced active records should be located near court and counter clerks who are continuously involved in the processing of case documents, in pulling case records for court hearings or trials, or in providing information to attorneys, litigants, and the public. Since active records are used by both counter clerks handling inquiries at the public counter, and other clerks working in private clerical work areas, the most suitable location for active records would be between the two areas. In fact, records storage cabinets or shelving units can be used as a visual separation between the two functional areas. The volume of active records would determine the storage system to be recommended. Flat lateral filing with closing covers, with or without locks in accordance with security requirements, provides the most efficient and economical system of storing easily retrievable court case files. An appropriate color coding and case number identification system would minimize misplacement of files as a result of careless filing. In most courts, no more than two years of case files need to be stored at this location.

In a major court location with high-volume case files, semiactive files that are not frequently referenced—say, those that are three to five years old—should be located in the court building if appropriate space is available.

However, records should not be stored in spaces that are suitable for and needed by personnel use. This rule is invariably broken when records storage is indiscriminately assigned space that is urgently needed for personnel expansion. Prime office space suitable for full-time personnel use is frequently occupied by file and storage cabinets that are frequently underutilized. Spaces that are suitable for urgently needed courtrooms and ancillary facilities are used instead for storage of active and sometimes inactive files, which can be stored elsewhere. For example, internal rooms within building service cores, mezzanine levels without windows, and basement storage space are often suitable records storage spaces within the court building.

Since it is recommended that public-oriented, high-volume clerks' offices be located on or adjacent to the main public entrance levels of the building in order to minimize elevator traffic to the upper floors, it is logical that active records storage space be provided on the same floors as the clerk's office. If the clerk's office were to be located on the ground floor, available space on that floor is usually so valuable that records storage space should be minimized. All records, other than the most frequently referenced ones, should be located in basement storage areas. Direct access from clerical space on the main entrance floor to the records storage space in the basement can be provided by means of either an internal private staircase or an elevator or booklift. The last mentioned is preferred, since there could be regular transfers of heavy case files, in addition to other documents and supplies. If the clerk's office could be located adjacent to the freight elevator, and the basement records storage space is also near such an elevator, the need for a costly internal elevator or booklift would no longer exist. The use of freight elevators for records transfer between basement storage and clerk's office on an upper floor requires a secured system of checking and monitoring records. While it is somewhat more costly to provide a separate booklift near the public counter area, such additional cost may be justified on the basis of increased records security and integrity. If a booklift is installed, care should be taken in its design to ensure that it is large enough to house at least two file carts as well as the person responsible for their transfer to and return from clerical work areas on the upper floor.

Records storage areas in basements are frequently assigned in a vague manner within large building storage spaces. In view of the fact that building storage, which may include combustible and flammable materials, is entirely different from case records, it is recommended that records storage space be completely separated from general building storage areas. Fire-extinguishing systems and equipment for the two spaces are also different; the system installed within the records storage area should not result in the destruction of court records by water damage from sprinklers.

Within certain jurisdictions, active case records may be housed within each courtroom unit during their pendency and active processing. In Houston, Texas, the court clerk for each civil district court is responsible for all active files of cases assigned to that court. The case files are stored in filing cabinets either in the courtroom or in a vestibule directly behind the judicial area of the courtroom. Since the court clerk's station is in the courtroom, the location of case file cabinets along the side walls within the courtroom, while convenient to the court clerk, is unsightly. Lack of storage space outside most courtrooms has resulted in such records storage within courtrooms. It would be desirable to provide a separate private office for the court clerk directly behind or adjacent to the judicial area of the courtroom so that all file cabinets and storage shelving units within the office can be locked after regular court hours. It is also recommended that the court reporter for each court be provided with private office space so that the stenotapes, recordings, and transcripts of active cases can also be locked up in suitably designed storage cabinets outside regular court hours.

With the increased use of microfilm, microfiche, microthin jackets, electronic data processing, and computer output microfilm systems, different space requirements must be satisfied. In many jurisdictions, the microfilming of court records simply produces a backup copy of the original case file documents, without any plan to destroy or relocate the original case files. This would increase, instead of decrease, records storage space needed within the clerk's office. Microfilming of records should be tied to a carefully established records retention-destruction plan, so that records could be destroyed upon microfilming in order to free the space for more productive personnel and court uses. Certain records need to be stored over a period of years after microfilming. Such records should be housed in warehousing space either in the basement of the court building, if such space is available, or in warehousing space outside the court building. Microfilming of certain currently active records would normally duplicate the original records without the capability of destroying these records for a period of time. Microfilming of disposed case records that can be destroyed would result in reclaiming new space for more productive uses.

In addition to the storage of microforms, which require only a minute fraction of the space needed for storage of hard-copy files, a substantial amount of space is needed for the viewing and examination of records, as well as for translating microfilm records into hard copies for certification. Microfilm readers, reader-printers, and CRT terminals tied to computerized information systems require tabletop work surfaces for public use. Instead of a simple work surface for the examination of the original case file, microfilmed cases are examined on readers or reader-printers, and a hard copy of any instrument in the case file can be produced by the reader-printer. In addition to this tabletop equipment, general work surface is also needed by users, resulting in the need for larger records examination areas adjacent to the public counter and supervised by the counter clerks. These records examination areas should be glazed to facilitate visual supervision, and should be near the storage areas for original case files as well as to microfilm storage facilities. Examining microformed case files and the use of CRT terminals for information retrieval requires a high contrast and low-light-intensity environment, as compared with high-light intensity needed to examine original case files on regular work surfaces.

Filming of current active case files, as instruments are filed, can result in substantial savings in records storage, providing case files can be located and stored in warehousing space outside the court building. Microfiche and updatable microthin jackets, while requiring high initial investment and being applicable only in high-volume clerks' offices, require a comparatively small space for their storage. The cost of constructing or leasing additional records storage space should be compared with the high initial cost of filming active and inactive court records. Such an evaluation should be made prior to arriving at a decision on the optimum method of records and information storage and retrieval.

Inactive-Records Storage

All inactive records stored in office space should be removed from the courthouse and stored in warehouse space. Except in rural courthouses, in which the number of noncourt personnel can easily be housed in these buildings, most courthouses and metropolitan justice complexes invariably experience overcrowded conditions soon after those buildings are occupied. Most noncourt departments have long outgrown their space in the courthouse and have moved to new administration buildings or are leasing commercial space in office buildings within the downtown area. While these agencies continue to pay high rent for commercial space, inactive records continue to occupy prime office space that could be used much more productively. This misuse of court space has resulted in the location of essential courtrooms and ancillary facilities in leased commercial space. In many major court buildings throughout the country, as much as 30 percent of net usable space is currently used to store court records. This is due mainly to the lack of court-approved records retention-destruction schedules, and to the clerk's insistence that all records are permanent and, therefore, must be stored near the office for convenient access and retrieval.

The relocation of inactive records from the court building may free space that is neither suitable to nor needed by the court system. Such space may be utilized by government departments presently leasing space in commercial buildings, thus reducing the amount of public funds expended on commercial leases. Even if inactive court records were to be relocated in leased warehousing space, there would be a cost saving, since the unit rental of warehousing space is considerably lower than that of prime office space.

In the design of a major court building where the construction of one or more basement levels does not present soil or foundation problems, and where the site is suitable for basement construction without major expenditure, it would be desirable to provide secured storage space for inactive court records in basement spaces that are not suitable for personnel and other court uses.

The design of a court records center for long-term records storage will be discussed in a later section of this chapter.

The Records Study

The jurisdiction involved in establishing a comprehensive records program must have access to a thorough and comprehensive records study before any specific design plans can be made. This is the only way a court can establish the parameters of the problem it faces and make valid judgments regarding the system to be developed. Records studies are neither complex nor difficult to carry out. However, they do require a concentrated effort on the part of personnel selected for that effort.

The court manager has three options to carry out that study.

1. *The study can be done "in-house"*—This may be a feasible alternative if there is someone available with expertise in this area or someone in whom the expertise can be developed. It is certainly the most economical route, at least in the short run. The pitfalls are obvious—if some appropriate person has been available all along, careful consideration should be given to the reason why nothing has happened before. Also, a completely "in-house" staff may not be able to see records problems from a fresh viewpoint and/or make its influence felt.
2. *A consultant can be hired*—If a court chooses to hire an outside firm or individual to do the entire job, two cautions should be observed. Be sure the consultant selected is responsible for system installation as well as recommendations. Be sure also to assign a court official who is in a significant position of responsibility, and who will have some continuing responsibility in records management, to work with the consultant. Good consultants welcome this interaction. Consultants have the obvious drawback of higher expense.

3. *A manufacturer's representative can become involved in the study*—
A satisfactory arrangement with one of the larger and more knowledgeable filing equipment manufacturers is a definite possibility. Most of these firms have sales representatives who are systems analysts in the area of records management. They are usually eager to work with the court on a survey of its records problems and make recommendations. This approach has the advantage of bringing in a skilled outsider, tempered by involvement with the court's in-house staff without the direct cost of paying a consultant. One disadvantage is that such firms would be interested in promoting the sale of their company's equipment.

The preferred method is the development of in-house expertise from the initiation of the program. This ensures that the system will, early in its conception, develop a program which relates directly to its needs. An added benefit is that designated court staff will become familiar with the system. Any records study must consider the following questions:

• *Inclusiveness*—Does the study deal with all factors that affect records flow? Does it deal with these factors from the time they enter the system until they exit? Is it applied equally throughout the court?

• *Information System*—How does the proposed records program relate to the information system? Does it facilitate information flow to the appropriate personnel? Does it tie in with the reporting and statistical analysis functions?

• *Indexing and Control*—Are records properly indexed so that they may be referenced by court personnel from the point of view of their own needs? Does indexing include items such as exhibits, depositions, and so on? Can a layman retrieve basic information from the system?

• *Equipment*—Is equipment appropriate for the task assigned to it, or is the court utilizing obsolete equipment? Does a change in the format require new equipment? Equipment costs account for approximately 15 percent of total records management costs, including the initial cost of equipment, the space it occupies, and the supplies to maintain it. The initial cost of new equipment is more than offset by the savings accrued to increased records management personnel efficiency.

• *Paper Proliferation*—Does the program control the volume of information entering the system? Is forms management a continuing part of a court's program? Does the records management program eliminate obsolete forms and revise current ones? Does it control copy machine use and electronic-data-processing (EDP) printout material? Does the records program prevent duplication of information available in official office files for personal files?

• *Records Manual-Retention Schedule*—Does the program include a records manual that outlines the system and establishes clear guidelines for all personnel? Is there a clearly delineated retention-destruction schedule covering all record material, and is it enforced? Is the schedule based on statutory authority or court rule?

- *Costs*—Does a court know the true cost of its records management program? Have space, equipment, personnel, and operating expenses for the program been computed?

Study Products

A useful records study should produce two specific products: a records inventory and a retention-destruction schedule.

Records Inventory

Early in the records study, the manager should develop a comprehensive inventory of the records held under the existing system. The inventory should determine the type, quantity, age, location, and condition of the records and the equipment in which they are stored. This inventory must be complete and account for each type of record held by the clerk. Once established, it must be continually updated by records personnel so that they are aware of changes in the records being maintained by the clerk.

This inventory should be reviewed by records personnel and court managers to ensure its accuracy and completeness. Agreement on the inventory should be reached before the study moves to the development of a retention-destruction schedule.

Retention-Destruction Schedule

Once the inventory is complete, a detailed retention-destruction schedule should be established. The schedule must be responsive to the legal and management requirements of the court records system. Important considerations are that the schedule deal with all types of records identified during the inventory, that the schedule be officially adopted by the jurisdiction, and that it be widely distributed to all personnel involved with records management.

The preferred method for establishing such a schedule is by administrative order and/or rule of court. The rule or order technique has three distinct advantages: the judges are aware of the program; the program is based upon specific authority; and, in many jurisdictions, it can be used to avoid or nullify conflicting statutes and practices which may be causing records management problems. Such a rule or order may be very specific and may include the schedule in complete detail. In other jurisdictions, it may be more appropriate to draw a broad order leaving the establishment of the detailed schedule to the records center.

Facility Ramifications

Both the inventory and the schedule have very significant consequences for facility design. The type, quantity, and condition of records and the location and equipment in which they are stored establish present needs as well as space and equipment requirements for long-range planning.

Once the retention-destruction schedule is established, facility design and capacity are a function of the time period of records retention, the type of records involved, and the condition of the records. An effective records program cannot be developed without this input in the early stages.

The Integrated Records Center

The vehicle which best utilizes court facility capacity is the integrated court records center. To provide a coordinated records program, any jurisdiction, regardless of size, should adopt a structure which oversees records management from creation through retention-destruction. That structure should be vested with all necessary authority to develop and enforce the records program. Few states can install such a program on a statewide basis. Problems of size and divided legal jurisdiction usually preclude such development. However, the concept can be adapted to any logical jurisdiction unit, such as an individual court, county, or municipality.

The integrated records center has four main components:

- An approved program, including a retention-destruction schedule
- Appropriate storage space
- Appropriate equipment
- Appropriate personnel

Program

The establishment of a program, including a retention-destruction schedule, has already been discussed. Its relevance here is that the results of the study should be implemented by records center personnel, and the study should be subject to continual review and updating.

Storage Space

The second component is the procurement of adequate and appropriate space for the operation of a records center. Space that is inappropriate for any other purpose may well be appropriate for records storage. Windowless internal space is often suitable for records storage while being substandard for virtually any other office use.

Space utilized as a records center must have suitable environmental conditions, relatively undivided area, adequate lighting, and a high level of security. Beyond these requirements, there are virtually no criteria that cannot be met with imaginative use of design and equipment. For example, one old midwestern courthouse, constructed with relatively low floor-load capacity, appeared to have no adequate space for the development of a records center. However, upon examination, it was found that there was a large amount of space available in the basement corridors of the building. The installation of relatively low-cost partitioning, upgrading of lighting, and shielding of certain heat and water pipes provided a useful storage area at very low cost.

Storage Equipment

Storage equipment has already been discussed. Detailed specifications are also included in a subsequent section on the designing of the court records center. In general, equipment used in records centers is less expensive and simpler than that used in general clerks' offices.

Records Management Personnel

The success or failure of a centralized records management program is affected more by the quality of personnel than by any other single factor. Approximately 85 percent of each dollar spent on records management is for personnel. The recruitment and training of records personnel must be given high priority if the program is to be successful. In most systems, records management personnel are generally among the lowest paid and least trained of all court employees. Consequently, personnel handling records have a high turnover rate through promotion to other positions within the court or by seeking other employment. If a judicial records program is to be successful, it must make the commitment to hire and maintain personnel at higher-than-average salary levels and to provide adequate training in records management. A typical staffing chart illustrating positions necessary for a typical records center is shown as figure 4.1.

There are two personnel functions necessary in any integrated records center development: supervision and technical services. The importance of supervision cannot be overemphasized. A resourceful individual given proper responsibility and authority can produce a meaningful records management program. The best-conceived and -designed program will falter without proper leadership. The records center supervisor must be properly trained, compensated, and clearly charged with overall responsibility for the entire integrated records program. It must be a full-time, professional position with clearly defined authority corresponding to the responsibility.

There are a variety of technical services necessary for the program. These will vary according to the scope of the program but will include some or all

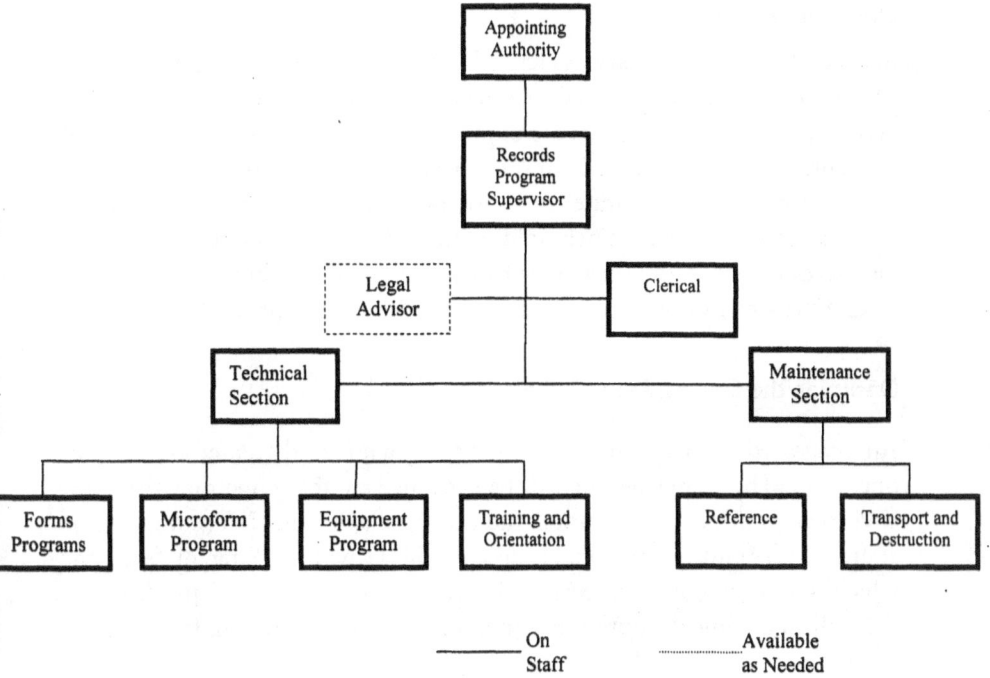

Figure 4.1. Typical Personnel Organization, Integrated Records Center

of the following: legal systems and procedures analysis, microform systems, forms design, equipment evaluation, security analysis, computer systems, and so on. Several of these abilities may be found in the same individual, but the list is illustrative of the range of an effective program.

In addition to appropriate supervisory and technical personnel, there is a need for a certain number of semiskilled personnel for records transport, retrieval, and destruction. Care should be taken that these people are well selected and trained. Although they may be low in the hierarchy of organization, they are a vital part of the system. Poor quality work at this level is probably more damaging than poor systems design.

The final group of employees in an integrated records management program are the employees within the individual offices serviced by the program. A system is not integrated if it does not involve these personnel directly. In most systems it is unlikely that office personnel will be employees of the records center. Office personnel must realize that they function specifically and continually with the records center program and that much of their technical direction comes from the center.

Operating Expenses

Beyond the usual expenses associated with the areas of space, equipment, and personnel, any centralized records program may have certain miscellaneous operating expenses that are unique. The most notable is the expense of the centralized forms program if the particular jurisdiction chooses to print and distribute large quantities of court forms. This is a major commitment and, unless forms are routinely sold to attorneys, will never be self-supporting. Beyond the cost of printing the forms, this decision affects facility design, since extensive storage and distribution facilities are required.

Designing the Courts Records Center

An integrated records system must have its own records center as a base of operation. The center design will be governed by the scope that the court envisions for a records operation and the space available. If a center is to be staffed with full-time personnel, design criteria will be different from one which is to be used by personnel within the system. The design specifications that follow assume the optimum conditions of full-time staff and satisfactory available space.

There are five criteria that must be considered when designing the records center:
- Size and type of space
- Location
- Internal design
- Equipment
- Security

Size and Type of Space

The space requirement is difficult to estimate. During the records survey, it is vital that projections of case filings be carried out. When considered in relation to the retention-destruction schedule, this projection should designate the amount of space required, or what the capacity for space being considered will be.

The most functional space for a records center is square or rectangular in shape. Ceiling heights should be sixteen feet or higher. There should be a minimum of pillars, posts, and other obstructions.

Location

Ideally, the center should be convenient to the main work area. However, it should be separate from that area, as some records center activities could be disruptive in a general administrative office. The best location within a build-

Records Management and Space Management / 159

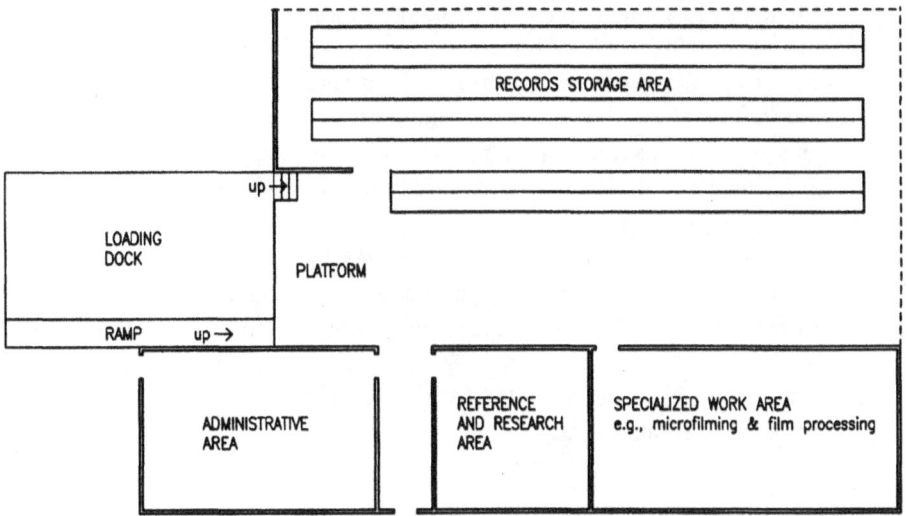

Figure 4.2. Diagrammatic Plan of Typical Records Center

ing is on the ground floor or in the basement. The factors to consider in locating a records center are floor loading, the movement of fairly heavy material in some quantity in and out of the facility, and accessibility of the clerk's office to the records housed in this center.

Internal Design

There are certain factors that should be incorporated in the design of any records center. Figure 4.2 shows the plan of a typical records center. Not all of the functions shown in this plan will be found in every records center. However, optimum design should include consideration of these services, if only over the long range.

- *Administrative Area*—Assuming full-time personnel, every center should have an area assigned for administrative purposes. This space should be functional and, if possible, separated from the general work area, with visual and acoustical privacy.
- *Reference and Research*—An area should be assigned to records reference for users of the center. This space should be close to the center entrance and have ample work area for the reviewing of records, including tables and chairs. If the center maintains copy capability, it should be located close to this area.
- *General Storage Area*—The majority of the records center space is assigned to general storage area. Figure 4.2 shows general storage space and its relationship to the total center area.

- *Loading Area*—If center volume merits it, a loading area should be provided. This is necessary for the receipt and processing of new records as well as records marked for destruction.
- *Specialized Work Areas*—Space should be provided for such specialized functions as microfilming and film processing. Such specialized areas may require hot and cold water, related plumbing, and special wiring.
- *Environment*—Certain environmental conditions must be maintained within the center. The humidity level should be adjustable through the use of humidifiers and/or air-conditioning system. Light levels should be a minimum of 30 foot-candles at desk level in the general storage areas and 50 to 100 foot-candles in the administrative and reference areas.

Equipment

The primary equipment of a records storage center is shelving and storage boxes. A typical single module of standard shelving measures 42 inches wide and 30 inches deep. If back-to-back shelving is possible, the addition of a 4-inch spacer between the units precludes storage box overhang, and the back-to-back module then measures 42 inches wide and 64 inches deep. Upright or vertical members of the shelving module should have standard shelf position holes 1 or 1½ inches apart to permit variable shelf spacing when necessary. The standard space between shelves should be 23 to 24 inches.

Shelving height depends on ceiling limitations, but for an assumed 16-foot ceiling height, upright or vertical members will be 14 feet 2 inches to 14 feet 9 inches. This will accommodate seven 23- or 24-inch shelves, a 3-inch rise from the floor to the first shelf, and an extension to the vertical members of 6 inches above the top shelf. This spacing allows clearance from lighting fixtures to meet illumination and fire code needs.

In the shelving arrangement in figure 4.3, the storage containers are housed two deep (per single-faced module), two high, and three wide. With a standard weight of 40 pounds per box, the shelf must support 480 pounds. The shelf itself should then be Class II (600-pound test) with bracing and stiffener bars along the front and rear underside lips of each shelf to preclude shelf sag and collapse.

Although wood shelving is available with 1-inch shelf centers, steel screw receptacles to prevent sag, 500-pound test weight shelves, and a fire performance better than steel, there is a mental (and occasionally fire code) block to using wood in records centers. Long-term appearance factors also favor steel.

There are numerous steel shelving manufacturers. They offer bolt-on or clip-on shelves; angle or T-bar posts; 1-inch or 1½-inch shelf-positioning holes or single fixed-position shelves. If the records storage center is liable to

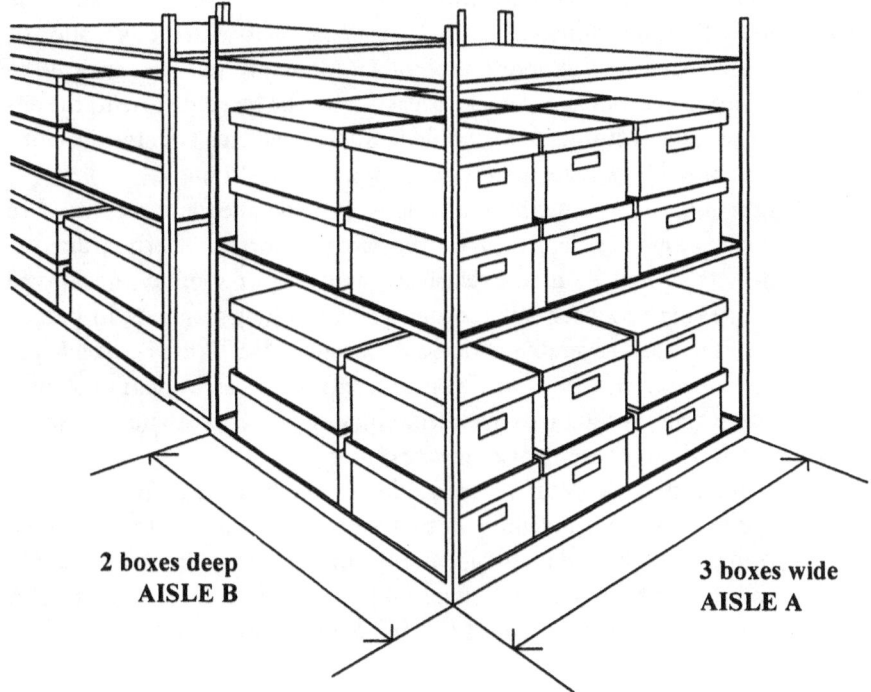

Figure 4.3. Records-Storage Container Arrangement

be relocated, select clip-on shelving. If the material stored requires variable shelf height, get the 1-inch to 1½-inch position vertical members. For appearance and less interference, select the T-type vertical members. Comparable systems from several manufacturers should be analyzed before making a final selection.

Storage boxes are available in a variety of shapes and sizes. The most common storage box is 12 by 15 by 10 inches. In certain situations, a center may require specialized storage equipment. Microfilm cabinets, EDP output containers, and similar equipment are all available from a number of manufacturers. However, the use of standard storage boxes should always be considered first for reasons of economy.

Any storage center will require a certain amount of file handling equipment, such as ladders, step stools, hand trucks, and so forth.

Security

One of the main design factors that contributes to the success or failure of a records center is the amount of security designed into the facility. Security considerations are of design, equipment, and procedures.

The center should be designed with limited access both into and within the center area. Entrance should be limited to a single door, with the exception of one-way fire exits. A vault door is preferable. All public functions such as the administrative and public reference areas should be located close to the entrance. The records storage area should be supervised on a twenty-four-hour basis and should be a regular stop on the watchman's rounds.

Certain equipment must be available to provide adequate security. Fire extinguishers and fire detectors are the most important. Carbon dioxide extinguishers should be used exclusively, as water or some chemical-type extinguishers may do more damage than a fire. Smoking should be forbidden or, at the very least, severely restricted to specified "safe" areas. Great care should be taken in the use of any heat source. If possible, burglar and automatic alarm systems should be installed. Equipment such as an internal intercom system is often necessary in a large center.

The final aspect of security is procedures. The records manager should develop clear internal guidelines as to access by individuals to the center. Monitoring of people and material entering and leaving the center, including a log and an in-and-out card system, will ensure good records control. A periodic review of security procedures and equipment is essential.

Exhibits Storage

An integral part of the records for any case is the exhibits. Whether they are civil or criminal, exhibits pose some unique problems for records management. This is particularly true of those which are an unusual size, perishable, valuable, dangerous, or some combination of these factors.

Therefore, in any records system, provision must be made for the receipt, proper handling, indexing, secure storage, and disposal of exhibits.

Receipt and Indexing

Exhibits must be handled in a standard manner and related to the case just as any document is. Exhibits should be indexed so that they may be identified with the appropriate case. This generally involves using the standard case number and affixing it to the exhibit so that it cannot be easily separated. A description of the exhibit should be included in the case file.

Secure Storage

A storage area for exhibits must be appropriate in size and equipment, and it must be secure. Very few court facilities have space designed specifically for exhibit storage. The most satisfactory space is equipped with shelving on which exhibits may be appropriately segregated. Shelving subdivided into "pigeonholes" is appropriate if the configuration is flexible enough to accommodate various-sized exhibits. Effective exhibit management requires the provision of a secure area. Too often the exhibits area is a subsection of a larger vault or storage area. This results in access to the exhibits area by a multitude of people. For all practical purposes, this destroys security in the exhibits custody area, as a shared responsibility entails no responsibility. Access to exhibits should be severely limited. Ideally, the exhibits room should be staffed on a full-time basis and exhibits moved in and out only by that person. In high-volume courts, this is often a possibility. In lower-volume courts, access should still be limited as much as possible. If it is not possible to limit room access generally, then an effort should be made to create smaller, secure subdivisions within the room.

In multistory court buildings, it might be appropriate to assign an exhibits storage room on each courtroom floor. This would eliminate the need for court clerks or court reporters to obtain exhibits from another floor. However, if it is not possible to provide the necessary level of security and supervision at each courtroom floor, then it would be preferable to centralize all exhibits storage at one location regardless of courthouse size. In other words, security of exhibits should have higher priority than convenience of personnel to exhibits storage locations. Criminal cases arising from theft of trial exhibits (drugs, precious metals, guns, etc.) as a result of negligence of court personnel who are assigned the responsibility for safety and security of exhibits are not uncommon.

All exhibits storage rooms must be of fire-rated construction and equipped with an appropriate fire alarm system and fire-fighting equipment (e.g., fire extinguishers). Exhibits that could be damaged by water should not be protected by a water sprinkler system, but by a fire alarm and appropriate carbon dioxide or foam system. An appropriate, sensitive burglary alarm system should be installed, especially in storage vaults for weapons, drugs, and precious gems exhibits.

Disposal

The final step in any exhibits management program is disposal. Accumulated exhibits consume valuable space. The crowding of accumulated, obsolete exhibits makes effective management of current exhibits more difficult. Some exhibits have value and should be returned to the proper parties. Many courts have developed rules governing exhibit disposal, and such disposal should be included in the records retention schedule. In civil cases there is no reason for retaining exhibits once an appeal has been taken or the time for filing that appeal has passed. At that point, exhibits should either be returned to the owner, destroyed, or sent to the appellate court. Criminal exhibits often pose a different problem. Dangerous, perishable, or valuable exhibits must be returned to owners or proper authorities before the appellate process is complete, particularly in light of postconviction relief problems. A successful technique for dealing with this material would be the "certified sample," or "certified photograph." Using such a system, jurisdictions retain a small portion of the exhibit or photographs of it and have them properly notarized regarding their validity and relevance to the case.

Close supervision of exhibit destruction is also vital. Many exhibits have a cash value either because they are valuable or prohibited, or both. The records supervisor should work closely with the court, the prosecutor, and the police to ensure the exhibits are properly destroyed. A certificate or notation verifying the method of disposal should be completed and retained with the final case record.

Trends in Records Management

There are two identifiable trends in records management that will have significant impact on court space design in the years ahead. The first is the realization that efficient court records storage depends on the development of a successful mix of filming and destruction of court records. The second is that technology may only be successfully utilized in an organization with a high degree of records management centralization.

Technological Application

There is the growing realization that few court systems can continue to retain all court records in hard-copy form. In most jurisdictions that is no longer a realistic option. Therefore, the trend is toward the development of a program that includes minimal hard-copy retention, some filming, and some destruction of some material, the last-mentioned sometimes following filming and sometimes being just simple destruction. A reasonable mix of retention, filming, and destruction will enable any system to control and manage its records volume in the years to come. That mix will vary in accordance with the unique needs of a given jurisdiction. However, a system that expects to successfully manage its court records must adopt such a technique.

Centralized Management

The second trend, based upon the increased use of technology, is toward centralized records management. The scope of centralization is not necessarily statewide or even countywide. However, the benefits to be realized from the increased use of technology are directly proportional to the extent of centralization possible. This trend toward centralization is inevitable for several reasons:

- The current trend in court management is increasing centralization, not necessarily statewide, but certainly on a regional level. Records management will be included in that trend. Court managers attempting to establish a records program are advised to consider some type of centralized system. Records affect all court functions either directly or indirectly and have major impact on space design and management. Just as an administrator would not consider fragmenting such areas as personnel, jury management, or information systems any more than necessary, fragmentation of records programs should not be tolerated.
- The uniformity that is required for an effective records system can only be accomplished with centralized management. This is particularly true in the input phase of the system, where the long-term format and content of the records system is determined.
- A system that is limited in jurisdiction is also limited in effectiveness. A subsection of a court will usually encounter significant difficulty in attempting to change its records-keeping system if the sections around it do not change.
- Records technology is expensive and requires proper utilization and relatively constant use to benefit from economies of scale. This is particularly true when it is equipment that requires operating personnel.
- Records management expertise in the court management area is hard to find. The centralized jurisdiction that pools the resources of small units has a better chance of finding and retaining appropriate personnel.
- A centralized, comprehensive records program can gather more support and utilize resources more efficiently than a fragmented effort. If a records management program is recognized as a priority centralized management function, it would be in a better position to obtain a fair share of court resources, including equipment, personnel, and space.

Facility Considerations

The continuing trend toward centralization will have a significant effect on the design criteria for court facilities. Facilities planners with centralized records management as a goal will find that this impact has two effects: the quantity and location of space needed, and the type of space provided.

Quantity and Location of Space

A records manager who is committed to centralized records management designed court space will find that the quantity of space required may change. Centralization implies that records will be removed from decentralized locations and consolidated in a central facility. Therefore, the court manager who has been maintaining extensive records in a particular courthouse will find that he or she can free space in that courthouse either by removing the records entirely or by filming them and working from the filmed copies on a day-to-day basis. However, the obvious corollary is that he or she will have to provide a larger single facility somewhere within the jurisdiction. Thus, the overall quantity of space devoted to records may not change; in fact, it may increase. The advantage is that space will be available where it is most needed for alternative purposes—in the local court facility.

Type of Space

The court manager will also be designing a different type of records space. It should be designed after the jurisdiction has developed an overall records program, based on the mix of records modes that the program will utilize. The manager will then be in a position to project gross space needs, equipment types, and space configurations, and to provide for the specialized areas, such as reference, microform, and records-processing and records-destruction spaces. This is a possibility only when the manager has developed a program that will remain constant over time.

5

Court Technology and Space Management

Introduction

The state of available technology has undoubtedly always been a major factor in space design. In early times, when natural light was the major source of illumination, workplaces had to be arranged in such a way that this source could be maximized. As effective sources of alternative light were developed, flexibility of design increased. Until recently, large quantities of paper records mandated banks of filing cabinets, readily accessible to workstations, occupying large amounts of prime office space. Electronic access to remote computer-based files has virtually eliminated such use of space in many facilities.

All aspects of court management are increasingly affected by technology, thus influencing the criteria for facility design for these court management functions. This influence raises such issues as (1) the amount of space to be allocated for a function, and indeed whether space for that function needs to be allocated at all; (2) the location of that space; and (3) the design of that space. The rapid rate of development in technology, and its increasing availability owing to falling costs, means that a facility planning process must include the highest-possible level of flexibility in space design. Lack of consideration of technology factors may result in a facility that will have a shorter useful life than users and funding authorities have a right to expect.

Characteristics of the Technology Environment

There are several aspects of the current technology environment that space planners must understand and incorporate into any facility planning project of significant scope in order to make that process effective.

The Rapidity of Change

As noted above, the rate of change in all areas of technology appears to accelerate exponentially. The office environment of 1960 was only marginally different from that of 1940. However, the office of 1990 bore little resemblance to that of 1980, and the technology-driven changes in the past ten years rival those of the previous ten. There appears to be little doubt that such a pattern will continue.

The Capability and Applicability of Technology

Technology is becoming increasingly capable. Not only are we able to meet in more effective ways needs that administrative functions have long had (e.g., the imprinting and preservation of the written word), we are constantly developing entirely new capabilities to address needs that are new to administrative responsibilities (e.g., computer-driven voice-print identification). Technology vests us with entire categories of new functions as well as expediting the carrying out of existing functions.

Just as significant is the trend to develop more and more of that technology for judicial management functions. In most areas of technology it is no longer necessary for the court manager to seek out technology applications in use in another discipline and adopt them to judicial management. It is the rare technology set indeed which has not addressed the unique needs of courts as it is developed and marketed. Thus, the judicial administrator involved in a facility design project has a full range of technology available to apply to identified needs.

The Affordability of Technology

Technology is increasingly affordable, in both its relative dollar cost and in its ratio of cost-effectiveness. Of the many examples of this phenomenon the best is probably the personal computer. In real dollars the typical PC in 2000 costs about half of what the typical unit cost in 1985. The level of increased capability is beyond description. Rapid changes in increased capability have major consequences for government-funded facility projects in that they broaden the options, making once-unavailable technologies available, which often results in savings in other major aspects of the project (e.g., the replacement of expensive "computer centers" with distributed database systems).

The Degree of Integration of Technology

Finally, and possibly most important, is the rapidly increasing integration of various technologies into what might be called "functional service packages." This is typified by open systems-design capabilities in computer hardware and software. However, it goes far beyond that. The marrying of voice, optics, data-compaction, and high-density storage in the initiation, processing, and storage of information allows the judicial manager to rethink all sorts of functions that affect facility design. The effect goes far beyond the traditional issues of where a particular function should be located in the new facility, in how much space, and how that space should be designed. It sometimes makes it possible to remove that function entirely from the facility by allocating it to space that imposes a much lower cost on the court (e.g., a remote records storage site for records that can be electronically transmitted to the court facility as needed).

Faced with so many technology options, all with the potential to have great impact on the design of a new or renovated facility, the judicial manager must be sure that any facility planning process well defines those functions to be included in the facility which lend themselves to the application of technology. To do anything less will more than likely lead to a design that not only does not take advantage of the technology of the day, but will lack the flexibility to adjust to the technology of tomorrow, which comes upon us at an increasing rate.

Technology Groupings and Their Impact on Space Management

Until fairly recently, technologies available to court managers, such as computer systems, security systems, and court reporter systems, could be discussed on an individual basis. However, as noted above, the growing integration of various technologies into what we have described as "functional service packages" makes such an approach less than useful when addressing a facility design project.

Therefore, the discussion that follows addresses prime judicial management functions and the groups of technologies that exist to expedite those functions. It will come as no surprise to judicial managers that these groupings revolve around the generation, exchange, and retention of data, a prime purpose of courts, which cuts across virtually all court functions, and which is most subject to rapid change impacting facility design.

Core Data Configurations

The day of the centralized computer facility, housing one or more mainframes and peripherals with a staff for its care and feeding, is rapidly fading. Changes in hardware, software, communications, and data entry technology are leading to increasingly decentralized systems.

Hardware

The general trend is a transition from mainframes to personal computers (PCs). The more recent development in that trend is the marrying of clusters of PCs into local area networks (LANs) and wide area networks (WANs). This development has major consequences for facility design. It is this technology which has eliminated the need for the traditional centralized computer facility by placing data storage and "computing power" at numerous local sites in a facility, and by linking those PCs together through an adjacent server, which is in turn tied to additional servers and PC clusters. Computer technology has enabled court managers to deliver a higher level of service closer to the end users than ever before. However, such configurations do not necessarily mean that less total space in a facility will be allocated to computer hardware, although that is often the case. It does mean that such space must be sited throughout the facility and that there are specific design criteria that must be applied to those spaces wherever they are located, just as there were specific requirements for the formerly centralized facility.

Of particular note to facility designers is the need to provide the "highway" that will link these new hardware configurations. At present that is either fiber-optic or twisted-pair cable (although some early wireless systems are available for limited applications). Either material may be used, although fiber-optic-cable technology does have some distance limitations. However, the more important consideration for facility planners is the anticipation of locations for the decentralized hardware sites and workstations in the new facility. It is obvious that the time to install conduit, access panels, terminal boards, and so forth is during construction—retrofitting is vastly more expensive. Erring on the side of overkill is no sin in this area. This "highway" development and layout is also one area in the planning process where a specialized consultant is well worth the investment.

Software

If the trend in data management systems is increasing decentralization, with its impact on facility design, then facility planners must pay more attention to software concerns than ever before. Effective decentralization depends on effective data management in all its aspects. Facility planners must work closely with MIS personnel in such areas as selection of database management systems and function-specific software packages. Although it is true that the rapid advancement to open-system technology makes the integration/communication of individual and function-specific software increasingly possible, it is still fair to say that adoption of common systems is a wise alternative. This is particularly important if a facility is to be designed assuming access and possible data entry from remote sites and entities, not actually part of the court system, such as law firms, other government agencies, and the like.

Data Entry

Basic decisions made regarding the management of data entry impact both facility design and technology selection decisions and must be addressed at the facility design stage.

Traditionally, courts tend to overwhelmingly centralize data entry functions. This takes various forms, but almost always involves the transfer of written data from such points as courtrooms, clerks' counters, law firms, and litigants, etc. to a central point where the information is entered into computer-based systems by a staff allocated to that function usually using some level of keystroke technology. The structural inefficiencies of such systems in terms of time and data transfer errors are well known. Even if the error rate can be contained, increasing case volumes make such labor-intensive systems decreasingly cost-effective. Therefore, more and more courts are adopting decentralized data entry. Direct entry from points within the system (e.g., courtrooms) and without (e.g., law firms, other court-related agencies, and individual litigants) is growing. The utilization of such technologies as bar coding, optical character recognition, various other imaging technologies, "smart cards," and so forth makes such change possible, and the level of reliability of these technologies is now quite high. The concern for facility planners is that they accommodate these developments in their design as a change that is either imminent or will certainly occur during the life of the facility. A simple example will suffice: If data entry is to be relocated to individual courtrooms for all events occurring in that room, how will that affect the configuration of those rooms? How will it affect the judges' bench and clerk's station? How much space should now be allocated in the central clerk's office for this function? Will clerks' office workstations have different requirements? What types, and how much data transmission capability must be installed?

Data Exchange

The second leg of data management that affects court space design is the exchange of data within the facility and between the facility and locations outside it. Assuming that an initial record has been created as discussed above, there will be a constant need from a wide variety of sources to reference that record for information and update purposes. Again, basic policy decisions by the court will drive system design, and that design will require certain technical capabilities. A variety of technologies are available and proven for such configurations, and the facility planner should consider each in light of defined system needs.

Fax Technology

Although fax technology is not new, fax applications have mushroomed in recent years owing primarily to improved telecommunications capabilities. In data systems that desire to retain hard copy yet want to allow increased data exchange, this technology has found a place. Examples include document filing from remote locations and nonjudicial agencies, calendar distribution, and arrest and search warrant circulation.

Voice Systems

Utilization of these systems has grown at about the same pace as fax technology. Ranging from simple telephone-answering or message-recording devices to relatively sophisticated menu-driven automated attendants, they have found wide application in courts for such functions as jury calls and attendance instructions, case-scheduling information, filing instructions, and directions to court locations. Although the technology is increasingly reliable and can result in significant personnel savings (thus impacting space allocation and design), care must be taken that such systems do not become so complex as to remove the human element from court operations. There is a growing body of evidence that persons requiring data and information access to courts become resentful of such systems, which tends to make the technology counterproductive.

Video Systems

Video applications are among the most rapidly growing in judicial facilities. They also have major facility design impact. Applications may be logically characterized as passive or interactive.

Among the passive applications are jury orientation material, courthouse directory or case-scheduling information (often made somewhat interactive by the use of touch screen/interrogation technology), and such courtroom presentations as depositions and accident simulation. The first and possibly most significant of the interactive applications was the recording of courtroom proceedings in lieu of stenographic or sound recording. Although still questioned by some within the court community (primarily those with a vested interest in the preservation of more traditional systems), the technology must be considered proven. It is also, like most of the technology included here, generally cost-effective. However, if such systems are selected as the method of choice, great care must be taken in interior space design in the areas in which they are to be used. Of particular note are adjacency and proximity requirements of participants, acoustics and lighting, power supplies, system redundancy, and the location of operating personnel.

Of more recent vintage are such interactive systems as transmission of testimony from remote locations, appearance of prisoners from remote holding areas within or without the court facility, and teleconferencing among judges, attorneys, and others for purposes of settlement, issue clarification, and so on. The extent of use of such applications can have major facility implications, as it impacts the amount and type of space to be included in the courthouse (e.g., does video prisoner appearance from a remote location impact the amount of prisoner holding area to be provided?).

Telecommunications

Virtually all of the technologies discussed above require great attention to the general area of telecommunications. Such applications as electronic mail, electronic fund transfer, case file reference and possible update, and document filing from internal and external locations are clearly upon us and are in the future of all courts. Great care must be taken during the program and design stages of facility development to see that the telecommunications infrastructure is adequate to meet present and future needs. The transition to such systems constitutes a major commitment from which there is usually no retreat. As the supporting infrastructure is literally and figuratively embedded in the facility, it is critical that facility project managers get it right the first time.

Data Retention

The final phase of data management is that of long-term data retention. This phase is discussed in the earlier section dealing with records management. However, some parts bear repeating briefly.

Traditionally, courts have retained large quantities of paper records over long periods of time. Despite our best efforts, this remains the case. The "paperless" court movements of the seventies and early eighties were interesting and ambitious ideas that were never really successful. The court or legal culture, conversion costs, shifting and sometimes unreliable technologies, and the dubious cost-effectiveness of such systems in increasingly lean judicial budgets worked against their success.

However, reliable technology now exists which, if properly applied, can result in "less-paper" courts. These are microforms and optical-disk-based data and image systems or systems that combine these technologies. The increased capability and flexibility of computer-based systems makes these technologies more feasible, as court records can be converted much more easily for film or disk formats. However, the more important development is major recent improvements in the ability of hardware and software to manipulate those media for data management, particularly in the areas of accurate indexing, retrieval, and (if such is desired) data update. Film or disk has progressed from a relatively static medium with the prime advantage of great savings in storage space to a dynamic management medium for active records with the bonus of greatly reduced—or at least remotely located—lower-cost, long-term storage capabilities. The consequences of such developments for space allocation and design with a judicial facility are obvious and should be a major consideration in the planning process.

Technologies in the Courthouse

Court systems have come a long way over the past thirty years in adapting new technologies and automation into operations. Even in the seventies, while the larger court systems became increasingly aware of what automation and technologies could do to improve operational efficiency, clerks in smaller communities and rural courts were continuing their entry of case activities in large, heavy, leather-bound record books. In the past fifteen years, almost all court systems in the United States have adopted some form of computer-based system, and certain systems have experimented with and installed new technologies that have been available in private industries for many years but were recently adopted to the needs of the court system. As we proceed into the twenty-first century, the technological and communications gap between the judicial system and the private sector will certainly be narrowed even further. Many state and county systems have, over the past decade, created their own internal management information system (MIS) to research, design, and monitor their automation and technology system on a statewide or countywide basis.

The following are brief descriptions of the new automation and technology systems being used in courts today and some predictions as to what new systems might be used in the twenty-first century.

Automation

All new court buildings or judicial complexes should be designed to provide the capability (convenient accessibility to power, communications, and data wiring and outlets) of providing a personal computer (PC) and telephone or intercom equipment at each workstation throughout the building. This would include all workstations in courtrooms, judges' chamber suites, clerks' offices, and all departmental support offices.

The degree of flexibility and convenience to provide power, communications, and data access on floors and walls depends largely on the functional and personal requirements of each court or department.

   a. In the clerk's office, the organization and layout of workstations in an open office setting undergo frequent adjustments and/or changes. Changes in grouping of clerical personnel in a working unit (that is, criminal, juvenile, calendaring, case-processing, and courtroom) invariably result in changing configuration of staff workstations. Consequently, clerks' offices usually require the highest level of flexibility in accessing power, communications, and data wiring and outlets. This can be accomplished by using a three-inch raised floor above the structural floor; modular wall partitions with base channels to house such wiring and outlets; or access to underfloor wiring channels embedded in floor finishes or under the structural floor in the ceiling space of the floor below. Vertical power poles are unsightly in an open office setting to accommodate wiring from the ceiling space above the workstations, and should be avoided through proper planning and innovative design of power, communications, and data distribution systems.

b. Computer equipment rooms that anticipate major changes in equipment and the types of power supply and cabling in the future will require the degree of flexibility that a three-inch raised floor provides. With the continuing miniaturization of computer equipment and data storage media, very large computer rooms in many high-volume metropolitan courts may become obsolete in the future, and such spaces could be converted into workstations for MIS personnel, meeting or training rooms for courts staff, and so forth.

c. Locations of power, communications, and data outlets in courtrooms and hearing rooms are reasonably well defined. Flexibility in relocating such outlets in the judicial area of the courtroom would not be as significant, since the locations' regular trial participants—judge, courtroom clerk, court reporters, witness, jurors, attorneys, litigants—are not usually variable once the courtroom is designed and constructed. The judge's bench, witness box, courtroom clerk's workstation, and the court reporter's workstation are invariably grouped together at the front end of the courtroom. Attorneys' and litigants' tables usually face the judge's bench and witness box. The jury box with at least 14 seats for a 12-person jury is usually to one side of the judicial area, on the opposite side of the wall from which in-custody defendants are brought into the judicial area, near the defense attorneys' table in a criminal trial courtroom. Even a movable podium used by attorneys during case presentation is limited to certain locations within the judicial area. Underfloor ducts providing power, communications, and data outlets at participants' location, and the use of the raised platforms under the judge's bench, witness seat, and the clerk's workstation, should provide adequate flexibility to accommodate all wiring and outlets necessary in the judicial area of the courtroom. In the spectator seating area at the rear of the courtroom, power should be provided at specific seats near the judicial area to accommodate the visually and hearing impaired and the news media.

d. In the law library, the bookstacks area would not require the same degree of flexibility as regular workstations in the clerk's office.

Study and carrel areas, where power and data outlets are required, are usually well defined, although such locations could change in time. More bookstacks would result in reduced study and carrel areas. It is important to define the area for regular bookstacks and the area for potential high-density book storage systems with manually or electronically operated bookstacks for books that do not require frequent access. Such systems would require much greater structural floor loading strength, which must be planned for during the design process. Similarly, it is equally important for the clerk's office to define, within the records storage area, the potential area for high-density file storage and structurally planned for the increased floor loading.

Technologies

Video Display Terminals and Monitors

The courts have increasingly adopted the use of technologies requiring video display terminals (VDTs) and monitors. The prevalence of workstations employing VDTs requires a studied design response addressing the special requirements of the equipment and its users. The following provides a summary of such basic lighting and acoustical design concerns.

Lighting for VDTs and Monitors. It is important to ensure optimal lighting conditions for the users of VDTs and monitors to minimize visual discomfort and the potential for long-term vision damage. Surveys have shown strong correlations between poor lighting on the one hand and user fatigue, eyestrain, and burning eyes on the other. Consideration of the following recommendations will help minimize visual discomfort:

- General levels of ambient light should be in the range of 30 to 40 foot-candles and should be produced by glare-free, diffuse luminaries. Adjustable task lighting providing about 70 foot-candles should be provided at each workstation.
- Glare and contrast should be minimized at the workstation. The brightness ratio between the VDT and keyboard, the worksurfaces, and the peripheral environment should be about 1:3:10. Matte surface finishes should be specified for workstations to prevent excessive brightness: panels and other surfaces immediately adjacent to the work surface be finished with materials having surface reflectances of 70 percent or less.
- Positioning of the workstation in relation to its light sources is also important. Lights located directly overhead should be placed such

that the angle of incident light on the VDT screen does not exceed 45 degrees vertical. To minimize glare, VDT screens should be placed at 90 degrees horizontal in relation to windows, and the use of adjustable window coverings should be considered.
- The spectrum range or temperature of lamps should also be considered in the lighting design. Spaces provided with relatively great quantities of natural light or employing a palette of cool colors should use lamps providing about 4,000 K (Kelvin). Spaces not closely affected by daylight sources can use warmer lamps of around 2,000 K.

Acoustics for VDT Workstations. Noise generated by people and equipment may cause acoustic discomfort such as distraction and loss of privacy. As discussed above, there are several ways to go about improving acoustical performance in work spaces. For instance, furniture and partitions can be placed in desirable positions and interior surfaces, materials, and finishes that inhibit noise can be provided.

The spacing of workstations is an important aspect of acoustic control and speech privacy. When positioning a VDT workstation, direct lines of sight with other workstations should be avoided. Additionally, a minimum spacing of 8 to 10 feet between workstations separated by acoustic panels or partitions will aid speech privacy, while separations of less than 3 feet will not significantly contribute to noise control.

Acoustical panels can effectively reduce ambient noise levels by blocking direct sound transmissions and absorbing reflected sounds. Such panels, either freestanding or integrated with furniture systems, can provide an effective acoustical control system, especially when used in concert with sound-absorbent materials applied to building surfaces. Ceiling surface materials and configuration can also be used to control transmission and reflection of sound.

Video Technology

Video technology is increasingly being used for judicial proceedings, and its use will continue to grow as the technology becomes more reliable and less expensive. Video has been used for the presentation of evidence and testimony, as the official record of the court proceedings, for accommodating an unruly defendant, and for public and media access to court proceedings. Closed-circuit television (CCTV) is also used for court security. Every courtroom and hearing room should be wired or, at a minimum, have conduits placed for audio and video recording and transmission of court proceedings. Cameras and microphones are usually fixed; they do not move to follow the action. The cameras are mounted at a high position on the wall and aimed so that all participants are in the field of at least one camera. All cameras operate continuously while the court is in session. The recording or transmission may include all cameras, or they may be switched by voice activation or other control device. A split-screen mechanism allows multiple camera angles to be viewed simultaneously. The microphones may be part of the courtroom sound-enhancement systems or a separate parallel system. Recording equipment is usually placed in the courtroom or it may be in a shared control room. Consideration must also be made for space to accommodate the storage and repair of equipment and supplies. Special attention must be paid to the lighting and acoustics for video recording. The intensity, color balance, and direction of the lighting will affect the quality of the video picture. The intensity should match the sensitivity of the cameras used; color should be balanced to project natural skin tones, and backlighting of the subject and glare on the monitor need to be avoided. The audio transmission should be direct from microphones with a minimum of background noise. Sound transmission in the courtroom or hearing room is especially critical when a voice-activated switching system is used.

At public-interest trials for which the number of spectators is much greater than the number of available seats in the spectator area of the courtroom, there are two ways of accommodating the additional number of spectators. First, one or more trial courtrooms could be planned to be larger than the regular trial courtrooms so that the larger judicial area can accommodate multiple parties or defendants, and the larger spectator area can seat a larger number of spectators during public-interest trials. All multiple-party and public-interest trials would be assigned to these special trial courtrooms. The problem with this approach is that these courtrooms would be very underutilized most of the time, as there are a very few public-interest trials. On the other hand, public-interest trials could generate such public attendance that even large trial courtrooms with spectator seating of more than 100 would still not be adequate. Furthermore, security risk increases as the number of spectators increases during an emotion-charged public-interest trial. A regular trial courtroom with seating for 50 to 60 spectators would be more controllable than one with double that seating capacity.

The second method of addressing this situation is to conduct the public-interest trial in a technologically equipped regular trial courtroom which would be linked by CCTV to a large conference or training facility located on the main-entry floor of the courthouse. Proceedings of the trial could be viewed by a much larger number of overflow spectators beyond the regular capacity of the trial courtroom, and the security risk in the courtroom would be minimized. In addition, these overflow spectators would be kept on the ground floor, which eliminates the need for their using public elevators to access the courtroom floor, thus decreasing the passenger loading on these elevators during peak use. Being on the main-entry floor would also provide these spectators access to vending, lunch, and toilet facilities, and greater flexibility for them to enter or leave the conference facility without interrupting the trial process in the courtroom. Depending on how this facility is designed and equipped, there could either be a large central screen or a series of smaller CCTV monitors mounted on the walls or ceiling throughout this large room. Lighting and sound would be controlled by a technician, and adequate provision would be made to accommodate the physically handicapped and the visually and hearing impaired. Should there be a security problem, this facility would be near the building security control center on the ground floor, where prompt response by security officers would be expected.

With TV videocameras gaining greater acceptance in courtrooms to record trial proceedings for the news media, a degree of order should be established for newsworthy information to be disseminated to the public with the least amount of disruption to the trial proceedings. For the large special-trial courtroom, a small news media room equipped with one-way glass could adjoin the judicial area of the courtroom so that news reporters and/or TV camera operators can view the proceedings through the glass separation. Sound is transmitted into the room by the use of speakers and headphones. Such a room has not been used frequently, since news reporters and TV camera operators prefer to be in the courtroom proper in order to feel and to report on the atmosphere as well as the proceeding of the trial. The court usually allows a single camera in the courtroom. This camera would be linked to a CCTV wall or floor outlet that transmits pictures of trial procedures taken by the camera to a central news media room on the ground floor near the clerk's office, from which news media crews could obtain factual information about any public-interest case.

This central news media room would have several semiprivate workstations in which news media crew members could use the equipped CCTV monitors and controls to view trial proceedings being conducted from various courtrooms, and to extract the videotaped portions that are considered newsworthy and that eventually would be aired by TV stations during the news hours. With sensational trials that require instant broadcast, the portions of trial proceedings selected could be transmitted directly from this news media room to a broadcasting van located outside the building. For this reason, it would be more convenient for the news media room to be located along an exterior wall of the building, so that the video link would be direct from the video outlet to the broadcasting van outside.

Video-Teleconferencing

Video-teleconferenced court proceedings are a cost-effective approach of conducting first appearances, arraignments, motions, and other court activities that do not require the physical presence of all participants in the same space. The rights of the defendants or litigants must be reviewed and accommodated or waived in each application. Video-teleconferencing is particularly useful when there are multiple court locations or if the jail is at a remote location. The factors that must be considered when determining if and how to implement a video-teleconferencing program include the following: alternatives for in-person proceedings, interfacing with other video systems, the record-playback system, transmission mode, and facilities.

Video-teleconferencing programs may be part of broader programs to utilize video in the courtroom. The record and playback equipment used in other applications may also be used for teleconferencing. If multiple participants are included, there are usually multiple cameras and microphones situated to cover the entire field. TV monitors are provided for each participant or located so that each participant has a clear, unobstructed view. The image displayed may be switched automatically to show the person speaking, or a split-image screen may be used to show all participants at once. A split image of the viewer (how that person appears to the other participants) may be included with either display approach. Transmission of the proceedings between sites may be accomplished by dedicated telephone lines, fiber-optic lines, or microwave transmission. The choice of transmission mode will depend on the distance and terrain to be covered, available infrastructure, desired picture quality, and project budget.

Facilities for video-teleconferencing may be dedicated and used solely for video proceedings or for in-person proceedings. The size of the space may be equivalent to a hearing or conference room. Video-teleconferencing proceedings could also take place in a courtroom. In new or remodeled court facilities, provisions could be made for future video applications by providing conduits for camera, microphone, and monitor hookup. The cameras, microphones, and/or monitor may be built in, or permanently fixed, in the room, or they may be portable units.

Other Court Technologies

Other areas of technologies applicable to the judicial system include the following:

1. Real-time reporting that connects the court reporter's stenographic machine to a computer can be provided. During a trial or hearing, the stroking of the keys would be instantaneously translated by a com-

puter program into an unedited English text shown to video monitors at various locations in the courtroom (e.g., judge's bench, jury box, clerk's station, and attorneys' and litigants' stations). For a hearing-impaired person, the proceedings of the trial or hearing could be read on the monitor practically as soon as the words were spoken. This would satisfy the Americans with Disabilities Act (ADA) requirements for the hearing-impaired or deaf person. At the same time that the proceedings were reported by the court reporter, a scopist could be editing the text in another room so that a fully edited transcript could be printed by the following day, if necessary.

2. Instantaneous display of exhibits on video screens or monitors during trials or hearings can be provided by means of a small videocamera mounted on a stand. The videocamera would be connected to a computerized program that instantaneously projects the exhibits onto various video screens or monitors at different locations of the courtroom. Instead of exhibits being passed from juror to juror in the jury box, small monitors would show close-ups of the exhibits, or portions of the exhibits, to all jurors simultaneously, which results in shortening the time for jurors, as well as for other participants, to view the exhibits. Such video monitors can also be located at the judge's bench, clerk's workstation, witness box, and the public spectators' area.

3. Adequate and flexible access to power, telephone, and data outlets is becoming increasingly important in courtrooms. Attorneys may bring compact laptop computers into the courtroom for quick legal research, access to centralized information systems, and communication through a built-in modem with their offices or with other offices nationwide or worldwide during the course of a lengthy trial. Such outlets should also be available in attorneys' conference rooms adjoining courtrooms, attorneys' meeting or lounge areas, law libraries, and multiple-use spaces such as conference or training facilities, jury assembly facilities, and so forth.

4. Computer-aided legal research (e.g., Westlaw and Lexis) contains computerized legal case information and decisions of federal and state supreme and appellate courts. As these computerized legal research systems expand in the future to incorporate an increasing amount of case law information and decisions from various states, and as attorneys and judges become more proficient in the use of computerized legal research systems, the amount of hardcover books may begin to decrease in law libraries, which may result in a decreasing need for expansion space for book storage.

Security Planning

The decisions underlying the development of the design for a new courts facility should address three primary goals regarding protection of the safety and security of facility users, facility functions and operations, and facility contents. The goals are the following:

- deterrence of actual or potential threats
- detection of breaches of security
- minimizing or eliminating the damage arising from such incidents

An effective security plan will incorporate architectural, technological, and operational components to form a comprehensive solution that avoids the atmosphere of an armed fortress. Using all three components, it will separate the circulation of people to minimize unauthorized public access to areas that need to be secure.

The Architectural Component

The architecture of the building is perhaps the most important component of the security system. By properly zoning activities and creating separation of different classes to and movement within the building, the architecture provides initial deterrence, facilitates detection, and minimizes the possibility of catastrophic damages to persons or property. Security-conscious design is also the most cost-effective of the three components of a security system. Thus, the approach to the design of a court facility should emphasize architectural solutions to potential security concerns and should use technological and operational solutions only to supplement and reinforce the architectural systems. Security-conscious design encompasses not only the interior arrangement and outfitting of the building, but also consideration of the building's landscape and exterior design.

The architectural component will typically incorporate a variety of mechanisms to contribute to the accomplishment of the three goals of security planning. These mechanisms may include the following considerations, although this list should not be considered exhaustive:

- The number of exterior entrances to the court facility should be strictly limited (ideally with provision of a single public entrance and a minimum of other staff and service entrances). It must be impossible for the public and certain unexempted staff to enter the court facility without going through the court facility's public entry screening station.
- The building's design should create separation between public, restricted, and secure access points and circulation patterns (both ver-

tical and horizontal) to reduce the possibility of unauthorized access to sensitive areas or undesirable mixing of incompatible groups. The design may not buffer zones or spaces to support this separation. These areas would occur in the form of reception spaces and securable soundlocks.
- Primary circulation should occur through corridors planned to incorporate a minimum of blind corners and places of concealment. Where possible and practical, the spaces adjoining these corridors should be provided with relites (interior windows) to allow casual surveillance by staff, serving both deterrence and detection functions.

The Technological Component

The technological component of the plan typically incorporates a variety of remote-sensing and communications systems. These would include the following:

- *Video Surveillance*—Video surveillance is generally used at building entries, in infrequently patrolled corridors and lobby areas, in courtroom holding areas, in judge and staff parking areas, at cashier stations, and for other areas and space uses that may require a relatively high degree of security.
- *Intrusion Detection*—Intrusion detection systems are primarily used to reinforce control of access to sensitive areas of the facility, or to areas of the facility that should not be accessible during certain time periods (that is, outside normal hours of operation).
- *Key-card, Code-Controlled, or Fingerprint-Locking Mechanisms*—Electronic systems can be used in concert with intrusion detection systems to accommodate variable levels of authorized access.
- *Threshold Audio Monitoring*—Threshold audio monitoring devices can be used in prisoner-holding areas, but may also be useful in infrequently accessed areas, as a backup or reinforcement of the intrusions detection system.
- *Concealed Silent Duress Alarms*—These alarms should be used in courtrooms, chambers, reception areas, work areas, and other selected locations and should be equipped with an inconspicuous indicator (such as a ceiling-mounted LED) within the alarmed space to allow operators to see that the alarm has been activated.
- *Personal Alarm ("Man-Down") Systems*—These systems can be especially useful for limiting the risks to individuals who might be exposed to potentially dangerous situations, such as a deputy escorting a prisoner or a judge who must traverse public areas.
- *Weapons Detection*—Physical searches and/or magnetometers and

X-ray machines may be used to detect organic-material and inorganic-material weapons.
- *Communications*—Telephonic and/or radio intercommunications to a central security or control station should be installed.

Duress Alarms

The occupants of some areas of the building may be exposed to the risk of robbery or attack and should be provided with a means of summoning security personnel for assistance. A method of providing for communication with security personnel is to provide a duress alarm near an occupant's primary workstation. The alarm should be located so that it can be activated without detection. When activated, the alarm signal should be received at a central security control center with a device that indicates the origin of the alarm.

The following spaces should be equipped with alarms:

- courtrooms, with provision at the clerk's and security officer's station as well as at the judge's bench
- judges' chambers and support offices
- public reception station and service counter areas
- cashier stations
- other areas of the building providing direct service to the public

Security staff responding to alarms should be able to unobtrusively obtain information regarding the circumstances of the alarm before making a decision about how to handle the situation. One method to accomplish this uses inactive telephone handsets as in-place microphones to monitor sound within the affected space from the security control station. In some areas, CCTV monitoring should be considered. A building-wide public address system should be provided to allow authorities to communicate with building occupants during emergencies. The emergency public address system is particularly important in public assembly spaces.

The Operational Component

The operational component generally consists of the provision of designated security staff as well as security-related training for nonsecurity staff. Although the designer does not have direct control over the implementation of the operational component of a security plan, it must be acknowledged that this component will be an important factor in the efficacy of any such plan. Nonsecurity staff would be trained to recognize suspect conditions, to inform security staff of potentially threatening situations, and to react to perceived security breaches in both active (e.g., evacuating an area) and noninterventive (e.g., summoning security personnel rather than attempting to break up a scuffle) roles as may be appropriate to specific situations. Designated security staff may serve at fixed stations (e.g., a central security control station, courtroom stations, and the public entry screening station) as well as performing regular patrols of both public and private areas. These personnel serve in both deterrent proactive and reactive roles. Court security is often the responsibility of a unit that transports prisoners to and from the court facility, maintains the central holding area, transfers the prisoners within the court building, and maintains general security for all areas of the building. Operating the security screening equipment at building entrance(s) and security monitoring of the exterior of courthouses is more often the responsibility of a court security division or a contract security company. However it is provided, the key factor is that the respective staffs be well coordinated, with clear lines of responsibility.

It should be noted that police officers or sheriff's deputies in the building to present testimony and to perform other official and nonofficial court business should not be considered to be part of the building's security force. They may not be familiar with court security procedures, their number cannot be depended upon, and they often are not easily identified.

Separation of Circulation

An important security consideration is the control of unauthorized public access to private areas of the building. Authorized movement from a public zone to a private zone should occur only through controlled interface areas, which can be staffed spaces to serve both control and informational functions (unauthorized movement between these areas should not occur). These stations should be linked to a central security control station by both telephone and concealed silent duress alarms. In the limited number of instances in which access to private areas must occur directly from uncontrolled public areas (e.g., a fire exit to the exterior of the building), technological detection and entry control measures should be taken, including the use of video surveillance, intrusion detection equipment and card- or code-controlled locking mechanisms.

Barrier-Free Access

All public service buildings, including courthouses and governmental facilities, should be accessible to all segments of society. This is especially important for court facilities. Unfettered access to justice is a right, not a privilege. In recognition of this requirement, most states and local jurisdictions have enacted regulations prohibiting creation of building conditions that present potential barriers to access. Most of these regulations have been made to conform to the Americans with Disabilities Act Accessibility Guidelines (ADAAG), published in 1991. Additional guidelines specifically addressing judicial facilities were published in 1994. States have issued guidelines; for example, specific statutory accessibility regulations for the physically handicapped in the state of Florida are presented in the *Accessibility Codes and Standards Handbook,* fourth edition (chapter 553, Part V, Florida Statutes).

The Americans with Disabilities Act (ADA) of 1990 extends civil rights protection to persons with disabilities. Title II and Title III of the ADA became effective in 1992. Title II covers guidelines for buildings and facilities of state and local governments, and Title III covers guidelines for new construction and alteration of public accommodations and commercial facilities. The law prohibits discrimination in employment, public services, programs, activities and transportation, public accommodation, and telecommunication. The ADAAG describes the physical standards for compliance to the law. The guidelines were developed and are interpreted by the Architectural and Transportation Barriers Compliance Board, an arm of the U.S. Department of Justice. The law required elimination of all barriers that may prevent a person from equal access to all public facilities and barriers that prevent employment or participation of a person who would otherwise be qualified or capable of participating. Compliance can sometimes take the form of physical adaptation of the environment or administrative solutions whenever feasible.

The greatest impact of implementing barrier-free accessibility standards is generally realized in providing access to people with limited mobility, especially where multistory structures are concerned. It should be recognized, however, that these are by no means the only people for whom accessibility is affected. Barrier-free access must also be ensured for people with nonambulatory disabilities such as sight and hearing disabilities, incoordination, reaching and manipulation disabilities, lack of stamina, difficulty interpreting and reacting to sensory information, and extremes of physical size.

Areas of judicial facilities requiring specific accessibility requirements for maneuvering will have a great impact on the layout of courtrooms. Adequate space must be provided for persons in wheelchairs to be accommodated in the spectator area of courtrooms as well as at all the courtroom stations. Currently the ADAAG allows only the judge's bench and the clerk's station to be adaptable, which is defined as "being easily made accessible." In existing facilities, portable ramps or lifts are currently allowed to provide vertical access to the witness stand and jury box.

Public access service counters, such as in the clerk's office, must provide lowered sections that accommodate persons in wheelchairs.

People with impairments affecting the arms or hands frequently experience limited dexterity and strength that restrict their ability to grasp and twist. Therefore, hardware and controls that do not require these movements are preferred.

Consideration must be given to those conditions which affect accessibility for the visually impaired. Clear and unobstructed pathways must be maintained and should be without protrusions such as benches, projecting signage, overhanging stairs, trash receptacles, and so forth. Consideration should also be given to the provision of textural, value contrasts and resiliency cues to indicate the presence of potential hazards, such as entrances, corridor intersections, and changes in floor level.

Visual warnings and directions should be provided for hearing impaired persons. Signage should be clear, easily recognized and obviously located; signage of adequate size and incorporating contrasts of light and dark are often usable by partially sighted persons as well as hearing impaired persons. A percentage of telephones should have amplification provisions for persons with partial hearing; consideration should also be given to provision of telecommunication devices for the deaf (TDD) in offices experiencing relatively high volumes of public traffic.

As is discussed above, it will be necessary to make provisions for hearing-impaired persons in the building's assembly-type spaces, some of whom may be adequately served by provision of headphone sound reinforcement systems. It will be necessary to make accommodation for court-appointed signers, especially as regards proceedings involving deaf defendants, witnesses, and jurors. The design of the courtroom layouts should address the need to place the signer within the reader's field of vision while allowing the reader to also view the speaker, in order to observe the speaker's gestures, facial expressions, and other visual cues. It should be noted that, in many cases, it will be necessary for the courtroom design to make provision for both signers and language interpreters. Outlets are also necessary in public meeting and jury spaces to accommodate personal communication devices.

It should be noted that provision of barrier-free access is required not only for public areas of a court facility, but also for restricted and secure areas. For example, facilities provided for jurors and alternates (including the jury assembly facility, jury deliberation rooms, as well as jury boxes in courtrooms) must be designed to allow the participation of physically handicapped jurors; and, in all prisoner holding areas, at least one of each type of cell must incorporate barrier-free design standards as must all related areas. Equal employment regulations may also require maintenance of barrier-free access in all or most staff areas to ensure that artificial barriers to employment are not erected in the workplace.

Conclusion

The matter in this chapter is based on two simple premises:

1. Technology-use decisions should be driven by broad-based policy and management decisions made by the court and related agencies prior to judicial facility design. Technology is a means to implement the objectives of efficiency, security, and above all, justice. Technology itself is not the objective.
2. Once the broad-based policy decisions have been made and objectives defined, appropriate technologies should be selected and incorporated into the basic program and design for the facility at the earliest stage possible.

In light of those premises, we have attempted to identify current technologies and evaluate where their placement in specialized areas (security, law libraries, etc.) seems most appropriate. We have included enough detail to make the project manager aware of various technologies' existence and to provide some description of their capabilities. It has not been our purpose to describe the technologies in detail, as the rate of change in all areas (capability, reliability, price, etc.) is so rapid as to make such discussions very soon irrelevant. The key message is to stress the impact the selection of appropriate technology will have on all aspects of facility design and management after occupancy. Technology by itself is often relatively inexpensive in the context of a total facility project. However, lack of its application, or selection of an inappropriate technology, can have very expensive consequences.

6

Statewide Court Management Projects

This chapter deals with the purposes, methods, and implementation of comprehensive statewide court studies and the relationship of such studies to space management. Statewide court studies have the following characteristics:

- They have broad functional scope, encompassing most areas of court management, and may include prosecution, probation, and defense.
- They encompass all levels of the court system and major auxiliary systems.
- They develop a broad systems approach to improvement, usually in conjunction with a planning process or promotion or implementation of court reorganization.
- They are logistically complex, thus requiring strong project management.
- They require a high degree of participation from judicial system personnel during data compilation and for enhancing the quality and acceptability of study recommendations.
- They require considerable sensitivity to local concerns, since major studies are threatening to many people and are thus subject to harsh criticism.
- They require indigenous political support for implementation, since they are, for better or worse, political documents.
- Finally, and perhaps most important, they integrate and prioritize needs of the whole system and lay the groundwork for a systemwide approach.

Origin and Purposes of Comprehensive Statewide Court Studies

Court Planning as an Impetus to Studies

During the 1970s, the Law Enforcement Assistance Administration (LEAA) presided over the comprehensive criminal justice planning process. It was apparent from the outset that many states lacked enough information on their courts to formulate a plan. LEAA encouraged and, in a few instances, mandated states to develop more information in the courts area.

As defined by LEAA over the years, courts included prosecution and defense. By tacit agreement, it also included civil courts, since there was general recognition that civil and criminal courts were interdependent. Under federal legislation allocating funds for judicial planning at that time, court studies appeared to be exclusively judicial in nature.

Court Reorganization as an Impetus to Studies

Court reorganization has pervasive ramifications and requires a broad information base. The trend toward court unification in the past quarter century has thus been a great impetus to comprehensive statewide court studies. These studies have been responsive to indigenous needs and are more focused and issue-oriented than broad planning studies. These studies have originated either as a catalyst to court reorganization, so that a constitutional convention or legislative body had comprehensive data on the need for organizational change, or as a means to provide facts necessary for the implementation of constitutional amendments restructuring the judicial system. The latter type of study tends to orient more toward matters of administrative detail (e.g., list of employees affected by changeover, detailed financial data for budgeting), whereas the former is normally more oriented toward jurisdictional and organizational facts. Both types of studies are similar, since they both relate to court reorganization.

Court reorganization studies tend to attract more political scrutiny than planning studies because they are generally perceived as more immediately threatening to the *status quo*.

Since the termination of LEAA funding in the early eighties, the responsibility of conducting statewide court management studies rests on the shoulders of the states and their court systems. Owing to lack of adequate state funding for the court system, very few statewide court management studies have been completed during the past two decades.

State Agency Impetus for Court Studies

Since comprehensive court studies were almost invariably federally funded, a state agency must serve as sponsor and grant recipient. Sponsorship of a state agency did not connote strong support of, or even high interest, in the project. In instances in which there is a lack of judicial support, a criminal justice planning agency occasionally provides the main impetus for a comprehensive study and serves as the grant recipient.

Normally, a state-level judicial body would assume a role in the project. The logical candidates for this role would be the highest state court or the state court administrator, but in some states the directing agency might be a judicial council or conference.

In some instances, the judicial body serving as the grant recipient might actually be only a conduit for transferring funds to an organization or committee actively concerned with the court study, such as a constitutional convention, an advisory committee on court reorganization, or perhaps even a judiciary committee of the legislature.

Purposes of Comprehensive Court Studies

The purposes of comprehensive statewide court studies vary with the timing of the study in relation to court reorganization, but may involve one or more of the following:

- developing a uniform comprehensive database where none had existed
- providing factual data to promote or implement organizational changes
- providing a system overview and a prioritized statement of needs
- providing an integrated set of action alternatives for the entire court system

Scope of Comprehensive Court Studies

Juvenile Justice

Juvenile courts have a special status, since they are at the core of a juvenile justice system that extends well beyond the normal confines of the courts. Juvenile courts may include juvenile probation and aftercare workers, counselors, special detention facilities, special methods of appointing defense counsel, various juvenile institutions, group homes, and foster-care facilities. Since the juvenile justice system is fairly self-contained and has very special characteristics, it is frequently the subject of special study. It is important at the outset of any comprehensive court study to determine an approach to juvenile courts. If resources are adequate, juvenile courts can be the subject of specialized study within the context of the broader study. If resources are too limited, juvenile courts must either be excluded or studied within their strictly adjudicative features. The latter course is preferable, since juvenile courts are too much a part of the judicial system to be ignored in any general court study. Most juvenile judges hear cases other than juvenile matters, while many judges are reluctant to handle juvenile cases. Jurisdictional and organizational questions exist as to whether juvenile courts should be part of limited-jurisdiction or general-jurisdiction courts. Juvenile courts also require special facilities, which affect courthouse construction and utilization. Thus, even if a comprehensive court study does not explore the full ramifications of the juvenile court system, it must at least explore the role of the juvenile court as it relates to the operation of the judicial system.

Extrajudicial Components

A court system can be viewed as a self-contained entity or as part of a larger legal subsystem encompassing prosecution and indigent defense. In strictly conceptual terms, the larger scope is appealing, since it recognizes that courts are but one institution operating within the context set by organized, substantive, and procedural law. In practical terms, it is usually preferable to deal separately with the judicial system, since related legal institutions may be in the executive branch of government or otherwise beyond control of the judiciary.

Broad-scale court studies may involve prosecution and indigent defense. Inclusion of indigent defense is supportable, since few states have a well-structured defense system and are, therefore, dependent on the courts to administer the system of indigent defense. The inclusion of prosecutors and the attorney general's office is less defensible, since prosecutors are organizationally and politically independent from the judiciary and are usually reluctant to be included in a study where the principal focus is on courts.

As a general rule, comprehensive court studies are best confined to those system components that are clearly judicial in nature or are subject to at least some degree of court control.

The Judiciary as a Special Component

How a major study views the judiciary is important. A court system can be studied from the perspective that judges are simply a manpower resource. This will normally result in studies of judicial time allocation, judge-to-caseload ratios, judge-to-disposition ratios, and judges-to-population ratios. In this type of study, judges are viewed as a system input. In most cases, it would seem advisable to view judges both as a resource and as part of the judiciary. In studying the judiciary, the project should focus on such factors as judicial selection, tenure, qualification, education, discipline, compensation, and retirement.

Depending on study purposes and the structure of the judiciary in a particular state, it is desirable for a major court study to have a separate section dealing with the judiciary.

Auxiliary and Supporting Systems

A comprehensive court study must, to some extent, encompass those organizations, agencies, and institutions that support or are closely linked to the judiciary. Among the support services that must be considered for inclusion are adult probation, jury systems, courtroom security and prisoner transportation, clerical support, court reporting, and court administration.

Of these support services, only court reporting can be considered an automatic inclusion, since court reporters are so intimately involved with the trial and appellate processes. Court reporting would include technological innovations for recording and transcribing testimony.

It also would be unlikely to exclude clerical offices, court administrative offices, or the jury system. There are, however, political situations in which it may be advisable to exclude clerical offices and to avoid analysis of the jury system, especially if state authorities wish to avoid assumption of financial responsibility for the jury system.

Adult probation should be included in court studies, since it deals with the sentencing power of courts and is subject to court control. However, it is usually under control of an executive branch agency of state or local government, and built into the machinery of the correctional system. While adult probation could thus be viewed as appropriate subject matter for a correctional study, it is so integral to the judicial function that it is difficult to exclude from a court study.

Other marginal inclusions in court studies are pretrial detention, prisoner transportation, and courtroom security, often the functions of a sheriff or other law enforcement agencies. As in the case of adult probation, these services are essential to court operations but usually beyond direct administrative control of the courts. Generally, these services should be included within a comprehensive study.

In addition to support services, consideration should be given to auxiliary organizations that might justifiably be included in a court study, including state and local bar associations, law schools, organizations of judges, judicial conferences or councils, judicial discipline or conduct commissions, judicial nominating commissions, judicial compensation commissions, and organizations devoted to law reform.

Law Reform and Rule-Making

A court study cannot be a purely organizational analysis. Invariably, it will involve some study of the law. Consideration should be given to rules of appellate, civil, and criminal procedure. This does not require the type of analysis that precedes drafting of new rules, but simply an identification of major procedural problems that obstruct or complicate court operations, suggest the need for major revision of rules, or are inconsistent with current norms of procedural fairness.

A crucial underlying factor in studying procedure is the assessment of the rule-making power of the judiciary, and the exercise of this power. Another important factor is substantive law reform. It should not be the function of a court study to assess the criminal code or civil substantive law, but it is appropriate and desirable to consider aspects of substantive law widely identified as having a very heavy workload impact or as causing congestion. Increasingly, judicial leaders are urging legislators to be aware of the impact of new legislation on the judiciary, and consideration of substantive law from this perspective should be an important feature of major court studies.

Vertical Scope

A comprehensive courts study normally encompasses the appellate courts, general-jurisdiction and limited-jurisdiction trial courts, and these courts' administrative structure. The administrative function would include assessment of the authority of the supreme court and state court administrator, and the exercise of authority at the lower court levels by the hierarchy of presiding judges, clerks, and/or trial court administrators.

A comprehensive court study may not focus primarily on one tier of the court system. For example, a study of limited-jurisdiction trial courts would almost inevitably involve general-jurisdiction trial courts, even though this might be a tangential inclusion.

The principal limitation placed on the vertical scope of comprehensive court studies is usually at the bottom tier of the trial court system, that is, municipal courts and/or justice of the peace courts. These courts tend to be numerous, widely diffused, and lacking in good documentation. A decision to include or exclude these types of courts is essential in determining project scope.

Geographic Scope

In general, a comprehensive courts study is statewide, but there may be situations that require the geographic scope to be slightly restricted. Some states have regions that are quasi-autonomous or that tend to be *sui generis* for some reason. They could be omitted from a study. Typical exclusions might be a metropolitan center with a fairly unique court structure, strong aversion to state control, and detailed data on its own operations. At the other end of the scale, a decision may be made not to include very small counties because of their very low workloads.

Time Frame

An important element of project scope is the time frame to be covered. Should the study look only at current data or data for the past two, three, or five years? Where the study includes workload data from trial courts, time scope is an important decision affecting the length of the study, manpower needed, and the complexity of data compilation and analysis. This decision is not simply a function of study methodology, but a fundamental choice on resource allocation and study scope. The final choice has to be based on the purposes of the study, the quality of the local database, and the resources available for data compilation.

Static/Dynamic Alternatives

Closely related to deciding on the time scope is a decision on whether the study should analyze caseflow and system dynamics. This has significant implications on the cost and complexity of the study, and on its outputs.

In general, a statewide study is a poor vehicle to analyze the dynamics of a system functioning differently in each county. If serious problems in system operation exist, they often surface in workload and backlog figures. More subtle problems of caseflow blockage require tracking of cases in each county of the state and studying local calendaring practices and caseflow procedures. This is rarely feasible at the state level, but the study may determine the extent to which system dynamics are to be addressed.

If the purpose of the study is to establish long-term goals and policies or to effect structural change, the added burden of addressing system dynamics seems inappropriate. However, if the purpose is primarily to improve caseflow on a statewide basis, then it would be necessary to gather case tracking and calendaring data on a county-by-county basis.

Subject-Matter Scope

It is difficult to define the scope boundaries of a court study. The possible data acquisitions are infinite in number. It is possible, however, to define the basic data necessary to present a picture of each type of court within the system:

Organizational or jurisdictional data
- original and appellate subject-matter jurisdiction
- powers and duties
- geographic jurisdiction and subdivisions of court
- organization of court, including terms of court, number and distribution of judges, and sitting locations

Administrative data
- location of administrative authority
- choice of presiding judge and powers of presiding judge in relation to other judges and court personnel
- divisions of court and transfer of cases
- rule-making powers of trial courts

- supervisory powers over lower courts
- powers and duties of clerks, administrator, and other personnel

Workload data

- filings and dispositions
- pending caseloads

Resources data

- judges in relation to workload
- manpower resources, including court reporters, secretaries, law clerks, clerical support personnel, bailiffs, referees, masters, and commissioners
- facilities and equipment
- records management system

The data collected in the above categories answer four basic questions about each court in the system:

- What are its powers and functions?
- How is it organized and managed?
- What is its workload?
- What resources does it have to meet the workload?

The answers to the above questions provide a necessary but inadequate factual base. Additional inquiry and analysis must be made to identify problems that do not surface in the basic data-gathering, and to assess needs in each basic area of court management covered by the data-gathering, for example, case statistics, personnel finances, facilities, and records. In short, the basic data must be supplemented and interpreted by observation and informed inquiry.

General Management Considerations

Comprehensive court studies have some unique managerial features. The management of such a study involves principles and techniques of general applicability, for example:

- development of a work breakdown structure (WBS) outlining and describing each task and subtask
- scheduling of tasks and key events based on milestones and deliverable product deadlines
- issuance of directives and assignment of responsibilities of project personnel
- direction of project personnel and monitoring of progress
- management of project logistics
- management of project records and data

- monitoring of costs and billing or drawdown
- liaison with sponsoring agency, advisory boards, and other organizations involved in the project

The WBS for a comprehensive courts study is a specialized task structure, as set forth in table 6.1.

Involvement of Judiciary

Importance of Involvement

A comprehensive court study must be able to have impact on the judiciary and the political decision-makers. A study may be methodologically perfect but fail to reach the right audience. To ensure some degree of implementation for a study's recommendations, it is essential to involve the judiciary and, if possible, legislative and executive branch officials who have the power to promote or impede improvements in the state judicial system.

The advantages of having judges participate in a courts study are numerous:
- Their participation will increase the likelihood of greater confidence in the study results and reduce the likelihood of strong opposition.
- The study will benefit from their practical insights.
- Judicial involvement will reveal practical constraints on change.
- Judicial participation will tend to increase the level of cooperation by judicial system personnel.
- The study recommendations will reflect a knowledge of the system that can only be derived from widespread contact with judges and other system personnel.

In addition to judges, other key groups in the judicial system, such as clerks and court reporters, should be involved. Clerks, in particular, are important to study success, since they control data sources and generally have political influence.

Method of Involvement

In a major study, any or all of the following methods may be used to involve key system personnel:
- personal interviews
- questionnaires and data sheets
- inclusion on advisory boards
- contact with leaders of judicial, clerical, or reporter organizations
- informal personal contacts

Prior to any of the above contacts, a general announcement of the study through the media and some written communication to system personnel

Table 6.1. Work Breakdown Structure—Comprehensive Courts Study

Task/Subtask	Product	Responsible Party	Time Frame
1. Develop Project Plan			
a. Define project goals			
b. Develop task structure, personnel assignments			
c. Develop project schedule			
d. Develop project monitoring procedures			
e. Develop liaison procedures with sponsor, advisory boards			
f. Integrate subtask products into project plan			
2. Data Collection			
a. Definition of data requirements/preliminary study outline			
b. Identification of sources			
c. Develop survey forms			
d. Prepare logistical plan for field survey/mail surveys			
e. Conduct test visits			
f. Revise forms/procedures; review with advisory board			
g. Orient data collectors			
h. Advance site preparation			
i. Conduct surveys			
j. Documentation of surveys			
k. Data accuracy check			
l. Follow-up			
m. Coding/keypunching			
n. Final edit routines			
o. Filing/storage			
3. Data Analysis			
a. Assignment of analytical responsibilities			
b. Identification of key issues/analytical models			
c. Generation of special analyses/tables			
d. Revision of study outlines/review with advisory board			
4. Preparation of Study			
a. Develop quality control and production plan/formats/writing assignments			
b. Aggregation of descriptive analytical material by study category			
c. Preparation of section drafts			
d. Substantive and procedural editing			
e. Review with advisory board			
f. Preparation of final study			
g. Final editing			
h. Final presentation of finished copy			
5. Study Implementation			
a. Preparation of strategy for implementation			
b. Review with advisory board			
c. Revision of strategy			
d. Development of coordination mechanisms to implement strategy			
e. Orientation/turnover to coordinator			

from the chief justice or state court administrator is necessary. To be effective, different groups in the judicial system may have to be approached in different ways by different officials.

Personal contact provides the most effective method of data compilation. For economic reasons, such contacts must be selective. The responsibility for interviews with key system personnel should fall on senior project personnel and should not be delegated to junior professionals, for the following reasons:

- The quality of the response is higher if a peer relationship is established.
- The quality of the questions and the evaluation of the responses are improved by the experience of the interviewer.
- The status of the interviewer indicates respect for the person being interviewed and raises the level of importance attached to the interview.
- The person being interviewed has a chance to appraise and develop some confidence in the persons responsible for the study.
- Perhaps most important, the persons in charge of the study develop a sense of the local environment and a feel for the problems.

Data Collection

Data Collectors

The quality of data collection is largely dependent on the training and experience of the data collectors. In a major court study, it may be necessary, for reasons of cost and lack of available in-house manpower, to recruit temporary help. These individuals may be local people or may be college or law students. An advantage of using local people is that they may have more acceptance in those regions where nonindigenous collectors would be poorly received. In some regions of the country this can be a very important factor. The advantages of using college or law students is that they would bring a certain, desirable level of education to the job. Also, college or law school students may accept a low wage, since by their participation they may get marketable experience and/or college credit. Where either local people or students are recruited, a good training program and on-site supervision is an absolute requirement in order to ensure the accuracy, consistency, and overall usefulness of the data collected.

The use of specially recruited collectors involves many risks and drawbacks:

- The quality of performance will vary, and some collectors may prove to be very inadequate.

- Uniformity and commonality in data collection will be difficult to maintain.
- If the data collectors are young, as in the case of college or law school students, their youth may impede their acceptance and their ability to perform.
- If students are used, the study schedule may have to be adjusted to school terms, which may be a serious constraint.
- Lack of experience may limit the recruits' ability to make on-the-spot judgments when problems arise in data collection.

Where cost and time factors permit, it is preferable for the organization in charge of the study to use its own personnel. This ensures better quality and more uniformity in results; it also reduces the need for intensive training.

Definition of Data Requirements

The tendency in any study is to collect too much data without being specific about the purposes for which data are collected. The antidote is to develop data requirements based upon a detailed table of contents and anticipating the types of descriptive data and analytical formats to be included. This exercise, while necessarily subject to modification based on the scope and quality of the data actually collected, is an essential stop in focusing the data-collection effort, designing survey forms, and determining the relevant data sources.

Identification of Data Sources

Data requirements are initially defined in the abstract and represent the ideal. In practice, the ideal is unattainable. The desired data may not be available or may be available at a cost that does not warrant compilation. It is necessary, therefore, to systematically identify the possible sources of desired data and to confirm the validity of these sources. A considerable amount of data may be available at the state level, so that data compilation is greatly eased. The key to most comprehensive studies is to maximize the utilization of the state-level data, data which are usually valuable to the project. Among the types of data frequently found at the state level are the following: auditor data on court finances, local budgets collected by state agencies, state budgetary data on courts, court statistics compiled by the state court administrator's office, state police crime and arrest statistics, motor vehicle statistics on traffic cases, vital statistics on domestic relations cases, statewide probation statistics, juvenile statistics, and various studies and reports conducted by the state criminal justice planning agency. By definition, all legal research is state-level, since it derives primarily from state legislation, supreme court rules, and reports.

What emerges from an analysis of data sources is a systematized listing of the following facts pertinent to each piece of required data:
- Whether data are available or unavailable
- If data are available, are they available at the state or local level? In what type of records? With what degree of difficulty can they be obtained?
- If the data are unavailable, can they be developed, as through interviews, questionnaires, and so forth?

A matrix with the following characteristics can be developed:

Development of Data-Collection Plan

Once data sources are identified, a data-collection plan can be designed. This plan categorizes data needs by type of data collection. What normally evolves is a multifaceted data-collection effort, each facet producing a designated portion of the required data.

Such a plan is largely logistical in nature and has, as its main purpose, the integration of a varied data-collection effort. The plan should identify each phase of the data-collection effort, the detailed subtasks, the responsibility for each subtask, the timing of performance, and the corollary management tasks. Typically, such a plan will encompass personal interviews, mail-out surveys, field surveys, legal research, and state-level data collection.

Depending on the degree of specificity required in the study, sampling offers great opportunity to develop adequate data, particularly workload and financial data. This is probably best done by collecting complete data in a selected sample of counties and projecting statewide total, but it is conceivable that a limited sampling of data in all counties could be used to project statewide totals. The key question is whether the study is designed to develop a database to be updated or to develop data adequate for general policymaking or planning purposes. In the latter case, sampling should be considered; in the former case, it would not meet the purpose of the study.

Development of Survey Instruments

Part of the preparation for data collection is developing structured survey instruments. The structure of these instruments will determine the success of the study. The data should be returned in a form that ensures easy checking, commonality in data, accurate and easy compilation, and cross-comparisons. Each type of survey has its own logistics, which should be covered in the survey plan.

Field surveys may require a number of different forms involving data to be collected from multiple sources. A data collector may be given a small booklet of forms with an instruction manual and some intensive training. Survey forms and procedures should not be given to data collectors until after they have been field-tested.

Table 6.2. Identification of Data Sources

Section of Study	Data Requirements	Available	Location	Data Source	Degree of Difficulty
Chapter 3, Circuit Courts	Filing and dispositions of civil cases, 1994–96	Yes	Circuit clerk	Docket books	Fairly routine county-by-county collecting
	Jurisdiction/organization of circuit courts	Yes	Law library	State code	Routine legal research
	Name/tenure/salary of judges	Yes	State administration	Personnel records, lists	Simple, one-shot collecting
	Judicial attitudes about court administration	No		Mail survey	Responses from survey form are difficult to analyze

Among the areas covered in a field survey booklet are the following: filings and disposition data; case age and backlog data; case processing times (usually a sample); jury utilization data; court cost data; budget data; listing and categorization of personnel; and facility characteristics and utilization data. Much of these data should be quantitative, some of them requiring extensive worksheets to aggregate totals on the forms. Such worksheets should also be submitted for backup.

Data-collection forms should be structured to facilitate data processing. They could be designed as direct input, but usually it is preferable to have the data coded centrally as a means of quality control. This additional step is necessary where data collectors are untried.

State-level data-collection forms should also be structured, as should interview forms. Design of mail surveys involves a special problem. If they are sent to judges, lawyers, reporters, or clerks and involve attitudinal research, social science techniques should be used to structure the questions and to weigh the responses. Where a sample is used, care must be taken to use a statistically defensible sample selection and not to bias the survey by the covering letter and phone follow-up. Mail-out surveys also involve problems of respondent identification, which can be a factor in the types of questions asked and the subsequent analysis. Members of the bar, for example, may be reluctant to criticize judges in signed statements.

Development of Controls

A comprehensive statewide court study can easily get out of control. The scope and complexity of the effort requires centralized management control. Among the controls that must be imposed are the following:

- Interviews and visits should be centrally controlled to ensure that officials are not bothered unnecessarily, that schedules of project personnel are coordinated, and that information and possible problems derived from phone contact are passed on to data collectors.
- Distribution or mailing of survey materials should be logged, as should receipts of survey material.
- All survey forms returned by data collectors should be subjected to a control check for comprehensiveness, internal consistency, and adherence to directions.
- All coding of data should be handled centrally, as should interchanges of data with input personnel.
- All filing and duplication procedures should be handled centrally to ensure that data reaches their intended destination.
- Expenses and financial procedures must be monitored centrally.

Conduct of Survey

Conducting the various surveys is the most time-consuming part of the project. It may involve many data collectors, visits to all counties and numerous state agencies, and contacts with hundreds of individuals. Data collection may last from four to six months, or even longer, depending on the project work scope and the anticipated project outputs.

A key element of a field survey is preparation. This includes letters and calls to the persons and agencies to be surveyed, elicitation of cooperation, and even advance data gathering. Of equal importance is the ability of the data collector to establish rapport and follow instructions.

Even under the best of conditions, there will be human problems, such as the recalcitrant clerk, the hostile judge, or the wary reporter. There will be logistical problems such as the unforeseen special term of court conflicting with the site visit. There will also be problems with incomplete or poor records impeding the ability of the data collector to perform. Even the best-laid survey plan is subject to constant change. Some troubleshooting will be required. A major courts study may evoke much opposition and cannot be left entirely to data collectors.

Editing and Follow-Up

There will inevitably be errors of omission and commission on the part of data collectors. It is essential that some person is charged with the review of every incoming data-collection instrument. There should be a formal edit procedure whereby the instrument is reviewed and accepted by the person charged with this responsibility. Ideally, a checkoff list for the reviewer should be prepared. If acceptance is denied, some form of follow-up should be initiated. When a set of completed data instruments is accepted as part of the study database, it should bear the signatures of the data collector and reviewer.

Storage

The end result of the data collection is a complete range of data organized within a file structure adaptable to analysis and report generation.

The filing system is of significance. It should have subdivisions corresponding to the study outline so that data are systematically arranged in the order in which they will be used. Data should also be arranged to facilitate ease of retrieval and geographic analysis.

Some types of data should also be organized by county and/or court level. State-level data should be arranged by agency or source (e.g., attorney general or state auditor). Each set of survey forms should be separately aggregated (jury forms, facility forms, etc.).

Most survey instruments have to be reproduced several times to accommodate filing requirements. The convenience that this produces in utilizing the data and writing the report is immeasurable. Where data are voluminous, their efficient organization determines their value to the analyst and writer.

Transforming Data into Study Products

The Raw Data

The data-collection effort will result in aggregation of data by categories corresponding to the outline of the system description, that is, by chapter and section. Some of these raw data will prove worthless owing to incompleteness or inaccuracy. Some data will prove to be marginally relevant. By a process of selectivity, the person assigned to develop each segment of the system description will eventually utilize the key data to produce part of the overall description.

Production Methodology

Comprehensive court studies are not virtuoso one-person efforts. They involve many people in the process of report generation and require tight central coordination.

The essential features of a good production methodology are coordination of different authors and deadline enforcement, format and typing control, and quality control.

Where multiple authors are involved, there will obviously be differences in style, problems of smooth transition from section to section, differences in writing speed, and subject-matter overlap. The project manager must, therefore, define subject-matter divisions, enforce deadlines, and assume responsibility for smooth interrelationships between various sections. Format control involves control over typing and diagrammatic and tabular presentation. Early in the study, the project manager must decide on such points of format as the following:

- style and size of type to be used throughout the project
- pagination methods (within chapter, consecutive)
- indentation format
- numbering and capitalization of titles
- footnoting (particularly if there are extensive legal footnotes)
- table format and numbering
- numbering and entitlement of special figures and drawings
- appendix formats

Maintaining tight format control from the outset minimizes later editing. Extensive use of appropriate software programs is essential, since constant reiteration is a feature of large-scale production. The flow of material to and from production technicians should be logged and drafts clearly dated and identified, or inevitably there will be loss of material or mix-ups in drafts.

Quality control is very difficult when end products are voluminous. There is a strong temptation to skimp on editing time. Editing of complex court project products should be at least 20 percent of the production time, since the following factors and actions must be taken into account:

- checking of format, including pagination and table numbering
- checking of subject matter (the subject manager has personal responsibility for content as well as form)
- legal editing, checking of footnotes for form and accuracy
- checking of corrections

A most complex aspect of editing a large document is the enforcement of editing decisions. As corrections are made, they must be fed back into the production process, and checks must be made to ensure that corrections have been properly made. One person must always have a complete set of all drafts in their most advanced state of preparation to ensure that orderly progress is made toward an error-free product.

The Basic Products

A comprehensive court study will produce a number of products. The basic product will be an objective, factual description of the system. Other products will include recommendations and an implementation plan.

System Description

The system description should be separate and self-contained because of its volume and inherent qualities. The system description is not an advocacy document but a coherent presentation of facts bearing upon the structure and operation of a court system. It is advisable to separate it from other study products urging specific changes and methods of implementation. These latter products, while necessarily based on the facts set forth in the system description, are usually political, and should be relatively small in size to facilitate their dissemination and comprehension.

Integration of Data into a Systems Description. A system description consists in large part of the orderly presentation of facts according to a preconceived format. This exercise involves some special analysis but is largely taxonomic. This is an important contribution, since the starting point for any type of systemic improvement is a coherent description of the status quo.

However, a system description cannot consist entirely of a factual presentation of jurisdictional, organizational, workload, and financial data. There must be some element of interpretation and judgment, including some special analyses and interpretative commentary that establish correlations, make interjurisdictional comparisons, show trends, and point out special operational or structural problems. This implies an informed intelligence to the study and gives the data vitality and meaning.

The problem is to achieve a balance between interpretative comments and conclusion- or solution-oriented statements. An analyst usually approaches a study with some preconceived personal opinions as to what a court system should and ought to be, but it detracts from the system description if the analytical formats, tables, and commentary are narrowly focused and highly judgmental in tone. The basic system description should do no more than set forth the facts and their probable meaning. Argument on behalf of specific remedial steps is best contained in other study products.

Recommendations

Concurrently with preparation of a system description, recommendations should be prepared. In a small report, recommendations can be contained in the report, but in a major court study, it is advisable to make recommendations a separate product.

The recommendations should be accompanied by a concise summary of the factual support data, a summary that can be based on either excerpts from the basic system description or their conclusion from factual statements, citing pages in the system description. Recommendations should be based on facts and low key in tone. Philosophical speculation, gossipy tone, accusatorial comment, and strident advocacy detract from recommendations.

The key to recommendations is their possible implementation. This requires that the recommendations be realistically prioritized, be considered in the light of their feasibility, practicality, and cost; be linked to some incentive or strategy for implementation; and attract support of some indigenous force likely to utilize the recommendations effectively.

Implementation Plan

Recommendations are not self-executing. A strategy for implementation is worthless unless there is some political force interested in and capable of implementing recommendations.

Assuming such support, one of the final products of the study should be an itemized cost and time-phased list of action steps to implement priority recommendations. Accompanying this short-term action plan should be a long-term strategy. This document should be a concise statement with great specificity on needed legislation, rules, administrative actions, and funding.

Evaluation

In a strictly technical sense, evaluation of a court study should be based on a formal research design integrated into the project to test stated hypotheses in quantified terms. Such a formal approach is not feasible, since the cause-effect relationship between studies and measurable system impact is tenuous.

How then can a study be evaluated? A study has only one measure. Either it was a catalyst for change or it wasn't. If the study recommendations were implemented or led to other ameliorative action, the study may be judged to have met its goals.

Role of Space Management in Comprehensive Court Studies

General Relationships

Court facilities are a major resource of any judicial system. Where facility resources are inadequate, court operations may be impeded, court reorganization may be inhibited, and implementation of certain procedural reforms—such as broader use of jury trials—may be rendered difficult. Therefore, a comprehensive court study must address court facilities.

Unless funds are unlimited, comprehensive court studies obviously cannot achieve the level of detail associated with a specialized facility study. Data collection must be more limited and clearly justified by its relationship to major issues.

There are three types of facility data that should be included in a comprehensive courts study:

- data on financing of court facilities
- data on utilization of court facilities
- data on adequacy of facilities

Facility Financing

Despite a strong trend toward state financing of trial courts, states are reluctant to assume the cost of court facilities. The burden of providing such facilities continues to be a local responsibility in most states.

The logic of unification calls for state assumption of facility costs, and this issue should be considered in any governmental court study. The questions to be answered are the following:

- What would it cost to assume the cost of existing facilities?
- What would it cost to upgrade existing facilities to meet minimum standards or to achieve regional consolidation of facilities?
- What is the best method for state assumption of this financial responsibility?
- What, if anything, can the state do to defray the cost of this added responsibility?

To determine the cost of assuming current court facilities, a general court study should gather information on proportionate court share of current courthouse maintenance costs, square footage of court facilities and market rental value of space in each county, list of outstanding bonded indebtedness on courthouses, and the use of public-building authorities and other courthouse funding and financing building devices.

It would be a heavy burden for a general court study to prepare costs of facility upgrading or regional consolidation—it would require the development of facility standards and a level of factual detail not realistically attainable in a generalized court study. However, a general study could propose various alternatives for state assumption of financial responsibility, including rental of space from localities; state assumption of court facility costs by paying for the *pro rata* share of all courthouse maintenance and for court facility renovation; preparation of a capital improvement budget for courts; state support of local courthouse bond issues; and the use of a state public-building authority with lease-back of court facilities.

A final consideration is an increase in the state share of court revenue to cover facility cost. A special fee for facility usage is a source of state revenue in North Carolina.

Utilization of Court Facilities

Most court facilities are grossly underutilized. In many rural areas, courtrooms are used for public meetings and many purposes of a nonjudicial nature. Ironically, court facilities, unused for long periods, may suddenly be subject to excessive demand during a term of court. For example, a county court and circuit court may be in session simultaneously with only one courtroom available.

It is, therefore, important for any general court study to develop data on the actual time each courtroom is in use during the year, distinguishing between jury courtrooms and nonjury courtrooms; the use of courtroom facilities by specific courts (circuit court, county court, juvenile court) and degree of shared use; and conflict situations in which two courts make demands on the same facilities during certain court sessions.

The data gathered on facility utilization may bear heavily on the following issues:

- The excessive supply of unused space may lend support for construction of regional court facilities
- The amount of unused jury courtroom time may be used to indicate that the system could, in many parts of the state, absorb an expanded number of jury trials without new construction.
- In a system with justices of the peace operating in outlying areas, the

data might justify centralizing those hearings that should be conducted on the record (e.g., a preliminary hearing in a felony case).

Courtroom utilization data are a valid indicator of judicial bench time, and consequently, some obfuscation of facts may be anticipated. Court minutes represent a good source of data, but actual observation is preferable, if economically defensible. Generally, courtroom utilization has to be estimated from interviews and an examination of relevant records, unless an ongoing method of recording utilization can be established early in the study.

Adequacy of Facilities

A key facility issue is the power of a state court administrator to set and enforce standards for facilities in order to ensure their adequacy.

A general court study may not be able to measure in detail the adequacy of court facilities. However, it can usually produce an inventory of existing court facilities, which will show that certain types of facilities are lacking in various locations (jury assembly rooms, witness rooms, jury deliberation rooms, judicial chambers, etc.), and an assessment of major deficiencies in courtrooms and other court-related facilities.

A general court study can provide rough facility inventory and define the need for upgrading facilities. In this regard it may be helpful to include questions on facility adequacy in any survey of judges or other court personnel. Realistically, however, general court studies cannot be expected to go beyond establishment of fundamental needs.

Relationship of Facilities to Study Design

Prior to any comprehensive court study, careful consideration should be given to the relationship of facilities to the overall study design. Some study issues pertain directly to facilities, while other issues involve facilities indirectly. These issues should be systematically enumerated as a prelude to defining the requirements for facility data and subsequent analysis.

Trends in Court Studies and Space Management

Future Court Studies

It is highly probable that the upsurge of interest in judicial planning will lead to a large number of studies and a great deal of data collection. It is by no means certain, however, that there will be an increase in comprehensive court studies, since they are costly, lengthy, and administratively difficult, and often excite concern.

A few states may launch massive studies, but it is more likely that studies and data-collection efforts will be discrete and narrow. Special-purpose studies are adequate for most purposes but may lack an overall management perspective.

Space management is of sufficient importance that either a comprehensive or special-purpose study should have a facilities component or a facilities impact statement. It is inconceivable, for example, that a jury management study would not in some way address juror facilities; that a records management study would ignore space trade-offs; or that a personnel study would ignore working space for court employees. As judicial management increases in sophistication, facility considerations should become an increasingly significant factor in most special-purpose studies and in every comprehensive study.

Unification Trends as a Factor in Space Management

The profusion of court facilities across this country is an indicator of the traditional fragmentation of court systems. Courts have been so intertwined with local government that they are located in municipal buildings, justice of the peace offices, county courthouses, and various specialized court buildings. The key court facility is the county courthouse. It is a focal point of legal and governmental activity and an important institution of local government. In many counties, it is still a major event when there is a term of court at the courthouse.

Courts have traditionally been an integral part of the county government and part of the courthouse milieu. Judges and clerks have enjoyed political status within county government and sometimes have wielded great power. This traditional pattern, however, is being eroded by the trend toward court unification under state control.

Inexorably, the nexus between courts and local government is being broken. Counties have found it increasingly difficult and costly to support courts, and the court function is gradually passing to the state level of government. This process is part of a general diminution in the power of county government stemming from the static nature of the property-tax base, declining population in rural areas, and a growing trend toward regionalization of services. Regionalization is partly a function of efficiency, and partly a function of a transportation technology, which permits broader service areas.

As courts disengage themselves from local government, a number of problems arise. Of these, one of the foremost is the question of facilities. State governments have shown a great reluctance to assume the cost of trial court facilities and have, for the most part, been content to leave this responsibility with local government. The reasons for this reluctance include politically frightening cost factors, poorly defined administrative mechanisms for state assumption of facility costs, and low priority assigned to facility needs.

Until such time as states face up to their responsibilities for facilities within a unified system, there are unlikely to be any major changes in the nature of court facilities. Existing courthouse facilities will be renovated and some new courthouses will be built, but funding and organizational constraints will continue to dominate space management.

Capital Improvement Programs

Unified state court systems sorely need capital improvement programs for court facilities. This will supply the long-term financial strategy now lacking. The next decade should witness some breakthroughs in financing of court facilities and the relationship of state funding strategy to local courthouse bonds.

Judicial planners are not presently thinking in these terms, but a good judicial plan should include not only projection of operating budget needs but also a capital improvement budget. At present, facility decisions are made locally with no coherent space management philosophy or funding strategy.

Dedicated Regional Facilities

Regional trial court facilities are considered futuristic. The conventional wisdom is that the legal system is too deeply intertwined with the county to permit such a radical development. Yet an almost inevitable corollary of state assumption of facility costs will be some consideration of supracounty facilities dedicated entirely to court purposes.

Regional facilities would encounter many obstacles within the present system of operation:

- juror selection is conducted on a county basis
- state laws often compel courts to sit in various county seats
- state constitutions often accord a criminal defendant a right to trial in a specific county
- venue is based on the county
- county chauvinism and provincialism are strong

The above obstacles notwithstanding, judicial planners have an obligation to think the unthinkable and to explore alternatives. From a strictly logical point of view, regional court facilities offer many advantages:

- resources could be focused on fewer facilities
- facilities would be dedicated to court use and could be constructed for that purpose
- court could be in continuous session
- scheduling conflicts would be reduced by centralized calendar control

A corollary regional issue is the handling of juvenile court facilities. Regional detention facilities are being created in some rural areas, raising the question of why there should not be a system of regional juvenile courts presided over by a full-time juvenile judge for the whole region.

Statewide Judicial Management and Space Management Projects

While statewide judicial management projects to date have not addressed the space management components to any extent, full integration of judicial management and space management concepts and solutions can be accomplished only through an integration of related judicial management and space management components.

This integration has not been accomplished for four reasons:

- *High cost in conducting detailed joint judicial management and space management projects.* The cost of conducting a comprehensive judicial system and space management project would normally be too high for any state to afford without the assistance of federal and/or private foundation funds.
- *The need for highly specialized consultants from a number of specialized disciplines in related fields.* Within the area of judicial management, personnel or consultants must be experienced in components such as caseflow, jury personnel, and records management; in information, data-processing, and communication systems; in budgeting, funding, and financing techniques; and in law and public administration. In the area of space management, the compilation of data, the evaluation and development of recommendations, and the recommending of solutions would require expertise in planning, statistics, projections, architecture, engineering construction, and project financing. The collaborative effort necessary for integrating an enormous amount of statistical data from various fields is difficult and complicated.
- *The need for complex intergovernmental agency involvement and cooperation throughout the project duration.* This need is especially felt during critical project funding, financing, and implementation.
- *The lack of appropriate administrative and management experience, and the reluctance of the court system to provide the necessary leadership.* For the successful development of such an ambitious and far-reaching comprehensive master plan, experience and leadership are needed and are often lacking.

The following chapter provides a detailed description of the work scope, methodology, organization, and management of statewide judicial facilities projects.

7

Statewide Space Management Projects

One of the major concerns of any state court system, and a special concern of state and trial court administrators, is the lack of adequate and suitable facilities for effective administration of justice. Most county courthouses were constructed toward the end of the last century and during the prewar period of this century. They were designed, structurally, to last for centuries. If our justice and social systems were to remain unchanged, these impressive and massive courthouses would probably continue to serve, quite adequately, the needs of the judicial system. While changes are slow within the judicial branch, major reforms over the past two decades have required serious reevaluation, not only of court procedures, administration, and programs, but also of the physical facilities in which justice is administered.

Through the tremendous strides achieved in the field of court management and judicial administration, largely due to the catalytic efforts of former chief justice Warren Burger, new concepts of judicial administration have been introduced and implemented in most of the fifty state court systems. Common business management techniques are being applied to court management. Prior to the late sixties, the judicial system, though viewed with awe and reverence, existed and operated in an "ivory tower" atmosphere, insulated in large part from the influence of external forces and yet financially dependent on the other two branches of government. The traditional concept of slow change in the judiciary still persists in many states today. However, the training of court administrators in recent years, specifically to manage court systems in a more scientific and effective manner, has drastically changed the organization, administration, and procedures of many state court systems.

With reform came improved organization. The need for a "unified" court system became the cry of the late sixties and the seventies, although such a concept was advocated many decades earlier by prominent jurists. A unified court system may mean many things to many people within the judiciary. For example, it could be a one-tier trial court with several functional divisions, or a two-tier trial court and a one- or two-tier appellate court. Regardless of terminology, each state undergoing judicial reform attempts to establish a unified court system in accordance with local needs and assessment of efficiency by the judiciary of that state.

On an operational level, the unified court system usually means centralized administration of the judiciary under the chief justice of the state's highest appellate court and the state court administrator, who normally serves at the pleasure of the supreme court or its chief justice. This centralized administration may or may not extend throughout the entire judiciary. In some states, the state court administrator has almost autonomous authority to administer the many components of judicial administration, including the management of court personnel, budget, salary, facilities, furniture, equipment, and supplies. The state judiciary prepares its own budget, submits it directly to the legislative assembly, and lobbies heavily for its passage. On the other hand, the state court administrator may act only as an executive assistant to the chief justice, with administrative responsibility only at the state supreme court level, and does not administer or manage the entire court system.

To the active and effective state court administrator, judicial reform and administration must be carefully integrated to serve the goal of better justice. Changes in criminal, civil, juvenile, and probate procedures may have significant impact on the assignment of judges and court personnel and on the use of facilities. Reorganization of the judicial system invariably has a significant impact on personnel and facilities. Court management programs involving improvement of case processing, jury and records management, and installation of technological systems and equipment require changes in the amount, as well as in the relationship, of spaces in courthouses.

Since court facilities are such an important component of judicial administration, why are many courthouses so inadequate, unsuitable, deteriorated, and poorly maintained? One of the main reasons is that, with few exceptions, providing court facilities is the responsibility of the local board of county commissioners or county supervisors or other local governmental entity. Invariably, the statutes would have the local community responsible for providing and maintaining adequate facilities for court use. As a result, in richer areas, large courthouses have been constructed with luxurious, but sometimes nonfunctional, facilities far in excess of what is needed, while many poorer jurisdictions are not even able to provide proper maintenance of their existing courthouses, which are left to deteriorate with age and fall into disrepair.

Another reason for the dilapidated condition of many courthouses is the inability of local authorities and judges to develop an amiable working relationship. It is not uncommon for local boards to deny that court's requests for capital improvement because such costs are not justifiable in terms of local priorities. Regardless of the reason, a poor working relationship between the executive and judicial branches has usually resulted in the latter being the loser. Even a court order may not be effective in requiring an antagonistic county board to take appropriate action. In most instances, nothing has been gained through confrontation. Improvement of judicial facilities can best be achieved through willing cooperation and understanding demonstrated by both branches.

In many instances, the local authorities and the court have not been sufficiently innovative in their thinking and planning approaches. There are several feasible methods of financing judicial facility improvements without major expenditure of local tax money. Long-term investment of capital improvement funds, phased implementation over a period of several years with proper long-term planning, utilizing revenue-sharing funds and public-building authorities to greater advantage, and establishing programs for college students to participate on minor construction and renovation work are but a few of many available methods of financing renovation and construction projects with reduced local expenditures. Of course, there are also state and federal sources of funding that are available if the local authority and the court are willing to collaborate and to invest the time and effort to obtain such funding.

The inequities of the quality of judicial facilities are apparent in most states. There are several methods of correcting such inequities. One obvious method is the assumption of the responsibility for judicial facilities by the state. This could be achieved through the state purchasing the courthouses at a nominal fee and being responsible for their maintenance, upkeep, and improvement, or through the state leasing the facilities occupied by the court system at fair rental values to be established, or through the state subsidizing needy local areas on a selective basis to ensure that judicial facilities are provided according to minimum acceptable standards and design guidelines.

The establishment of facility standards and design guidelines for the judiciary would not be beneficial unless the judiciary or the state is willing and has the authority to enforce their application in courthouse renovation and construction projects. The state court administrator should be the overseer of all such projects to make sure that plans and designs of court facilities satisfy the requirements set forth in adopted standards and guidelines. If the state should assume the responsibilities for judicial facilities, the state court administrator, with the help of experienced consultants, should be given the authority to approve, modify, or reject designs for renovation or construction projects at early planning stages.

For the state to play a more active role in the area of judicial facilities, there is the need for a comprehensive master plan with integrated short-term improvements of local courthouses and long-term development of judicial facilities on a statewide basis. This plan must be feasible, flexible, and economical—it should be feasible for implementation within the existing political and administrative structure of the state; it should be flexible enough to accommodate the changing needs of the judiciary; and it should be accomplished at the lowest cost. In other words, the plan must be operationally optimal and cost-effective.

Because centralization of administration is believed to provide a more effective and economical method of providing justice, many state court systems have tried over the years to achieve this goal. Yet few to date have succeeded. However, there is little doubt that the trend of the future will be toward centralization of judicial administration and consolidation of personnel units and facilities to maximize effectiveness and minimize duplication and unnecessary expenditure. With this premise, it is crucial that state court systems, in the process of reform and reorganization, be cognizant of the advantages of and need for a statewide judicial facilities planning and management project, preferably conducted in conjunction with court management programs on a statewide basis.

Goals and Objectives of Statewide Projects

The ultimate goal of statewide court projects is the full integration between court management programs and space management projects on a statewide basis. The judiciary has not yet reached this level of sophistication and awareness. To conduct such integrated statewide projects is also very costly in large states with a great number of counties and courthouse locations.

It is essential that each state, in its attempt to achieve its unified court system, know in some detail existing court facilities at each court location throughout the state, and the means by which these facilities are made available. As discussed in the previous chapter, if the reorganization of the judicial system results in centralizing administration, consolidating facilities into regional trial centers, or creating administrative judicial districts, the impact on facility needs would be very significant. If the state is ignorant about existing court facilities and their utilization, the implementation of any reorganization plan would be very difficult. Consequently, one of the first goals of a statewide project is to develop a complete inventory of all court and court-related facilities through specially designed data sheets and questionnaires, and through personnel surveys of existing facilities and interviews of current staff.

Once the inventory is completed, the information should be organized in a format conducive to analysis, retrieval, and update. To keep the inventory current, its format must allow for easy information update. This could be accomplished either manually or by automated data-processing systems. If the state court system has an automated court management information system, the facility inventory information could be incorporated within the same system. This would encourage future integration of court management and space management information in developing solutions to related management and facility problems.

Based on the inventory and an in-depth analysis of court organization, administration, operations, personnel, equipment, furniture, and facilities, the next major task is to develop judicial facility standards and design guidelines for statewide application in preparing recommendations for short-term and long-term facility improvements. There are three levels of facility standards: space standards for individual spaces; component and facility standards (e.g., courtrooms and ancillary facilities); and space standards for courthouses of various sizes (e.g., single-courtroom and multicourtroom courthouses). The facility requirements of the Americans with Disabilities Act (ADA) have significantly affected facility standards in recent courthouses. Judicial facility standards and design guidelines should remain flexible over the duration of the statewide project. Once the comprehensive master plan has been finalized and the standards and guidelines adopted, their application to the design and planning of courthouse construction and renovation projects should be enforced and monitored.

Another major task of statewide projects is the development of a comprehensive short-term improvement plan containing recommendations for each courthouse location. These recommendations include minor renovation and departmental space reorganization that can be implemented at minimum cost. If counties are responsible for providing adequate and suitable court facilities, such costs should be well within the financial and budgetary constraints of the individual local governments, provided they investigate innovative alternative sources and methods of funding. If the court system continues its present operation, the implementation of these recommendations and suggestions should adequately accommodate the short-term needs of the court system.

The ultimate objective of such a project, however, is to prepare a master plan that integrates short-term facility improvement with long-term implementation of a judicial facilities master plan. In order to accomplish this, future needs of the court system have to be projected over a period of time, usually at five-year intervals over a twenty-year planning period. In addition to the analysis of historical demographic and economic growth trends and parameters, consideration of the following factors would be very important in projecting future caseloads and workload and personnel and facility needs: anticipated changes in the judicial system, including new bills being considered by the legislature; court rules that may change procedures and operations; administrative changes in case assignment and personnel facility use; and possible adoption of technological changes including records imaging, data processing, videotaping, and real-time reporting.

With projected personnel and facility needs, and having developed facility standards and design guidelines, the next major task is the development of a preliminary and substantially detailed judicial facility program of facility needs, taking into account possible changes in its organizational structure as well as in operational and personnel needs. The facility program contains all essential and measurable information required for the development of the comprehensive statewide master plan. It includes facility program tables, personnel organizational charts, and functional and spatial relationships diagrams. The facility program logically leads to the development of the comprehensive plan, which integrates short-term facility improvements with long-term facility development, based on anticipated policy and budgetary decisions.

Having developed a feasible comprehensive master plan, the most vital goal is to implement it. Cost estimates, including construction, renovation, maintenance and annual operating expenses, and depreciation costs, should be prepared. If there are alternative plans, various cost estimates should be developed for comparative purposes. Depending on the direction of state participation, it might be essential to develop the criteria for assessing fair rental value of judicial facilities owned and operated by local governments. If the state should decide to assume the cost of operating and maintaining local court facilities, the basis for the state to purchase or reimburse would need to be determined. Methods of financing and funding judicial facilities projects should be evaluated at local, state, and federal levels, and recommendations should be made on the most economical method of implementing the comprehensive plan in the sequence that would provide the court system with suitable and adequate facilities. Government-judiciary working relationships in facility renovation and construction projects should be analyzed, and an atmosphere of cooperation and collaboration between branches of government should be established. Since the implementation of the comprehensive master plan may span several fiscal years, a schedule of phased implementation, based on anticipated budgetary constraints of the state, should be prepared to aid long-term financial planning.

To summarize, those persons carrying out a statewide judicial facilities planning and management project should do the following:

1. Complete a detailed inventory of court and court-related facilities at each court location throughout the state.
2. Develop a system of judicial facilities information for rapid analysis, and convenient storage, retrieval, and update.

3. Establish facility standards and design guidelines for court facilities of different sizes and functions for statewide application.
4. Recommend short-term improvements that could be quickly implemented at existing judicial facilities locations with minimum local expenditure.
5. Project court personnel and facility needs of the judicial system over the planning period, at five-year intervals.
6. Prepare a comprehensive statewide master plan, integrating short-term improvements with long-term facility needs of the judicial system, based on anticipated policy and budgetary decisions regarding the future direction of the judicial system.
7. Recommend the most feasible and economical implementation process, including cost estimates; fair rental values; method of local, state, and federal participation; financing, funding, and budgeting of facility projects; phased implementation scheduling; and government judiciary relationships in the implementation process.

Methodology and Tasks

The activities sequence chart (figure 7.1) and the project work plan and time schedule (table 7.1) show the tasks, subtasks, and activities to be performed in conducting a statewide judicial facilities planning and management project. The activities sequence chart shows the activities to be performed by the consultants as well as those to be performed by the court project liaison and by personnel in local court facilities statewide.

The following is a summary of the more significant tasks of the project arranged in approximate sequence:

- Organize project planning, coordination planning, and task scheduling.
- Develop, test, and distribute initial data sheets, questionnaires for key personnel, and building- and space-use information sheets for statewide initial data compilation.
- Review and analyze available and compiled initial data and information.
- Develop and test detailed survey questionnaire for statewide survey of judicial facilities.
- Conduct statewide on-site survey of court and court-related facilities.
- Organize, analyze, and evaluate data and information compiled:
    - Analyze anticipated changes in the judicial system.
    - Analyze court organization, administration, and management systems.

- Analyze common and special problems and deficiencies.
- Analyze departmental functions, personnel, and facilities.
- Develop a judicial facilities information system for easy analysis, and convenient storage, retrieval, and update.
- Establish judicial facility standards and design guidelines for statewide application.
- Apply judicial facility standards and design guidelines to improve the quality of existing facilities.
- Develop short-term improvements at minimum expenditure for short-term implementation.
- Prepare program of personnel and facility needs, projected over the planning period, at five-year intervals.
- Develop comprehensive long-term statewide master plan of facility management, based on anticipated changes in the judicial system.
- Recommend feasible and optimum implementation process:
  - Determine construction, renovation, operation, maintenance, and other costs.
  - Define criteria for assessment of fair rental values of judicial facilities.
  - Evaluate methods of financing, funding, and budgeting of judicial facilities.
  - Schedule phased implementation of comprehensive master plan.
  - Recommend improvements in government-judiciary relationship for implementation of comprehensive master plan.
  - Determine need for in-house space management capabilities within state court administrator's office for future coordination and supervision of comprehensive master plan implementation.

Description of Tasks

Project Planning and Data Compilation

The approach in conducting statewide judicial facilities projects should be cost-effective. The goals of each state conducting such a project could be quite different, and the approach should be sufficiently flexible in order to accommodate the specific needs of the particular state court system. For example, the goal of one state might be to establish judicial facility standards and design guidelines; another to compile a useful facility inventory; a third to plan for more effective statewide security systems in courthouses; and a fourth to develop a comprehensive master plan for phased implementation.

The project planning, coordination, and scheduling phase of statewide judicial facility projects is a crucial phase of the project. A firm with extensive

Figure 7.1. Statewide Judicial Facilities Project—Activities Sequence Chart

TASKS	I: PROJECT PLANNING, COORDINATION & SCHEDULING 1/2 – 1 MONTH (1st Month)						
CONSULTANTS		STUDY & EVALUATE available information/ reports, etc.	STUDY Judicial System	STUDY & EVALUATE floor plans & building data			SCHEDULE tasks and subtasks of project
MEETINGS & REVIEWS	INITIAL MEETING to define work scope & project methodology						
PROJECT LIAISON	APPOINT Project Liaison		PROVIDE available relevant information/ reports, etc.	NOTIFY court personnel about project, request data and floor plans		COORDINATE & monitor floor plans & data	
COURT/ COUNTY PERSONNEL STATEWIDE					PROVIDE available relevant information & court facility floor plans		

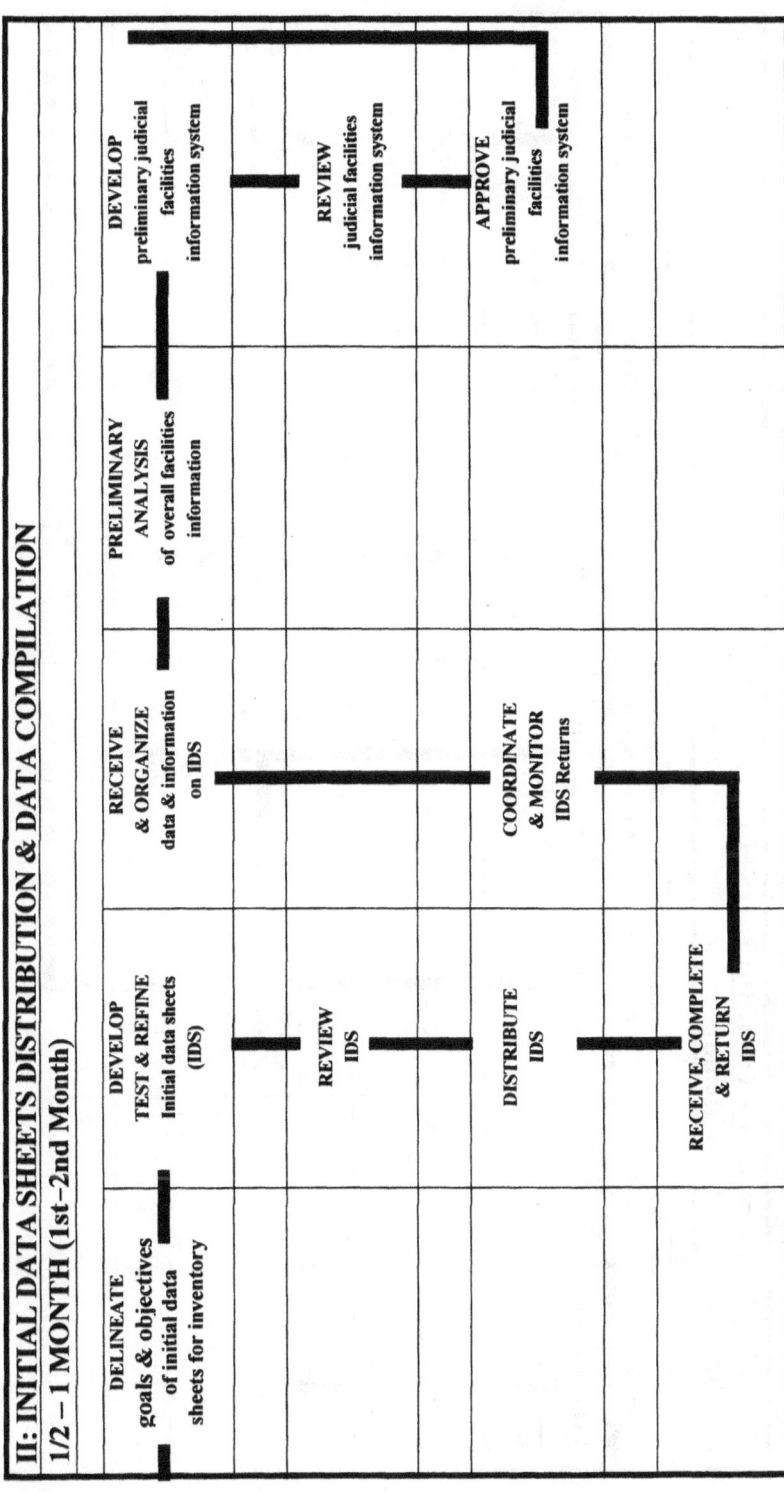

Figure 7.1—*Continued on next page*

Figure 7.1—Continued

III: STATEWIDE SURVEY OF JUDICIAL FACILITIES
1 – 6 MONTHS (2nd–8th Month)

PLAN for site visits to all court locations	DETAILED scheduling of site visits	DEVELOP, TEST, & REFINE Detailed Questionnaire	FINALIZE travel arrangements for site visits	CONDUCT site survey & data compilation; SKETCH facilities	ORGANIZE & ANALYZE data and information	DEVELOP Judicial facilities information system
REVIEW plan for site visits						REVIEW Compiled facilities & information system & inventory
NOTIFY & ARRANGE for site visits by consultants		MAKE TRAVEL ACCOMMODATIONS arrangements for project team				CHECK inventory for accuracy & applicability
			PREPARE for site visits	CONDUCT site visits with consultants		
				SUPPLY relevant information and data		

IV: DATA ANALYSIS AND EVALUATION							
3 – 8 MONTHS (3rd–10th Month)							
ANALYZE judicial system	ANALYZE anticipated changes in judicial system	EVALUATE impact of changes	EVALUATE population & economic growth of state & counties	PROJECT needs of judicial system: caseload, personnel, facilities	ANALYZE Caseflow operations & anticipated changes	ANALYZE common problem & deficiencies & suggest solutions	
▬▬▬▬▬	▬▬▬▬	▬▬▬					
				▬▬▬			
▬▬▬▬▬▬▬▬▬▬▬▬▬▬▬▬▬▬▬			INTERMEDIATE REVIEW if necessary				
PROVIDE detailed information on judicial system & anticipated changes		CONTINUAL EVALUATION of analytical process & analysis results					
▬▬▬▬							
		EVALUATE & PROVIDE FEEDBACK on process if necessary					
▬▬▬▬							

Figure 7.1—*Continued on next page*

Figure 7.1—Continued

V: ESTABLISH FACILITY STANDARD & DESIGN GUIDELINES
1 – 3 MONTHS (6th–12th Month)

CONDUCT departmental & court analysis: personnel responsibilities, facility relationships, findings	DELINEATE flexibility of standards & guidelines	ANALYZE IN DETAIL operations, activities, people, and spaces	REVIEW available standards & guidelines for individual spaces	ESTABLISH facility standards & design guidelines for individual spaces	ESTABLISH Standards & guidelines for combined & grouped facilities in locations of different sizes	TEST standards & guidelines
REVIEW analysis, projections, problems, deficiencies, changes, solutions			INTERMEDIATE REVIEW if necessary			REVIEW facility standards & design guidelines for the judicial system
APPROVE analysis, projections, problems, deficiencies, changes & solutions			REVIEW findings, standards, & guidelines when necessary			APPROVE facility standards & design guidelines by Supreme Court
OBTAIN selected feedback if necessary						OBTAIN selective feedback on standards & design guidelines if necessary

VI: APPLICATION OF JUDICIAL FACILITY STANDARDS & DESIGN GUIDELINES
3–9 MONTHS (7th–20th Month)

REVIEW overview charts, tables & information on statewide judicial facilities	RECOMMEND method for adoption & application of standards & guidelines	APPLY standards & guidelines to specific problems & deficiencies	DEVELOP short-term master plan improvements at min. cost to counties	PROJECT long-term facility needs taking into account anticipated changes	PREPARE master plan of judicial facilities in the state
			REVIEW short-term master plan		REVIEW master plan & projected needs
		REVIEW application of standards & guidelines	APPROVE short-term master plan		APPROVE facility master plan
		OBTAIN selective feedback on application of standards & guidelines			

Figure 7.1—*Continued on next page*

Figure 7.1—Continued

VII: IMPLEMENTATION PROCESS
2–4 MONTHS (9th–22nd Month)

COST/RENTAL					FINANCING & BUDGET	
ESTABLISH construction operation & maintenance costs	ESTIMATE replacement values for court facilities	ESTABLISH criteria for setting fair rental values for court facilities	ESTABLISH fair rental values	APPLY fair rental values to all court locations	OUTLINE & EVALUATE financing methods	BUDGET construction and/or renovation expenditures
		REVIEW criteria		REVIEW fair rental values for court facilities		
PROVIDE available information		REVIEW & APPROVE criteria		REVIEW & APPROVE fair rental values for court facilities	PROVIDE available information	
PROVIDE available information					PROVIDE available information	

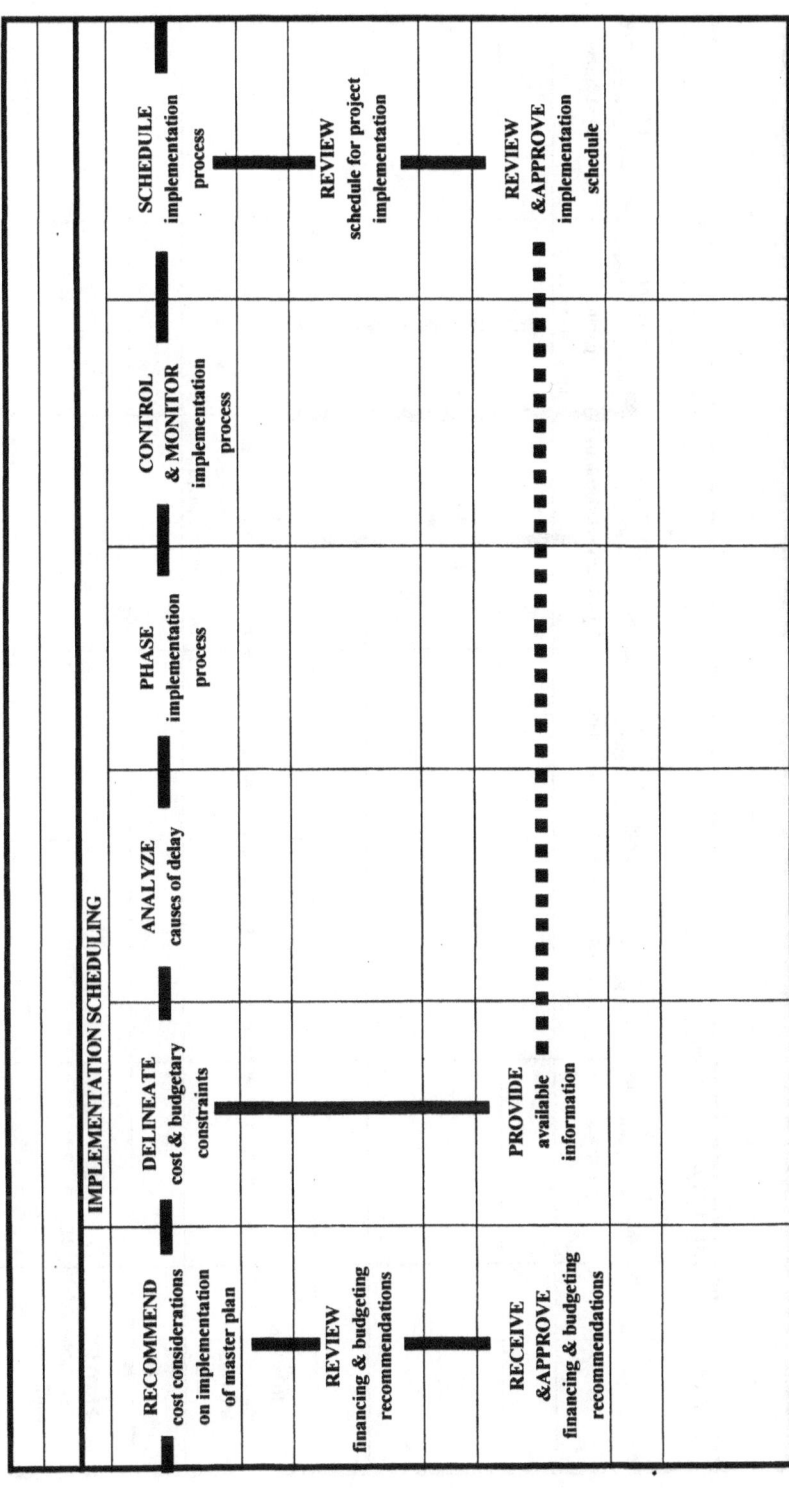

Figure 7.1—*Continued on next page*

Figure 7.1—Continued

GOVERNMENT – JUDICIARY RELATIONSHIPS					IN-HOUSE CAPABILITIES	
DEFINE problems & deficiencies	EXPLAIN relationship problems	IMPACT of government - judiciary relationships	SUGGEST implementation schedule	SUGGEST Improvement of government - judiciary relationships	DEFINE extent of client's in-house capabilities in space management	DETERMINE cost of providing such capabilities
				REVIEW government - judiciary relationships		
PROVIDE available information				REVIEW & APPROVE recommendations on relationships	PROVIDE available information	
PROVIDE available information						

VIII: FINAL REPORT PREPARATION PROJECT
1–3 MONTHS (11th–24th Month)   (End of 12th–24th Month)

TASKS						
CONSULTANTS	PREPARE draft report and manual	REVISE draft report and manual	COMPLETE final manuscripts	COMPLETE final evaluation report		
MEETINGS & REVIEWS	REVIEW draft report and manual	REVIEW MEETING	FINAL REVIEW of contents & format	REVIEW MEETING on publication of manuscripts		
PROJECT LIAISON	REVIEW & COMMENT on draft report and manual	SUPPLY COMMENTS on draft report and manual	REVIEW & APPROVE final manuscripts	ARRANGE for publication of manuscripts	TERMINATE PROJECT	
	DEFINE client-consultant relationships in the implementation process					
	REVIEW implementation process & scheduling					
	REVIEW & APPROVE implementation process & scheduling					
COURT/COUNTY PERSONNEL STATEWIDE						

Figure 7.1—*Continued on next page*

Table 7.1. Project Work Plan and Time Schedule Tasks and Subtasks	Lapsed Time (Months)	Project Time Sequence
I. Project Planning, Coordination, and Scheduling • Appoint project liaison to coordinate project and to collaborate with consultant's project team. • Notify court locations of nature, scope, and impact of project. • Request architectural and contractual documents of court facilities, where available. • Review available reports and relevant information, including annual reports of court system. • Meet with project liaison and administrative director regarding approach, methodology, and scheduling of project. • Define overall time scheduling of project and major goals and subgoals to be accomplished within schedule.	½ to 1 month	1st month
II. Initial Data Sheets Distribution and Data Compilation • Review the approach, methodology, data, and findings of previous facilities and management studies. • Delineate goals and objectives of information to be compiled by initial data sheets. • Develop, test, and refine initial data sheets and questionnaires for distribution. • Distribute initial data sheets and questionnaires through project liaison. • Coordinate and monitor initial data compilation efforts. • Receive and organize completed initial data sheets and questionnaires. • Prepare preliminary analysis of overall statewide judicial facilities information. • Advise court system regarding findings, results, and next phase of project.	½ to 1 month	1st to 2nd month
III. Statewide Survey of Judicial Facilities • Notify and arrange for site visits and interviews—require close collaboration between project liaison and consultant's project team. • Provide detailed scheduling of site visits by project team; finalize method of data compilation. • Develop, test, and refine questionnaire or detailed data sheets for statewide survey.	1 to 6 months (depends on number of counties and size of courthouses)	2nd to 8th months

Tasks and Subtasks	Lapsed Time (Months)	Project Time Sequence

- Make travel and accommodations arrangements for project team; rent cars for statewide travel.
- Conduct on-site survey of operation, activities, caseload, personnel, facilities, equipment, and systems.
- Sketch facilities and building layout at court locations without architectural plans.
- Organize and arrange compiled data and information for detailed analysis.
- Develop preliminary judicial facilities information system, possibly an integral part of judicial information system, if necessary.
- Review compiled data and information with court system.

Data Analysis and Evaluation

Analyze the jurisdiction and responsibilities of the judicial system
- Outline the historical growth and changes of the judicial system.
- Define the jurisdiction and responsibilities of the judicial system.
- Evaluate the impact of the system on the planning and design of judicial facilities.

Analyze the anticipated changes in the judicial system.
- Discuss anticipated changes within the judicial system.
- Critically evaluate the impact of these anticipated changes on operation, caseload, personnel, and facilities.
- Assess the population and economic growth of the state and counties.
- Project the critical and priority needs of judicial system as a result of these anticipated changes and growth factors—caseload, personnel, and facility projections.

Analyze court caseflow operations.
- Present and analyze information compiled on processing of various types of cases.
- Develop tables on sequence of operations, activities, people, and facilities involved in case processing methods.
- Analyze the projected changes in caseflow operations as a result of anticipated changes in the judicial system.
- Evaluate possible improvement in caseflow operations.
- Analyze common problems and deficiencies.
- Conduct overview analysis of problems and deficiencies in court facilities of various sizes, locations, and activities.

3 months (depends on scope of project; some overlap with Task III) — 3rd to 10th months

(continued)

Table 7.1—Continued Tasks and Subtasks	Lapsed Time (Months)	Project Time Sequence

• Review common problems and deficiencies such as inadequate facilities, improper facility assignment and use, lack of proper security, lack of storage facilities and poor environmental conditions, etc.
• Suggest and evaluate alternative solutions to problems and deficiencies.
• Prepare departmental analysis of functions, personnel and facilities.
  • Delineate functional, personnel, and facility components.
  • Prepare personnel organizational charts showing present and projected personnel and lines of responsibility.
  • Prepare lists of responsibilities and duties for various positions.
  • Prepare facility tables showing spatial, accessibility, environmental, and communication needs on a statewide basis.
  • Prepare functional and spatial relationships diagrams to show how functions and spaces are related within the judicial system.
  • Prepare summary tables of facility requirements for small, medium, and large courthouse locations.
• Organize findings and conclusions of functional, personnel, and spatial requirements.		

V. Establishment of Facility Standards and Design Guidelines • Delineate degree of flexibility for application of standards and guidelines. • Analyze in detail operations, activities, people, and spaces. • Review facility standards and design guidelines already established for other states. • Establish facility standards and design guidelines for individual court spaces in the state. • Establish priorities, criteria, and guidelines for planning, design allocation, and use of facilities. • Establish facility standards and design guidelines for combined and grouped facilities at different court levels and at locations of different sizes. • Review facility standards, design guidelines, and priorities with court system.	1 to 3 months (some overlap with Task IV)	6th to 12th months
VI. Application of Judicial Facility Standards and Design Guidelines • Review overview charts and information of judicial facilities statewide, based on earlier data organization. • Recommend method or approach for adoption and application of standards and guidelines. • Apply minimum acceptable standards to existing court locations to	3 to 9 months (some overlap with Task V)	7th to 20th months

Tasks and Subtasks	Lapsed Time (Months)	Project Time Sequence

Evaluate the improvements needed to upgrade existing facilities within existing judicial system operation.

Develop short-term master plan of facility improvements for the state. Most of the improvements should be implementable, as much as possible, by local boards of county commissioners.

Project long-term facility needs for the judicial system over the next 25 years, at 5-year intervals, taking into account anticipated changes and their impact.

Prepare long-term master plan of judicial facilities development over the next 25 years, taking into account possible changes and reorganization of the judicial system.

Prepare preliminary cost estimate for the implementation of both short-term and long-term master plans. Review short-term and long-term master plans of judicial facilities with court system.

II. Implementation Process

Calculate construction costs and fair rental value of judicial facilities.
* Establish unit construction, operation, and maintenance costs of court facilities.
* Estimate replacement values, operation, and maintenance costs of court facilities.
* Establish criteria for the setting of fair rental values for court facilities.
* Establish fair rental values for court facilities in the state.
* Apply fair rental values to all court locations to estimate total cost to the state in assuming the cost of operating the court system.

Analyze financing and budgeting of judicial facilities.
* Outline methods of financing judicial facilities, including the use of public building authorities, pensions and retirement funds, leasing and renting of commercial space, turn-key operation, popular vote, and state/federal appropriation, investment, etc.
* Do comparative study of various methods of financing judicial facilities master plan in the state.
* Budget for judicial facilities planning, reorganization, renovation, and construction projects.
* Consider practical costs of implementing improvements of judicial facilities in the state.

Set up project implementation scheduling.

2 to 4 months (some overlap with Task VI)

9th to 22nd months

Table 7.1—Continued Tasks and Subtasks	Lapsed Time (Months)	Project Time Sequence

• Consider costs and budgetary constraints in implementation scheduling.
• Determine parameters that cause delays and variations in time and cost of implementation.
• Analyze quality control and monitoring of the implementation process—personnel and project management.
• Review government-judiciary relationships in the implementation process.
  • Examine existing legislative-judiciary relationships—problems and deficiencies.
  • Determine relationship problems in facility projects in the state.
  • Analyze improvement of government-judiciary relationships and its impact on facility projects.
  • Suggest methods of improving government-judiciary relationships in order to expedite the implementation process.
• Assess in-house capability within the court system in judicial space management.
  • Define the extent of in-house capability in judicial space management within the court system.
  • Calculate the cost of providing such in-house capability within the court system.
  • Consider the court system–consultant relationship in the implementation process.
• Finalize review of implementation process recommendations with the court system.		

VIII. Report Preparation and Revision Process • Progress reports—submission and review • Draft final report—submission and review • Preparation of final report for printing and distribution • Distribution of final report	1 to 3 months (some overlap with Task VII)	11th to 24th months

experience and expertise in this field would be able to analyze critically the approaches and methodologies used in previous projects, and to evaluate results and recommendations of previous project reports in order to develop a more concise and effective methodology for conducting the proposed statewide project. The ability to pinpoint essential information and to compile data in a readily transferable format between fieldwork and in-office data-organization activities can only be gained through practical experience from conducting major statewide projects. To complete a statewide project on time, within budget, and to specification, there are numerous details that need to be attended to; many alternative approaches to data compilation, organization, and analysis that need to be considered; and many alternative methods of coordinating on-site survey efforts that need to be weighed.

Tremendous effort and care goes into the development of the initial data sheet, questionnaire for key court personnel, building- and space-use information sheet, and other data formats. The ability to design and use these sheets and questionnaires effectively may result in a substantial reduction in on-site survey time. Knowing the limits that court personnel will go to in spending time and effort in completing data sheets and questionnaires is crucial to the success of compiling data supplied by court personnel. Data sheets and questionnaires should be kept concise and simply stated. A one-page data sheet should not take more than fifteen minutes to complete. Such data sheets and questionnaires should be distributed, completed, and returned within two or three days. If more time is allowed, the tendency would be for the sheets and questionnaires to be put aside and forgotten. If survey data sheets and questionnaires are developed in final format prior to distribution, and if project team members know exactly how the compiled data and information are to be organized, analyzed, and presented, data-organization and data-presentation work in project offices could be in progress simultaneously to on-site survey and data compilation. This generally means that more time spent on the project planning and coordination phase may result in substantial time and cost savings in subsequent phases.

Rushing into on-site surveying without adequate project planning and coordination usually proves fatal to the project. Voluminous data are compiled without knowing, in detail, why they are compiled or how they are to be used for analysis. When this happens, much more time is spent on extracting essential information from the massive amount of data compiled, and the methodology and recommendations tend to be controlled by the type of information and data already compiled instead of their dictating the essential information to be compiled in the first place.

Project methodology should be developed and carried through as far as possible to the conclusion and final outputs of the project. In a statewide judicial facilities project, an important decision is whether the information gathered for each local area should be analyzed and presented on a local or statewide basis. This decision can influence the design of data sheets, questionnaires, and final presentation format.

With careful planning and organization, useful information, such as local government profiles essential to the projection of future needs, could be organized prior to on-site survey work. A folder containing essential and available information for each local government would be available to the project team during its on-site survey. This results in reducing the amount of routine and repetitive on-site work and minimizes the amount of survey time needed at each court location.

Judicial Facilities Information System

The establishment of a judicial facilities information system is essential to the overall planning of the judicial system. In a state with a court management information system, facilities inventory information could be incorporated into the existing system. Each court management program, whether it be jury, caseflow, personnel, or records management, invariably has an important facility component that, in the past, has frequently been neglected. Where necessary, system improvements should be accompanied by facility improvements.

The statewide judicial facilities information system (SJFIS) is not only useful to planning programs at the state level, but is equally important to the county or city boards and court system at local county or city levels. When a courthouse is to be renovated, added to, or reorganized, a well-organized and current facility information system will provide local and court personnel, as well as architects and planners, with essential information not only on the physical size and condition of existing spaces, but also on the deficiencies and constraints of the courthouse and recommended short-term and long-term improvements. This system should also provide information on court operation, functional and spatial relationships, and facility standards and design guidelines. Since such information could be provided from a central source, the SJFIS would eliminate, or at least minimize, the duplicating effort of obtaining similar information in each local government involved in a renovation or construction program.

Data Organization, Analysis, and Evaluation

Data organization, analysis, and evaluation is both an art and a science. The scientific method in compiling essential information can make organization, analysis, and evaluation of that information an artistic endeavor. The primary reasons for performing this task are to develop judicial facility standards and design guidelines for statewide application and to develop a comprehensive master plan integrating short-term improvements with long-term facility development.

Organization of data in a statewide project should be by local area, with graphic and tabulated information made interchangeable for comparative purposes. Selected tables and figures for each court facility could be extracted and combined to form a statewide inventory. Profile information, summary tables of initial data sheets and questionnaires, on-site survey information, floor plans, and photographs of the facilities could be organized in a report for local area. This would enable each area to update the facility information system on a regular basis, with the state court administrator's office coordinating such information from all local areas at state level.

Analysis and evaluation of statewide data and information is intricate and complex. It involves a systematic and comprehensive approach to delineating causes of problems and deficiencies and to developing cost-effective solutions. This task begins with the analysis of the judicial system—its jurisdiction, organizational structure, and responsibilities. Detailed analyses are made of anticipated changes within the judicial system as well as of external pressures to alter its direction and their impact on administrative and operational procedures, and on personnel and facility assignment and utilization over the short and long term. Careful evaluation should be made of court management systems and programs being conducted or contemplated. These systems and programs may create special personnel and facility requirements for the judicial system.

Another important analysis is the delineation of existing operational, administrative, and facility problems and deficiencies, the determination of their causes, and the development of optimum solutions to alleviate or eliminate them. Physical problems and deficiencies common in courthouses include space inadequacy; facility misuse; poor functional and spatial relationships between existing facility uses; lack of separation of circulation patterns for improved courthouse security; mismanagement of space; lack of proper building maintenance; lack of building evacuation procedures for emergency situations; and lack of compliance with local building codes, ADA requirements, and fire regulations. Administrative and operational deficiencies include insufficient personnel in certain departments, lack of uniform operational and administrative procedures, antiquated records storage and retrieval system, outdated system of jury selection and assembly, and so on.

Since the facility program for both short-term and long-term facility improvement is based on departmental analysis, functional, personnel, and facility analysis of each court and each related department directly affect the establishment of facility standards and design guidelines. The initial data sheets and questionnaires for key personnel supply detailed information on duties and responsibilities of each position within the judicial system. They provide information on the amount of space occupied; furniture and equipment use; storage, car parking, and eating facilities available; and their adequacy and suitability. Useful information is also available on the relative significance of relationships between people, spaces, and departments; subjective responses regarding problems and deficiencies; and on improvement suggestions. Departmental analysis yields personnel organizational charts showing positions, lines of responsibilities, functional groupings, and existing number of persons in each position level; preliminary facility requirement tables based on analysis of department deficiencies and needs; and spatial relationships, accessibility, and circulation (SRAC) diagrams showing the significance and proximity of spatial relationships and the level and separation of public, private, and secure access and circulation systems required for the type of courts involved.

Judicial Facility Standards and Design Guidelines

The establishment of facility standards and design guidelines has long-term statewide impact on the design and planning of courthouse construction and renovation projects. Standards and guidelines must be sufficiently flexible so as not to inhibit the creativity and innovation of local project architects involved in the design of court facilities. On the other hand, all important elements of design and planning should be fully incorporated in these standards and guidelines for application to the design and planning process. Once standards are established and adopted by the court for statewide application, a mechanism must be established, either through legislative or judicial action, to enforce, monitor, and coordinate their application in the design of new facilities as well as the renovation of existing court facilities.

The three types of judicial facility standards are for individual spaces, judicial spatial components, and combined components in courthouses of various sizes and types. Facility standards for individual spaces include size of courtroom, jury deliberation room, judge's chamber, and so on. Judicial space components could be a "judicial component," which includes a courtroom; its ancillary facilities, such as jury deliberation room, judge's chamber, prisoner-holding facilities, attorneys' conference rooms, and witness rooms; and related support facilities, such as office space to house the number of court and court-related personnel in various departments required to support the operation of the one trial courtroom unit. For example, there could be 0.5

supervisors, 2.5 probation officers, and 1.2 secretarial and clerical personnel needed in the probation department to support a criminal court trial courtroom. The third level of standards includes the definition of sizes of courthouses. A small rural courthouse could have a courtroom and a hearing room, serving two judges; a medium-size courthouse could have three courtrooms and one hearing room for four to five judges; and a large courthouse may have five to eight, or more, courtrooms and hearing rooms. By defining the number of judicial components in each size courthouse, it is possible to develop space standards for small, medium-size, large, and metropolitan courthouses. By using these three levels of standards and assuming certain use patterns of court facilities, it is possible to accurately assess the amount of space needed to add a trial courtroom in an existing courthouse.

Projection of Future Needs

The next step in this planning process is the projection of future needs. The longer the period of projection, the greater the degree of inaccuracy. In general, projections are made over a 20- to 25-year period. Although the life span of a building is closer to 50 years, it is not expected that the building will remain functional over its entire life span. With rapid changes in technological and management techniques, the needs of the court system over a 25-year period become increasingly difficult to project with any degree of accuracy. The purpose of projections, however, is not to pinpoint the needs of the court system in, say, the year 2025, but to determine a range of possible directions and anticipated changes within the court system that may need to be accommodated in the court building being planned today. Having projected the range of directions and changes likely to occur in the future, it would then be possible to design and plan a structure or a complex of structures sufficiently flexible so that they could be expanded, reorganized, and renovated at reasonable cost in the future to accommodate changing needs.

Projection of facility needs follows a sequence of steps. Analysis is made initially of historical population and economic growth over the previous twenty to thirty years. Population information is broken down by age group, sex, race, education, and income levels. For example, to project juvenile caseload, information on population between twelve and eighteen years old is analyzed in regard to growth trends and factors influencing growth or decline of population within that age group. Historical economic development and factors influencing economic growth or decline are evaluated in detail. Economic indicators and trends for future development of industries are analyzed to determine their likely impact on population growth. Workforce, unemployment rate, and family and per capita income are also analyzed to develop an economic profile of each county, community, or region. Population and economic projections are essential to developing court caseload projections. Correlations can be established between population or economic parameters and volume of case filings and dispositions for each type of case.

Caseload projections, however, are influenced more significantly by changes in the judicial system than those in population and economic growth. While correlations established between certain aspects of population and types of caseloads or workload within the judicial system, changes such as the creation of a traffic violations bureau outside of the system to handle traffic violations would have an immediate and significant impact on the caseload of the limited-jurisdiction court. The creation of a small-claims court would have a similar effect. Changes in the jurisdiction of the court, such as the reduction of marijuana possession from a felony to a misdemeanor or violation, may shift a considerable number of cases from general-jurisdiction to limited-jurisdiction courts. Population and economic projections should complement anticipated changes of the judicial system in order to more realistically project future court caseload, personnel, and facilities.

Once filings and dispositions for each type of case have been projected, it is possible to establish personnel needs over the project planning period. Departmental analysis of survey information and information obtained from the initial data sheets and questionnaires for key personnel enable the consultants to determine the workload capacity of present court personnel. Certain standards, such as maximum number of cases or weighted caseload that can be handled by a judge, are then applied to projected caseload to determine the number of judges and support personnel needed during the planning period.

Personnel space projections within each court or department are derived from personnel projections and established space standards of individual spaces. In addition to personnel space, however, combined-use spaces such as courtrooms, hearing rooms, conference rooms, and so on, are projected and added to the projected personnel space to arrive at the total amount of space needed by the court system over the planning period.

Development of a Comprehensive Statewide Judicial Facilities Master Plan

The development of a comprehensive statewide judicial facilities master plan is basically a presentation of the optimal solution to accommodate the projected personnel and facility needs of the judicial system over the planning period. Projections are translated into a detailed facility program that contains all measurable information necessary for the development of the comprehensive plan. This plan integrates short-term improvements and long-term judicial facility development. It contains recommendations ranging from minor improvement of rural county courthouses and major renovation of metropolitan courthouse complexes to extensive reorganization and construction plans of judicial facilities. The comprehensive master plan is a feasible action plan, scheduled for phased implementation over a projected period and within available budgets.

In major renovation projects, certain departments must be relocated before space is available for renovation. This sequential implementation process may require many years to complete. Unless all occupants of the courthouse could be moved temporarily to an available building while the courthouse is being renovated, a tightly controlled sequence of the implementation projects would have to be adhered to in order for the plan to be fully implemented without major disruptions to efficient court operations.

Recommending the Implementation Process

Recommending the implementation process involves many related elements. Unit construction, renovation, annual operating and maintenance, and other costs have to be estimated. Cost estimates will depend on whether the local government continues to provide, maintain, and upkeep judicial facilities in courthouses or whether the state participates in the maintenance and operation of these facilities. The state could purchase courthouses at a nominal price and be responsible for their operating and maintenance, in which case the nominal price would have to be established, and decisions would have to be made on leasing space back to local governments to house their departments. Another possibility might be for the state to lease the space required by the judicial system, in which case fair-rental-value criteria for judicial facilities would have to be established. Fair rental value of judicial facilities in existing courthouses should not be based solely on square footage of space, but on functional space, conditions of facilities, and degree of usage. For example, a 2,400-square-foot courtroom should not have a higher rental value than a 1,600-square-foot courtroom, if it can be established that a 1,600-square-foot courtroom is adequate for conducting jury trials and hearings, and assuming the amount of usage of both courtrooms is identical. Should the organization and administrative structure of the court system change and administrative judicial districts with major trial centers be established, major construction or renovation projects would be recommended. Alternative methods of financing and funding such projects would have to be identified and evaluated, and the most feasible and economical methods recommended. These methods may include the creation of a public-building authority to construct courthouses that would be leased on a long-term basis to the court system through the state or county. The lease money provided by the state or county would be used to retire construction bonds over a period of years, at which time the state or county would own the building. Another method might be the use of revenue-sharing funds and other possible sources of federal and state funding. Borrowing from the state's pension and retirement funds may yet be another feasible method of financing large courthouse projects. Long-term investments of capital funds could yield investment income for renovation projects. State appropriation and regular bond issues voted for by the people would be the more regular method of funding. However, it is increasingly difficult to obtain construction funds through these regular sources. In recent years, a design-build, turnkey approach involving private financing by developers has become a viable, though expensive, financing option. The selection of methods of financing and funding judicial facilities projects is perhaps the most important task that could move the master plan from planning phase into implementation phase. This task should be carefully planned from the beginning of the project so that a feasible method of financing and funding could be determined by the time planning is completed and implementation is ready to proceed.

In major renovation projects, implementation should be phased according to the sequence of implementation contained in the comprehensive plan. Even if funds are available, this phased implementation program must be adhered to if court operation is to continue during building renovation without major disruption. Phased implementation usually means higher unit renovation costs as a result of overtime labor and more frequent delays. Heavy renovation work that is particularly noisy may have to be completed outside regular work hours, resulting in high labor costs. Renovation of courtrooms may have to be carried out during the summer recess or regular holidays. Major renovation of a large courthouse may require several years to complete, and the cost and inconvenience involved should be weighed against the rehabilitation potential of the existing building. The questions to be asked are whether the existing building, after major renovation at high costs and over a long period of time, will be adequate and suitable to house the projected needs of the court system, and whether court operations will be improved by such extensive renovations. The costs of such a project should be weighed against the advantages of designing and constructing a new courthouse on another site. When the new building is completed, the court system and its personnel would merely move into the new building, leaving the existing building to be renovated in one phase for other governmental uses.

Implementation of court facility projects is frequently delayed or abandoned because of conflicting government-judiciary priorities and working relationships. In many instances, the local government makes the decisions on facility improvements in the local courthouse. A new, ambitious presiding judge dissatisfied with existing facilities may either negotiate in an amicable manner with the local government or be confrontational when the local government does not agree with him or her. In some instances, members of the local government are antagonistic toward the court system because of personal dislike of a particular judge, a bad experience with the court system, or other reasons. On the other hand, the judge may have requested better facilities repeatedly without results, and decides that drastic actions must be taken if improvements are to be made.

At another level, the state or city public works department is used to conduct planning and programming of office and school buildings and considers the planning and programming of court facilities in the same category. It is not uncommon for the public works department to contract with a local architectural firm that has no previous court space management experience to design the courthouse. Judges and other users of the proposed facility are usually not consulted to any meaningful extent. When the building is completed, the court system is simply informed to occupy the building, or part of the building. While such instances are becoming less frequent because users are more frequently consulted as to their needs, court facilities continue to be designed and constructed by people with little or no knowledge of the court system and its complex operations. There is a real need for procedures to be established which would encourage an atmosphere of cooperation and collaboration between the executive, legislative, and judicial branches of government in the implementation of statewide judicial facilities programs. Most conflicts in government-judicial relationships have been the result of misunderstanding between agencies and their lack of knowledge of one another's operations and needs. An established procedure of input, review, and evaluation throughout the planning, programming, design, and implementation phases of facility projects would be most helpful in improving the quality of judicial facilities at state and local levels.

After the completion of the planning and programming phase, it would be beneficial to the court system to involve the consulting firm of the planning and programming phase in the implementation phases of the statewide judicial facilities project. The coordination and supervision of the implementation phase is complex, and requires the expertise of the consultant's project team, which has become experienced and knowledgeable in the specific state court system. Involvement of the project team should be planned for from the start. The consultants will be more careful in formulating their recommendations if they know in advance that they will also be responsible for their implementation. Adequate funding should be requested and obtained in advance in order to proceed into the implementation phase without incurring lengthy delays, which could be disastrous to the momentum achieved during the planning phase.

It is equally important for the court system to develop, during the planning phase, some in-house capabilities in the area of judicial space management. Since the consulting firm may not be available after a period of time, more than one staff member of the state court administrator's office should be trained by the consultants during the planning phase. They would eventually coordinate the implementation phase of the plan as well as provide information to other counties requiring subsequent assistance in the area of judicial space management. Even if the consulting firm continues to be involved in the implementation phase, there is always the need for a project liaison from the state court administrator's office to serve as the direct contact for the consultants.

Project Products

The statewide judicial facilities project normally has the following products, arranged in their proper sequence:

1. *Completed initial data sheets, questionnaires for key personnel, and building- and space-use information sheets*—This information provides data and information for organization and analysis. It is generally more useful to the consultants than to the court system.
2. *A complete detailed statewide inventory of court and court-related facilities*—When inventory information and data are organized and presented in final format, it becomes a valuable planning and information tool with a wide range of applications.
3. *A judicial facility information system*—A judicial facility information system is a refined format of inventory information and data organized for efficient analysis, storage, retrieval, and update. This system is designed to suit the specific local requirements of the state court system, and provides up-to-date inventory information for a wide range of applications.
4. *Facility standards and design guidelines for statewide application*—This is a valuable tool for the judicial or the executive branch to regulate the standards to be met in all courthouse renovation and construction projects. If the state court system has the authority over the functional and design quality of court facilities, a set of feasible and applicable facility standards and design guidelines will, over a period of time, raise the quality of judicial facilities throughout the state.
5. *Projection of future personnel, equipment, and facility needs*—Be-

cause buildings are built to house judicial functions over a long time period, efficient planning to satisfy short- and long- term needs of the court system is essential. Projections with reasonable and acceptable assumptions provide the three branches of government with valuable information on anticipated rate and amount of growth or decline, and allow more flexible buildings to be built to adequately and suitably accommodate changing needs over the projected period.

6. *Plan of short-term improvements of existing judicial facilities for minimum-cost implementation*—This plan provides each local unit with specific recommendations on short-term improvements that can be implemented at minimum cost. Such recommendations include reorganization of department for more efficient operation, creation of private and secured patterns of circulation to improve courthouse security, and more efficient layout of courtrooms, jury deliberation rooms, judges' chambers, and so forth, for better utilization.

7. *Comprehensive master plan*—The comprehensive master plan integrates short-term improvements of existing facilities with long-term development of judicial facilities, according to anticipated changes within the judicial system. This plan is a feasible action plan presented in various formats to suit different groups of people involved in its implementation. In general, the comprehensive master plan could be presented in a final report with voluminous support data; an executive summary of the report prepared for easy comprehension of major recommendations of the plan by people who do not have time to read the detailed report; conceptual drawings showing the salient aspects of the master plan; scaled planning models of typical facilities to show alternative spatial and circulation solutions; and videotape presentation on television monitors to demonstrate applications of facility standards and design guidelines as well as to show sophisticated and innovative space management concepts, approaches, methodologies, and solutions for judicial facilities projects.

8. *A feasible implementation plan*—Perhaps the most important output of any statewide judicial facilities study is the implementation plan. Short-term improvements at minimum cost usually can be implemented without disrupting court operations, and minor repairs can be implemented over a short-term period. However, in major renovation of existing buildings, a comprehensive master plan can only be implemented in scheduled phases, which are determined by funds available and degree of disruption tolerated by various court-related departments. Preliminary cost estimates of the plan are also presented in a phased implementation program. Methods of financing

and funding judicial facility projects are evaluated and the optimum method recommended, substantiated, and presented. Improvements in government-judiciary relationships are also presented to expedite the implementation process.

Project Evaluation

Several levels of evaluation should be established to review, evaluate, and approve each major step of project progress:
1. consultants' in-house evaluation
2. evaluation by court project liaison
3. evaluation by the court administrator's office or by a steering committee
4. evaluation by the highest court of the state

Consultants' In-House Evaluation

Initial evaluation should occur at two levels within the consulting firm. Work generated by project team members should be evaluated on a regular basis by the project coordinator for that team. All recommendations, suggestions, standards, guidelines, applications, master plans, and implementation methods should be evaluated by the project coordinator. Regular discussion sessions and close working relationships are usually developed between the project coordinator and team members during the project. Project outputs are the result of a close collaborative effort between coordinator and team members.

To ensure that a more objective evaluation is made of essential work products at crucial points of the project, a second-level evaluation is necessary. A senior member of the firm, designated as project director, should be informed regularly of project progress. Since this person is usually not as involved in the details of the project, he or she would be in a better position to provide a more objective evaluation of project outputs generated by the project team.

The involvement of the project director, however, does not begin at the evaluation phase. He or she is usually the person responsible for, or involved in, developing the project for the firm. Therefore, he or she is more familiar with the client's requirements than members of the project team are. The project director will define the goals, approach, and methodology for the project and work closely with the project coordinator and team members to ensure that their ideas on how the project is to be conducted and the final products to be generated are fully understood by team members from the outset of the project. The following are the project product stages that require sequential review and evaluation:

1. development of initial data sheets and questionnaires but prior to mailing to court personnel statewide
2. reorganization of information compiled through data sheets and questionnaires for preliminary analysis
3. development of on-site survey data sheets and questionnaires, but prior to site visits to compile detailed information
4. development of a method and various formats for reorganization and presentation of information and data compiled from site visits
5. reorganization of information compiled through site visits
6. completion of the statewide judicial facilities inventory for review by the project liaison
7. development of the statewide judicial facilities information system (SJFIS) as an integral part of the court management information system, if such a system exists in the state
8. development of draft judicial facility standards and design guidelines for statewide application
9. completion of judicial facility standards and design guidelines for review by the project liaison
10. development of the draft master plan for short-term improvement of existing facilities at minimum cost
11. completion of the master plan for short-term improvements for review by the project liaison
12. definition of assumptions and parameters for use in projection of future facility needs of the judicial system
13. development of preliminary population, economic, judiciary caseload, personnel, and facility projections
14. completion of projections for review by the project liaison
15. development of a draft comprehensive master plan, which integrates short-term improvement with long-term facility development
16. completion of the comprehensive master plan for review by the project liaison
17. development of a draft implementation plan, which should contain cost estimates, project implementation scheduling and phasing, recommended government-judiciary relationships to expedite implementation plans, and recommended financing and funding methods to realize implementation plans
18. completion of draft progress and final reports and presentation materials for review by the project liaison
19. completion of programs and final reports and presentation materials for review and approval by the project liaison, the state court administrator, and the highest court of the state

Evaluation by Project Liaison

The project liaison would be responsible for the review and evaluation of consultants' finding, recommendations, and outputs. While the review and evaluation of consultants' outputs at crucial points of the project must of necessity be thorough and analytical, regular review and evaluation throughout the project could be conducted on an informal basis. A close working relationship is essential between the consultants and the project liaison if the project is to be completed successfully and with maximum benefits to the judicial system. Recommendations generated from the project should be viewed as the results of this collaborative effort between the consultants and the project liaison. It is only through this effort that final results, recommendations, standards, master plan, and implementation schedule can be made to suit the specific needs of the state judicial system.

For the project liaison to function effectively as a reviewer and evaluator of consultants' work, it is essential that the following factors be considered:

1. The court project liaison should be a senior staff member familiar with the operation, management, personnel, and facilities of the court system. The liaison should have convenient access to all available information and statistics required by the consultants for the statewide project. The liaison should also know how the state court administrator and the justices would react to consultants' inquiries, findings, and recommendations. In other words, the liaison's evaluation of consultants' work should reflect the general thinking of the court system. The consultants should be able to develop sufficient confidence in the evaluation and judgment of the project liaison to be able to proceed with subsequent phases of the project without undue delay.

2. The project liaison should spend considerable time at the beginning of the project becoming familiar with the concepts, approaches, methodologies, tasks, and outputs of the statewide judicial facilities project. The liaison should be trained by the consultants to evaluate the technical aspects of consultants' recommendations and determine whether such recommendations would suit the management goals of the court system. This is especially important if the project liaison were to become the coordinator of comprehensive master plan implementation. The liaison has to be familiar with the plan; the application of facility standards and design guidelines to all renovation and construction projects; the coordination of implementation process; and, if necessary, the regular updating of the master plan and its facility program.

Evaluation by the State Court Administrator's Office or by a Steering Committee

After initial review and evaluation by the project liaison, relevant and important findings and recommendations developed during each major phase of the project should be presented to the state court administrator or a project steering committee, either at regularly scheduled review meetings or at special meetings called by the state court administrator or by the chairperson of the steering committee. Findings and recommendations must be reviewed and evaluated without delay so that the project can proceed to subsequent phases without undue interruption. To prevent such delay, the state court administrator or the chairperson of the steering committee or a designer should be able to meet directly with the project liaison and the consultants' project coordinator during unforeseen emergency situations to arrive at decisions, if necessary without having to wait for the regular meeting or to call for a full meeting.

Careful evaluation of project outputs and consultants' recommendations should be made by the state court administrator or the steering committee at the following crucial points of the project:

1. after the completion of the draft statewide judicial facilities inventory
2. after the completion of the draft statewide judicial facilities information system
3. after the completion of the draft judicial facility standards and design guidelines for statewide application
4. after the development of the draft master plan for minimum-cost short-term improvements of existing facilities
5. after the completion of draft population, economic judicial caseload, personnel, and facility projections
6. after the completion of the draft comprehensive master plan that integrates short-term improvements with long-term facility development
7. after the completion of the comprehensive master plan for statewide judicial facilities development
8. after the completion of a draft implementation plan and schedule
9. after the completion of the draft final report and presentation materials
10. after the completion of the final report and presentation materials

In addition to evaluating project products, the steering committee or state court administrator should also actively participate in determining how the statewide project should be conducted in order to yield maximum benefits to the judicial system. Valuable insights into the specific character of various court locations and methods of dealing with difficult personalities and situations would be most helpful to the project team's on-site efforts.

If a steering committee is created to supervise and direct the statewide project, members of the committee should be selected carefully. Since one of the major goals of the project is that the master plan be implemented expeditiously and in its proper sequence to provide adequate and suitable facilities for the judicial system statewide, the steering committee should consist of people from the state legislature, federal funding agencies, and local government, in addition to representatives from the various courts and related departments. This would create greater awareness of judicial facility problems among government representatives who will eventually be responsible for funding the implementation of the master plan. By being involved in this planning process, and by learning about common problems on a statewide basis, the representatives may be in a better position to help the judicial system in obtaining necessary funding for implementation. It would also encourage communication among representatives from all branches of government in the development of solutions that would affect the facilities of all branches of government. Instead of an atmosphere of confrontation and distrust, a basis for frank discussion and cooperative efforts would provide an important step toward implementation.

The size of the steering committee should be kept small, preferably no more than seven persons; otherwise it will become too unwieldy and difficult to organize and coordinate. This committee should consist of people who are able, in various ways, to effect the eventual implementation of the comprehensive master plan. They should demonstrate their willingness to collaborate with other committee members in an effort to improve the quality of judicial administration and facilities.

Evaluation by the Highest Court of the State

It is likely that the highest court of the state, usually the supreme court, would give final approval to the work completed and products submitted, based on the recommendations of the state court administrator and/or the steering committee. In some states, the judicial council, or its equivalent, would be responsible for the approval of the consultants' final report and presentation materials.

It would be especially important for the highest court of the state to review the facility standards and design guidelines developed by the consultants and evaluated and approved by the project liaison, state court administrator, and/or the steering committee, especially if the standards are to be adopted by the court for statewide application to courthouse renovation and new construction projects. If requested, the consultants should assist the state court administrator or the steering committee in presenting findings, recommendations, standards, master plan, and implementation scheduling to the highest court at appropriate times during the course of the project.

Since the highest court of the state represents the third coequal branch of government, and since the chief justice of the state court system can usually be persuasive at the state legislature—besides being influential within the judicial system—it is essential that the highest court of the state, and in particular the chief justice, endorses and supports the statewide judicial facilities project and approves the state judicial facilities master plan and its implementation plan.

Court Participation

The extent of court participation has already been outlined in figure 7.1, Statewide Judicial Facilities Project—Activities Sequence Chart, and in table 7.1, Project Work Plan and Time Schedule. The complexity and magnitude of this project warrant a more detailed discussion of court participation throughout the project.

Project Coordination and Monitoring

For the statewide judicial facilities study to be conducted successfully, each phase of the project must be properly coordinated and monitored. While the consultants' project coordinator would manage the various tasks and subtasks to be performed in accordance with project agreement, the project liaison should provide appropriate coordination and monitoring of the project and serve as the vital link between this planning phase and the subsequent implementation phase of the project.

The project liaison is responsible for the overall supervision and coordination of the project. He or she is the consultants' direct contact throughout the project, and should collaborate closely with the consultants' project team, through its project coordinator, to ensure that the project progresses according to established activities and time schedule. The liaison is involved in regular meetings with the project team and provides the necessary input, suggestions, advice, and information to the consultants in order to maximize their time and effort.

Upon project commencement, the project liaison would write to the key contacts at each of the court locations included in the project to inform them regarding the nature, scope, approach, and expected benefits of this project, and at the same time to solicit local support for the project. Initial data sheets, questionnaires for key personnel, and building- and space-use sheets would be forwarded to each court location through the project liaison, who would coordinate and monitor the return of completed data sheets and questionnaires and follow up on delinquent returns.

During the data-compilation phase, the project liaison would inform each court location in advance of the approximate schedule of site visits. This schedule is usually prepared by the project team and approved by the project liaison, who arranges site visits and appointments. A project staff member would call the contact person at each court location a day or two before the site visit. Any on-site problems encountered by the consultants during the data-compilation phase are referred to the project liaison.

Throughout the analytical and planning (short- and long-term) phases, the project liaison provides the courts' inputs, ideas, the information to expedite project progress. The liaison serves as the initial reviewer of consultants' findings, suggestions, and recommendations, and as the consultants' conduit to the administrative office, the courts, and court-related governmental and private agencies.

To perform these tasks effectively and efficiently, the project liaison should be knowledgeable in court jurisdictions, operations, caseloads, caseflow, personnel, equipment, systems, and facilities within the judicial system. Past experience suggests that an alternative project liaison should be appointed to provide necessary continuity throughout the project, should the primary project liaison be unavailable or absent when problems arise and inputs are urgently required by the consultants.

The project liaison usually spends a considerable amount of time at the beginning of the project to make sure the project is on the right track. Once the data-compilation phase is under way, the liaison's time commitment need not be more than 10 to 15 percent of his or her full-time job for the coordination and monitoring of the project. However, if it is decided that the project liaison should have a working knowledge of space management concepts and methodologies and travel with the project teams during on-site visits, the percentage of time spent on the project would be increased, depending on the degree of involvement and the number of sites visited.

Product Review and Evaluation

The products of the project should be reviewed and evaluated by the state court administrator or a project steering committee. In most statewide judicial facilities projects, the state court administrator or the administrative director of the courts is normally responsible for the review and evaluation of consultants' outputs on facility standards and design guidelines, suggestions, and recommendations, short- and long-term master plans, and implementation and financing of these plans.

In a recently completed statewide judicial facilities study, a committee consisting of three judges, a representative of the boards of county commissioners, a state legislator, the administrative director of the courts, and a selected number of his or her senior staff were responsible for the review and evaluation of project progress. One advantage of this approach is a view toward implementation, as evidenced by the representative of the county boards and the state legislator. The former represents the groups of county commissioners who are responsible for provision, upkeep, and maintenance of local county court facilities, while the latter is in a position to exert significant influence on the state legislature when funding is needed for the approved and adopted implementation program. The chairman of this steering committee would convey the recommendations of the committee to the judicial council or the highest court of the state for its consideration and possible action.

Either method of project review and evaluation is feasible and applicable, depending on the ultimate goals and objectives of the project, as envisioned by the state court administrator and the highest court of the state.

Review and evaluation meetings should be conducted according to a set schedule during the course of a statewide project. Additional meetings could be called by the state court administrator or the chairman of the steering committee when necessary. Specific review and evaluation meetings are indicated on the activities sequence chart for the project (figure 7.1). Critical meetings would occur at the conclusion of the data-compilation phase, at the development of facility standards and design guidelines, and at the completion of draft short-term minimum-cost facility plans, draft long-term maximum efficiency statewide plan, and at the completion of the draft implementation plan.

Project Input and Feedback

Input and feedback by court and personnel are also shown on the activities sequence chart. Major inputs occur during the data-compilation–site-visit phase of this project. Key personnel at each court location spend around thirty minutes, depending on the size and complexity of each facility, to complete the initial data sheets and questionnaires. During the data-compilation–site-visit phase, the project team spends between one and three person-days at each court location, depending also on the size and complexity of the court facilities. It is estimated that the project team spends approximately half the time of the site visit interviewing court and county personnel, and the remaining time updating or sketching floor plans, compiling data and information through observation and measurement, photographing exterior and interior views of court and court-related facilities, and completing initial analysis of facility problems, deficiencies, and preliminary short-term solutions.

During data analysis, standards and guidelines development, and preparation of short- and long-term master action plans, a representative cross section of court locations should be contacted to solicit feedback on consultants' findings, standards, guidelines, recommendations, short- and long-term planning solutions, and methods of implementation. Detailed application of facility standards and design guidelines should be planned in selected court locations, and the results should be presented to local court and county personnel for their reactions. This close working relationship between the consultants and local court and county personnel is essential for evaluating the applicability, feasibility, and comprehensiveness of the master plan. The project staff should study local codes and regulations to ensure that recommendations and solutions to facility problems and deficiencies are practical and implementable within the requirements of local codes and regulations. The project teams should also spend time, where necessary, to explain in detail their approaches and recommendations so that court and local government personnel would be able to understand clearly their impact. In other words, the consultants should concentrate on each local court location to ensure feasibility of the master plan at both state and local levels.

Project Implementation

Implementation of short-term minimum-cost recommendations may proceed during the course of the statewide project. Should this occur, it would be desirable for the project liaison to coordinate such efforts, so that the facility standards and design guidelines developed during the project could be applied to the development of renovation plans for short-term improvements. While most local government will continue, at least in the foreseeable future, to be responsible for the provision, upkeep, and maintenance of adequate judicial facilities, the state court administrative office could, if it chooses, assume a more positive role in providing technical assistance and information transfer to local court locations so that the quality, as well as quantity, of judicial facilities could be improved.

Statewide judicial facility projects can also provide an opportunity to promote the work and programs of the judiciary. The consultants should inform court and local government personnel at each court location that the statewide project is sponsored by the state judiciary and that the recommendations, solutions, and action plans are not only for statewide application, but for the individual local court locations throughout the state. The statewide judicial facilities project can be a most valuable public relations tool for the courts system. The consultants should provide both short-term recommendations and long-term action plans for each court location within the overall scope of the comprehensive master plan for the state. Minor involvement of the project liaison and of local court and local government personnel would be necessary to ensure feasibility and applicability of consultants' recommendations.

Successful implementation of a statewide judicial facilities master plan requires the active participation of the state court administrator's office throughout the process. Consultants contracted by the state to develop the statewide judicial facilities master plan usually move on to conducting other projects elsewhere once the master plan has been completed and approved by the judiciary. Implementation of the master plan over many years requires the continuity and consistency that the state judiciary should provide.

If the judiciary is interested and committed to the overall improvement of judicial facilities statewide, a unit of the state court administrator's office, headed by an assistant court administrator and consisting of professional and technical staff (such as architects, planners, engineers, CAD operators, and administrative and clerical staff), should be created as soon as possible during the early stages of the statewide judicial facilities planning project. This unit would collaborate with and monitor the efforts and work products generated by the consultants hired by the state to develop the master plan. By the time that the master plan is approved and funded for the initial fiscal years by the state legislature, this unit's staff would already have become familiar with the details and nuances of the master plan, including its recommendations and implementation schedule.

The implementation of such an ambitious master plan on a statewide basis will require the joint commitment of the state legislature and the state judiciary over many fiscal years and legislative sessions, and only an in-house unit, staffed with professionals and technicians with the appropriate and needed skills and experience, would be able to provide the continuity and sustain the tenacity required to guide the implementation of the statewide judicial facilities master plan to its successful conclusion. While consultants, including architects, engineers, and planning teams, would be contracted to provide professional architectural and engineering services for specifically identified courthouse construction and renovation projects, the coordination, monitoring, and supervision of all the intricate details, funding, and scheduling of the master plan can only be effectively and productively organized and managed by a competent in-house unit within the state judiciary.

If the state judiciary has sufficient confidence in the ability and experience of the consultants, the training of the unit's staff could be provided within the consultants' contract. A close collaboration between the unit's staff and the consultants during the master planning phase would prepare the in-house staff to assume the subsequent day-to-day operation and implementation efforts after the consultants have completed their work. The consultants could be retained to conduct periodical implementation review and sporadic training programs, if necessary, during the master plan implementation process.

Project Effort and Cost Considerations

In general, statewide judicial facilities planning and management projects require a project time period of between 12 and 24 months, depending on the size of the state in terms of number of counties and court locations, and on the complexity of the judicial system. However, regardless of the number of courthouses in the state, there are minimum time and effort requirements for certain major tasks to be accomplished. These cannot be reduced no matter how few the number of court locations within the state. For example, the time period required for the initial project planning and scheduling process, the development of initial data sheets and questionnaires for key personnel, and the development of facility standards and design guidelines is fairly constant for all statewide projects. Consequently, a project involving 20 counties might require half the project time of one involving 100 counties. Major time savings in smaller states can accrue during site visits and data compilation, projection of future needs, and the development of a short- and long-term facility master plan.

To become attuned to the detailed organization and management of the court system in a small state, and to complete a statewide judicial facilities study according to the work scope outlined earlier, the minimum project time period would be around 12 months. A 30- to 50-county state would require around 15 to 18 months, and a 60- to 100-county state would require a minimum of 18 to 24 months. These time periods cannot be substantially reduced by adding more personnel to the project team. Additional personnel can reduce the time spent on repetitive tasks such as data compilation and organization of data. Detailed planning and evaluation work necessary to develop master plans can only be accomplished successfully by experienced personnel who are familiar with the project, and since major planning decisions are made by the project director and the project coordinator, many of the tasks cannot be expedited by additional personnel.

Another important consideration is the fact that adequate time is needed for detailed analysis and evaluation, development of alternative solutions, and determining optimum recommendations. If these tasks are rushed because of project time constraints, the quality of outputs could be adversely affected, and recommendations might not be as cost-effective as they would be if more time were given to their analysis and determination.

The cost of statewide judicial facilities studies varies with project scope, time constraints, and degree of assistance provided by the state court administrator's office. Consulting firms also have varying fee structures. It is not uncommon for one firm to submit a bid price that is more than double the lowest bid. The court system should select a firm with proven experience in statewide judicial facilities projects. Since the concept of statewide judicial facility studies is a relatively recent innovation, expertise in conducting such projects efficiently and economically can only come with experience gained from conducting similar projects in other states. Having experienced a statewide judicial facilities project, a consulting firm should be able to analyze and determine the flaws, problems, and inefficiencies at various stages of the project, and to develop and refine approaches and techniques to overcome predictable problems in future projects. Improvements in method and techniques in conducting large statewide judicial facilities projects can result in substantial savings in project time, personnel efforts, and overall costs. Firms with no previous experience in statewide projects are not aware of such problems and inefficiencies, and the court system would be burdened with an inferior and impractical product. When this occurs, the selection of an inexperienced firm based solely on the lowest bid price results in wasting the entire cost of conducting the project, with no benefit whatsoever to the court system.

8

Changing Concepts and Trends in Judicial Space Management

Over the past quarter century, there has been intensive improvement of judicial facilities. Improvements have been in the form of reorganization, renovation, and new construction. System and spatial reorganization in court buildings has lessened space misuse as well as space shortage. Improvement in space use can alleviate space-shortage problems. Buildings with inactive records occupying private office space show a lack of proper space management. Space-use priorities and spatial relationship requirements are essential to optimum space allocation and management, and to minimizing space-use problems in existing buildings.

Rehabilitation Potential of Existing Buildings

Renovation of existing court buildings without the involvement of experienced judicial space management consultants has invariably resulted in nonfunctional and uncoordinated facilities. Courthouse renovation should be based on the concept of rehabilitation potential. Since courthouses are commonly measured in terms of number of courtrooms, which to a large extent determines the structure of the building, one method of determining rehabilitation potential is the suitability and adequacy of the existing building to accommodate a projected number of courtrooms. Forced adaptation of unsuitable spaces for use as courtrooms has frequently resulted in acoustical, visual, motion, and functional problems during trials and hearings. A more reliable method of determining rehabilitation potential is to evaluate whether the existing building can be adapted feasibly and economically for efficient court and court-related operations. Court facilities for handling criminal cases involving detained defendants require at least three separate modes of circulation: public; private, or restricted; and secure. Public circulation involves public lobbies, elevators, corridors, and spaces that are freely accessible to the general public. Private, or restricted, circulation involves private lobbies, controlled elevators, corridors, and spaces that are freely accessible to appropriate court staff, but off-limits to the general public. Judges' chambers and clerical personnel work space are private space with restricted access. Secure circulation involves secure lobbies, elevators, corridors, and spaces used for movement of prisoners, sequestered jurors, and grand jurors and secret witnesses during grand jury hearings. Figure 8.1 shows a courthouse security model of the three circulation patterns.

The configuration and size of the existing building, the location of vertical transportation systems and equipment, and the structural and design constraints of an existing building will determine the degree of rehabilitation potential for court and related uses.

Other criminal courts buildings, such as the Pinellas County Criminal Courts Complex in Clearwater, Florida, have introduced a fourth circulation system, for judges and chambers staff, which is separate from the restricted corridor directly behind the courtrooms for jurors, attorneys, and other court staff. Other circulation systems in courthouses include separate freight elevators for freight service from this building loading area, and staff service elevators between clerk's office and courtroom and chamber floors.

New construction may involve an addition to an existing building, the construction of a separate building, or the construction of a complex of buildings. With the continuing rise in labor and material costs, more and more state, county, and city governments are investigating optimum allocation and utilization of existing resources. Reorganization and renovation of existing facilities at lower costs are generally preferred over most costly new construction. Evaluation of rehabilitation potential assists in determining whether funds could be better spent in renovation or in new construction. Buildings with low rehabilitation potential are potentially unsuitable for efficient judicial use, and expenditure of even large sums would not significantly improve their suitability and adaptability. When such situations occur, new facilities are indicated. Renovation cost is comparatively low for a building determined to have a high rehabilitation potential for court use.

Determining Building Adequacy

A problem that frequently plagues the court system is the lack of a logical approach and methodology for determining at what point in time an existing building becomes inadequate, and a new addition or building becomes necessary. Traditionally, consultants have relied on personnel and space projections of court needs over a planning period of twenty or more years to determine the year that the existing building would become inadequate for accommodating future court space expansion. By comparing the projected space needs with the available space in the existing building, the year that the existing building becomes inadequate can be derived theoretically.

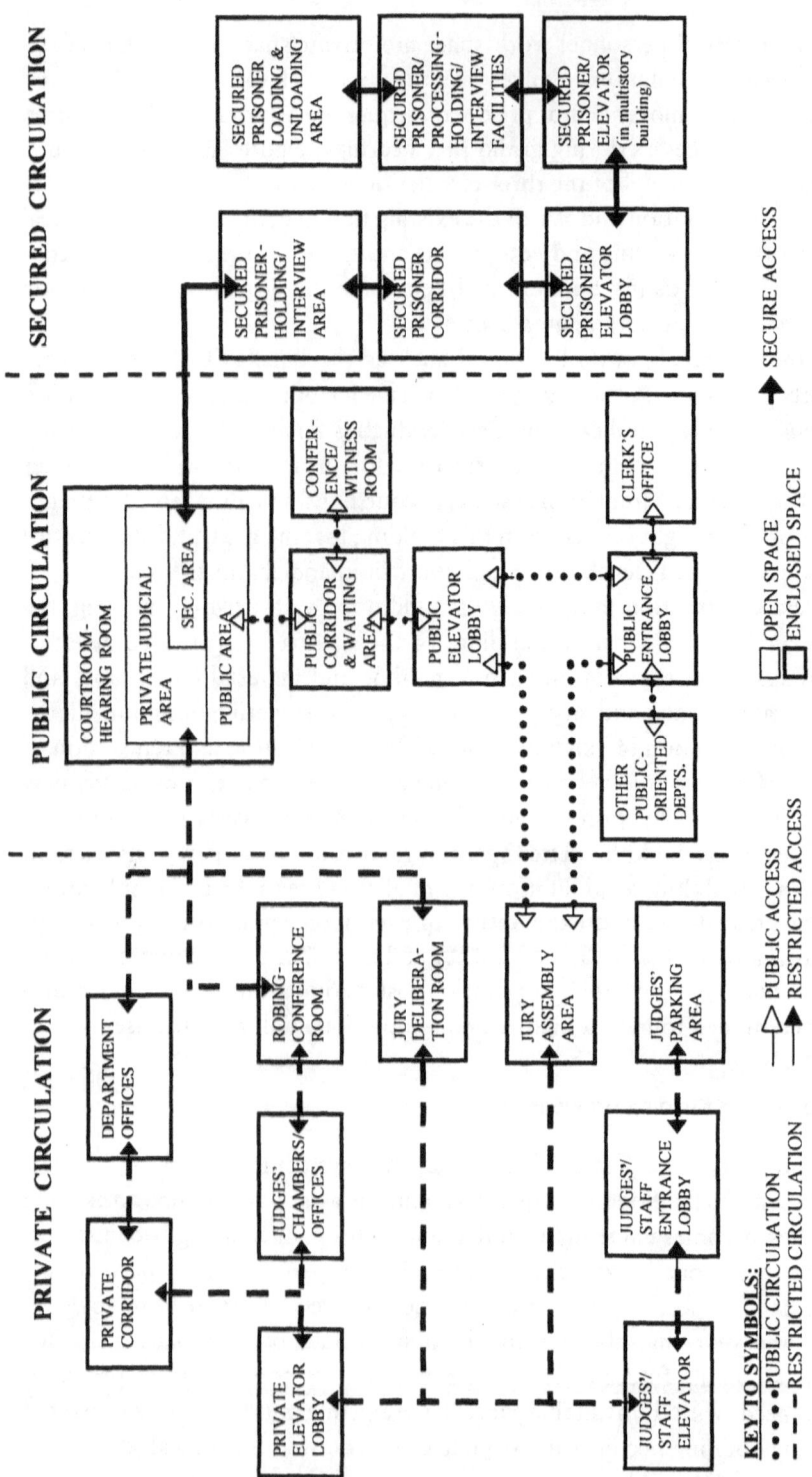

Figure 8.1. Courthouse Security Model of Circulation Patterns

There are several problems in the use of that approach and methodology. First, the method of deriving space projections based on population projections, economic indicators, and caseload or workload, and personnel growth is no better than an educated guess, especially when significant administrative and operational factors that may alter these projections are not taken into account in the projection process. The longer the time period over which space needs are projected, the less accurate the projections. Second, the traditional linear trend or straight-line projection, based on historical population, caseload, and personnel data, presumes that factors influencing rates of change in the past will continue to apply to projections of future needs. While changes in judicial administration, operations, technology, and personnel needs were not substantial prior to the late sixties, changes in the eighties and nineties have been so dramatic in many locations that projections based on historical data in the sixties and seventies would not have been accurate. Third, projections derived from this approach, if applied to the determination of when a building becomes inadequate, would be inaccurate because of the inherent inaccuracy of this approach for long-term projections.

A recent innovative approach developed in this area is based on the logical assumption that each trial courtroom, the common unit of measurement of courthouse size, has to be supported by a certain amount of ancillary and related space, which varies according to the type of cases regularly conducted in that courtroom. For example, a courtroom handling criminal felony trials involving detained defendants would need considerably more ancillary and support spaces than one handling civil cases. In some jurisdictions, quasi-judicial personnel such as masters, magistrates, or referees are appointed to conduct specific hearings in civil, traffic, juvenile, probate, and domestic relations cases in smaller nonjury hearing rooms. Consequently, both regular trial courtrooms and hearing rooms must be considered in determining maximum building capacity.

A criminal trial courtroom of 1,600 square feet of net space may require at least a similar area for ancillary facilities which include the judge's chamber, private offices for judicial support staff, jury deliberation room, attorneys' conference and witness room, and prisoner-holding, supervision, and interview facilities. Ancillary facilities should be contiguous or near trial courtrooms. In addition, departmental support may include two assistant district attorneys, one assistant public defender, one probation officer, five clerks, and so on, to adequately support the efficient operation of a trial courtroom. These departmental support spaces may add up to three to four times the size of the courtroom. Consequently, a 1,600-square-foot courtroom may need 4,500 to 6,000 square feet of total ancillary and support space.

With this in mind, the planning of an existing building should be approached from the point of view of maximum and optimum capacity. The first step would be to delineate the spaces that are being used as, or that are potentially suitable for conversion into, trial courtrooms. This would determine the maximum number of adequate and suitable courtrooms that could be accommodated in the existing building.

The next step would be to determine whether the width and the existing configuration of the building would provide for the number of separate circulation systems that are essential to the efficient and sole operation of specialized courts such as criminal or juvenile courts.

The remaining available space would be for ancillary and support function. For the maximum number of courtrooms to function efficiently, each must have, in close proximity, adequate ancillary facilities. Most departmental support spaces can be more remotely located from the courtrooms. Some support departments, such as public defender's office and the department of probation, can operate more effectively outside of the courthouse. In any case, by dividing the available support space in the building into the standard space requirements for each type of trial courtroom, the optimal number of trial courtrooms that can be adequately serviced by ancillary and support facilities can be calculated. If this optimal number of courtrooms is larger than the maximum number of courtrooms assessed for the building, there is more than adequate support space to service the maximum number of courtrooms. On the other hand, if the reverse occurs, there is not enough support space to service the maximum number of courtrooms, and the optimal number must be used as the maximum capacity of the building.

Through this method, it is possible to determine accurately the maximum number of trial courtroom units that can be accommodated in an existing building. Based on historical data on (a) how often judgeships have been created over the past ten years, (b) an analysis of how conservative the state legislature has been in the creation of new judgeships, (c) the number of cases that can be handled by each judge, and (d) the future projection of number of judges, it should be possible to develop the average number of years between appointment of new judges. Once this is determined, it would be possible to define when planning and programming efforts will have to begin if a new building is to be completed at approximately the time that the existing building becomes inadequate. For example, if the optimal number of trial courtrooms in the existing building is twenty, and if a new judgeship is expected on an average of one every two to three years, assuming a new courtroom is needed for each new judge, it can be concluded that when the eighteenth courtroom is occupied, planning and programming work should begin so that when the twenty courtrooms in the existing building are fully occupied, a new building would have been completed and ready for occupancy. It is generally accepted that the project time period from planning and programming to completion and occupancy of a major new court building is between four and five years.

This approach eliminates the uncertainty of long-term projection. The optimal number of trial courtrooms and ancillary and support facilities that can be accommodated is factual, based on detailed structural, functional, and spatial analysis of the existing building. While the extent of support facilities per trial courtroom may vary with systemic and operational changes, and with the relocation of support departments (such as public defender's office and probation department) to spaces outside of the existing courthouse, the optimum number of trial courtrooms can be easily adjusted according to these variations. This approach also eliminates the inherent inaccuracy in projecting the year that additional facilities are needed. By defining the maximum capacity of the existing building, and by delineating the parameters that govern the planning and design of a new facility, the time for a new facility is dependent on how close the court system and its related departments are to the maximum capacity of the existing building.

Integration of Justice System Component Facilities

The integration of courts, corrections, and law enforcement facilities is likely to gain momentum in the future. Because courts are the responsibility of the judicial branch, while correction and law enforcement are usually included within the executive branch of government, coordinated joint programs and operations in most states are rare. The separation-of-powers doctrine is invariably applied to each of the three major justice functions. In spite of the fact that their operations overlap in the processing of criminal cases, there are many locations where communication between them is nonexistent. In the planning and design of major justice complexes in metropolitan centers, steering or advisory committees consisting of representatives from all justice agencies have been formed with varying degrees of success. At the state level, Alaska is perhaps the only state that has made serious attempts at relating the spatial requirements of all three major justice components. A project in the seventies produced comprehensive facility standards and design guidelines for all courts, corrections, and law enforcement facilities for statewide application, based on an in-depth analysis of organization, administration, operation, personnel and space allocation, and utilization. Upon completion of a detailed review process, these standards and guidelines were adopted as an integral part of the administrative policies of the executive branch. All justice facilities, regardless of whether they are new or renovated, were planned and designed in accordance with these standards and guidelines, once they were adopted.

It may be some years before such a bold integration of closely related justice facilities becomes a common occurrence in other states. The location of regional justice centers, including the use of shared facilities to minimize duplication and to reduce construction costs, would result in substantial long-term cost savings to the state. As more justice administrators and planners appreciate the benefits of comprehensive planning to the overall development of justice facilities on a local, county, or statewide level, more functional and economical justice facilities will be planned, programmed, designed, and constructed. In metropolitan centers, as administrators and planners become more cognizant of the complex inter- and intrarelationships among justice components and their subcomponents, and of the greater functional advantages gained through optimal design of closely interrelated facilities, advisory and steering committees will become a more effective vehicle in guiding complicated justice complexes to their successful completion.

Regionalization and Facility Consolidation

The concept of regionalization was derived from the assumption that administration and operation in a decentralized justice system are inefficient and uneconomical. In most states, each county or parish has its own form of local government, justice system, law enforcement department, courthouse, and jail. In well-populated, highly productive, and high-income local areas, the existence of a courthouse (in some cases, a large justice complex) to house an active and well-coordinated justice system could easily be justified, and regionalization of the justice system may have no operational impact on its operation. However, local government could be affected significantly by major administrative changes. For example, in the state of Georgia, in which most of the 159 counties are rural counties with small population and limited projected growth, it was recommended that the state be divided into ten regions, each with one or more counties or judicial circuits, based on population, caseload, and other considerations. The justice system of each region would be managed by a regional court administrator, and one or more trial centers would be located in the more populated cities or towns. The existing courthouse could be used to house other county functions, with the justice system retaining some space for handling local cases such as small claims, traffic, juvenile, uncontested domestic relations, and nonjury cases.

Regionalization will benefit mainly those rural counties that are too impoverished to adequately maintain and operate their justice systems and their county courthouses. While regionalization creates geographic areas larger than individual counties, it is expected that local government will continue to exist without major changes. Regionalization of the judicial system does not necessarily mean handling all cases in one location. Such a centralized system would not be functionally, economically, or politically acceptable.

In most states, changes in the existing justice system toward regionalization may require many changes in constitutional, statutory, administrative, and operational areas. The state constitution may require jurors to be selected from citizens residing in the county in which a case was commenced or a crime suspect was arrested. The centralization of judicial facilities in one county within a region would either require that the constitution be amended (a long and difficult process) to allow jurors to be selected from the broader geographical area of the region, or that jurors continue to be selected from the county of case origin and transported to the trial center located in another county for trial, in which case no constitutional amendment would be required.

Another impediment to regionalization is the statutory requirement that a person be tried in the county in which the crime was committed. While it is possible that minor traffic and misdemeanor cases and preliminary hearings of major criminal cases could continue to be conducted in the courthouse within the county in which those cases originated, conducting major cases in a central court location that serves the entire region may necessitate changing the statute by legislation to permit a person to be tried within the "region" instead of the "county" in which the crime was committed.

Traditionally, the sheriff has the statutory responsibility for the care and custody of the courthouse and jail, for attending all courts of record held in his or her county, and for obeying the lawful orders and directions of the court. The sheriff is normally paid by the county to perform these services. His or her office also receives fees for service of summonses and warrants. With regionalization, consolidation of major trial activities in one location within a region would substantially reduce the fees paid to the sheriff in the outlying counties as a result of shorter court sessions handling minor cases at those locations. One method of overcoming this problem is for the sheriff's office to be responsible for process serving of cases originating in that county, and for the sheriff or deputy sheriff to attend court sessions when cases from his or her county are involved. This would mean substantial personnel resource and travel time. Another method would be the creation of a group of court officers consisting of deputy sheriffs from all counties within the region, organized in such a manner that the workload for each county would be roughly proportional to the number of cases generated from each county. Fees would then be distributed to the various counties according to workload.

In some states, the constitution may have already made provision for consolidation of prosecution and public defense functions. Unlike the jury venue problem, there would not be the need for a constitutional amendment in order to consolidate these functions within a system reorganization or facility consolidation plan.

Other statutory changes that may be needed before implementation of a regionalization or consolidation plan would be the appointment of a court clerk for each region instead of each county, perhaps with deputies at each county to handle clerical matters on an as-needed basis; the repealing of any statute that requires the election of a resident judge for each county (as in Illinois), and instead legislating for the election of one or more circuit judges within a region or selection district; and the possible need to change present circuit boundaries to regional boundaries. The need for statutory and/or constitutional changes will depend on the extent and nature of the regionalization and consolidation plan.

Beyond legal and political considerations, the most important consideration is economic comparison between the present system of operation and the projected regionalization system and facilities consolidation. To improve the present system, the quality and quantity of present judicial facilities may have to be improved substantially. Existing facilities can be renovated, added to, or replaced. The extent of renovation will depend mainly on the quality, adequacy, and appropriateness of the existing facilities. Real space shortage can only be remedied by adding to the existing building, renting, or leasing commercial facilities adjoining or near the county courthouse, or the construction of a new court building on a new or existing site. Long-term leasing or renting of commercial facilities, even when they are designed in accordance with court specifications, is uneconomical owing to escalated leasing costs compared with lower long-term annual operation and maintenance costs of a government-owned building, even though the initial construction cost may be high. By amortizing the initial construction cost over a thirty- to fifty-year life span, the depreciation costs should be less than the annual leasing cost. The only cost outlay would be for annual operation and maintenance, which should be considerably less than annual leasing costs. In the case of a state or county maintaining state- or county-owned buildings, respectively, when the maintenance crew is already in existence, the apportioned cost of maintaining such buildings should be lower than contract maintenance (including janitorial services for individual buildings).

The degree of feasibility in renovating existing court facilities depends largely on their rehabilitation potential. While it is possible, though not always desirable, to hear civil cases in criminal courtrooms, the reverse situation does not apply in cases in which prisoners are involved. Consequently, conversion of office space into court facilities to handle civil cases does not necessarily mean that the same facilities could be renovated to hear criminal cases. If the rehabilitation potential of existing facilities is low, it may not be beneficial to spend large amounts of funds on renovation. The cost of major courthouse renovation could be as much as, and perhaps even more than, the cost of constructing a new facility or a new addition. If circulation separation to improve courthouse security is an important consideration, and if the constraints in renovating existing facilities would not substantially improve this situation, then it would not be desirable to renovate the building. On the other hand, if only minor renovations are needed to substantially improve existing court operation, the building has high rehabilitation potential and should be renovated.

A feasibility evaluation of system regionalization and facility consolidation has to go far beyond construction or renovation costs and annual operation and maintenance costs of buildings. In urban settings, such costs are only a small fraction of overall costs of the justice system. In the state of Alaska, the addition of a judge would require an estimated 3,500 to 4,500 square feet of net usable space for the judge and support staff. During the eighties, the cost of providing such a facility in certain parts of Alaska was close to $1 million. Over a ten-year period, the operation and maintenance cost of the facility would be between $1.5 and $2 million. In addition, the operating cost to the court system, including the salaries and fringe benefits for the judge and support staff, as well as other costs such as traveling, administrative, and operating costs, was estimated to exceed $5 million over the same 10-year period. In the mainland states, where the unit construction and operating cost is considerably lower than in Alaska, the difference between building construction and maintenance costs on the one hand and the operating costs of the judicial system on the other may be even more pronounced. This requires that the state legislature, when creating new judgeships, be fully aware of (a) the economic impact of their decisions, (b) the need for adequate facilities to accommodate the additional judges and their staff, and (c) the cost for proper long-term maintenance of the facilities once they are built.

Beyond these tangible costs, which can be measured in reasonably accurate and definitive terms, there are many social costs that are less obvious, but are nevertheless equally important contributors to the feasibility evaluation of system regionalization and facility consolidation. In comparing existing operation and facilities on a county basis with regionalization of several counties and consolidation of judicial facilities into one major facility located in the most populous county, the following conditions are likely to occur.

Consider a county in which the existing county courthouse is located in the county seat centrally situated in the county. The maximum distance from the county boundary to the courthouse is assumed to be 50 miles. The mean distance of travel to the courthouse is less than 10 miles, since most of the population is assumed to be concentrated at the county seat and its surrounding areas. Most of the attorneys in the county have their offices around the courthouse, many of them within walking distance of it.

Table 8.1, presenting comparative costs between the existing system (with five separate counties) and the regionalization-consolidation system (five counties with one major trial center in the most populous county at the center of the region) reveals a much higher cost for the latter. Travel, time, fee, and salary costs of the major participants in the judicial process indicate that the existing system of operation ($1,314,304) is about $1,053,290 less than the regionalization-consolidation system ($2,367,594). This is equivalent to an 80.14 percent increase over the cost of the existing system. The only cost advantage in favor of the regionalization-consolidation system is the lower cost for judicial and support staff as a result of better resource utilization and reduction in amount of travel between counties. Such savings are offset by major cost disadvantages to jurors, attorneys, witnesses, and the public.

Judicial Cost Considerations

If one considers only those costs that directly affect the court system, a different conclusion can be drawn. Since a high cost percentage in this analysis is from travel time and cost, provided in large part by attorneys, litigants, witnesses, and jurors, direct costs to the court system or to the state are shown on table 8.2.

Based on this information, it can be concluded that the regionalization-consolidation concept can result in cost savings to the court system, depending on whether the increased travel costs of jurors and witnesses are to be reimbursed by the court. It is assumed that a regionalized judicial system facilities consolidation at a regional trial center should result in increased efficiency in the use of available court personnel and other resources. Fewer personnel are needed in a centralized facility than when they are dispersed in a decentralized system of small and inefficiently operated county courthouses.

For this example, the regionalization-consolidation concept is applicable only to rural counties that have low caseloads and low rates of jury trials and counties that are not financially able to support, operate, and maintain underutilized court facilities. A coordinated and cooperative effort between several such adjoining counties to implement a tailor-made regionalization-consolidation plan, designed specifically to accommodate the peculiar needs of these counties, may result in substantial cost savings to the counties, and eventually to the state, if the latter were to assume greater financial responsibilities for the state court system in the future.

Table 8.1. Cost Comparison of an Existing Court System with Regionalization/Consolidation Concept*

Courthouse

Existing System
The courthouse in a particular county seat is centrally located within the county. Maximum travel distance is 50 miles, mean distance less than 10 miles.

Regionalization/Consolidation
In a region of five counties, the courthouse in the most populous county is centrally located. Maximum travel distance is 150 miles, mean distance 80 miles from adjoining counties, and less than 10 miles within county with courthouse in its county seat.

Jurors

Existing System
500 cases, of which 50 go to jury trials: 20 12-member jury trials and 30 6-member jury trials. Jury panel for 12-member jury trial is 20 and for 6-member jury trial is 15. Consequently, total number of jurors serving on jury panels is 600 + 450=1,050 for the year. If the number of jurors assembled for jury trial is 25 percent higher than those served on a jury panel, the number of potential jurors assembled would be around 1,300. Based on an average of 10 miles of travel distance (20 miles round trip), the amount of travel distance for jurors would be 26,000 miles per year. If each juror has to make an average of 3 trips to the courthouse, this number would become 78,000 miles per year and for 4 counties would be 312,000 miles per year. At the central county, with an estimated 1,875 jurors, there would be a travel distance of 1,875 x 20 x 3=112,500 miles per year. Total travel distance for jurors is 312,000 + 112,500=424,500 miles per year.

Regionalization/Consolidation
500 cases per county of the 4 smaller counties, each with approximately the same number of jury trials. Consequently, there are 200 jury trials, 80 12-member jury trials, and 120 6-member jury trials from the 4 counties. Total number of jurors at the trial center, with a savings of 30 percent because of more effective jury management system, would require 70 percent of 1,300 x 4=3,640 jurors. Amount of travel at an average of 80 miles (160 miles round trip)=582,400 miles per year. If the average number of trips made per case is reduced to 2, the total travel distance would be 1,164,800 miles per year. Caseload for the main county: 1,000 cases of which 70 cases are jury trials: 30 12-member jury trials and 40 6-member jury trials. Total number of jurors 900 + 600=1,500 for the year. Number of potential jurors would be around 1,875. Based on an average of 10 miles of travel distance (20 miles round trip), jurors' travel distance would be 37,500 miles. If the average number of trips per case is 2, total distance would be 75,000 miles per year. Total number of jurors for the region is 3,640 + 1,875=5,515 jurors, and the total mileage of travel=1,164,800 + 75,000=1,239,800 miles.

Attorneys

Existing System
For the 500 cases, if the number of attorneys involved is 3 per case, the number of attorneys would be around 1,500. If the number of trips made by each attorney per case is 3, the total number of trips would be 4,500. Based on a mean distance of 2 miles between

(continued)

Table 8.1—*Continued*

attorneys' office and the courthouse (4 miles round trip), the number of miles traveled by attorneys would be 18,000 miles per year. For 4 counties, the number would be 72,000 miles per year.

Regionalization/Consolidation
For the 4 surrounding counties, the average number of attorneys (3 per case) for the 2,000 cases would be 6,000. If the system is improved so that the number of trips by attorneys per case is reduced to 2, the number would be 4,000 visits with an average travel distance of 80 miles (160 miles round trip), the total travel distance of attorneys would be 640,000 miles per year. At the central court center, the 1,000 cases would require 2,000 attorney visits. At 2 miles per visit (4 miles round trip), this could be equivalent to 8,000 miles. The total distance for attorneys would be 640,000 + 8,000=648,000 miles.

Witnesses

Existing System
For the 500 cases, if 150 cases go to trial and if the average number of witnesses called per case is 3 per side (or 6 per case) the total number of witnesses would be 900 per year. Based on an average of 10 miles per trip (20 miles round trip), the distance of travel for witnesses would be 18,000 miles. If each witness has to make an average of 1.5 trips for each case, this distance would be 27,000 miles per year per county. For the 4 counties, total witness travel distance would be 27,000 x 4=108,000 miles. For the central county, the travel distance for the 1,500 witnesses, based on 1.5 trips per witness per case, and 20 miles round trip, would be 45,000 miles per year. The total witness travel distance for the 5 counties is 108,000 + 45,000=153,000 miles per year.

Regionalization/Consolidation
Based on the same 150 trials (both major and minor) at each of the 4 locations, but assuming that 50 trials are local in nature and nonjury, and can be heard in the local county courthouse, 100 trials would be conducted in the trial center. This would mean that each of the 4 locations would have 200 witnesses per year, based on an average of 4 witnesses per case or 2 per side. The distance of witness travel would be 200 x 10 or 2,000 miles. Based on 1.5 trips per case, this distance of travel would become 3,000 miles per year. At the trial center, the 100 trials from each county would require 600 witnesses. Based on 1.5 trips per witness per case and an average travel distance of 80 miles (160 miles round trip) to the trial center, the travel distance of witnesses for each of the 4 counties would be 144,000 and for all 4 counties would be 576,000 miles per year. At the central county, with 250 trials of which 75 are jury trials, the number of witnesses (average of 6 per case) would be 1,500. Based on 1.5 trips per witness per case, an average distance of witness travel at 10 miles (20 miles round trip), the distance of witness travel in the central county would be 45,000 miles per year. Consequently, the total travel distance for witnesses in the region would be 576,000 + 45,000=621,000 miles per year.

Judges and Court Staff

Existing System
The circuit judge is a resident judge of the county. He or she may be assisted by one or more associate judges. The circuit judge spends two days per week during the court term in this county. The other three days he or she is assigned to two other counties. This means that he or she has to travel an average of 80 miles or 160 miles round trip 3 days each week. Assum-

ing he or she does not travel home the 2 nights he or she is away, the total mileage per week would be 240 miles. If he or she works 10 months each year, the number of miles traveled would be 240 x 43=10,520 miles. If a court reporter/secretary travels with the judge, an additional 10,520 miles would be recorded. Based on an average travel time of 40 mph, the amount of time spent in traveling would be 6 hours per week or 258 hours per year. This is equivalent to ¾ of a workday per week spent in traveling between counties. For the 6 circuit judges in the surrounding locations, the total amount of traveling would be 63,120 miles per year. The same amount would have to be added for court reporter/secretary's traveling with the judges. There would be one circuit judge per county, and two circuit judges in the central county, a total of six circuit judges. An associate judge would be retained at each county to handle minor cases of local nature.

Regionalization/Consolidation

Judges and court staff would be located in the trial center for the entire week or the entire court session. The judges who reside in the surrounding counties would need to make the round trip each week, or 160 miles per week, 6,880 miles per year. With the 3 circuit judges traveling from the surrounding counties, the total amount of traveling would be 6,880 x 3=20,640 miles per year. With the 2 resident circuit judges in the central county, the amount of traveling should not exceed a total of 4,000 miles. The total traveling of the 5 circuit judges would be around 24,640 miles per year. Because of the regionalization/consolidation, the total number of circuit judges could be reduced to five, or even four if proper scheduling of cases and resources are implemented. There would be no change in the number of associate judges.

Public

Existing System

Public traveling to the courthouse would be much more difficult to estimate. There would be more public attendance within each county when all trials are conducted in each county than if all major trials are conducted in the trial center of the region. Assuming that each of the 500 cases attracts 2 public members (including family, relatives, friends, etc.) and that the 150 trials attract 4 additional public (both family and general public), the total number of public would be 3,000 per year. If 3 of the 6 public members need to visit the courthouse twice per case, the number of public visits would be 4,500 per year. Assuming an average distance of 10 miles (20 miles round trip), the total travel distance for public would be 90,000 miles per year for each county, or 360,000 miles per year for the 4 surrounding counties. In the central county, due to the doubling of caseload, we can assume that the number of public could be roughly doubled (180,000 miles per year). Therefore, the total for the 5 counties would be 540,000 miles per year.

Regionalization/Consolidation

With greater travel distance from the surrounding counties to the central location, it can be assumed that the number of public (outside of relatives and friends) from these counties would be substantially reduced. Assuming the total number of public from each of the 4 surrounding counties is 2,000 per year and the number of trips per case is 1.5, then the total number of public trips would be 3,000 per year. Assuming an average distance of 80 miles (or 160 miles round trip), the total travel distance would be 480,000 miles per year for each county, or 1,920,000 miles per year for the 4 surrounding counties. In the central county, the number of public trips would remain at 180,000 miles per year. The total public traveling in this system would be 2,100,000 miles per year, which is nearly 4 times the number of the existing judicial system.

(continued)

Table 8.1—*Continued*

People—Costs

Existing System	Regionalization/Consolidation
Jurors	
424,500 miles at 40 mph=10,612.5 hours Time cost at $5=$53,062.50 1,300 x 4=5,200 jury days (four counties) 5,200 + 1,875 (central county)=7,075 jury days Based on $15/jury day: Jury fee=7,075 x $15=$106,125 Reimbursement of travel at 15¢ per mile: 424,500 x $0.15=$63,675 Total jury cost for five counties=$222,862.50	1,239,800 miles at 40 mph=30,995 hours Time cost at $5=$154,975 5,515 jury days at $15=$82,725 Reimbursement of travel at 15¢ per mile: 1,239,000 x $0.15=$185,970 Total jury cost for five counties=$423,670.00
Attorneys	
18,000 x 4=72,000 miles per year (4 counties) plus 36,000 miles for main county per year At 40 mph=2,700 hours Time cost: 2,700 hours at $25 per hour=$67,500 Travel cost: 108,000 at 15¢=$16,200 Total attorneys' travel cost for 5 counties = $83,700 (Assume that the amount and value of time spent on court business remain the same for both systems)	Total travel distance=640,000 miles At 40 mph=16,000 hours Time cost: 16,000 hours at $25/hour=$400,000 Travel cost: 640,000 at 15¢=$96,000 Total attorneys' travel cost for 5 counties= $496,000
Witnesses	
Total travel distance for the 5 counties = 153,000 miles per year At 40 mph=3,825 hours Time cost: 3,825 at $10=$38,250 Travel cost: 153,000 at 15¢=$22,950 Witness fee: 7,650 witness days at $30= $229,500 Total witness costs=$290,700	Total travel distance=621,000 miles per year At 40 mph=15,525 hours Time cost: 15,525 at $10=$155,250 Travel cost: 621,000 at 15¢=$93,150 Witness fee: 5,850 witness days at $30= $175,500 Total witness costs=$423,900
Judges	
Total travel distance for 5 counties = 63,120 miles per year At 40 mph=1,578 hours Time cost: 1,578 at $25=$39,450 Travel cost: 63,120 at 15¢=$9,468 Salary: 6 judges at $45,000=$270,000 Fringe benefits: 30% of salary=$81,000 Total cost=$399,918	Total travel distance=24,640 miles per year At 40 mph=616 hours Time cost: 616 at $25=$15,400 Travel cost: 24,640 at 15¢=$3,696 Salary: 5 judges at $45,000=$225,000 Fringe benefits: 30% of salary=$67,500 Time cost=$311,596
Court Reporter/Secretary	
Time cost: 1,578 at $8=$12,624 Travel cost with judge, no charge Salary: 6 reporters at $20,000=$120,000 Fringe benefits: 30% of salary=$36,000 Total court reporters' cost=$168,624 Total judge and court reporters' cost=$568,542	Time cost: 616 at $8=$4,928 Travel cost, no charge Salary: 5 reporters at $20,000=$100,000 Fringe benefits: 30% of salary=$30,000 Total court reporters cost=$134,928 Total judge and court reporters' cost=$446, 524

Table 8.1—*Continued*

Public

Total travel distance=540,000 miles/year
At 40 mph=13,500 hours
Time cost: 13,500 at $5=$67,500
Travel cost: 540,000 x 15¢=$81,000
Total public cost=$148,500

Total travel distance: 2,100,000 miles/year
At 40 mph=52,500 hours
Time cost: 52,500 at $5=$262,500
Travel cost: 2,100,000 x 15¢=$315,000
Total public cost=$577,500

Summary

Jurors	$222,862	$423,670
Attorneys	$83,700	$496,000
Witnesses	$290,700	$423,900
Judges and court staff	$568,542	$446,524
Public	$148,500	$577,500
	$1,314,304**	$2,367,594**

Source: Space Management Consultants, Inc.; Illinois Statewide Judicial Facilities Project, Phase Two Summary Report, 1978.
* Cost figures are based on 1978 cost information for this specific project.
** Cost difference between the two systems is calculated to be $1,053,240 for one year, which represents an 80.14% difference between the Existing System and the Regionalization/Consolidation System, the latter being the higher-cost system.

Table 8.2. Costs to Court System between Existing and Regionalization/Consolidation

Participants	Existing System	Regionalization/Consolidation	Remarks
Jurors	Jury Fee: 7,075x$15=$106,125 Reimbursed Travel: 424,500x 15¢=$63,675	5,515x$15=$82,725 1,239,800x15¢=$185,970	If reimbursed by court
Witnesses	Witness Fee: 7,650x$30=$229,500 Reimbursed Travel: 153,000x 15¢=$22,950	5,850x$30=$175,500 621,000x15¢=$93,150	If reimbursed by court
Judges	Total Cost: $399,918	Total Cost: $311,596	
Court Reporter/ Secretary	Total Cost: $168,624	Total Cost: $134,428	
Total Cost to Court	$904,167	$704,249	Excludes reimbursed travel costs
	$967,842	$890,219	Includes jurors' travel cost
	$990,792	$983,369	Includes jurors' and witnesses' travel costs

Source: Space Management Consultants, Inc.; Illinois Statewide Judicial Facilities Project, Phase Two Summary Report, 1978

Facility Cost Considerations

In the area of facility costs, it can be assumed that each local government (e.g., county or parish) in most states has its own courthouse, which requires a certain degree of improvement, renovation, and possible expansion. Based on an analysis of facility needs and recommendation on facility improvement for rural areas with low caseloads and underutilized court facilities (combining short-term, intermediate-term, and long-term facility improvement), renovation and construction costs of several courthouses can be, in many instances, much higher than the renovation and construction costs of a regional trial center. It can also be assumed that the regional trial center would not necessarily be a new building; it could be a renovated existing courthouse with high rehabilitation potential and with the possibility of expansion on the site to accommodate projected growth needs. While the creation of such a regional trial center may incur substantial capital costs, the renovation and construction work recommended for these other county courthouses could be substantially reduced. Depending on the condition of these other courthouses, the cost savings resulting from reduced renovation and construction work to several courthouses may be adequate to cover the cost of renovating the regional trial center.

The regional trial center should be fully utilized by handling the more complicated criminal and civil cases. All major trials would be conducted by judges and juries at the trial center. Cases that can be handled more effectively at the local level, including traffic and ordinance violations and small-claims, probate, and juvenile matters, should remain at the local courthouses. With the regional trial center handling the more complicated cases, local facilities needed in the county courthouse could be reduced. There would not be the need for a large trial courtroom; nearly all limited-jurisdiction cases could be heard in smaller hearing rooms, conference rooms, and judges' chambers. In many courthouses, portions of existing court facilities could then be returned to the local government for reassignment to other functions that otherwise might have to continue leasing commercial office space.

System Cost Considerations

If overall system costs were to be considered in this analysis, the regional trial center concept would involve considerably more travel time and costs to case participants as well as to the general public. This high cost of travel between the outlying counties and the regional trial center is the major contributor to the high overall system cost of the regionalization-consolidation concept. In addition to these cost considerations, there are other less tangible social costs that cannot be measured easily in terms of monetary value. For example, the consolidation of facilities in a central location may cause serious inconvenience to jurors, attorneys, witnesses, and public irrespective of the extra costs involved in time and travel between the surrounding counties and the trial center.

Consideration should also be given to prisoner security and transportation costs. If prisoners continue to be housed in local jails and are transported to the trial center only on the date of appearance, there may not be the need for a regional detention and holding facility near the trial center. Prisoner-holding and detention costs would remain the same. However, there would also be considerable prisoner transportation and supervision costs, including the purchase of suitable prisoner vans or cars, additional security precautions during transportation, and additional personnel costs during transportation and in the trial center. After their court appearance, the prisoners would have to be returned to the local area in which they are detained.

While this system may result in higher security and transportation costs, it has two advantages:

- Defendants are held in facilities located in the area in which they reside. Their relatives and friends could visit them on a daily basis. This strengthens the defendants' community ties. If they were to be housed in a regional detention facility requiring long distances of travel, there would be less frequent visits.
- It eliminates the need for a costly new regional detention facility.

Video-arraignment procedures involving video links between the jail and the video-arraignment courtroom(s) in the courthouse would significantly reduce prisoner transportation between the jail and the courthouse for preliminary hearings and arraignments. The number of prisoners transported to the courthouse for trials and hearings is only a small percentage of those attending arraignments and preliminary hearings.

If a regional detention facility were to be constructed adjoining or near the trial center, all prisoners arrested within the region would be transported to this facility to be detained until they are released on bail, on their own recognizance, when their cases are dismissed, or when they are acquitted of the charges against them. A regional detention facility could serve as a prisoner-holding facility while defendants await trial, or it could also be a combined pretrial and postsentence facility in which both defendants awaiting trial and prisoners serving short sentences are housed. Such a regional facility would house all those arrested within the region. Once the prisoners are properly processed, they remain in the facility until they are released by court order. The advantage of this system is that the prisoners are housed near the trial center, and could be transported through secured corridors, tunnels, and so forth, between detention and court facilities without the use of vehicles. The security personnel in this detention facility would be responsible for the transportation and supervision of prisoners, and the local authorities of the surrounding areas within the region would not have further responsibility over the prisoners once they are handed over to the regional detention facility personnel. The arresting officers, of course, may appear as witnesses during hearings or trials. The staffing of the regional detention facility could be accomplished either by creating a separate correctional unit at the regional level, or by the expansion of the existing sheriff's staff in the area where the detention facility is located. Unless the state legislature acts on bills to create such regions, the selection of any area within a region for expansion of its sheriff's department would no doubt create serious political and economic problems and objections from the sheriffs in the surrounding counties.

Even with the creation of a regional detention facility, the local jails would continue to house the few defendants to be tried on minor charges in the local courthouses. These defendants are normally released on their own recognizance. Some are detained for a specific reason, such as inability to raise the necessary bail or the need to detain them for their own and others' safety. If funds are available, the local county jail could be renovated and converted to office space for other use.

Local Autonomy Considerations

Another factor against the regionalization-consolidation concept is the desire of each local area to have its own courthouse. In many states, this is traditional. Historically, the county courthouse served as the focus of community activities and, in many cases, as its main source of entertainment. As the churches were the center of people's lives in the Middle Ages, the local courthouse has been the symbol of strength of local government and had significant impact on the lives of the citizens. Politically, the local government does not wish to lose any of its power and autonomy. The local courthouse belongs to them, and they are responsible for the care and custody of the building. Through this means, the local government is able to exert a sense of control, whether real or imaginary, over judicial facilities. To lose the major part of the judiciary to a centralized trial center could be viewed as equivalent to the loss of control over the local court system. Beyond the need for statutory or constitutional changes, there is also the need to show the local governments that the regionalization-consolidation concept would result in economic as well as other advantages to them. If this cannot be accomplished, then the regionalization-consolidation concept is not a feasible alternative to the existing system.

The above hypothetical application of the regionalization-consolidation concept provides a basis for cost comparison and system evaluation. The application of this concept has its limitations and constraints. Experimentation of concept application to specific locations, accompanied by careful and complete documentation, would be the first step toward an evaluation of the extent of applicability of the regionalization-consolidation concept.

Fair Rental Values of Judicial Facilities

A systematic method of determining the purchase or leasing of locally owned judicial facilities should be developed if the state is to assume the responsibility for operating and maintaining all court facilities statewide. To arrive at fair rental value for court facilities, criteria should be established to evaluate the capability of each courthouse to provide adequate and suitable spaces for the efficient functioning of the court system.

Existing courthouses vary widely in age, condition, size, adequacy, and suitability of court facilities, and are not conducive to a single standard rental value. Flexible rental values should be established to compensate for inconsistencies created by local governments of similar populations and caseloads having court facilities that are either oversized or undersized for their particular needs, based on established facility standards and design guidelines for the particular courthouse size. Therefore, a fair-rental-value index should be established which reflects the courthouse's capability to provide adequate and suitable facilities that will meet facility standards and design guidelines required by the court system. In determining the improvements necessary for each facility to meet these minimum facility standards, the age and physical condition of the facility and the suitability and adequacy of existing court spaces should be taken into consideration. By using these standards, all facilities throughout a state can be assessed on an equal basis.

It would be beyond the scope of this discussion to recommend actual rental values for existing facilities throughout a particular state, since basic rental values vary widely across the state as a result of differences in rural and urban market values and in local conditions. If and when the state should assume the cost of operating and maintaining all local court facilities, the fair-rental-value index could then be applied to the basic unit rental cost in each area to derive the actual fair rental value of each court facility.

Analysis of Fair Rental Values in the Illinois Statewide Project

In the Illinois Statewide Judicial Project, each of the departmental functions (judicial, clerical, prosecution, etc.) for all counties was evaluated in terms of its departmental summary factor, which is the sum total of work necessary to be completed within that particular function to meet minimal standards. The summary factors for each court facility were added up to reflect the total amount of project work required to be completed in each court facility. This total was then compared with the maximum total possible for the corresponding class or size of facility to obtain a percentage of the maximum total. For example, Alexander County is within the Class A range, small courthouses with one to two courtrooms, and has a total of 2,160 departmental summary points out of a maximum of 4,210. Therefore, the department total is 51 percent of the maximum total value for Class A (table 8.3). This value is important when assessing the amount of work required within a particular facility to bring it up to minimal standards, compared to the maximum value, which represents the scope of work required to completely replace an existing facility with new construction. The maximum value for Classes A to D is as follows:

Class A (1–2 courtrooms)   4,210 points
Class B (3–6 courtrooms)   4,750 points
Class C (7–13 courtrooms)   4,975 points
Class D (13 or more courtrooms) 4,975 points

To determine the fair rental value index, the percentage of building value to maximum value was multiplied by the evaluation factor (a number on a scale of 1 to 10), which represents the physical condition of the facility: this calculation was necessary so that the fair rental index would reflect the amount of work needed within the buildings, as well as its physical and environmental conditions.

Once the fair-rental-value index has been completed, counties were arranged by these values in numerical sequence—see table 8.4, Priorities for State Leasing of County Facilities. This table categorizes the counties into three major groupings by their fair-rental-value index: facilities requiring minor renovation (1 to 300 range), facilities requiring moderate renovation (301 to 600 range), and facilities requiring major renovation or construction of new building (601 to 1,000 range). These ranges were determined by reviewing the actual recommendations made for each county within each subgrouping as indicated in the table (that is, 1 to 100, 101 to 200, 201 to 300).

Development of Branch Court Locations

Many local governments in various states use branch or field locations to handle a wide range of judicial procedures. Branch courts are utilized for a variety of reasons. Among them are the needs to provide judicial services for population concentrations outside the range of convenience from the main court facility, to relieve overcrowding and congestion at a courthouse, and to

Table 8.3. Analysis of Fair Rental Values for Court Facilities

Circuit	County	Class	Evaluation Factor	Departmental Summary Factor									Total	% of Maximum Value	Evaluation Factor x % of Maximum Value**
				Judicial	Support	Clerical	Prosecution	Defense	Probation	Law Enf.	Bldg. Svcs.				
1st	Alexander	A	4	1350	0	440	105	70	120	45	30	2160	51	204
	Jackson	B	4	2000	336	320	700	160	240	240	45	4071	95	380
	Johnson	A	9	2000	210	640	385	50	120	180	225	3810	90	810
	Massac	A	6	1500	150	400	70	70	120	240	45	2595	62	372
	Pope	A	10	2000	210	640	420	70	120	240	300	4000	95	950
	Pulaski	A	6	2000	120	360	420	70	120	60	120	3270	78	468
	Saline	A	5	800	120	720	446	70	120	0	0	2276	54	270
	Union	A	7	1400	96	400	350	70	150	240	45	2751	65	455
	Williamson	B	2	350	72	120	280	70	45	18	0	955	22	44
2nd	Crawford	A	9	2000	180	280	280	70	120	0	90	3020	71	639
	Edwards	A	9	400	60	320	280	70	120	0	165	1415	34	306
	Franklin	B	10	2000	210	800	420	120	180	210	300	4270	100	1000
	Gallatin	A	10	1100	108	320	35	70	120	60	210	2023	48	480
	Hamilton	A	8	2000	96	160	84	70	120	180	240	2950	70	560
	Hardin	A	10	2000	120	640	280	60	105	150	120	3475	83	830
	Jefferson	B	7	2000	120	240	280	70	120	15	45	2890	68	476
	Lawrence	A	6	100	180	280	210	70	120	0	45	1005	24	144
	Richland	A	8	2000	96	140	280	70	120	0	45	2771	66	528
	Wabash	A	2	100	0	520	350	80	135	0	0	1185	28	56
	Wayne	A	8	100	0	200	245	70	120	45	75	855	20	160
	White	A	5	1500	96	480	280	70	120	0	30	2576	62	310
3rd	Bond	A	9	2000	102	480	315	70	120	0	240	3327	79	711
	Madison	D	7	2000	600	800	700	200	300	300	75	4975	100	700
4th	Christian	B	7	350	0	520	35	80	120	0	45	1150	27	18
	Clay	A	8	1500	96	280	245	70	120	30	270	2611	62	496
	Clinton	A	9	1800	180	480	420	120	180	0	180	3360	80	720
	Effingham	A	10	2000	210	640	420	120	180	0	300	3870	92	920
	Fayette	A	6	350	72	280	280	70	120	0	45	1217	29	174
	Jasper	A	9	2000	96	320	280	70	120	60	105	3051	72	648
	Marion	B	7	2000	900	280	280	70	120	0	45	2885	68	476
	Montgomery	A	8	2000	210	800	420	120	180	270	300	4210	100	800
	Shelby	A	7	2000	93	240	280	70	120	180	60	3046	72	504

Source: Space Management Consultants, Inc.; Illinois Statewide Judicial Facilities Project, Phase Two Summary Report, 1978.
*Fair Market Value

Table 8.4. Priorities for State Leasing of County Facilities

Number of Facilities Requiring Minor Renovation						Number of Facilities Requiring Moderate Renovation			
1–100		101–200		201–300		301–400		401–500	
Carroll	21	Bureau	120	Alexander	204	Edwards	306	Greene	432
McLean	27	Henry	130	Lasalle	204	Jo Daviess	306	Cumberland	441
Williamson	44	Moultrie	135	Logan	216	Macon	310	Morgan	455
Randolph	46	Lawrence	144	Kendall	222	White	310	Union	455
Stephenson	50	Henderson	152	Iroquois	225	Pike	322	Pulaski	468
Wabash	56	Adams	156	Marshall	225	Perry	342	Jefferson	476
St. Clair	62	Wayne	160	Kane	228	Schuyler	343	Marion	476
McHenry	63	Grundy	165	Peoria	245	Piatt	344	Gallatin	480
Will	64	Hancock	186	Saline	270	Massac	372	De Kalb	483
Cass	66	Christian	189	Tazewell	270	Washington	376	Clay	496
Fulton	84	Ford	190	Lee	288	Edgar	378	Mercer	496
Winnebago	90	Livingston	195	Ogle	288	Putnam	378	Kankakee	497
Lake	96			Rock Island	294	Jackson	380	Woodford	497
						Kane	390	Stark	500
						Coles	392		
						Mason	392		
						Scott	399		
						Sangamon	400		

Source: Space Management Consultants, Inc.; Illinois Statewide Judicial Facilities Project, Phase Two Summary Report, 1978.

accommodate the public and local police agencies by providing more conveniently located court services. Consequently, branch courts have a significant impact and need to be addressed in the comprehensive county, regional, or statewide judicial facilities master plan. It follows that for the master plan to be optimally implementable, branch locations, where applicable, must be evaluated as an alternative in developing the county's solution to future space needs. The operations at these branch locations could range from conducting weekly jury and nonjury trials for most types of cases to nonjury matters involving traffic and small-claims cases as infrequently as once a month.

Incorporating the branch court unit locations into a master plan requires completion of the following tasks:

Number of Facilities Requiring Major Renovation or Construction of New Building								
501–600		601–700		701–800		801–900		901–1000
Shelby	504	Menard	608	Bond	711	Johnson	810	Effingham 920
Clark	520	Crawford	639	Clinton	720	Hardin	830	Pope 950
McDonough	528	Jasper	648	Boone	736			Calhoun 1000
Richland	528	Madison	700	Champaign	800			Franklin 1000
Dupage	546			Montgomery	800			Monroe 1000
Douglas	552			Whiteside	800			Vermilion 1000
Hamilton	560							
Jersey	560							
Macoupin	560							

- an analysis to determine whether a branch court location in the county can be justified, based on criteria for the establishment of branch courts
- determination of the operations of the branch locations, based on functional guidelines
- development of spatial standards and design guidelines for branch court facilities
- adjustment to the master plan for inclusion of specific branch courts

To accomplish these tasks, this section develops the necessary factors and processes to evaluate the need for and space requirements of a branch court location. This results in a planning tool with which to design a flexible solution to future space needs.

Criteria for Branch Court Development

To incorporate a branch court location into a court system, the system must first analyze whether a branch location is justified by evaluating it with appropriate branch court criteria. Analysis of existing branch court locations throughout a state would reveal that branch courts are utilized for a variety of reasons, including alleviating present space deficiencies in the main court location and accommodating areas of strong political influence. Some of these reasons have little relevance to the efficient functioning of the court system and should not be viewed as appropriate guidelines for the development of branch court facilities. The purpose and criteria for the development of the branch courts should be as follows:

- to increase the efficiency and effectiveness of the justice system
- to provide better judicial services to the population
- to handle concentrations of caseload activity remote from the central courthouse location
- to eliminate congestion at the main court location

These criteria identify the following factors for determining whether a branch court location is warranted.

- distance of the location from the main courthouse facility
- case-filing activity generated by the neighborhood
- trial activity generated from case filings
- convenience of access and available transportation to and from main courthouse facility
- amount of local police activity likely to be generated at the proposed branch court location
- amount of attorney business likely to be generated at that branch court location
- percentage of population to be served by that branch court location

The efficiency of the justice system depends on the degree of operational integration among its many components (courts, prosecution, law enforcement, correction, etc.). In many locations, considerable police and prosecution time is wasted by having to make frequent trips to the main courthouse to process minor cases. Branch court locations to which local police agencies and lawyers have convenient access can recapture a significant amount of this time. Therefore, the justification of branch court locations for this purpose depends partly on the number of police officers involved in required appearances for traffic and other minor cases as well as on the distance and directness of travel between the main courthouse and the branch location.

In some areas, the county seat does not represent the concentration of population within the county. This situation requires residents in high-population-concentration areas to travel long distances to conduct court business. In such a situation, a branch location provides more direct local contact with the court system. This permits greater familiarity with the court process and easier access with less travel time. Beyond time and distance, the amount of court activities will have to be evaluated to assess whether a branch court location can be economically justified in terms of personnel and facility use.

Congestion at the main courthouse usually occurs in large urbanized centers. With high land costs in the downtown area, car parking is usually at a premium, and construction of parking garages requires substantial initial expenditure of funds. For minor court activities, the time spent on finding a parking space and in waiting at the counter or in the courtroom far exceeds the amount of time needed to complete court transactions. This is especially troublesome for people who can get to the courthouse only during the lunch period or outside regular business hours. A branch location in such a situation would reduce parking requirements for visitors and would reduce the peak loads at the main courthouse by dispersing necessary court transactions to branch locations that handle local court business.

Functional Guidelines

After establishing that a particular location meets the criteria for a branch court, the next step is to determine how that court should function (see table 8.5). Because of the present variety of purposes for which branch courts are utilized, they operate within a wide range of schedules, some handling the full spectrum of court procedures. In many cases, handling certain court procedures at branch locations reduces the efficiency of the system and requires additional personnel time. For example, if jury trials were to be conducted at branch court locations, the expenses involved in organizing jurors at different locations, and the additional clerical personnel necessary for processing legal documents, may not justify decentralization of jury trial for the convenience of local population. Therefore, to establish branch court locations from a functional standpoint, the following guidelines, based on maintaining the efficiency of the court system, should be used:

- the schedule for court should be regular, whether it be daily, weekly, monthly, or on a less frequent basis
- branch courts should handle limited types of cases for the locality, including traffic, small claims, and ordinance violations
- branch courts should not handle jury trials

- branch courts should not handle criminal case procedures involving appearances by defendants in custody except for the initial court appearance
- clerical functions should be maintained centrally, with clerks at branch locations only during court days

Regular schedules for branch court locations should be developed to handle sufficient caseload activity generated at the location. The caseload activity should warrant at least a half-day court session. Any lighter court activity cannot justify the traveling time of court personnel. The schedule should be coordinated with other locations in the county handling similar case types. This would allow all judicial departments to assign personnel to handle a combination of locations without duplicating effort and wasting time. Schedules should also be coordinated with judges' assignments so that a judge can travel a developed circuit if there are sufficient branch locations. Regular schedules also assist in coordinating the court system with police departments, private attorneys, businesspeople, and related county government agencies.

Restricting case types at branch locations helps maintain efficiency in the processing of many case types. Case categories such as civil cases over a certain monetary amount, felonies, juvenile cases, and domestic relations cases have procedures that require a high degree of coordination between all court-related departments. In addition, these procedures also require certain specialized services that operate better in central locations (e.g., psychiatric and psychological counseling, defendant detention, case research, intake diversionary programs). Traffic and small-claims hearings are of short duration and do not require continual updating of schedules, while major civil and criminal cases have numerous procedures that may result in case processing spanning periods of months or even years. Hence, it would be more difficult to coordinate such procedures during the limited branch court schedule, since each procedure could take up most of the allocated court time. In conclusion, branch courts should handle the numerous local cases involving the least difficult and least time-consuming procedures.

Conducting jury trials in branch court locations contradicts one of the above-listed guidelines. They require maximum coordination between the court departments as well as the largest number of participants. Jury trials also require a full range of trial facilities and an adherence to stricter design standards and guidelines in order for trial procedures to function efficiently. Jury deliberation rooms, enlarged courtrooms to accommodate jurors and more trial participants, special prisoner-holding facilities, and more attorneys' conference and witness waiting rooms would increase renovation, con-

Table 8.5. Functions, Spaces, and Users—Branch Court Function

Function	Space Description	User
Adjudication	Nonjury courtroom for bench trials, motions, hearings and other court proceedings. High-volume court room for traffic, small claims and misdemeanor court proceedings.	Judges, state's attorney, public defender/counsel, litigants, defendants, witnesses, circuit clerk, court reporters, bailiffs, sheriff's or city police deputies, probation officers, news reporters, relatives, public.
Courtroom Support	An attorney's conference room for discussions with clients during court proceedings. A waiting area for witnesses, including storage area for personal belongings, and private toilet.	Public defender/counsel, litigants, defendants, witnesses, bailiff or court officer, attorneys, public.
Security	Station within the courtroom for observation of court participants and the public. Temporary holding facility with toilet for detaining prisoner awaiting court appearance.	Bailiff, court officer, sheriff's/city police deputies, public defender/counsel, prisoner.
Chambers	Executive private work area for legal research. Conference and meeting area with staff and visitors. Storage area for personal items, records. Work area for court reporter/secretary. Reception area for staff and visitors.	Judges, secretary, court reporters, court officers, clerks, visitors.
Clerical	Reception and waiting area for visitors. Public counter for receiving necessary files and filling out forms. Open work area for clerical staff. Storage area for records. Storage area for supplies and forms.	Court clerk, clerk-typist, public, attorneys, court reporter.
Prosecution/Defense/Probation	Private work area for conferring and working. Reception and public waiting area for visitors. Clerical work area for secretary/receptionist.	State's attorney, public defender, probation officer, secretary, public, witnesses, defendants, attorneys.

Source: Space Management Consultants, Inc.; Illinois Statewide Judicial Facilities Project, Phase Two Summary Report, 1978.

struction, and annual operation and maintenance costs. Jury trials also demand greater security precautions involving the separation of public, private, and secure circulation patterns. These requirements would make it difficult and costly to provide part-time or occasionally used facilities.

Increased security is one of the main reasons why criminal procedures should not be included in branch court schedules. Criminal procedures require the transfer of a defendant from a detention facility, which can be well removed from the central court facility. Transportation of prisoners, especially by means of vehicles, increases the difficulty of maintaining an acceptable level of security and at the same time increases the time and cost involved.

The clerical function is one of the operations that can be performed most efficiently at a centralized location. Schedules should be coordinated with all departments, and central records should be maintained for the convenience of related departments as well as of the general public. Having additional locations for case processing increases and duplicates the procedures necessary for the filing, processing, and retrieval of records. Invariably, this duplication of effort results in additional time and the need for more clerical staff. Clerical functions at branch locations should minimize the procedures that are later performed at the main clerk's office, and should essentially handle only those cases scheduled at the branch court location. Where it is possible to maintain the single centralized function, the clerical function at the branch court location should operate by having a traveling clerk carry those cases that are scheduled for that session of court on that particular day. This procedure eliminates the duplication and simplifies the process by reducing the coordination effort required.

Branch Court Facility Standards and Design Guidelines

The development of space standards and design guidelines is based on the procedures. Operations of branch court locations involve similar personnel, activities, and functions as the main court location, except on a limited scale.

This section presents the branch court facility standards and design guidelines, in tables and diagrams, developed for the state of Illinois (see tables 8.6 and 8.7 and figures 8.2 and 8.3).

Implementation Process

To effectively develop a branch court location, the three steps are as follows:
- determine whether a branch court location is needed
- develop the court procedures to be followed at the branch location
- develop the facility guidelines that would dictate the size and composition of the facility

Table 8.6. Design Guidelines—Branch Court Function

Court Function	Location Accessibility	Delineation & Scale	Flexibility	Furnishings & Equipment	Services
Adjudication	The basic courthouse guidelines for nonjury or high-volume courtrooms are applicable for the Branch Court Function. Special considerations include:				
		If multipurpose meeting room is needed, space should be sufficient to locate a judicial area for participants, separated from public seating by at least an aisle but preferably a low railing.	Courtrooms, whether used daily or occasionally, should be multipurpose, can be used for public meetings, counsel conferences or classroom/lecture space.	Furnishings in multipurpose courtrooms should be moveable to accommodate a variety of activities including lectures and public meetings. An occasionally used lecture platform with suitable office furniture is required to differentiate the judge's bench and the witness area.	
Courtroom Support	The basic courthouse guidelines for courtroom support space are applicable for the Branch Court Function. Special considerations include:				
			Ancillary space used infrequently by court should be designed as multipurpose space to be used by the city/county when not in use by court		

(continued)

Table 8.6—Continued

Court Function	Location & Accessibility	Delineation & Scale	Flexibility	Furnishings & Equipment	Services
Security	The basic guidelines for courtroom support space are applicable for the Branch Court Function. Special considerations include:				
		For only occasional prisoner detention, one of the attorney conference rooms should be made secured to hold prisoners when necessary.			
Chambers	The basic guidelines for judges' chambers are applicable for the Branch Court Function. Special considerations include:				
		Chambers need not contain informal conference area but only informal meeting of one or two visitors. Chambers should be 170 to 220 square feet.	Ancillary space used infrequently by court should be designed as multipurpose spaces to be used by the city or municipality when not in use by court.		
Clerical (Reception)	The basic guidelines for the clerk's office are applicable for the Branch Court Function. Special considerations include:				
	Reception area should not only have central access to office, but access to courtroom waiting area.	Counter should have cashier's station for collection of traffic fines and payments.			

	If only a part-time facility, clerk's office should also function as reception area for judges' chambers.	
(Record storage)		Storage should be provided by file cabinets, but if area is used only part-time, secure closet should be provided for safekeeping of records when office is closed.
Prosecution Defense Probation	The basic guidelines for specific functions and General Building Guidelines are applicable for Branch Court Function. Special considerations include:	
	Office should be provided in close proximity to courtrooms along public corridor.	Office should maintain staff involved at Branch Function.
	Full-time office should be accessible to public while courtroom areas are closed.	Full time office should provide private areas for personnel equivalent to areas at central location.
		Office should have combined reception/clerical working area.
Public	The basic guidelines for reception area in General Building Guidelines are applicable for Branch Court Function.	

Source: Space Management Consultants, Inc.; Illinois Statewide Judicial Facilities Project, Phase Two Summary Report, 1978

Table 8.7. Space Standards Summary—Branch Court Function

Space User	Court Function	Space	Special Equipment	Standard Area (sq.ft/person or space)	Facility Code
Branch Location Used Periodically					
Judge	Chambers	Private Office		170 to 220	PE-2,P-1
Judge's Secretary/ Court Reporter	Chambers	Work Area	Tape Machine	70@	AC-1,AC-2
	Adjudicative	Courtroom	Movable Furniture	900 to 1200	CC-3
	Courtroom Support	Attorney Conf. Room	Security Hardware	75@	CR-6
		Public Waiting Area	Movable Seats	10@	
	Security	Prisoner-Holding room	Wash Basin/Water Closet Unit, Secured Seating	70	PTI-1
Court Clerk	Clerical	General Work Area		55 to 70@	AC-2,AC-3
		Record Storage	Record Storage Equipment	30 to 45	
		Public Counter		55@	
		Public Reception Area		20@	
Branch Location Used Daily					
Judge	Chambers	Private Office		170 to 220	PE-2,P-1
Judge's Secretary/ Court Reporter	Chambers	Work Area	Tape Machine	70@	AC-1,AC-2
	Chambers	Reception Area		20@	
	Adjudicative	Courtroom	Movable Furniture	900 to 1200	CC-3
	Courtroom Support	Attorney Conf. Room		75@	CR-6
		Witness Waiting Room		100@	WW-1
		Public Waiting Room	Movable Seats	10@	

	Security	Prisoner-Holding Room	70	PH-1
		Secure Interview Room	100@	S1-1
Court Clerk	Clerical	General Work Area	55 to 70	AC-2,AC-3
		Record Storage	60 to 100	
		Public Counter	55@	
		Public Reception Area	20@	
		Supply Storage	10 to 25	
Assistant State's Attorney	Prosecution	Private Work Area	140@	P-2
State's Attorney Clerical Staff	Prosecution	Private Work Area	140@	P-2
	Prosecution	Clerical Work Area	55 to 70	AC-2,AC-3
		Reception Area	20@	
		Record Storage	15 to 30	
Assistant Public Defender	Defense	Private Work Area	140@	P-2
Probation Officer	Probation	Private Work Area	140@	P-2
Probation Clerical Staff	Probation	Clerical Work Area	55 to 70	AC-2,AC-3
		Reception Area	20@	
		Record Storage	15 to 30	
Public	Public Participation	Reception Lobby	8 to 10@	

Wash Basin/Water Closet Unit, Secured Seating Glass Panel, Intercom (Security)
Record Storage Equipment (Clerical)
Secure Record Storage Equipment (Prosecution Clerical)
Public Seating Facilities, public toilets (Public)

Source: Space Management Consultants, Inc.; Illinois Statewide Judicial Facilities Project, Phase Two Summary Report, 1978.

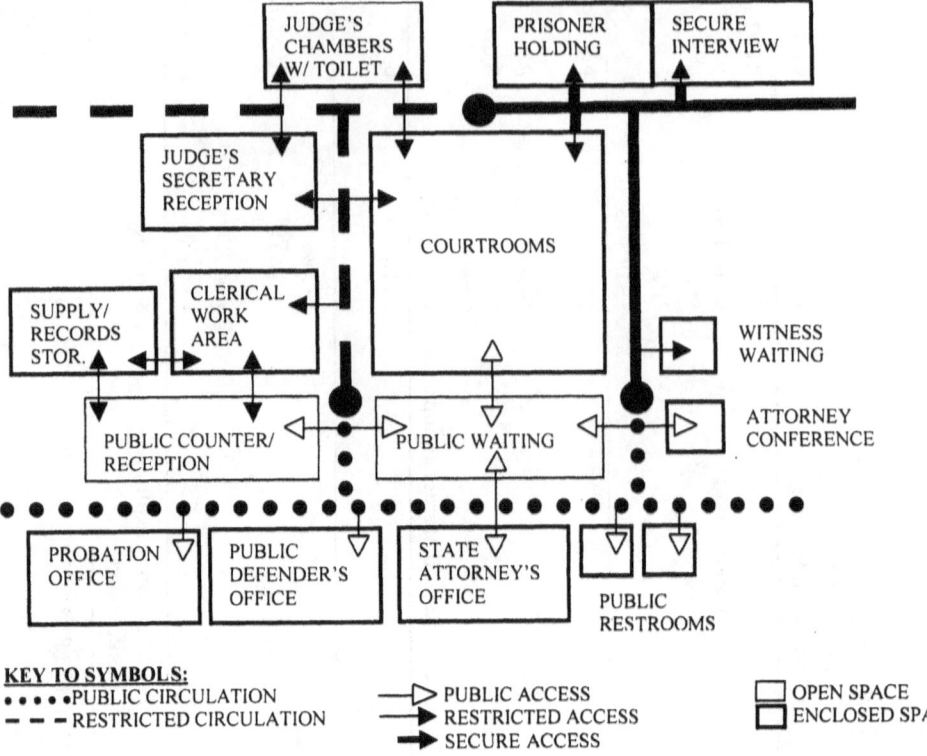

Figure 8.2. Branch Court Function—Facility Used Daily

To implement the branch court as an integral part of the judicial facility master plan for the county, it is crucial to evaluate the impact of the location on the projected space and personnel needs outlined in the facility program for that county. To do this, one needs to examine the effects of branch facilities on the specific court functions.

Judicial Function

The caseload generated by the county would not change with the introduction of a branch court; therefore, the workload that determined the judge and support staff allocations would remain the same. The number of courtrooms required at the main facility would be reduced by the amount of activity handled by the branch court. If a branch court operates twice a week for two full days, it would be safe to assume that time would have been scheduled in a courtroom in the main courthouse location. Therefore, the reduction would be two-fifths of the full use of a courtroom. For example, if a ten-courtroom county established five branch locations, each functioning two

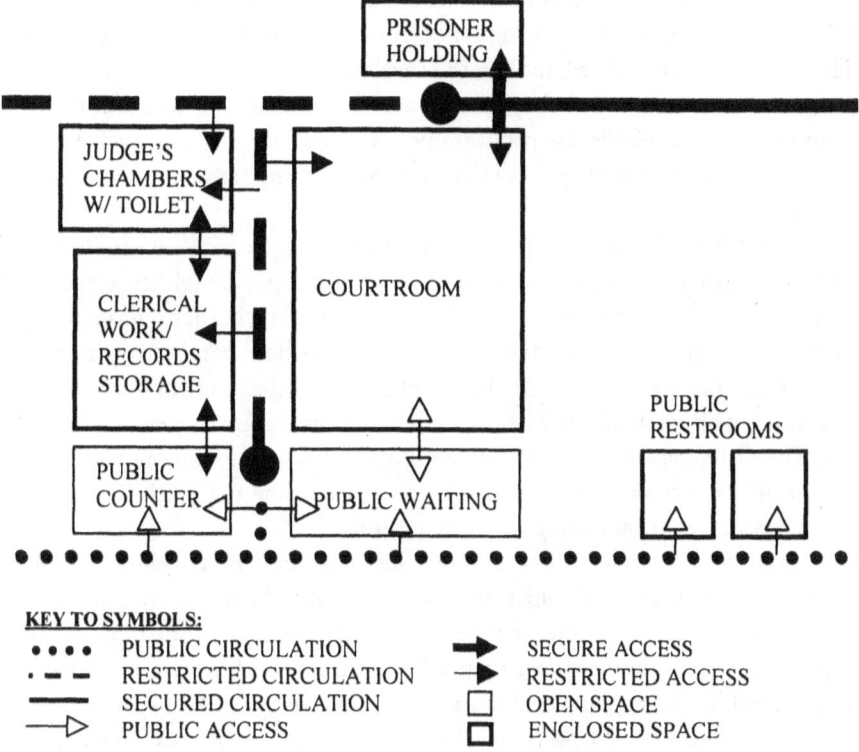

Figure 8.3. Branch Court Function—Facility Used Periodically

days a week, the courtrooms needed in the main location would be reduced from ten to eight by the two-courtroom activity handled by the branch courts. The need for ancillary spaces at the main courthouse would be reduced, corresponding to the decrease in the number of courtrooms. Judges' chamber requirements would depend on whether the judges travel regularly or only occasionally. If the judges travel one or two days each week, they would require home offices to conduct a large percentage of their work. However, if judges travel on a near full-time basis, their home office requirements would be minimal, as they would utilize chambers at branch court locations for most of their work. Adequate chamber facilities should be made in the main court facility for visiting judges on special or temporary assignment.

Clerical Function

Depending on the type of clerical activity conducted at branch locations, the clerical personnel may need to be adjusted. If the branch court operates on a part-time basis, with clerical personnel needed only for the days when court is in session at the location, then no additional personnel would be required. The court clerk would be handling the caseload at the branch court in essentially the same manner as they handle a court schedule in the main courthouse location. If efficiently programmed, the loss of time for travel should not have a significant effect on clerical personnel requirements at the main facility.

If the branch location requires a full-time clerk's office to handle case processing, there would be an increase in the total personnel needed in the department. The activity performed by a clerk handling branch court activity cannot compensate for the activity that would have been handled by the clerk in the main facility where he or she could assist in other clerical duties when necessary. This normally results in much better utilization of clerical personnel. The difference in personnel utilization would depend on how efficiently the branch court operates, and how much free time the clerk has at the branch court location during the slow periods.

Spatial requirements at the central clerk's office would change significantly only if the branch courts process a substantial caseload of particular types of cases. For example, if the branch courts handle all or most of the traffic and small-claims cases, then all spaces involved in case processing, such as public waiting, general work, and active records filing spaces at the central location, would be reduced by the percentage of space needed to process traffic and small-claims cases. Central records storage and calendaring, as well as supervision and administrative functions, would remain at the main facility, and no changes in spatial requirements would be needed.

Prosecution—Defense—Probation Functions

With no changes in caseloads, there would be no significant changes in the personnel of the state attorney's office, the public defender's office, or the probation department. These departments would function more efficiently if they maintained resource functions at the department's central facility. Therefore, the only change in space needs would be if the offices maintained permanent field offices at the branch court location. Requirements for private staff offices would be shifted to the branch facility and eliminated from the main office. Reception, clerical work areas, and record storage and staff service areas should not change to any extent.

Law Enforcement Function

The processing of the workload generated by the branch court location would be handled by the local police agencies. There would be no changes in the personnel or spaces required in the main facility except where there is a significant reduction in the number of courtrooms. If the number of courtrooms should be reduced as a result of branch court locations, there would be a reduction in the number of bailiffs required, but not in proportion to the number of courtrooms for branch courts that do not handle jury trials.

Branch Courts—Conclusion

For the implementation of a branch court to be totally effective in a master plan, it should be developed as an integral part of both the short- and long-term planning process. Before major improvements to the court system are initiated, the local area should have developed a policy and plan for the use of branch court locations, if they are necessary. They should also have assessed the possible locations of branch courts, and evaluated when each location should be developed to best accommodate future space needs. Major factors that should be considered in such a planning scheme are as follows:

- to make the solution as flexible as possible to incorporate future changes and shifts in population and procedures
- to understand that branch courts will be an effective tool only if provided with an efficient, coordinated process and suitable facilities
- to develop branch locations on a minimal basis when all other effective alternatives have been evaluated and eliminated from consideration

9

Intergovernmental Relationships and Their Impact on Court Facility Development

This chapter discusses how the judicial branch of government, through the separation-of-powers doctrine and its corollary, the doctrine of the inherent power of the court, combined with a strong base of intergovernmental relationships, can have impact on the renovation of existing judicial facilities or the construction of new ones.

Anyone exploring these issues should be familiar with the judiciary's awkward position in the governmental structure. On most issues, governmental power rests with the party who controls the purse strings. In such context, the judiciary's position is weak and vulnerable. The judiciary possesses no taxing power to coerce the funding of resources through the use of the veto, as can be done by the executive branch. The judiciary's real power, if such be a power, is the threat of litigation to compel, through its inherent power, the payment or appropriation of funds necessary to support its operations. This threat, to be successfully used, can be resorted to only in cases of extreme emergency. Even in such cases, the court will have to generate broad public support if it hopes to be successful.

The Judicial Branch—Its Role in Judicial Facility Development

Over the more than two hundred years of judicial history in this country, actual application of the separation-of-powers doctrine has been limited and has given rise to extensive debate and comment by legal scholars as to its real success. Today, with escalating caseloads facing courts at all levels and with governmental dollars and budgets constantly shrinking, it may become necessary to resort to use of the doctrine as an accepted means by which judiciaries can achieve their desired goals and objectives.

Separation of Powers—What Is It?

The separation-of-powers doctrine is the constitutional theory upon which our government at both federal and state levels is founded. It holds that the three branches of government, that is, the executive, legislative, and judicial, are separate, equal, and coordinate. Each branch, under the theory, is free to set its own destiny and manage its own day-to-day affairs without fear of control, restriction, or reprisal from the other two. This is the so-called checks-and-balances doctrine, which purports to guarantee that one branch of the government will not assume larger powers than the other two branches and by so doing put them in a subservient position. In practice, however, the doctrine is often abused by both the legislative and executive branches, particularly in the funding of the judicial branch.

The doctrine has met severe tests in the past quarter century, particularly at the federal level during the Nixonian crisis of the post-Watergate days. As a result, more people have become attuned to the doctrine, its nuances, subtleties, and potential uses.

Essentially, the power of the judiciary under the doctrine is to "emphatically . . . say what the law is." It is a power inherent to the judiciary even when such an interpretation checks the activities of another branch of government or contrary to a view taken by another branch of the government.

Even in enforcing the separation of powers, courts must intervene in the operation of other branches. This is no inconsistency in constitutional theory, since complete separation was never intended and overlapping functions were created deliberately.

How Is the Doctrine of Inherent Power Developed from the Separation of Powers?

It is axiomatic that if the action of one branch of government undermines or infringes upon the operation of another branch, such action is destructive to our system of government and poses a threat to the very existence of the governmental structure. Each branch of government possesses broad authority to stand up to the other branches and check arbitrary activities on their parts. However, the judiciary is severely limited in performing this function because of its passive role in the governmental budgetary process. In order to ensure its survival, the judiciary must develop a process and course of action particularly when the legislature provides insufficient funds for the operation of the judicial branch. Thus, the development of the doctrine of inherent power.

Courts should exercise the doctrine only when necessary to "preserve the efficient and expeditious administration of justice and protect it from being impaired or destroyed."

In *O'Coins, Inc., v. Treasurer,* a retail merchant in Worcester, Massachusetts, sought to compel the county treasurer to pay for a tape recorder and three tapes, which he had sold to the local superior court. The Supreme Judicial Court of Massachusetts held that among the inherent powers possessed by every judge is the power to protect his or her court from impairment resulting from inadequate facilities or a lack of supplies or supporting personnel. The court stated:

> It is axiomatic that as an independent department of government, the judiciary must have adequate and sufficient resources to ensure the proper operation of the courts. It would be illogical to interpret the constitution as creating a judicial department with awesome powers over the life, liberty, and property of every citizen while, at the same time, denying to the judges authority to determine the basic needs of their courts as to equipment, facilities and supporting personnel.

The power and authority described by the Massachusetts Supreme Judicial Court is the so-called doctrine of inherent power of the court, that is, a court possesses an implied or inherent power to, among other things, compel the expenditure of public funds for its survival or existence. The actual number of cases decided on such interpretation of a court's inherent power has been few and development of the doctrine probably is not yet complete.

An examination of those cases that have relied on the doctrine indicates actual use of the doctrine and its consequent deviation from the normal political process generally ends up impacting a very carefully developed governmental budget, thus making the courts responsible, at least in the eyes of the legislative and executive branches and probably in the eyes of the public, for increased taxes and diminished funding for other public services.

Use of the doctrine by state courts extends at least as far back as 1838, when the Supreme Court of Pennsylvania upheld the authority of a trial court to sequester a jury and require county commissioners to pay the expense incurred.

Cases have been used to compel the payment of the costs of recording or transcribing testimony; the payment of printing or publication costs; the payment of costs of investigations, examinations, audits; the payment of the cost of employing necessary court personnel, including clerks, secretaries, bailiffs, referees, probation officers; the payment of criminal defense expenses, including the expenses of appointed counsel; the payment of miscellaneous expenses; the payment of the expenses of prosecution; and, in limited instances, the payment of the cost of remodeling, repairing, or refurbishing courthouses and courtrooms. One commentator notes that the use of the doctrine and the litigation that has evolved from it is "more bountiful in legal rhetoric than in practical consequences."

In *Carlson v. State* a judge of the city court of Hammond, Indiana, brought a mandamus action to require the city council to provide funds for the operation of his court after the council had reduced his budget request. The judge based his action on the court's inherent power to compel sufficient appropriations. The Indiana Supreme Court articulated sound reasoning in support of the judge's exercise of power when it held it to be "axiomatic that the court must be independent and must not be subject to the whim of either the executive or legislative departments." This is particularly true because courts are frequently called upon to rule on the acts of those officials controlling public funds and must, therefore, be free to act in such cases without fear of retaliation.

More recent cases have reached similar results but have cautioned that while the power exists and can be applied to ensure the continued operation of the judicial branch, it is not unlimited and extends only to those expenses reasonably necessary for the proper function and administration of the court and that it must be exercised responsibly in the spirit of mutual cooperation among the various branches of government.

In *Commonwealth ex rel. Carroll v. Tate, supra,* the judges of the Court of Common Pleas of Philadelphia sought mandamus to compel the mayor and City Council of Philadelphia to appropriate additional funds they believed necessary for the administration of the court. The Supreme Court of Pennsylvania found that the requested funds should be appropriated by noting that the judicial branch has the inherent power to determine what funds are reasonably necessary for its efficient and effective operation. However, they took pains to point out that the court must do more than just assert the need for additional funds and that the burden is on the court to establish that the money it requests is reasonably necessary for the efficient administration of justice.

The Supreme Court of Washington went even further in limiting the exercise of inherent power in *In re Juvenile Director, supra.* In that case, county commissioners sought to reverse the order of the trial court judge directing them to increase the salary of the court's juvenile probation officer. The court held that the burden of proving the reasonableness of the request rested on the court and that the burden must be carried with evidence that was clear, cogent, and convincing. Such a limitation on the court's inherent power shows that courts and judges do not lightly exercise their powers.

Can the Inherent Power of the Court Be Used to Mandate Facility Renovation or Development?

It is accepted constitutional theory that the inherent power doctrine is more than sufficient to ensure the provision of facilities in which to hold court; facilities that are adequately furnished and kept in good repair and maintenance: "A duty to provide a suitable and convenient place for the holding of the courts necessarily includes the duty to provide a proper and sufficient courtroom with facilities for conducting trials by jury, including an adequate and sufficient jury room and the necessary conveniences." While the general rule is well stated and can be found as the statement of legislative intent in many state statutes, few attempts have been made under the auspices of the doctrine to require the building of completely new courthouses. A review of the literature and cases shows that little has been written on the subject, the most recent mention being Colorado Supreme Court justice Jim R. Carrigan's pamphlet *Inherent Powers of the Courts* (American Bar Association, 1980). Justice Carrigan cites a case, *Passaic County Bar Association v. Board of Chosen Freeholders*, which was settled by the construction of a new courthouse, thus avoiding litigation on the issue of the court's inherent power. In a second case cited by Justice Carrigan, *Ableman v. Mirrors*, members of the local bar association sued county officials to require construction of a new courthouse. In a letter from Judge Vincent Bifferato to then attorney Carrigan dated May 31, 1972, Judge Bifferato stated, "As soon as service of process was made . . . the matter settled and county officials then assumed responsibility for construction of a new courthouse." Again, litigation was avoided and we have no statement from a court of higher authority regarding the application of the doctrine as it relates to the construction of new facilities.

The oldest cited case that discusses use of inherent power to compel construction of court facilities is *Board of Commissioners v. Gwinn*, in which the circuit court entered an order that its courtroom was unsafe and unfit for further use. The court further appointed an architect to draw up plans to be followed by the commissioners and directed the sheriff to superintend construction of the repairs. The practical effect of following the architect's plan was gutting the existing courthouse and reconstruction to suit the judge. The Indiana Supreme Court held the court's power to order needed repairs did not justify building a new courthouse under the guise of repairing the old courthouse. The court did note that the circuit judge had the power to order repairs of the courthouse and that such power arose out of absolute necessity and was incidental to the jurisdiction of the court and, in fact, inherent in the court. The power could not be impaired by legislation but was limited and confined to repairs extending no further than to afford that temporary protection required to enable the court to continue to operate and provide fair administration of justice. In this particular case, the court found that there was no necessity or justification for the exercise of the power beyond minimal repairs necessary to ensure the continued operation of the court, observing that if the commissioners failed to make necessary repairs, the court could order such repairs as would afford temporary relief, and if they failed to rebuild the courthouse upon its destruction, the court could secure other quarters for temporary use by the court until proper authority could rebuild the courthouse.

Indiana seems to be the one state that has had some success in this area. In *In the Matter of Repairs and Rehabilitation of the Facilities of the LaPorte County Circuit Court,* Judge Alvin M. Smith mandated the air conditioning, remodeling, and modernizing of a seventy-five-year-old courthouse, citing as support for his action *Castle v. State.*

In *Castle,* the Indiana Supreme Court reversed a felony conviction because the court failed to provide the accused a speedy trial, the failure being due to inadequate facilities. The court held that it was the trial court's duty to exercise its inherent power "to ensure the efficient administration of justice" and "to see that the court was properly equipped in its accommodations and furnishings so as to be able to act effectively as a court."

Aside from the cases cited from Indiana, it appears that most courts have been fearful to tread upon the prerogatives of the legislative and executive branches of government without a public outcry and demonstrative support for new or renovated facilities. In *Nienaber v. Tarvin,* a circuit court judge imprisoned certain members of the city council of Covington for contempt in failing to obey his order to furnish the courthouse. The Kentucky Court of Appeals (that state's highest court) found that while the city did have an obligation to furnish a suitable courtroom, clerk's office, and other offices or buildings necessary for conducting the business of the court, the circuit judge was without authority to mandate provision of public expense for the refurnishing and rearranging of the courtroom. This function was vested solely in the council. The court stated that recognition of such power for the judge "would involve vesting in him arbitrary power over the property and liberty of citizens . . . and disregard of that other time honored principle, that taxpayers have the right, through their representatives, to determine when and in what amount, money collected by taxation shall be expended."

In *Committee for Marion County Bar Association v. County of Marion,* the Marion County Bar Association filed a motion in the Common Pleas Court to require the county commissioners to furnish an elevator to the second and third floors of the courthouse. The trial court ordered the commissioners to proceed, finding the elevator to be a facility that was essential to the efficient performance of the functions of the courts of the county. The commissioners appealed, and the Ohio Supreme Court denied the validity of the trial court's inherent power in this particular case, stating that while it did not wish to be misunderstood concerning the nature of the court's inherent power to require the furnishing of reasonable improvements, it found "no precedent that recognizes any inherent power of a court to provide a substantial addition to its courthouse building, especially where applicable statutes provide that other officers are to have discretionary powers with respect to providing such courthouse and determining its style, dimensions, and expense."

What the few cases that deal with this issue seem to imply is that use of the court's inherent power to require the construction or renovation of facilities may threaten rather than strengthen judicial independence. This is so because a court's mandating such actions involves it more substantially in the governmental budget process and may ultimately require increased taxes from the citizenry to pay for added costs mandated by the judiciary. Because the judiciary is generally isolated from public opinion concerning the appropriation of funds, it should approach this area carefully. Without caution, the judiciary runs the risk of developing a public image of partiality to its own cause, which could severely damage the public's support for judicial programs. Because the question is basically political, courts should only invoke the doctrine in cases of extreme emergency or neglect by the executive and legislative branches and when all other established means have failed.

If a court wishes to utilize its inherent power to mandate the construction of a new facility or renovation of an existing one, it must be willing to show that the building or its improvement is reasonably necessary for the holding of court, the efficient administration of justice, and the fulfillment of its constitutional duties. Even when the court so determines, it would be wise to remember that the public, particularly in states or jurisdictions where there is an elected judiciary, will be the final arbiter of an interbranch dispute over whether to improve or build a court facility. Thus, it is "incumbent upon the courts when they must use their inherent power to compel the funding to do so in a manner which clearly communicates and demonstrates the grounds for the court's action."

This discussion leads one to the conclusion that the doctrine probably is not sufficiently broad to allow for its general use to compel the construction or renovation of judicial facilities. Even so, it can be used as a tool by the judiciary to facilitate requests to the executive and legislative branches and compel them to respond to judicial facility needs in a timely and reasonable fashion. As a tool, it should be promoted and given extensive public visibility. The executive and legislative branches should not be allowed to lose sight of the fact that the ultimate power for determining a reasonable need for judicial facilities rests with the judicial branch and that, if the judicial branch demonstrates such need, it is incumbent on the executive and legislative branches to respond. Most legislative and executive officials, like their counterparts in the judiciary, are not anxious to publicize intergovernmental disputes. Therefore, given appropriate pressure from the judiciary, they will usually provide the judiciary with the necessary facilities.

Who Is Responsible for Articulating the Need for New or Improved Judicial Facilities?

Any number of reasons can give rise to a request for new or improved judicial facilities, including an inadequate number of courtrooms, inadequate space for support staff, or inadequate security. However, the usual reason for requesting additional judicial facilities is when the number of judges serving a court is enlarged by legislative action. Generally, on such occasions additional funds are required to construct additional courtrooms or court facilities. Such action can be characterized as a knee-jerk reaction and points to a larger problem—the lack of any real judicial planning within most jurisdictions, and in particular, the lack of either short- or long-range planning for judicial facility needs. Under the separation-of-powers doctrine, such planning is not the responsibility of the legislative or executive branches. Accordingly, it is the responsibility of the judiciary to develop a well-documented action master plan to ensure legislative and executive acceptance of its facility requests.

Most courts have little or no appreciation for current and future facilities requirements. Judicial officials should be responsible and responsive to the needs of the citizenry by developing a facility master plan that states short- and long-term facility requirements of the courts, provides a year-by-year capital improvement budget for implementing recommended improvements, and enlists citizen support to convince the executive and legislative branches of government of the validity of the judiciary's needs. Assuming that the judiciary wishes to exercise its responsibility for making the determination of need for additional facilities, minimum statewide judicial space standards and design guidelines provide the essential tool necessary for evaluating short- and long-term facility needs.

How to Prove the Need for Improved or New Court Facilities?

Once it is determined that new or renovated facilities are needed, the fact still remains that appropriate officials in the executive and legislative branches will have to be convinced as to the need for new or improved judicial facilities. Unfortunately, most judiciaries have not developed comprehensive facility master plans, and the court finds itself in the position of having to convince the other branches of its facility needs in short order, with little supporting documentation, and without affording the other branches any means of anticipating expenses. It is, therefore, necessary for the judiciary to know how to use the executive and legislative process, and be able to articulate to appropriate executive and legislative officials' judicial requirements in terms they most readily understand. Generally, this involves a discussion of caseloads, backlogs, and the growth rates the judicial official reasonably expects will take place in the foreseeable future.

The usual method for justifying the need for new or improved facilities involves projecting an increase in the number of judges required to serve a particular jurisdiction. For example, if ten judges working at maximum capacity can dispose of twenty thousand cases filed without building up a backlog, a doubling of filings would theoretically mean a doubling of the current number of judges. From a practical standpoint, the number of new judicial positions created is likely to be fewer. The increase in the number of judicial positions would require construction of appropriate courtrooms and ancillary facilities. By documenting projected judicial needs and the cost of implementing the needs, the judiciary is in a much better position than if future needs are vague and anticipated budget nonexistent.

Other factors would be points of inquiry by the executive and legislative branches before they decided whether to support judicial requests for additional judicial positions and their attendant requirements for additional facilities:

- the number of support personnel required to assist the judges
- the space requirements for judges and support personnel
- the breakdown of projected caseloads by types of cases
- administrative improvements being considered to make the judges more efficient in their handling of projected caseloads
- evaluation of the efficiency and suitability of current facilities
- the space and equipment requirements for records and exhibits storage
- the space and equipment requirements for developing court support technologies
- anticipated technological developments to assist the judiciary in raising disposition rates

These factors and others would certainly be considered by the legislative and executive branches when they consider requests for additional judicial personnel and related facilities.

Another factor that may influence the legislative and executive decisions is that in most facilities throughout the United States, the judiciary share facilities with the executive and legislative branches. A feasible alternative to the construction of additional judicial facilities would be the relocation of executive and legislative facilities utilizing space in the courthouse. This transfers the burden of acquiring new facilities from the financially hard-pressed judiciary to the legislative and executive branches of government.

Because increasing caseloads are the rule, not the exception, and because the legislative and executive branches often seem incapable of responding to judicial needs when such needs are urgent, those branches of government should be prevailed upon to assist the judicial administrator in evaluating alternative methods of handling increases in caseloads.

These factors and considerations are good tools for use by the judicial administrator in dealing with the legislative and executive branches.

The Impact of Court "Reform" on Court Facility Development

The past two decades have seen many jurisdictions "reform" their courts. This has included, in most states, the implementation of the unified court concept, that is, centralized control of the administrative operations of the judiciary. Centralized control has resulted in some changes of funding court operation, but such changes have not shown a marked improvement in the ability of the judiciary to obtain funding for its operations. In fact, many states still fund judicial activities and functions primarily from local government sources. However, centralized funding of court systems continues to increase. Accordingly, any judicial facility development, be it at the state or local level, should take this factor into consideration.

Cost-Effectiveness—A Critical Factor

The judicial administrator can accurately document and justify facility needs, generate the support of pressure and lobby groups, have the support of custom and traditions when it comes to the building of new courtrooms for additional judicial personnel but still fail to obtain the necessary funds. It is becoming clear that, in these days of shrinking government budgets, the judicial administrator must be able to talk in terms of cost-effectiveness. Even cost-effectiveness may not be sufficient if other political considerations dictate that a new facility should not be built or existing facilities renovated. Nevertheless, without a demonstration of cost-effectiveness, a judicial facilities request is quite likely doomed before it is ever started.

The Executive Branch—Its Role in Judicial Facility Development

The executive branch of government plays a larger role in judicial facility development than one might expect. This is because the judicial branch of government has not been adequately staffed or professionally capable of fulfilling many of the tasks that the executive branch has traditionally performed in the area of facility development. In some jurisdictions, the judiciary has totally abdicated its responsibilities to the executive branch. However, as state judiciaries have acquired professional staffs and have become capable of dealing with such issues themselves, they have on occasion clashed with established methods of doing things through the executive process. Because of such potential for conflict, the judicial administrator should understand the executive process and utilize it to the benefit of the judiciary.

Executive Branch Responsibility Preceding the Appropriations Process

The functions of the executive branch are not really difficult to understand, but are generally difficult to work with because the executive branch is subject to more, and more varied, change than either the judicial or legislative branches of government. This is due to the nature of the political process, which mandates periodical changes in the executive administrations. Those changes, although at times quite subtle, alter the way the executive branch operates.

Often, officials of the executive branch have less knowledge of the judicial process than their counterparts in the legislative branch. A primary factor is the lack of involvement with the judicial branch except when required to appear in a judicial forum as a litigant. Generally, the only other executive branch involvement with the judicial branch is at budget time. In many states, the executive branch maintains the power to revise judicial budgets, which means submitting reduced judicial requests to the legislature.

In the past, and in most jurisdictions even today, facilities planning done by the executive branch frequently does not include planning for specific judicial needs and seldom considers the unique requirements of the judicial process. When a judicial official articulates the need for renovation of existing facilities or construction of new facilities, the reaction of executive officials is generally to give the matter cursory attention, particularly in states where the executive has no revisionary power over the budget requests of the judiciary. In many cases, the judicial request is simply submitted by the executive branch to the legislative branch of government without comment. This is in keeping with specific statutes, found in most jurisdictions, specifying the method by which capital requests are to be presented to the legislative body. In the past, courts have generally not been willing to challenge such statutes, particularly when the legislative branch of government has also followed similar statutory restrictions itself. The executive branch is generally willing to transfer responsibility for decision making on a judicial facility request to the funding authority—the legislative branch.

Executive Branch Responsibility after the Appropriations Process

Once the legislature has funded the renovation of an existing judicial facility or the construction of a new facility, the judiciary finds itself, once again, facing an executive process that must be understood if the judiciary is to have meaningful input in the development of its own facilities.

In most states the executive branch is responsible for site selection and a determination of the space adequacy for governmental "agencies," including the judiciary. The judiciary should participate directly in this process in order to articulate its criteria for locating a court facility as well as its functional and spatial needs. Such criteria and needs are vastly different from the usual governmental office building requirements. For example, the court facility should be located near its primary users, that is, the prosecuting authority and the attorneys who most often utilize the facility. It is for this and other reasons that most court facilities are located in the central core of an urban area, not the cheapest or most cost-efficient site to acquire. The final decision on site selection should be made jointly by the judiciary and the executive branch, based on factors of accessibility, convenience, and economic consideration, as well as suitability of the site for actual construction.

Once a site has been selected, planning and design of the facility follows. Most architects and engineers employed by the executive branch have little or no experience with the judicial process and no knowledge of the unique technical requirements of the judiciary. Accordingly, without sufficient input from the judicial branch, the executive branch response to judicial requests and needs tends to be the same as it would be to a parks department or a revenue department; it is no different from the response to the day-to-day requirements of a working executive branch agency.

If a judicial facility program and master plan is available, the executive branch will usually utilize it. However, without sufficient input from the judiciary, the executive branch's interpretation of the program and plan may be different from that of the judicial branch. The executive branch probably will not go out of its way to assist in the development of such a plan and may not recognize a separate judicial facilities plan because of the tendency for most executive officials to view hostilely the notion that the judicial branch is somehow different from other governmental entities.

The first stage in the design process is the development of schematic plans, drawings, and layouts, which usually are presented to judicial officials for input. Once the schematic plans have been reviewed and revised and the final schematics approved, the project architectural firm then prepares contract documents, including working drawings and specifications that generally adhere to minimal state standards for the construction of state-owned facilities. Following final approval of the working drawings, actual construction takes place under the supervision of the executive branch.

In many jurisdictions, this process could take place without input from the judiciary. In most cases, the one-sided problem is not because the executive branch desires it that way, but because of the inability on the part of the judicial branch to articulate its particular facility needs in the context of the requirements of the executive branch. Most judges, judicial administrators, and other judicial officials have little expertise for facility management or design and, accordingly, have not had a great deal of input in the development of new facilities. In cases of renovation, the judicial official generally has more meaningful input because of his experience with the deficiencies he or she has observed over a period of years in the existing facility, deficiencies that, in many cases, have resulted in the requests for improvements. In any event, judicial officials must learn to use the executive process to their advantage just as they must learn to navigate the shoals of the legislative process.

The Legislative Branch—Its Role in Judicial Facility Development

After a determination has been made by the judicial branch that it is in need of renovated or new facilities, and after the executive branch has concurred with (or at least decided not to resist) that decision, the focus of attention turns to the legislature, which must actually pay for the renovating of existing court facilities or the building of new ones. Assuming the judiciary has met its responsibility as a coequal governmental partner, how will the legislature respond to that request? The answer to this question depends largely upon the way in which the judiciary approaches the legislative branch and makes use of the legislative process. Before the judiciary can be effective in its dealings with the legislative branch, it needs to understand its procedures, intricacies, and points of pressure and response. These factors translate into a need to have an intimate knowledge of the legislature's organization and procedures.

The Importance of Understanding Legislative Composition

Personnel composition of the legislature is generally more transitory than that of the judiciary but less transitory than that of the executive branch. However, some elements remain the same. The number of members in the legislative body generally does not change from session to session. This gives the judicial official a starting point in terms of the number of legislators needed to be persuaded concerning the validity of the judiciary's request.

The political party distribution within the legislature and the party in power will change from election to election. However, given the one-person, one-vote decisions of the U.S. Supreme Court, the makeup of the legislature as it relates to urban, suburban, and rural membership is not likely to change appreciably, allowing the judicial official to make decisions based on geographical considerations, with little concern for a marked geographic shift in the membership of the legislative body.

The occupations of legislators are also important considerations, particularly because of the differing views that persons with specific occupations will have of the judicial branch. In most legislatures, there has been a decline in representation from the legal profession, due in many cases to the so-called sunshine laws, which require disclosure of financial interests by legislative members. Such a requirement, for many members of the legal profession, creates serious ethical conflicts, which cause them to leave the legislative branch. However, most legislative bodies still have some representation from the legal profession and those members should be assiduously courted to support decisions by the judicial branch of government to seek legislative appropriation for the construction and/or remodeling of judicial facilities. These individuals are a key to the judiciary's success. Without their support, any judicial facility project is probably doomed to failure at the very outset.

The Importance of Understanding Legislative Organization

The organization of the legislature is also a critical factor in determining whether a judicial facility request will be successful. A strong individual or collective leadership is a key to the success of the judiciary's presentation to the legislature. Without the support of leadership, there is little chance of success. With its support, success may come with little or no effort. However, most legislatures, even with a strong leadership structure, function through the committee process.

Most facility requests initially are dealt with in the legislature by the so-called ways and means or appropriations committees. The committee chair exercises tremendous influence on the destiny of the judicial facility request. Most chairs have been selected by the majority party because of their particular areas of interest or expertise, as well as their longevity as members of the legislative body. They are usually seasoned politicians and strong individuals whose importance should not be ignored.

At the state level, differences exist in the organizational procedure between the two houses of the legislature. Such differences generally mandate the development of a different approach to each house except in cases in which one has to deal with a joint budget committee.

Other Important Legislative Considerations

The past decade has seen a marked growth in legislative budgets for professional staff assistance, giving greater ability to nonlegislators for influencing legislative decisions. Many legislators will not act on an issue without substantive review by their staff. Staff members are, in fact, elevated to a quasi-legislative role and add another level of bureaucracy through which the judiciary must function in order to achieve success with its requests. Therefore, it is critical to the judiciary that the legislative staff be familiar with the judicial branch of government, its methods of operation, its personnel, and its perceived needs. Without the initial support of legislative staff, it is unlikely that judicial requests of any kind will be successful.

The most powerful staff member in the legislative branch is usually the chief of staff for the legislative budget committee, whether it be a joint committee, a committee for each house, or, in the case of local governmental entities, the legislative body's budget director. This individual must be kept apprised of judicial needs. Without his or her support, the committee chair is not likely to be supportive of the judiciary's request; without the support of the committee chair, the majority party is not likely to be supportive; without the support of the majority party, there is little or no chance of success with the entire legislature; and, without support of the legislature, there is obviously no opportunity to have the request presented to the executive department for final approval.

The judicial official contemplating making a request for judicial facility improvement should also be cognizant of subpower groups within the legislative process—the interparty coalitions put together on specific issues. From time to time, matters come before legislative bodies which transcend traditional party alignments and create temporary coalitions. On judicial issues in particular, such coalitions frequently develop because of the vestiges of influence the legal profession still has in the legislative body. In such instances, and even where a less than substantial number of attorneys are members of the legislature, interparty coalitions may prove beneficial to the judicial branch of government. Such coalitions have on occasion sparked controversy within a legislature whose members feel that the judiciary receives favored treatment by the legislative branch as a result of such coalitions. For whatever reason, if a coalition exists or can be structured, the judicial administrator should not hesitate to take full advantage of it. It may simplify the job of the judicial administrator in attempting to steer a judicial facility request through the legislature, and may result in success of the request.

A champion for judicial facility requests may also come from temporary coalitions that can be formed on the basis of ideological grounds. If there is a strong movement within the state to provide speedier disposition of criminal cases, it may be opportune for the judiciary to respond with a request for new or additional facilities based on a need for new judges to handle increased caseloads and to provide a more speedy disposition of cases. A temporary coalition may result when legislators from a metropolitan area deem it necessary to transcend party lines to obtain funds for new facilities in order to facilitate the addition of new judicial positions or support personnel badly needed to attack the increasing judicial backlogs, the albatross around the neck of metropolitan courts. Interest or power groups, such as those for labor or agriculture, may occasionally help develop a coalition of special interests to assist in supporting judicial requests. Such coalitions may be put together to achieve specific goals, but all have the inherent danger of trading off more than is achieved. They are included in this discussion to show the lengths to which judicial officials may have to go to attain legislative success. Extreme caution should be used in dealing with coalitions in the legislative process because of their potential for future adverse affects on the judicial process.

Other important aspects of the legislative process are nonlegislative sources of assistance and their potential impact on legislative organization and processes to the benefit of the judiciary. As mentioned previously, legislative representatives of the legal community tend to coalesce behind judicial requests and provide invaluable assistance in promoting judicial requests before a legislative body. In addition, the organized state and local bar associations will usually provide assistance when approached by the judicial branch.

Other groups that can be of invaluable assistance to the courts in promoting their facility needs before the legislature include some activist political groups, such as the League of Women Voters, and professional organizations such as judges' and prosecuting attorneys' associations.

The news media may also provide assistance, and its appropriate use cannot be overemphasized as a tool of the judiciary in dealing with the legislature. However, caution should be exercised when using the media, owing to the inability of many of its members to understand the subtleties of judicial process and its requirements any better than the average citizen. Over a period of years, judicial administrators who are willing to invest the time and effort can develop working relationships with the media and utilize them to promote improved judicial facilities through editorials and favorably written articles.

The judicial official should also have intimate knowledge of legislative publications and how to determine the status of a bill without unduly burdening the legislative staff. The official should be a subscriber to and an avid reader of the legislative digest, calendar, status sheets, and journal, as well as press reports concerning legislative activities.

The Legislature as a Creature of Process

Probably more than any other branch of government, the legislative branch follows a set process in determining which requests or pieces of legislation will ultimately become law for a particular jurisdiction. Thus, even with a thorough understanding of the composition and organization of the legislature and the various impacting entities, many judicial facilities requests will fall on deaf ears because of failure by the judiciary to follow the process set forth by the operating rules of the legislature and by tradition and custom. Because of the inclination of the legislative branch to be a creature of process, it is much easier to kill legislation than it is to pass it. In short, the odds favor failure over success. Accordingly, judicial officials who are developing a facilities program not only should understand the organization and components of the process but also should be intimately familiar with the procedures followed by the legislature. These include the preparation of specific legislation authorizing or approving the facilities plan, the committee process, procedures for taking a bill from the committee of origin through the rules committee, special procedures on the floor of a particular house of the legislature, any differences between the procedures of the two houses, and, if necessary, conference committee procedures.

Timing of Legislative Contacts

Timing of legislative contacts is probably as important as any other factor in the judicial-legislative process. At the state level, because legislatures generally are not full-time bodies but meet for only a set time period each year, it is extremely important to lay adequate groundwork for a request prior to the beginning of the legislative session. Even in states with a full-time legislature, or, at the local level, where legislative bodies tend to meet year-round, there is such a need. Probably the easiest, best, and most utilized method for affecting legislative expectations concerning a judicial request is the use of interim study committees. This method may take any of several forms, including staff analysis, but most likely will include consideration by an interim committee composed of members of both political parties, and in many cases of both houses of the legislature. Interest groups composed of such people as attorneys, judges, and in some instances lay citizens should also be encouraged to participate in the interim study process. It is through the use of this process that the judicial administrator makes the most appropriate use of various lobbying or power groups. Generally, the presentation of a well-prepared and articulated case to interim committees will result in a favorable recommendation to the full legislature. Thus, it is necessary for the judicial administrator to take advantage of the interim committee process and the committee's concomitant ability to make use of resources outside the normal legislative process. Legislators and their staff members usually have more time to consider judicial facilities requests in the context of an interim study than during the ongoing rush of a legislative session. This process should guarantee a strong voice for judicial requests during the regular session.

The Legislature's Perception of the Judiciary

Another important consideration in legislative judicial relationships is the context in which the legislative branch views the judicial branch. Legislators and legislatures are somewhat defensive about the judiciary's ability to mandate support for its processes, including funds to guarantee the operation of the judiciary by use of its inherent power. The legislature's perception of inherent powers probably extends only to such areas as procedural rule making, control of personnel, and auxiliary court services and not to the question of what is an adequate funding level for the judicial branch. Because of such divergent views of the separation of powers and the inherent power corollary, the judiciary must appeal to legislative perceptions of what the judicial system is supposed to do, such as to reduce crime, provide quick redress of citizens' grievances, and so on. This appeal should be as low key as possible.

The judiciary should make every effort to avoid confrontation with the legislature. It should work within the process set up by the legislature to facilitate reasonable consideration of its requests. The judiciary may often appear to legislative bodies and legislative officials as arrogant, shortsighted, and interested only in short-range solutions to judicial problems. Judicial officials who present requests to the legislature must consider this negative possibility and approach the legislative branch cautiously.

To facilitate its approach, the judiciary should develop an internal process to articulate its needs prior to dealing with the legislature. The judiciary must become familiar with its own needs and expectations and must be able to articulate them in the appropriate manner and to develop a program to present both short- and long-range goals and judicial objectives. Included in these goals and objectives should be a judicial facilities master plan, with pertinent information on the development of such a plan and the considerations entering into its preparation and use. It is important to judicial-executive-legislative relationships to understand how judicial staff can be used in plan development and other facility project needs.

The Need for and Uses of In-House Staff and Consultants

The judiciary generally has little input into the planning, design, or redesign of courthouses. In most cases, the executive branch selects project architects and engineers, who often have little or no appreciation for the judiciary's specific needs, to design the court facility. The executive reacts this way because the judiciary has not developed in-house expertise to articulate its current and projected needs. A court system, particularly one with statewide jurisdiction and responsibility for developing facilities programs, should develop in-house space management capability to coordinate the development of building programs, the preparation of short- and long-range facilities plans, and the implementation of facility renovation and construction programs.

In-house staff should be responsible for coordination of the implementation of the facilities master plan and its regular reevaluation and updating. Such staff should have background and experience in the fields of management and administration and particularly in the coordination of facility projects within the judicial process. This quickest way for the judicial administrator to gain such expertise is to acquire the services of an experienced consultant. This will allow the administrator to build his or her in-house capabilities over a period of time while satisfying immediate planning requirements. This allows administrative staff to become familiar with methodologies and techniques utilized by the skilled professional facilities consultant. As the staff develop their own expertise, they will be able to update the information available to them and to reevaluate the facilities master plan developed by the consultant.

Development of a facilities master plan and in-house capabilities allows the court to address the budgetary process with more confidence in its ability to articulate its needs, particularly to executive branch officials. It also enables courts to take better advantage of facility services offered by the executive branch of government, including architectural and engineering services, which are either maintained at a staff level by the executive branch or contracted out to architectural firms, many of which, being unfamiliar with and inexperienced in the area of judicial facility design and management, positively need direct contact with the judicial branch.

Because the executive branch probably is unwilling to spend a great deal of money on predesign research into the unique needs of the judiciary, it is necessary for in-house staff to work with the officials of the executive branch to make such information available. It is important that executive officials learn very early in the process that, though it may not require any special knowledge or expertise to design a state office building, it does take special knowledge and expertise to design a court facility. The unique needs of the judiciary require very specific design and space requirements, and without expert assistance, the executive official or the everyday architect or engineer will not be able to address the specific needs of the judiciary. Inevitably, the design will accommodate neither the present needs of the judiciary nor its future needs.

In dealing with the executive branch staff, the judiciary can get much greatly needed assistance from a private consultant. On a project-by-project basis, the court should request that the executive agency obtain the services of an experienced consultant to collaborate with the executive branch architects in designing and building a facility that will accommodate present and future court needs. This is particularly important for projects in which the judicial facilities master plan has been developed with the assistance of a consultant. Hopefully, the project consultant will feel responsibility to the judiciary to ensure that the project architect retained by the executive branch incorporates the facility program recommendations into the facility plan, design, and contact documents.

To ensure that the facility program developed by the consultant is fully and accurately incorporated into the design of the court building, it would be more advantageous for the judiciary, rather than the executive branch, to hire the consultant. If the executive branch or the project architectural firm hires the consultant, the consultant's direct responsibility would be to the executive branch or project architect. Should a disagreement arise regarding the interpretation or application of the facility program, the consultant's role would be subordinate to that of the architect and the relationship would not be beneficial to the judiciary. The consultant can be more objective in reviewing architectural plans if he or she is the judiciary's consultant and represents the interest of the judiciary. Since the judiciary is the user of the facility, and consultants develop the facility program, it is beneficial to the judiciary to be the consultant's client in order to ensure that the approved facility program is fully and accurately accommodated in the building design.

Conclusion

The relationship between the executive, legislative, and judicial branches of government is founded in a centuries-old theory and philosophy—the equality of each in relationship to the other. Scholars have often discussed this relationship and used many phrases to describe it, among them "checks and balances," "coequality," "separation of powers," and so on. The key to the relationship is mutual respect between each branch and the ability of each to assert its "equalness" when the need to do so arises.

As the history of governmental relations has developed in this country, such ability has been less available to the judiciary and has resulted in the development of a judicial doctrine of necessity—the doctrine of the inherent power of the courts. The doctrine can be, and on occasion has been, used successfully by courts to compel the payment of funds necessary to ensure the functioning of the judiciary. It has been used only in isolated cases that usually do not involve large expenditures of money. The thrust of most inherent power cases and the writings of most legal scholars caution against undue reliance on the doctrine, suggesting that the judiciary would be wiser to rely on the good will of the other branches of government to achieve needed levels of funding and support.

To acquire such support for its programs, facilities, or otherwise, the judiciary must carefully prepare its case and document its needs. It must understand the organization and procedures employed by both the executive and legislative branches and take advantage of such knowledge. Even with adequate, careful preparation and a logical, timely presentation of its programs, the judiciary cannot hope to achieve success in its intergovernmental relationships without an increasingly professional and capable staff to improve its relationship with the executive and legislative branches.

Increased caseloads and associated increases in professional staff have caused judiciaries in all levels to seek additional and more adequate facilities. Most judiciaries lack the expertise to develop an adequate statement of facility needs and identify the most appropriate response to those needs.

Even when the judiciary is capable of articulating its needs, the legislative and executive branches have been unwilling to accommodate judicial requests without severe scrutiny and, in many cases, wholesale revision. Such attitudes have, in the past, caused judicial officials to resort to an assertion of their inherent power to achieve their perceived needs. On most occasions, judiciaries have not actually exercised the power, rather they have used the threat of its application to get the legislative and executive branches to logically discuss and respond to judicial requirements.

The usually responsive attitude of the legislative and executive branches to the threat of utilization of inherent power is fortunate for the judiciary because few would be willing to assert that the power is of value as anything more than a threat. If the judiciary actually has to respond to use of the power, it will have failed in its intergovernmental relationships and damaged our structure of government. Court support needs and judicial facilities will be obtained through the governmental process only by means of adequate preparation of a statement of judicial need, and a thorough and timely presentation based on knowledge of and cooperation with the legislative and executive branches. The court official who sits back and waits for success in the governmental arena on the basis of the judiciary's inherent power will not find it.

Summary Checklist for More Effective Judicial-Legislative Relationships

As discussed above, the judiciary needs to understand the legislative process, how it works, its intricacies, and points of pressure and response before it can deal effectively with the legislature. The following checklist is intended to serve as a departure point for the judicial official who must deal with the legislature and the legislative process. The checklist raises questions that a judicial official should have answers to before embarking upon presentation of any judicial program.

I. Legislative Composition
    A. How many members are in the legislature?
    B. What is the legislature's political party distribution?
    C. What is its geographic makeup?
    D. What are the occupations of the members of the legislature?

E. What is the percentage of minority group representation in the legislature?
II. Legislative Organization
 A. Who are the legislative leaders?
  1. How are they selected?
  2. What are their functions?
 B. Legislative committees
  1. How many and what is the subject matter of their jurisdiction?
  2. How are members of the various committees selected?
  3. What is the significance of the committee and what is its role in the legislative process?
  4. What special procedures are required by the budget committee?
 C. Relationship between two houses of legislature at state level
  1. Does each require a different approach?
 D. Special legislative bodies: Do they play a role in facility decision process?
  1. Joint committees
  2. Study committees
  3. Interim committees
  4. Executive-legislative committees
  5. Special committees
  6. Others
 E. Legislative staff
  1. How is the legislative staff selected and how does it function?
  2. What is the degree of responsibility to committee or legislature as a whole?
 F. Legislative procedures
  1. What are the general elements and key steps in the legislative process?
  2. How is legislation prepared?
  3. How is legislation assigned to committee?
  4. Are there special procedures required with regard to budget and court facilities matters?
  5. Importance of keeping posted on legislative process
   a. Use of official documents, that is, daily calendars, journals, legislative status sheets
   b. Other sources of information including press, lobbyists, etc.
   c. Other reference materials that may be of assistance, that is, legislative rules, procedure manuals
  6. What presession activities occur which will impact on facility requests?
III. Center of Power and Potential Friction Points in Judicial-Legislative Relationships

A. Identify the power centers and distribution of power
   1. Is power concentrated in a few hands or distributed more widely?
   2. Is there a formal power concentration, that is, is this fostered by formal legislative organization and procedures or is it more de facto?
   3. Which legislators constitute the real leadership or what formal position do they hold and how are they selected? (Does this differ from that procedure specified by rule?)
   4. What is the importance of seniority in the legislative process?
   5. What are the key committees?
   6. How are minority party committee appointments determined?
   7. What is the relationship of the judiciary committee chairman to the power structure, and is he or she willing to play an active role in advocating a judicial facility request to the appropriations committee?
   8. Are there interlocking power relationships between the two houses of the legislature, and how are leadership differences between the two houses resolved?
   9. What is the influence of outside groups and individuals, that is, lobbyists, agency heads, judicial officials, and others? Upon whom are they effective and why?
   10. What is the role and importance of the legislative caucus and the power concentration and distribution? Are real leadership decisions made by the caucus or is the individual legislative leader more powerful?
   11. What is the influence and role of the governor on the legislative process?
   12. What is the effect of the relative party strength and power concentration distribution on legislative decisions?
B. Sub–power groups and potential sources of friction and dispute
   1. Intraparty coalitions, both formal and informal
      a. Is their basis ideological, geographic, occupational, or other?
      b. What is the purpose of the coalition?
      c. What are areas of controversy that create coalitions?
      d. What is the effect of power concentration and distribution on the coalition and on legislative process and procedures? What is the influence of outside groups and individuals?
   2. Interparty coalitions—do they exist and are they more than informally agreed upon coalitions for specific issues?
   3. Are there interhouse coalitions?
C. Importance of presession and interim legislative activity
   1. How is the legislature organized in the interim between legislative sessions?

2. Are there special subcommittees that deal in the interim with the state's budget and, more particularly, facilities requests? If so:
    a. What is the composition and function of the study committee?
    b. How are members selected and what is their relationship to the power structure?
    c. Does the legislature generally accept their recommendation when the formal session has convened?
    d. What kind of staff services are provided to the interim committees, and what is the influence of staff on those decisions?
  D. The legislative view of the courts
    1. What is the context of the legislature's perception of the court's role in the legislative process, more particularly in the development of court facilities?
        a. Is the framework provided by constitutional and statutory provisions or based primarily on recent efforts at reorganization and reform?
    2. How does the legislature perceive the doctrine of separation of powers as regards:
        a. The court's rule-making power
        b. The function of court personnel
        c. The court's fiscal control of legislative appropriations
        d. The court's use of auxiliary services (probation, detention facilities, etc.)
    3. How does the legislature perceive the purposes of the court system, that is, what is the court system supposed to do?
    4. Is the legislature currently interested in judicial reform, and if so, is it high or low priority?
        a. Does the legislature wish to accomplish such reform piecemeal or comprehensively?
        b. How do they perceive their role in perfecting such change?
IV. Nonlegislative Sources of Information and Assistance
  A. Other groups that may be of assistance in promoting judicial facility requests to the legislature
    1. Bar associations
    2. Civic groups
        a. League of Women Voters
        b. American University
        c. Association of University Women
        d. Junior Chamber of Commerce
        e. State Granges
        f. Others

3. Judges' associations
4. Prosecutors' associations
5. Probation, correction, and parole organizations
6. News media
7. Executive branch agencies

Table 9.1 provides a methodology and procedures to improve cooperation between courts and governmental agencies in implementing judicial facility projects.

Table 9.1. Methodology and Procedures to Improve Cooperation between Courts and Governmental Agencies in Implementing Judicial Facility Projects

Major Operations	Detailed Procedures	Admin. Office of the Courts	Consultant	Architect	Dept. of Admin.	Division of Bldg.	Contractors
Comprehensive Plan of Statewide Court Facilities	Develop comprehensive facility plan	X	O				
	Establish priorities of facility needs	O	O				
	Coordinate phased implementation of plan	O	X				
Initiation of Facility Projects	Obtain court input on a continuous basis	O	X				
	Verify facility requests if necessary	O	X				
	Evaluate needs according to priorities in comprehensive plan	O	O				
	Develop methods of solving problems	O	O				
	Obtain current unit construction and operating cost from the division of building	O	O			X	
	Compute costs of facility construction, renovation and operation needs	O	O				
	Prepare draft capital improvement and operating budgets	O	X				
	In-house evaluation of budgets	O					
	Present court's budget to supreme court	O					
	Revise and prepare final budget	O					
	Submit budget to governor's office	O			X		
	Work with legislature on court's program requests	O	X		X		
	Submit governor's state budget to the legislature				O		

(continued)

Note: O indicates primary tasks. X indicates secondary tasks.

Table 9.1—Continued

Major Operations	Detailed Procedures	Admin. Office of the Courts	Consultant	Architect	Dept. of Admin.	Division of Bldg.	Contractors
	Appropriation and approval or modification by legislature	X			O		
	Responsible for managing the state budget	X			O		
	Decide on method of financing	X	X		O		
	Sell bonds according to cash flow needs				O		
Site & Space Selection Process	Preliminary consideration of potential sites	O	O		O	X	
	Visit and evaluate feasible alternative sites	O	O		O	X	
	Make decision on courthouse site	O			O	X	
	Notify owners of site regarding decision	O			O		
	Publish decision in local newspaper	O			O		
	Negotiate terms of transaction	O	X		O		
	Establish time schedule for project	O	X		O	O	
	Obtain bid waiver, if necessary	O			O		
Court's Input in the Planning & Design Process	Develop facility program of needs	X	O		X	X	
	Review and approve facility program	O			X	X	
	Develop schematic plans and layouts	X	O	O		X	
	Collaboration between architect and consultant to the court system	X	O	O			
Court's Space Standards & Design Guidelines	Develop standards and guidelines	X	O			X	
	Develop functional and spatial relationships	X	O				

Decision of Occupancy of Existing State Buildings

Task							
Review, approve, and adopt standards, guidelines, and relationships	O					X	X
Collaboration between division of building and court in determining building occupancy	O	X				O	
Appoint representative of the division of buildings to collaborate with the manager	O					O	X
Determine priority of space allocation and use	O	X				O	X
Planning and construction of separate court buildings to improve court image	O	O				X	O

State, Court, Architects, and Consultants Relationships

Task							
Input from experienced consultants	O	O	O				
Appoint architectural firm	X				O	X	X
Specify special consulting services	O				X	X	
Hiring of consultants	O	O	O			X	X
Collaboration between architect and consultant	X	O	O			X	X

Schematic Plans and Final Design

Task							
Obtain input from users in the court system	O	O	X				
Develop schematic plans for renovation	X	O	O			X	X
Develop schematic plans for new building	X	O	O			X	X
Review of schematic plans	O	O				O	
Revise schematic documents		O	O				
Develop final schematic documents		O	O				
Construct architectural model of project		O	O				
Make changes and revisions		O	O				

Working Drawings and Specifications

Task							
Prepare working drawings and specifications				X	O		

(continued)

Table 9.1—Continued

Major Operations	Detailed Procedures	Admin. Office of the Courts	Consultant	Architect	Dept. of Admin.	Division of Bldg.	Contractors
	Provide special consulting services	O	O				
	Review of working drawings and specifications	O	O			O	
	Final approval	O	X	X		O	
	Provide input for time scheduling	O	O	O		X	
	Provide input for phasing of renovations	O	X	O		X	
	Finalize construction time schedule for project	X	X	O		X	
Furniture Purchase	Prepare annual contract award manual				O		
	Prepare purchase requisition form (PRF)	O					
	Translate information on PRF into bid forms				O		
	Input on bidding constraints	O	X	X			
	Prepare bids						O
	Evaluation of bids	O					
	Award bids—notify successful bidders	X			O		O
	Obtain insurance and bonding				O		O
	Order furniture						O
	Inform court regarding status of order	X			X		O
	Deliver furniture						O
Bidding Process	Advertise in local newspapers in consecutive weeks	X			O		O
	Prepare bids	O					
	Evaluate bids		X	X	O		
	Input regarding specific contractor	O			O		

Task	1	2	3	4	5	6	7	8
Award bid—prepare contract or lease	O					O	O	
Approve contract or lease						O	O	
Sign contract	O					O	O	
Obtain necessary insurance and binding	O							

Building Construction, Renovation, and Change Order

Task	1	2	3	4	5	6	7	8
Assign project engineer	O			O	O			O
Inform court of project status	O			O	O			
Initiate change order	X	X						
Clarify change order	X	X						
Prepare request for proposal			X					
Prepare drawings of major changes	O							
Pricing of changes in change order			X					O
Approve change order	O			O				O
Incorporate changes in construction/renovation	O							O
Inform court of status of change order work	X			O				O

Key and Locks Schedules

Task	1	2	3	4	5	6	7	8
Set up keys and locks schedule	O		O	O			O	O
Input of lock schedule into working drawings and specifications	O			O				
Control assignment of keys	O							

Inspection of Completed Building

Task	1	2	3	4	5	6	7	8
Notify completion of project	X		O	O		O	O	O
Set date for final inspection	X		O	O	O	O	O	O
Inspect building	O		O	O			O	O
Make list of deficiencies	O		O	O			O	O
Correct deficiencies			O	O	O			
Issue acceptance date of completed building	X			O				

Moving and Occupancy

Task	1	2	3	4	5	6	7	8
Arrange for moving of department	O					X		O
Move department	O					X		O
Occupy building	O							

10

The Financing, Funding, and Budgeting of Judicial Facility Projects

It takes money to build a courthouse. It takes money from various sources, but the principle source is the taxpayer. Taxpayers pay their taxes because they have to, not because they want to. It follows that the hardest part in bringing about the creation of a new judicial facility is obtaining the money to achieve the construction of the facility.

Budgeting is the process whereby the cost of doing something is identified for some future action and that cost is related to the available sources of revenue. Budgeting is not an expenditure of money; it is planning for the expenditure of money. The creation of a judicial facility requires that at an early stage of the project a budget be prepared and the necessary dollars be budgeted.

In a governmental setting, budgets are normally prepared to the greatest degree of sophistication in the executive branch. Budgeting is, or can be, accomplished to a lesser degree of sophistication within the judiciary.

The terms *funding* and *appropriations* are used interchangeably. These two terms denote that the money is provided for a given period of time to accomplish a given purpose. While obtaining the appropriation from some governmental body is difficult, it is essential to accomplishing the goal of providing adequate and suitable facilities. Obtaining funds from other sources requires the action of a board of directors, a board of trustees, a judicial council, or a public-building authority.

Financing, as used in this context, means the obtaining of funds to begin a judicial facility project and to make payments to consultants, architects, engineers, and contractors. This is viewed as short-term financing, in contrast to long-term financing, which would allow the cost of the project to be spread over a much longer time period.

Financing in a governmental setting is normally determined at the time of the appropriation; however, the method of financing can affect the receptivity of policy makers to authorize the project.

Philosophies and Concepts

When renovation of an existing courthouse or construction of a new judicial facility project is contemplated, the parties involved sometimes overlook the following four basic steps that bring about a successful project:

1. obtaining the funds for facility planning
2. budgeting for the facility
3. obtaining funds for construction
4. financing the construction

In each of these steps there are a variety of philosophies and concepts that are applicable.

Obtaining Funds for Facility Planning

The most obvious source of funds for facility planning would be the regular appropriation process at either the state or local level. The appropriation can be identified for a specific purpose or it can be obtained within a broader category. Nonetheless, should the appropriation source be used, it is important to request sufficient funds to accomplish the necessary planning effort. If the original request is inadequate, it would be much more difficult to obtain additional funds at a later date.

Another source for facility planning (and possibly without local cost) would be to use an available technical assistance program. Such assistance in recent years has been available from national judicial organizations or federal agencies. However, such assistance tends to be limited in scope because of funding shortages. Technical assistance for space planning is available in some states from the state court administrator's office. At the local level, technical assistance for a judicial facility can also be obtained through the retention of a consulting architect who has knowledge in this specialized field, using local funds.

The third source of funds for facility planning can be either state or federal grants, which could be used to hire experienced judicial space management consultants to provide the necessary professional services. One of the problems in obtaining such grants is the difficulty and frustration encountered by personnel in the preparation and processing of grant applications. For assistance in this area, experienced grant writers, architects, or court administrators can be helpful, to varying degrees. Delays due to numerous bureaucratic procedures in the approval of grant applications contribute significantly to funds not being available when they are badly needed.

The fourth source of funds for the planning of a judicial facility is an emerging concept of the state government creating an architectural planning revolving fund. The concept is to have a revolving fund established from which monies can be used to hire consultants for the purposes of judicial facility planning. When and if the project is authorized, the architectural fee for the project would be reduced by the amount spent in planning, and the revolving fund would be replenished by that amount. There may be some objection to this technique inasmuch as architects do not normally view specialized program planning as a regular portion of their contractual fee. The revolving fund concept, however, is useful to the extent that it provides monies for facility planning at a sufficiently early stage without a cumbersome budgeting or appropriation process involving large numbers of policy makers.

A fifth source of funding for facility planning and preliminary architectural design is the creation of a court building or library fund, which could either be a percentage of filing fees, a special fee paid by attorneys and users of the judicial facility, or special funds earmarked for this purpose. States such as Florida and Arizona have utilized this source of funding for planning, design, and construction of court facilities.

Public-building authorities are a sixth source of funding for facility planning. Planning and design costs are integral parts of total project costs for which revenue bonds are issued and sold by the authority.

A seventh source of funding for facility planning and design would be unexpended and unobligated funds at the end of each fiscal year, if such exist. Alaska has utilized this source of funding successfully. In Arizona, there is a public works fund, which has carryover monies that can be used to fund facility planning, design, and construction.

Budgeting for the Facility

Once a judicial facility is planned, it becomes necessary to budget for the facility based on cost estimates derived from the planning phase. The necessary funds must be included within some budget so that its costs can be balanced against available revenues.

In a governmental setting, annual and biennial (two-year) budgets are common. At times it is argued that there should be budgets established for longer periods of time. However, such an argument quickly runs into major obstacles because policy makers of governmental units can only obligate funds for the period of their incumbency. There is usually a turnover of elected officials because of constitutional or statutory requirements, and elected officials are therefore reluctant to obligate monies for periods longer than one or two years.

It is helpful, nonetheless, to have a comprehensive improvement program for short-term and long-term renovation, construction, or replacement of judicial facilities within a jurisdiction. This improvement program can be in the form of a long-term capital improvement budget for tentative approval, which would be substantiated with documented needs and projections. It should identify which existing courthouse is to be renovated or replaced at what time, provide time schedules for the renovation and construction of new facilities, or show alternatives for possible consolidation of facilities in the future.

At some early point, a judicial facility has to be budgeted for the estimated square footage shown, potential locations discussed, functional and facility needs documented, and amount and sources of money identified. All these items bring about the unique process of the political system. It is not necessary to go into all the details of this political process, but it is not possible to budget for a judicial facility without involving politicians, whether they be elected officials, community leaders, members of the bar, or judges. All the parties must move in the same general direction, or else the project will not move forward.

Obtaining Funds for Construction

At this point, it has to be assumed that funds have been obtained for facility planning and that the budget for the facility has been secured. The next step is to obtain monies for construction.

If the judicial facility is to be built with general fund monies, the construction monies would be available by a direct draw upon the state treasury. This is normally done through a voucher process.

In some cases the judicial facility can be built with monies obtained from a bond issue. In that event, the proceeds of the bonds might be deposited locally, or the drawdown of monies for the actual construction might be obtained from the financial organization that sold the bonds. Again a vouchering process is the norm, with associated documentation being necessary.

A second source of funds for judicial facility construction would be a public-building authority. In this case, some quasi-governmental units may be established to construct the facility. The disbursement of monies is commonly through the authority rather than through the judiciary. If a public-building authority is used, the judiciary will be required to make rental payments to the authority for the eventual amortization of the investment. This method of funding has been used in the state of Rhode Island for several courthouse construction and renovation projects.

A third source of funds is grants from other governmental units and foundations, and bequests from estates (although it is unusual for a bequest to be made for judicial facilities, as most such money seems to flow to colleges and universities). Obtaining grants usually requires completion of lengthy and complicated grant applications, which must be approved at many levels before the award is made. Federal grants are the most typical. However, some states are moving toward grant arrangements for areas that are economically hard hit and that are beyond the financial capabilities of those states to help.

Yet another source of monies for facility construction is through lines of credit from financial institutions. Lines of credit can be established if it can be shown that there is a workable method by which the short-term loan can either be paid back or converted into a long-term obligation such as bond security. In some cases, a line of credit can be established whereby monies are made available, assuming a continuing income in the area of sales tax, revenue-sharing, or federal grants. A major program of courthouse construction has been funded in this manner in Cook County, Illinois, a county with home rule powers.

Financing the Construction

It is common for short-term facility construction financing to be converted into long-term financing upon completion of construction. In the event that construction monies are obtained from general fund appropriation, interim short-term financing would not be necessary in most cases.

Should the facility be constructed from bond proceeds, then either a drawdown of the bond monies or short-term loans would be necessary. Bond monies are generally available if the proceeds of the sale of bonds have been deposited in the treasury. As an alternative, bond monies may be obtained from the financial institution that sold the bonds as a service to the governmental unit. If bond monies are delayed, short-term loans or direct appropriations could be used after obtaining necessary approvals.

One further technique for obtaining short-term construction monies would be to begin charging prepaid rents for agencies that would be leasing space within the structure upon its completion. This is a difficult alternative in view of the argument that payment of rent for space not yet occupied is unfair. It is feasible, however, for courts to charge a facility fee as part of the filing fee. The funds derived from such fees could then be used for facility renovation and construction. This method is being used in several states, including North Carolina.

Another source of construction monies would be reserves that a governmental unit might have retained from various sources. These reserves might be monies that have been accumulated for the purpose of construction, or were commonly used for such purpose, to be replaced later by long-term loans.

If a structure is being constructed through the use of grants, then the drawdown of grant monies can be used for financing construction. Appropriate documentation and certification is necessary to ensure that grant conditions and budgets are being met.

A recently developed financing method for courthouse design and construction is design-build, in which a private developer is involved as the prime contractor, who would finance the construction of the project. The government would lease the facility for a period of time that would retire the debt and would eventually obtain title to the property, or the government could purchase the courthouse at a predetermined price. This financial arrangement may take a variety of forms, based on the financial capability of the government and the results of contract negotiation with the developer. While this method of financing could substantially reduce the initial capital expenditure by the government, the long-term financial costs and overall debt or purchase price would invariably be much higher than the initial capital or construction costs of the project.

Another recent financing method for courthouse design and construction is the use of an at-risk construction management company, which not only provides a guaranteed maximum price (GMP) for the completion of the project, but would finance or arrange for the financing of the construction of the courthouse. The construction management company would also provide value management, project scheduling and budget control, and coordinating and monitoring all subcontractors' efforts from the schematic design phase to the completion and occupancy of the building. Similar to the design-build concept, the government would lease the facility for a period of time that would retire the debt and would eventually obtain title to the property, or the government could purchase the courthouse earlier at a predetermined purchase price. This financial arrangement may also be structured in a variety of agreements between the government and the construction management company, depending on the financial capability and needs of the government. This method of financing would invariably be higher than the initial capital or construction costs of the project.

Common Problems in Funding Court Facilities

Lack of Expertise

In general, there is an exceptional lack of expertise in the individuals involved in establishing the need for renovation of an existing courthouse or construction of a new judicial facility. This lack of expertise can be found within the legislative body that must obtain or appropriate the funds for a facility. It can be found within the judicial branch, where judges or their staffs are seldom involved in the planning for and implementation of renovation of new construction projects. Few people are capable of coordinating, promoting, authorizing, budgeting, and financing efforts that are so essential to the implementation of major renovation and new construction projects.

Lack of Facility Program and Standards

Associated with the lack of expertise comes a general lack of any kind of formalized program or facility standards that could provide guidance in establishing the facility needs of the judicial system. In the government environment, formalized building programs are not often seen. In the same manner, it is rare that there are facility standards that identify the inadequacy of present structures. One of the primary goals of statewide judicial facilities projects is to establish facility standards and design guidelines for statewide application.

Lack of Planning

There can also be found in the government setting a lack of planning. Each branch of government tends to maximize its own needs and tends to take only a short-term view of its future, even though the structures eventually built tend to have very long lives. It is important that planning be done in order to show the need for monies within given time periods, and also to allow decision makers (such as the county commissioners or state legislators) to absorb and embrace the concepts of comprehensive space management, funding, and financing alternatives and building life cycle cost analyses.

Lack of Continuity

Another problem in our current system of providing money for court facilities is the general lack of long-term follow-through on the part of the individuals involved. Elected officials tend to view their length of service in terms of their elected term. To plan beyond that time period may involve making decisions for someone else, who eventually may take credit for any improvements, or who may even change or void these decisions. There is also a general lack of citizens' involvement in the process of facilities planning. It is rare that a facilities committee exists, much less one that would include citizens from the community at large. The problem boils down to a situation where no one is continually responsible for judicial facilities improvement, and it usually takes a catastrophe, such as a fire or condemnation, to bring about community involvement. Continuity in project management is crucial to the successful implementation of statewide judicial facilities master plans.

Lack of Priorities

A clear-cut set of priorities on facility needs and expenditures seldom exists within the judicial system. It is difficult to set priorities for the expenditure of monies within the jurisdiction. For example, it would be difficult to determine if the county board members rate the purchase of a road grader higher than the remodeling of the courthouse. Likewise, it would be equally difficult to obtain from the judiciary the priorities on whether or not the judges would prefer a pay raise before they would submit a request for a new judicial facility. A detailed list of renovation and construction projects, arranged according to priority needs, should be an integral part of any statewide judicial facilities master plan.

Confusion between Branches of Government

A high level of confusion exists between the branches of government. If a multiuse facility is involved, the legislative branch may feel that it should be under their control, since they appropriate the monies, while the executive branch may feel that they operate the building and, therefore, should control it. The judiciary may throw up their hands in despair and add to the confusion by stating that the demands of the judiciary should be met through the use of court orders. A more clearly defined working relationship between the three branches of the government is essential to the implementation of judicial facilities projects.

Lack of Coordination

A lack of coordination exists between the courts and the support elements within the courts. Judges often feel that their main responsibility is to handle judicial business and allow the support elements to operate as best they can. There are numerous support agencies which obtain their budget directly from county commissioners rather than working through the judiciary. Clerks of court, particularly if elected, feel a level of independence that allows them to proceed with their objectives without coordination with either the judiciary or the executive branch. Greater coordination and collaboration are necessary if the courts and their support elements are to obtain the necessary funding for courthouse improvement. A master plan supported by the courts and their related departments has a much better chance of being funded than when each component develops and presents its own plan that is not coordinated with others within the court system.

Inadequate Information on Sources of Funding

In addition to confusion and lack of coordination, there is generally inadequate information on the availability of funds. Without an action plan, the source of funding for a new facility is often unknown. This is true not only of locally generated funds, but also of grant funds from various federal programs. The mechanism for either specially or statutorily authorized bond monies is often not controlled by the local government jurisdiction.

Political Conflicts

Finally, there is the ever present possibility of political conflicts between individuals within each branch or between the branches of government. Political conflicts include partisan politics, political conflicts resulting from changes in the power structure, geographic or locational factors, alterations to the informal power structure within the community, and conflicts between elected and appointed officials. These political conflicts have to be resolved, and are sometimes key factors in whether or not a judicial facility is funded and built.

Financing Techniques—Implementation and Constraints

There are at least a dozen alternatives to obtaining funds for judicial facilities, and each one has certain characteristics of implementation and certain constraints that must be recognized (see table 10.1). What follows is a discussion of each alternative, with an indication of present trends and suggestions for implementation, as well as statements on appropriate constraints that should be observed. In addition, the probability of implementation is evaluated, based upon the present state of the art of financing judicial facilities.

Direct Appropriation

Direct appropriation of funds by the state legislature or by local county and city government for capital improvement would be the most desirable funding method for constructing a new courthouse or of renovating an existing court building. However, as expenditures increase at a faster rate than revenue, direct appropriation for capital improvement projects becomes increasingly difficult to obtain. Because of competing needs of various state, county, and city departments for funds to improve all kinds of facilities, the construction or renovation of a county courthouse is usually low on the list of priorities, certainly far below capital improvement needs for roads, schools, and hospitals. The competing needs for limited available funds have resulted in intense lobbying by the various departments.

It has not been traditional for the judiciary to join in the lobbying for a larger share of the capital improvement funds, and the need for facility improvement of the court system has largely been ignored. The judiciary is frequently at the mercy of the administrative office of the executive branch, both at state and local levels, for providing necessary court facilities. To obtain adequate and suitable court facilities in which to operate efficiently and effectively, much greater effort has to be initiated by the judiciary to obtain the necessary funds for capital improvements. (The unified Alaska Court System has senior fiscal and legal staff working at the state capital while the legislature is in session. This lobbying effort has resulted in the court system receiving substantial state funds for capital improvement projects). The days when the judiciary remained aloof and remote from the other branches of government, relying on the legislative assembly to appropriate whatever funds it considered the judiciary needed, are gone in most states. There has been a much greater awareness of the need for adequate funds for carrying out the wide range of court-related programs, and also a much greater willingness on the part of the judiciary to assume a more active role than in the past in making sure that judges and court personnel are paid reasonable salaries and that the physical environment in which the court operates reaches minimum standards, at the very least.

If some federal funds are available for the implementation of judicial facility projects, state or county matching funds may still be needed, usually through direct appropriation. With few exceptions, providing adequate facilities for use by the court system is a county responsibility. It is, therefore, unlikely that the state would appropriate funds for this purpose unless the state assumes the operational and fiscal responsibility for statewide court facilities. If and when the state assumes responsibility, the possible consolidation of court facilities in fewer locations, and the more efficient allocation, assignment, and utilization of available space, would result in lower long-term capital improvement costs as well as lower annual operating and maintenance costs to the state.

Special Bond Issue for Courthouse Construction

Bond issues for courthouse construction invariably have to be approved by voters in the county or state through a public referendum. Very few special bond issue elections have been successful in obtaining voter approval over the past few years. This is primarily due to the reluctance of the voters to approve capital improvement projects that would result in increasing their property and other taxes. Another reason for the low approval rate of special bond issues for courthouse construction and improvements is that voters may be unaware of the urgency and importance of such a bond issue. Not many of the voters have had experience with the court system, and the occasions when they are involved in the judicial process, such as having to pay fines for traffic violations, usually do not leave them with favorable impressions. Such resentment, coupled with a general lack of understanding of the needs of the court system, usually has the tendency to generate negative votes.

Special bond issues for courthouse improvement and construction may have a better chance if the court system assumes a more active role in the preparation for such bond issue elections. Most voters are ill-informed about the facility needs of the court system. Efforts should be made, preferably

Table 10.1. Alternative Methods of Funding and Financing Judicial Facilities

Funding & Financing	Legislation/ Referendum Needed	Agency Involved	Personnel Involved	Constraints & Problems	Recommendations on Applicability			Remarks
					Rural	Urban	State	
Appropriations	Yes	Legislature, County board	Legislators legislative staff, governor, county board members and staff	Reductions, vetoes, competition for limited funds	Yes	Yes	Yes	Judiciary competing with other agencies for available state/county funds. Requires detailed justifications and lobbying efforts.
Public-building commission	Yes (public referendum)	Commission	Commissioners and staff	Possible lack of judicial involvement	Yes	Yes	No	Requires public referendum. Voters reluctant to give too much power to commission in capital improvement projects. Judicial involvement essential.
Capital development authority	Yes	Authority	Authority board members and staff	Possible lack of judicial involvement	No	Yes	Yes	Judicial involvement essential.
Bank credit	Depends on county authority	Legislature or county	Commissioners or authority.	Need home rule authority	Yes	Yes	No	Legality will vary

						from state to state.
State revenue sharing	Depends on legislation	Legislature, county board	Legislators, legislative staff, governor, county board members, and staff	Reductions, vetoes, competition for limited funds.	Yes	Yes	Yes	Not available in all states. Judiciary competing with other agencies for available revenue sharing funds. Requires justification and lobbying efforts.
Bond issue	Yes (public referendum)	Legislature, county board, bonding institutions	Legislators and county board members, and staff bonding agency	Voter reluctance to possible tax increase	Yes	Yes	Yes	Requires public referendum and intense lobbying by judiciary and related personnel. Public education/communication programs essential.
Borrowing from pension funds	Yes	Legislature, county board, pension fund, administration	Legislators and staff, county board members and staff pension fund administration and staff.	Statutory requirements	Yes	Yes	Yes	Cost of borrowing from pension funds usually less than from private lending

(continued)

Table 10.1—Continued

Funding & Financing	Legislation/ Referendum Needed	Agency Involved	Personnel Involved	Constraints & Problems	Recommendations on Applicability			Remarks
					Rural	Urban	State	
								institutions. Not legally permissible in all states.
Appropriating or borrowing state trust funds	Yes	Legislature, county board, trust fund administration	Legislators and staff, county board members, and staff trustees of funds	Appropriateness of trust funds for court buildings	Yes	Yes	Yes	Limitations on how trust funds could be used. Cost of borrowing from trust funds usually less than from private lending institutions.
Fees and fines collected by court	Yes	Judiciary, legislature, county board, court staff	Legislators and staff county board members and staff, court staff	Statutory requirements. May not be adequate at locations with most urgent needs.	Yes	Yes	Yes	May encounter opposition from bar association and citizens. May not provide adequate funds at locations with the most urgent need. Statewide allocation of funds.

Federal funds, grants, and requests	Depends on federal sources	Judiciary, governor's planning office, regional boards, county boards	County board members and staff, court staff, governor's planning office staff and federal office staff	Sporadic funding, long review process, limitation in use of funds	Yes	Yes	Yes	Federal grants funding usually provided on project basis. Funds for statewide use would be for statewide planning projects or for implementing statewide master plan.
Investment or surplus funds	No	County board, auditor's and treasurer's office	County board members, auditors and treasurer's office, and staff, other county offices.	Sporadic, difficult to invest sufficent funds	Yes	Yes	No	May not be adequate funds at locations where improvements are most urgently needed.
Leasing from developer or construction manager	Depends on county authority	Legislature, executive and judicial branches, county board	Legislators, executive and judicial personnel, and county board members	High-cost design problems	Yes	Yes	Yes	Short-term private leases may be beneficial while adequate facilities are designed and built. Long-term leases are very costly to the state and county.

Source: Space Management Consultants, Inc.; Illinois Statewide Judicial Facilities Project, Phase Two Summary Report, 1978

through either the court administrator's office or the judicial planning unit (if one exists), or both, to organize a statewide or countywide program of education and public relations development. Well-prepared presentations of educational materials pertinent to the special bond issue should be presented by trained volunteers to citizens and special interest groups. Judges should communicate on a regular basis with state legislators or county commissioners and other state and county officials who are usually equally ill-informed of the justice system and its needs. Meetings should be conducted with organizations such as the League of Women Voters, the Rotary Club, and the Lion's Club, to inform their members as well as to solicit their active support. The support of the news media is especially important, as favorable news reporting on the bond issue may reach and influence a wide spectrum of voters. This type of effort, if organized and carried out throughout the county or state in which special bond issue elections are conducted, could make a significant difference to the outcome of those elections.

Federal Funds

A limited amount of federal funds are available for judicial facility planning, renovation, and construction. The National Justice Institute (NJI) and other funding agencies have been providing limited funds for short-term, high-impact technical-assistance projects to all areas of court operations, including facilities planning. Such funds are used solely for brief planning studies that result in specific recommendations to solve facilities problems. These funds cannot be used for implementation, renovation, and construction purposes, which are considered to be the responsibility of the local, county, or state government. One major problem in using technical assistance funds is the intense competition for very small amounts of grant funds, which usually means that counties requiring such assistance urgently do not receive assistance at the appropriate time. Other problems include lengthy delays in processing applications and the inevitable lack of information on specific locations and problems when all fifty states compete for limited funds. Such technical-assistance projects are designed to study problems over a few days and to recommend improvements in the form of a brief report. The amount of funds allocated to each project involving space management and facility improvement is invariably inadequate for consultants to complete the necessary tasks without incurring financial loss. For these reasons, technical-assistance projects for other than the most minor facility problems in rural courthouses are not an effective means of improving short-term and long-term problems in county courthouses. Technical-assistance projects in the future should be more flexible, less encompassing, and preferably supervised and directed by individual states with adequate information on local conditions.

With the expenditure of major federal funds for a statewide judicial facilities project, resulting in the development of a statewide judicial facilities master plan with project priorities for phased implementation, perhaps more federal funds could be set aside for the implementation of the master plan. Any such funds should be used to encourage local counties to provide the necessary matching funds, so that the funds could benefit a maximum number of projects. Federal funds should be used as an incentive for local counties to commit their efforts and their funds to courthouse renovation or construction. In rural counties where local funds for such purposes are not available and where improvements are urgently needed, either the state should provide matching monies for federal funds or the county should find alternative means of funding facility improvements, including the possibility of raising the tax rate if it is well below the tax limit for that county.

Federal funds from Highway Safety, HUD, and HHS are known to have been spent on courthouse improvement in several states. Highway safety funds have been used extensively in the improvement of traffic court facilities. HUD and HHS funds have been spent on improvement of the urban environment, including the improvement of courthouses located in urban centers. In 1977, the Congress appropriated $4 billion in project funds to stimulate the national economy by providing jobs in the construction industry. Some of this money was spent on the improvement of existing court facilities as well as on the construction of new buildings. For example, a new Circuit Court Building was constructed in Salt Lake City, Utah, through the use of such funds. That project would not have been possible without such federal assistance. The renovation of the courthouse in downtown Baltimore was also completed with similar funds. It is hoped that programs to improve urban centers will include major court facilities in large cities, in which space shortage problems have become critical. Sufficient funds should be provided for their improvement, renovation, and construction.

Public-Building Authorities

Another technique for financing court facilities is the creation of public-building authorities, which are usually quasi-governmental units outside of the regular governmental setting. Experience has shown that public-building authorities are usually created when there are statutory difficulties in raising bond monies for construction or where the local elected officials are hesitant to be exposed to criticism for authorizing large construction projects. These authorities are usually independent bodies that raise their own capital through bond sales and who construct the facility and lease the structure for various uses to retire the bonds over a set time period. The use of public-building authorities seems to be directly related to the statutory limitations in a given state. The trend seems to be that more states will establish building authorities when no other reasonable alternatives to raise the funds for building construction are available.

While public-building authorities are very useful for independent handling of the financing and construction of a judicial building, they are sometimes criticized for not being directly responsible to the voters. Members of public-building authorities are usually appointed, which isolates the selection process from voter impact. Public-building authorities have, on occasion, become very independent and have proceeded with the construction of a building even though the citizens, on a previous popular vote, had voted against the construction of the same building.

A further limitation relative to the use of the public-building authority for the construction of a judicial facility is that the members of the public-building authority are appointed by the legislative or executive branch. It is rare that there is direct representation by someone from the judiciary, either a judge or court administrator, except in an advisory capacity. There is also a natural tendency for these authority members to be oriented toward the needs of either the legislative or executive branch, rather than toward the needs of the judicial branch. This lack of representation of the judiciary on a building authority is a serious constraint to the use of this method of financing construction; however, a building authority should be considered if permitted by state laws and when no other possibility is available.

With the continuation of the present system of locally financed courthouse improvement, it is likely that more public-building authorities will be created in the future. In order for this to occur, citizens would have to be educated in its concept, advantages, and impact. Citizens will have to be informed that financing courthouses does not necessarily mean an increase in taxes, since the bonds are retired through revenue derived from the leasing of these buildings.

Should the state assume the responsibility of financing the improvement, renovation, and construction of courthouses, the concept of public-building authority remains applicable, on a statewide basis, as has occurred in the state of Rhode Island. A public-building authority or the equivalent at state level would be much more effective and efficient in implementing a judicial facilities master plan, and in the overall improvement of court facilities on a statewide priority basis, than would individual counties attempting to create their own public-building authorities.

Capital Development Authorities

The state of Illinois created a capital development board in 1974 to raise monies at the state level for the construction of facilities at the local level.

Basically, this is a form of revenue sharing and utilizes the financial clout of the state to support the financially hard-pressed local units of government. One of the rationales used for creating such an authority is that economy of administration and construction is possible through centralization of the development of specification, the letting of bids, and the supervision of construction. This method of financing should be monitored closely, as there is great potential for improved efficiency by professionals overseeing all aspects of building construction. Although there might be some objection to the concept from local officials, the fact that the state provides funds would assist local officials in accepting the concept.

The Capital Development Board in Illinois was created as a central agency for the improvement and construction of all state-funded buildings. State-guaranteed bonds are issued and sold under special authority, the proceeds from which are used to construct state buildings. The buildings are owned by the state once the bonds have been retired. Interest payments on these bonds are made through state legislative appropriations.

A capital development authority may include in its responsibilities the construction of highways, schools, state buildings, and the acquisition of park lands, as well as the construction of local judicial facilities.

Some of the same constraints associated with public-building authorities apply to capital development authorities. Usually, the amount of bond monies available is very great relative to what is available at the local level. The capital development authority is under the direct control of the governor and is oriented toward achieving executive objectives. Again, it is unusual to have judicial representation on a capital development authority or on its staff. The lack of judicial representation and the primary concern with major nonjudicial construction projects make it difficult for a judicial facility to become a high-priority project.

A capital development authority would be more likely to include a judicial facility project on its schedule if judicial needs are clearly documented and estimated costs are specified at the appropriate time. Besides being directly beneficial to the community, large sums of money provided for roads and schools undoubtedly result from extensive lobbying efforts by the highway and school associations. The judiciary is usually ill-equipped, and frequently reluctant, to compete with that quality of lobbying.

Using Bank Credit for Courthouse Construction

Cook County in Illinois has home rule authority that allows it to operate very much like a private corporation. A consortium of several banks provides the county with a credit line for the construction of courthouses and other public buildings. This is equivalent to an interim construction loan at a very low interest rate based on 60 percent of prime rate. Since this is tax-free interest to the banks, the actual return to the bank for their money is also quite favorable.

When a new courthouse or renovation project is needed, the county draws on this reserve, and the work proceeds to completion. After the project is completed, the full amount of expenditure for the project, including construction costs, architectural and engineering fees, interest over the loan period, and other related costs would be accurately calculated and capitalized over the life span of the revenue bonds, which are then sold in the bond market. Proceeds from the selling of these bonds would pay off the indebtedness incurred over a specified time period. Since there is no problem in selling Cook County bonds, there is little risk to the banks providing this credit line to the county.

This is perhaps the least expensive and most efficient method of financing public-building and courthouse construction. There is no need for a public referendum, and bank credit is considered to be more efficient than and advantageous over the public-building authority method, in that the interest rate is lower; the financing terms are more flexible; planning, design, and construction are within the direct control and supervision of the county board and not through a quasi-governmental agency; and the bonds are marketed with full faith in credit of Cook County.

Use of Fees and Fines Collected by the Court

In some states, a library fee is charged local attorneys, either as a separate annual fee or as a part of the filing fee. Such a fee is generally used for the upgrading and improvement of the law library within the court system. In a large urban county, the amount of library fee per year could be substantial. A similar arrangement could be made to set aside monies for courthouse renovation or construction. Users of the facility would be required to pay a separate courthouse fee or the fee could also be a part of the filing fee. In rural counties, the amount of fee would not be substantial, and only minor renovation costs are likely to be covered. However, if federal funds are available, this fee in a rural county could be used as matching monies for a larger amount of federal funds, which might then be adequate to complete major renovation or construction. In large urban counties, the amount derived from such a courthouse fee could be substantial. If this fee could be accumulated over a number of years and if the amount is carefully invested at a reasonable rate of interest, there could be an adequate amount of funds for major renovation or construction, as well as for matching monies to obtain even a larger amount of federal funds, provided such funds are available. The Guam Judicial Complex was constructed through a federal loan which was repaid through the raising of court fees and fines, the proceeds from which are paid into a judicial building fund.

Investment of Surplus County Funds

Where there are surplus county funds, interest from these investments could be used to renovate as well as to operate and maintain the county courthouse. Unfortunately, owing to the relatively low tax rate on total assessed value of all properties in most counties, there are very few counties with surplus funds. In small counties, the investment of small amounts of surplus funds would not yield sufficient funds to cover the costs of major renovations. In large urban counties, the proper investment of large amounts of surplus funds arising from an increase in the tax rate could provide a substantial amount of interest which, if accumulated over a number of years, should provide sufficient funds for major renovation or new construction of court facilities.

Borrowing from the State Employees' Retirement Pension Fund

The state employees' retirement pension fund usually earns a relatively low rate of interest. If it is possible to borrow from such a fund at a higher rate of interest, it would be beneficial both to the fund, which would earn a higher rate of interest, and the court system, which would have a valid source of funding. The pension fund would view this as an investment with a higher rate of return. The money borrowed from this fund would be used to construct the new court building. The state court system would lease the building, or part of it, on a long-term lease agreement, which would have been executed prior to the construction of the new buildings. The lease money, which would have to be provided by the legislature, would be used to repay the loan. The benefit to the state and court system from this source of funding is that the rate of interest, while higher than what the fund would normally earn, would still be considerably lower than money from private lending institutions. The state of Alabama uses this method of financing office buildings within the state capital.

Appropriating or Borrowing from State Trust Funds

In some states, special trust funds are set up to hold money accumulated from gasoline taxes, road and bridge tolls, and so forth. The monies in these trust funds earn interest. The general assembly may appropriate monies from the road fund to improve roads and highways. Portions of the court system's annual operating budget may be derived from the road fund, the theory being that the court system handles traffic cases, which are usually generated from local roads and highways, and therefore, the road fund could be used to defray traffic court expenses. If the general assembly wishes, it could appropriate any surplus monies from these trust funds for the construction of public buildings, including courthouses. If necessary, the court system could lease the new facility at an appropriate lease rental, which would add interest monies to these funds, much in the same manner as borrowing from the pension fund. The lease money, however, has to come from the legislature in the form of general operating funds of the court system, or from county funds specially designated for this purpose. Approval for expenditure of such funds for lease payment would have to be obtained from the legislature or the county board prior to entering into a lease agreement involving buildings built from borrowed state trust funds.

Rental of Facilities by States

Some states with unified court systems have developed a procedure for providing sufficient funds for court facilities by leasing local facilities through the use of state appropriations and other sources of funding. In this manner, the state court system is responsible for local facilities. Rather than construct facilities at the local level with state funds, the court leases facilities from a local government jurisdiction. The greatest use of this concept is seen in unified court systems, and it is presumed that further development toward the state assuming the costs of unified court systems will bring about a continued trend toward the leasing of local facilities. It is important to realize, however, that leasing of court facilities is practical only on a short-term basis. Long-term leasing may become more costly than constructing a new facility owned by the state and would commit the state to leases that run beyond the term of office of the legislators who approve these leases.

When a state court system leases judicial facilities from local jurisdictions, the state court system contracts for a given amount of space in a local courthouse and makes regular lease payments. Usually, the space to be rented is identified, a price is established, and the responsibilities of both parties are set forth. Such responsibilities would include provision for building maintenance, heating and air conditioning, lighting, janitorial services, and replacement of expendable items such as carpeting.

Minimum functional and space standards are essential to ensure that the state is getting adequate space for the rent that is being paid. The standards have to be clearly documented in order to satisfy pragmatic considerations of local officials. Criteria for the assessment of fair rental value of statewide judicial facilities, based on size of facilities, frequency of use, and condition of facilities are necessary. The lease rent can include an amortization of necessary remodeling and thereby allow the distribution of the cost of improvements over a period of years. It seems reasonable that a local court jurisdiction could spread the costs of improvement over a period of ten or twenty years, thereby keeping the annual rental rate fairly low. Such a long payout period is reasonable in a governmental setting, in contrast to a private transaction, where the payoff usually occurs within a shorter time period.

While the leasing of facilities by the state is a possibility, the problem generally seems to be that a scarcity of funds at the state level for new construction corresponds with a scarcity of funds for leasing of the facilities. In terms of the financing priorities for the courts, salaries and necessary operating expenses must be accommodated first, usually leaving very little for facility improvement or construction, including leasing of additional space. However, there is an advantage to spreading out the cost of the facility over many years rather than facing a large capital expenditure, which carries with it the hesitation to spend great sums of funds on construction. What is sometimes overlooked in the political process is that the annual cost of providing a judicial facility, over the long term, is low in relation to the cost of the salaries of the judges and nonjudicial personnel. If the cost of salaries represents 60 percent of the cost of operating a judicial system, then it is estimated that the cost of the facilities, amortized over a sufficient number of years, represents a small percentage of the cost of operating the system.

Leaseback from Private Developers

A commercial counterpart of local facilities rental by the state is the procedure whereby a court system will lease back a building that has been constructed by a private developer for the specific purpose of providing judicial space. Some unified court systems have used this procedure. A problem associated with this method is that judicial facilities are usually multiuse and those agencies sharing facilities with the judiciary are hesitant to become involved with either the financial transaction or lease-back or the planning and design of the facility. When a facility is for the exclusive use of the courts, a specialized building can be constructed by a private developer to the specifications set forth by the courts.

Again, this leads to the conclusion that the judicial system must have a set of facility standards in order for the private developer to provide a building that is adequate and suitable for court use. Without these standards, it is more than likely that the developer will provide a building that maximizes rental profits and flexibility for future use of the building beyond the court's lease period. If a short-term lease is being considered, the developer will place an emphasis upon the future use of the building, and the judicial system's needs would be in conflict with the needs of the private developer.

It can be presumed that the leasing of a facility from a private developer is more expensive than renting facilities from another governmental unit. The reason for the increased cost is that the private developer is required to borrow money in the private market to finance the construction at a higher rate than a governmental unit. A private developer would expect a reasonable rate of return on his or her efforts and risks and would also plan for the structure reverting to him or her at the end of the court's lease, at which time the developer would have to incur costs to renovate the facility for possible private use. Another cost factor is that the private developer may continue to lease the building beyond the point at which the investment has been recouped, and such continuing lease payments would be costly to the court system. If a lease-purchase arrangement could be set up whereby the structure is sold to the court system for a predetermined price before the expiration of its lease, this added cost feature would be minimized. An at-risk construction management company can also provide this method of financing, together with a guaranteed maximum price for the completion of the project.

Regionalization and Consolidation

Traditionally, judicial facilities in most states have been provided at the county level. A concept that has been considered for the past two or three decades is the consolidation of judicial facilities to serve regions, each consisting of several counties. The argument is that it is economically and administratively unsound to develop facilities on a county basis when the low workload and the high annual costs cannot justify a separate facility in each county. The alternative proposed is to provide a regionalized facility that would serve a given population in several counties.

Regionalization is very slow in gaining acceptance because it is immediately attacked as taking the judicial services away from the local citizens. Most county officials jealously guard the prerogatives and responsibilities of their counties and look upon regionalization as an erosion of the county structure. The trend continues, however, and can be expected to continue as responsible county boards face the economic reality of providing sporadically used court facilities.

Often a regional facility is proposed to serve the judicial needs of the citizens of two or more counties. The regional facility would replace older and smaller court facilities in each of several counties by renovation and/or new construction at one location. Unless satellite local courtrooms are used for certain types of cases, a regional facility would involve higher traveling expenses than citizens were previously accustomed to.

The concept of system regionalization and facilities consolidation may be more acceptable if it is directly related to the court structure, such as the circuit court, which cuts across county lines. Such a trial court facility could be used to handle all major trials for the entire circuit, which would consist of several counties. The existing local county courthouses would continue to handle lesser matters and could be used to accommodate noncourt county functions.

As judicial systems become unified, there seems to be a greater preponderance of single trial courts of general jurisdiction, perhaps with divisions within them. This allows for regionalized facilities for such trial courts. Another factor favoring regionalization of judicial facilities is the trend toward state financing of court systems, with the resulting greater control of the facilities that are provided. For example, in rural states, it is unlikely that a state court system would want to finance judicial facilities in each county. In urban states, a judicial system may consider specialized buildings for certain types of cases, with satellite court facilities distributed throughout the urban area to properly serve the local court needs of the city.

Judicial Orders

The concept of the inherent power of the court implies that it is possible for a judicial system to order the remodeling of existing court facilities or construction of new facilities. A rule of court or a court order can be made by an individual judge or agreed to by a multijudge court at either the trial or appellate level. A rule of court or court order would order some governmental unit or branch of government to provide or improve judicial space.

It is probably true that a court can issue such an order. The action would be official and the document would be very impressive. It would probably create headlines in the local newspapers. The officials served with the court order would probably be in a state of shock. In spite of the publicity, the orders would, in all probability, be ignored.

The issuing of an order that involves a substantial expenditure of money by another branch of government is usually a futile process and is seldom used. There have been instances where a court has ordered that all court-generated monies be set aside for the purposes of construction, but that technique is probably a practical limit on what can be done through court orders. One problem is that a court order or rule of court is considered by the public to be arbitrary. The issuing of a court order or rule does not usually involve public hearings, and the court's action could easily be misinterpreted. If a court order was issued after public hearings, then the technique might prove to be more useful.

However, for a state judicial system to improve all court facilities, it is essential that a rule of court be created to endorse a set of statewide facility standards and design guidelines. The court would put the various jurisdictions on record that the court wanted to upgrade facilities and that they were aware of which facilities were substandard. The adoption of such standards on an official basis by the judiciary can form the basis for the development of a master plan for judicial facilities.

11

Implementation of Judicial Facility Projects

Court facility project implementation is a very complicated and frustrating experience for the court administrator, judges, and the architects and engineers involved. In general, judges and court administrators are primarily responsible for the planning and financing tasks, while the architects and engineers are responsible for the design and construction tasks within the implementation process. The client, which could be the federal, state, county, or city government, or a user agency, is responsible for the development of the facility program from which the building or building complex is designed. Perhaps the most serious impediments to successful and functional design of court facilities are the inability of the court system to articulate its facility needs to the project architect in terms that the architect can understand, and the similar inability of the architect in translating the facility program into a feasible architectural solution.

Judges are trained to judge cases and to settle disputes. Court administrators are trained to manage the court system. Their backgrounds are usually in related fields of law and/or public administration. Architects are trained as generalists with a broad knowledge of many related fields. Of necessity, they are involved in the design of many types of buildings. The design of a courthouse is but one of the many types of buildings for which an architectural firm is responsible. Unless architects are also learned in the law, which is unlikely, or unless they have been involved in lawsuits, they are unfamiliar with the judicial system and its complicated operations. Without a working knowledge of the court system, the architect is not equipped to design a functional and feasible court facility unless assistance is obtained from consultants experienced in this specialized field. The problems between the court system and the architects frequently develop as the result of participants' overstepping the bounds of their expertise and experience. Judges and court administrators may impose their personal ideas on what they perceive the courthouse to be, or architects may design a building that imposes serious constraints on the efficient operation of the court system.

To bridge this interdisciplinary communication gap, it is essential that a consultant with extensive experience in court operation or court management and space management or architecture be involved as an intermediary between the court system and the local project architectural firm. The main tasks to be performed by the consultant would be to translate the needs of the judiciary into a detailed facility program that can be readily understood by the project architect and engineers; to develop essential functional and spatial relationships, accessibility, and circulation (SRAC) diagrams that would serve as valuable design tools; to provide pertinent planning and design information that would aid the architects and engineers in the development of the architectural and engineering solutions; and to collaborate with the project architectural firm in ensuring that the requirements and intent of the facility program are fully and accurately incorporated into the design solution and contract documentation of the project.

The implementation of any court facility project requires the integration of the four major ingredients:

- adequate funding for project implementation
- cooperation between the court system and other governmental agencies involved
- management and administrative skills in managing court facility projects
- effective site selection process

Adequate Funding for Project Implementation

Methods of obtaining adequate funding have already been discussed in detail in a previous chapter on budgeting, funding, and financing of court facility projects. Phased implementation based on available funding will be discussed in more detail here.

In major construction or renovation projects, it is uncommon for the state, county, or city to appropriate, or even commit, all necessary funding for a major project involving many millions of dollars. The first 18 to 24 months of a major courthouse project are assigned to planning, programming, and design documentation phases. Contract documents for a major project may be ready for bidding purposes between 18 and 24 months from project commencement. This means that only planning and design funds are needed in the first and second budget requests to the state's legislative assembly or to the local county board. Funds for the construction of the facility would be requested during the subsequent legislative session. It is essential, however, to inform the legislative body (that is, the state assembly or county board) regarding the anticipated preliminary overall cost of the project so that legislative members would not be unprepared for a major general funding appropriation or bond issue after the planning and design phases are completed.

Construction of a major courthouse or justice complex can also be phased over a period of years when available funds are not adequate to complete the project in one phase, when renovation tasks must be phased according to the relocation schedule of existing tenants or occupants of the building, or when the project is so large and complex that separate construction contracts are awarded for various phases of construction. For example, in the renovation of a major existing courthouse, renovation work on a certain area may not be possible until another area has been renovated so that the functions housed in the first area can be relocated. This kind of renovation project may take several years to complete, and if the projects can be properly phased and scheduled over those years, a separate budget could be prepared for each legislative session once the overall project cost had been determined and the legislature has approved and committed funding over the entire renovation time period.

In major construction projects, separate construction contracts may be awarded for the foundation, superstructure, building systems and equipment, and building finishes. These contracts can also be phased over a period of time and appropriations can be obtained on an annual or biennial basis. On the other hand, if a bond issue is involved, it would be desirable to obtain the entire funding through a single bond election. Bond issues rely heavily on public opinion, which can change on a day-to-day basis. Reliance on bond issue monies to be available on an annual basis would be entirely unrealistic. For a major courthouse project, a construction management firm is sometimes used to provide a guaranteed maximum project price so that a realistic cost figure can be placed on the bond issue to be voted upon by the citizens of the state, county, or city.

Another interpretation of phased implementation is the construction of facilities in phases, in accordance with the projected needs of the court system. For example, court facilities to accommodate the short-term (five-year) needs in the first phase should be constructed over the initial two to three years. It may be projected that the growth of the court system may require substantially more facilities beyond the first phase: the construction of an addition above the existing building, or a horizontal extension of the existing building, or a separate building attached in some manner to the existing building, and other possible options. When the site is limited and the expansion of the court facilities can only be in the vertical direction, it is more economical, and certainly less disruptive to existing court operation, to construct the structural shell as part of the phase one project in order to adequately house facility needs of subsequent phases. Subsequent construction of additional floors above an existing building, even with adequate structural capacity to support the new floors, is invariably disruptive to court operations. It can create major dust and noise problems, and can be very costly, owing to new construction connections, strengthening of structural elements, replacement of mechanical services and equipment at roof level, and overtime work when heavy construction is prohibited during regular court hours.

Construction of a structural shell and unfinished space is costly from the point of view of additional construction without the space being utilized over an extended time period. This situation becomes even more unpalatable to the citizens when other county or state departments are housed in leased facilities while one or more floors of the courthouse are left incomplete and unoccupied. One method of remedying this situation is to complete the floors to house noncourt county or state functions on a temporary basis, with the understanding that they would have to be relocated to other facilities when the court system requires the use of that space. The additional cost of completing the additional floors, amortized over a period of years, should be compared to estimated savings in the cost of leases if county or state functions were housed in the courthouse over a predetermined time period. If the savings are substantial, and if the funds can be obtained to complete those additional floors, then the extra initial capital cost to the entire project can be justified. However, if the additional construction cost far exceeds the savings in lease rental, then the county or state would need to make a management decision on whether to construct the additional uncompleted floors and to justify that decision. If there is adequate horizontal expansion space on the courthouse site, then it might be preferable to construct a building to adequately accommodate the short-term needs of the court system, leaving the long-term needs to be housed in a separate building, or an addition to be connected to the existing buildings, at a later date. This concept is being used in the Pasco County Courthouses in New Port Richey and Dade City, Florida.

Another consideration in relation to the construction of additional space in the courthouse is the possibility of leasing the completed office space to private organizations such as local law firms, title search companies, and others that may have functional ties to the justice system. This could present several problems. These organizations and companies would normally lease office space from privately owned buildings near the courthouse. If they were to lease space in the courthouse, especially at a lower lease rental than that paid to private owners, a higher vacancy rate and a more competitive lease rental for office space might result, which could have a significant adverse impact on private investments in the community. There would, no doubt, be strong opposition to the construction of the additional space in the courthouse by local businesspeople, who would view this as creating unfair competition by the government against the private sector. Since the government is a proponent of a free enterprise economy, any competition created by the government would not be tolerated by the private sector. In several recent judicial complexes the public has been encouraged to patronize local restaurants and cafeterias by not providing a large separate cafeteria within the complex for public visitors. Local business concerns encourage the construction of a downtown judicial complex not solely for the prestige of having an architectural monument in the downtown area, but for the rejuvenation of the business district by bringing more people into the financial business area, and by using the court complex as a potential business generator. This was clearly demonstrated by the construction of the Garrahy Judicial Complex in a previously blighted area in downtown Providence, Rhode Island. Professional and business development has rejuvenated that area over the past twenty years since the completion of the complex.

Successful phased implementation requires that a master plan of the entire project be prepared. To maximize the benefits of limited funding, short-term recommendations must be integrated at the early phase of a long-term implementation process. For example, it would not be economical to renovate, at great expense, space for a courtroom over the short-term when the long-term recommendation is for the space to be used as offices. Since the construction and finishing costs of courtrooms are considerably higher than those of office space, it is more efficient to place courtrooms in their permanent locations than to provide courtrooms on a temporary basis. Based on minimum requirements of regular trial courtrooms, it is likely that only certain locations and spaces in the court building are suitable for permanent courtrooms. Such spaces should be assigned to permanent courtrooms, to the extent that courtrooms are needed, before their assignment to other uses.

Cooperation between the Court System and Other Governmental Branches

Cooperation between judicial and administrative personnel within the court system and between the court system and involved legislative and executive agencies has major significance in facility project implementation. This has already been discussed in chapter 9, "Intergovernmental Relationships and Their Impact on Court Facility Development." A divided or fragmented court has little chance of success in convincing an unsympathetic state legislature, county board, or city council on the facility needs of the court system. The legislative and executive branches may capitalize on the lack of unity among the judiciary to deny requests for adequate funding needed to improve existing court facilities. In one jurisdiction, a unified court rallying behind the chief justice with a single goal for improved facilities would have convinced the legislature to approve a new court building. Because several judges openly expressed their satisfaction with existing facilities and indirectly expressed their opposition to the proposed new building, the legislature decided to provide only limited short-term expansion space within a multiagency office building instead of a new court building that would have more adequately accommodated long-term expansion and the operational needs of the judiciary.

Within the court system, most judges are individuals with strong personal viewpoints; some are not team players. Traditionally, each judge has his or her own courtroom, ancillary facilities, and support staff and is used to running the court according to his or her method of operation. In many states today, this situation has not changed dramatically. Judges often do not realize or admit that budgets simply cannot afford to provide a large courtroom for each judge, especially when many courtrooms in major courthouses are underutilized. Some standards define four hours of courtroom time per day as full utilization of a trial courtroom. This assumes that the judge spends half of his or her time working in chambers. It further assumes that the four hours of courtroom time are spread out throughout the day, and that the judge should have the flexibility and convenience of using a courtroom at any time that a courtroom is needed. In most rural areas, where there is only one judge and one courtroom, the extent of courtroom use is determined by the workload of that community. If the county has a very small caseload and the judge is either part-time or is assigned part-time to other, higher-volume counties, then the courtroom is unused for a large portion of the time. In that situation, the only remedy would be to design the courtroom as a multipurpose space that could be used for other court-related or county functions when it is not being used as a courtroom. This may require that the furniture in this multipurpose courtroom be movable so that courtroom furniture, if inappropriate for other functions, can be moved aside when court is not in session. This is only feasible when the court system has designated specific court sessions throughout the year, and there are lengthy time periods that the courtroom is not needed for court use.

In major multicourtroom courthouses, many courtrooms are frequently underutilized. Courtrooms are unused for days if the regular judges occupying those courtrooms are sick, and for entire weeks if they are on leave or on vacation. At some locations, judges on leave or on vacation instruct their support staff to lock the courtroom and to make sure that other judges do not use their courtroom and ancillary facilities while they are away. These judges assume that the courtrooms assigned to them are theirs. This assumption, of course, is erroneous. Courthouses are designed to accommodate the judicial system. Judges, like everyone else in the system, are either state or county employees and temporary users of these facilities. Judges at state or local levels are appointed or elected to a specific term of office. Consequently, judges' chambers and support facilities designed to suit the specific needs of individual judges are not only undesirable and costly, but also set a precedent with serious detrimental and costly consequences for subsequent assignment and use. In one jurisdiction, judges were permitted to bring in their individual interior decorators to pick the colors and finish materials for individual chambers and support offices. The result was chaotic, with chambers and offices decorated in different materials, conflicting colors, and uncoordinated furnishings. By setting such a precedent, future judges would also demand that their offices be redecorated according to individual tastes. This will result in unnecessarily high recurring expenditure to the state, county, or city.

Courthouses and court complexes are not apartment buildings with each tenant given the flexibility to decorate his or her individual apartment. Even in apartment buildings, there are certain constraints in the treatment of hallways and drapes in order to maintain an accepted degree of design uniformity and visual consistency. Courthouses are public buildings, usually monumental in scale and design. They are designed for public use and constructed with public funds. Managers of public funds are obligated to ensure that such funds are used effectively in the construction of court facilities. Public officials, in making decisions on the allocation of public funds, have the obligation to ensure that court facilities are used in an optimal manner. In most court departments, office space is occupied on a full-time basis by court employees working regular court hours. The only spaces that are subject to scrutiny are courtrooms, judges' chambers, and ancillary facilities such as conference or witness rooms, prisoner-holding facilities, and jury deliberation rooms.

While it is important that judges have convenient access to a courtroom, not all judges need a courtroom on a full-time basis. Judges may spend full days in the courtroom trying cases. There are other days when a judge works in chambers or hears cases in other counties, and the courtroom may be left unused. An efficient scheduling system of judges' case assignment and courtroom utilization is essential for optimum courtroom utilization. Instead of creating specific courtrooms for visiting judges, these judges should be assigned regular courtrooms not being utilized by regular judges. In the state of Alaska, this assignment system resulted in two additional courtrooms, which were assigned to visiting judges, being available for the newly appointed full-time judges.

A more radical method of optimizing courtroom utilization is to remove judges' chambers from the courtrooms so that the assignment of a specific courtroom to each judge on a continuing basis is eliminated. In the Garrahy Judicial Complex in Providence, which houses the Family, District, and Workers' Compensation courts, judges' chambers are grouped together on a floor separated from the courtroom floors. This design provides the flexibility for a more effective judge and courtroom assignment system. If a judge does not require a courtroom because he or she is working in chambers or trying cases in another county, the unused courtroom would be assigned to any full-time or visiting judge for that day. This means that if several judges do not need courtrooms for a particular day (or weeks if they are on vacation or at training seminars), an entire floor of courtrooms can be closed down so that operating and maintenance costs for that floor would be minimized for that day or week. If one judge requires the use of a courtroom for a short trial during the morning, the same courtroom can be assigned to another judge for other matters in the afternoon. It is essential that the environmental and electrical systems for each courtroom or courtroom suite are individually controlled.

In addition to the advantage of improved courtroom utilization, better shared facilities such as judges' conference rooms, staff lounges, and law library can be provided, and the level of privacy and security of judges raised. All public access to private chambers and work space can be supervised and controlled at a single point by a bailiff or receptionist. All judges would have convenient access to secretarial and court administration staff. Transportation to the judges' chamber floor would be by means of private judges' and staff elevators. On the other hand, the separation of judges' chambers on a separate floor from trial courtrooms necessitates small judges' conference and/or robing rooms to be provided adjoining courtrooms for judges to confer with attorneys, witnesses, and so forth during court sessions.

Within the court system, judges are invariably the most outspoken in terms of voicing their needs. Most judges are primarily interested in the design of their courtrooms and chambers, and usually have very peripheral knowledge of or concern for the adequacy of other related facilities, such as the clerk's office, support offices, and so on. For this reason it is essential that user input in a major court facility project involve more than judges. A facility committee for the project may include representatives from the clerk's office, public defender's office, district attorneys' and attorney general's offices, adult and juvenile probation and pretrial departments, and so on. The lack of planning and design input from all user agencies to be accommodated in the courthouse is by far the most significant contributing factor to a poorly designed and nonfunctional court facility.

Cooperation between judges and other departmental personnel does not always exist. During a meeting on facilities planning, court support staff representatives are sometimes reluctant to express their views in the presence of judges. Consultants usually obtain a more reliable and perceptive assessment from key departmental personnel during subsequent meetings, without the presence of judges. This situation invariably occurs in projects involving a strongly political and vocal judge. In deference to judicial position, departmental personnel are reluctant to publicly contradict the views of the judge. The dominance of the judge at meetings on facility improvement may not be as pronounced if the representatives are heads of departments and if they had previously served on other committees with the judges. A clearer definition of roles and the development of mutual respect between members of a facility committee would reduce the tension and uncertainty among members. Once a responsibility-sharing relationship has been established among committee members, planning and design input can become a collaborative effort between these members and the consultants.

A court inspired by a coordinated effort to improve facilities usually has a much better chance of obtaining the necessary funding from the state legislature, the local board of county commissioners, or city council. When all related departments act as a single organization to lobby for urgently needed facilities, legislators, county commissioners, and city council members are more likely to lend a sympathetic ear. This is especially true when the courts, corrections, and law enforcement components of the justice system join together to present an integrated and comprehensive criminal justice plan to the state or local government for appropriate funding.

In many states, effective communication does not exist between these three components of the justice system. Each department has its own budget and deals directly with the executive and legislative branches. Since there are significant functional relationships among the three components of the system, a uniform criminal justice facilities master plan integrating the short- and long-term facility needs of the entire justice system would have significant impact on the legislative or county board assessment of funding priorities. In the state of Alaska, where a concerted effort was mounted to establish facility standards and design guidelines for statewide court, correction, and law enforcement facilities, it was the first time that representatives from all three components of the criminal justice system met around a conference table to discuss facility problems of mutual concern. A farsighted and strong administration or executive at state level, with a unified statewide court, correction, and law enforcement system, together with a collaborative effort among heads of these three criminal justice components, is essential to the development and implementation of a comprehensive statewide justice system facilities master plan. There has not been a similar plan subsequent to the completion of the justice facilities master plan for the state of Alaska.

In the state of Rhode Island, the chief justice of the state's supreme court and the state court administrator, both former prominent legislators, were instrumental in persuading the governor to activate a Public Buildings Authority, which was created by the legislative assembly in the fifties but was never activated as a means of financing public buildings without the requirement of a public referendum. Since the hope of financing the courthouse through a public referendum or legislative appropriation at the time of the project was extremely remote, the use of the Public Buildings Authority was the only realistic and feasible way of funding public buildings in Rhode Island. The state's supreme court worked very closely with the executive and legislative branches over a period of two years before the Public Buildings Authority was activated by the governor's appointment of members to the authority. Close collaboration between the court system, the Public Buildings Authority, architects, consultants, and engineers was the major ingredient of successful project implementation in the early eighties.

Conflicting Priorities within the Court System

Conflicting priorities regarding space management exist in the court system. Court administrators and county commissioners often place space management low on their priority list of goals to be accomplished. The court administrator may feel ineffective in effecting changes in an unfamiliar area and may also feel that other court management problems have higher priorities. County commissioners have space management low on their priority list mainly because construction and renovation projects are usually costly, and the commissioners are responsible for paying for such improvements. Political considerations also influence the attitude of county commissioners in allocating public funds for judicial facility improvements.

On the other hand, judges, court personnel, and users of court facilities usually have judicial space management high on their priority list of court improvement. This is because their performance and attitude can be influenced by the environment of their facilities. A comfortable interior climate, glare-free lighting, effective noise insulation and reduction, pleasant atmosphere and appearance, adequate and suitable facilities, equipment, and furniture, and effective security design and precautions contribute substantially to the well-being, productiveness, and efficiency of court personnel, and to that of visitors to the courthouse, too.

There is a clear need for neutralizing conflicts within the judicial system. Space management should not be viewed as an isolated planning problem to be solved by various parties with conflicting priorities and interests. Space management problems should be organized for comprehensive planning analysis. Possible solutions to these problems should be developed and evaluated according to the comprehensive space-use plan of the entire building. It may not be possible to implement these solutions at once; they can be implemented in phases according to available budget. The priority of their implementation would be assessed according to the urgency of need in relation to the overall goals of the judicial system.

Management and Administrative Skills

Project management and administration skills are essential to the successful design and construction of court and related facilities. The court administrator is usually the person responsible for working with consultants and the local architectural and engineering team. In the state of Alaska, the manager of material operations is responsible for the implementation of all judicial facility projects, which range in scope from fixing damaged building equipment in a small rural court facility to renovation and reorganization of departmental space and to construction of major court facilities. Working closely with the deputy administrative director responsible for fiscal affairs, and with the court system's space management consultants, the manager of material operations ensures that all facility development and improvement projects are planned in accordance with established facility standards and design guidelines, and implemented with optimum efficiency and expediency.

The combination of management and administrative skills with professional experience in judicial space management is essential to successful facility project implementation. The manager of facilities operation deals, on a daily basis, with building contractors, architects, engineers, representatives from state public-building agencies and related departments, property owners, and local county and city officials. He or she is involved in a multitude of both general and specific tasks that frequently require the technical expertise of professional consultants. At the same time, this manager receives regular requests for assistance from all court and court-related departments throughout the state, and has to assign priorities in accordance with budgetary constraints and funding availability. He or she is intimately involved in the preparation of the annual capital budget for submission to the legislature. The approval of this budget constitutes the budget for building improvement and equipment purchase for the following fiscal year. While it is the responsibility of the administrative director and his or her deputies to lobby for the capital budget at the state capitol, the manager of facilities operation is responsible for providing the necessary support information. Space management consultants retained by the court system also assist in the preparation of necessary facility and personnel analyses and recommendations.

In most states, and at local county and city levels, an in-house staff specializing in facility management is not usually available within the court system, and the court administrator frequently becomes responsible for the initiation, planning, and implementation of facility improvement projects. The degree of success achieved in these projects is largely dependent on the administrative and managerial ability and experience of the court administrator in coordinating political, professional, and financial pressures exerted by various forces, internal to as well as external from the court system. In many situations, facility improvement projects are channeled and guided by a judicial facilities planning committee, consisting of representative judges from the various courts as well as representatives from the involved departments. The ability of the court administrator acting as project initiator and coordinator for the court system, to coordinate the frequently conflicting needs expressed by various user agencies and by architects and consultants, can often mean the success or failure of the projects. Knowing the personalities within such a committee, and the attitudes of key members of the legislative and executive branches with regard to much-needed support for funding appropriation, is essential to the successful implementation of court facility projects and master plans.

Local counties and cities are controlled politically by boards of county commissioners (or supervisors) and city councils, respectively. Few judicial facilities projects have been funded by such boards and councils through confrontation between the judiciary and the executive branch. Many more projects have been completed through a spirit of harmonious cooperation and collaboration. The needs of the court can be skillfully satisfied by the court administrator, working in collaboration with consultants and with key administrative and political personnel of county or city departments and of funding agencies. As a result, the court system benefits in the form of county board and city council willingness to appropriate adequate funds for the completion of essential facility projects. By effectively utilizing consultants' expertise, the court administrator can become a skilled negotiator for the court system. Knowing the funding capability limit of indebtedness, probability of bond issue passage, and other constraints in funding possibilities is essential to successful negotiation.

Beyond the funding process, project administration becomes a crucial ingredient in project implementation. Establishing a communicative working relationship with the facility consultants hired to develop facility standards and design guidelines and to prepare the detailed facility program of projected personnel and space needs is invaluable. The administration has to be intimately involved with the necessary function and spatial relationships and with the security requirements throughout the court building. The court administrator's input is essential to the schematic design and the design development of the building, to ensure that the requirements of the court system are properly and fully incorporated. The court administrator or other designated person should be involved in the selection of the architectural firms, project or construction management companies, and building contractors for court facility projects, and should make frequent on-site inspections, preferably with consultants and architectural or engineering representatives, so as to satisfy the court system that all construction or renovation works are being completed in strict accordance with contract documents approved by the user agencies. The court administrator's office is responsible for phasing the relocation and moving in of courts and related departments, and for ensuring that they are properly settled into new or renovated space provided. These responsibilities in project administration require experience and knowledge in court management and space management integration.

Construction Management Considerations

Construction management (CM) has become an important process in project implementation. The complexities of major renovation and construction of specialized facilities such as court buildings require the careful scheduling and coordination of the numerous trades and professions involved in such projects. CM techniques, when properly applied, can result in a more efficient implementation and construction process, which is necessary if the project is to be completed within an established time period and at a predetermined budget.

CM companies have been formed in recent years to provide this specialized service to architectural firms and clients involved in major architectural projects. One of the functions performed by many of these companies is the preparation of a guaranteed maximum price (GMP) at an appropriate stage of project design documentation. This enables the client/owner to budget adequately in advance of actual construction or renovation. For a government or quasi-government agency whose source of project funding is from the selling of bonds, a GMP would enable bonds for a sufficient amount to cover the cost of the various design and construction phases of the project to be approved and sold at one time. However, a prudent approach should be followed when using CM companies to obtain this GMP. Unless the company is experienced in all phases of CM relating to court buildings, and has the appropriate in-house cost-estimating expertise to develop a realistic and coordinated project price, the company's approach might be to use potential external contractors to develop cost estimates for the numerous building components that make up the court building. At design development stage, subcontractors invariably would tend to be high on their cost estimates. This may be due to the inadequate information at such early project stage, to the subcontractors' natural instinct to protect themselves from possible cost overrun due to underestimation of costs, or to the contractor's lack of experience with the system, equipment, and/or materials used in the construction or renovation of a court building.

The cost estimates of potential subcontractors, together with the CM company's cost estimates, form the basis for the GMP. In addition to the cost estimates for the various project components, the CM company would also add its fee and, usually, a contingency sum for unforeseen project expenditure.

An incentive for CM companies to submit a high GMP is an agreement, that if the project were to be completed within the guaranteed price, the company would receive a certain predetermined percentage of the difference between the guaranteed price and the actual project price. This kind of incentive is counterproductive and is a serious disadvantage to the client/owner. By increasing the cost estimate to an unusually high guaranteed price, the CM company fully protects itself from cost overruns. Since most, if not all, projects are thus protected, the construction company would inevitably benefit from the cost savings as a result of the building being completed below the guaranteed price. This is not a true cost savings to client/owner, but greater profit to the CM company for overpricing the cost of the building in the first place. This factor should be considered in any agreement with a CM company, and such a provision should be eliminated or limited if the project is to be completed at the lowest possible cost.

While the hiring of CM companies is the responsibility of the government or quasi-government agency acting as the client or owner, it is essential that the court system and the project architects and consultants provide the necessary input in the selection of the CM company. The architectural firm should be responsible for the review and evaluation of the work sheets and cost estimates submitted by the CM company and, if necessary, either the architectural firm or the client/owner should hire an external auditor to review the worksheets and cost estimates when questions are raised regarding certain aspects of the GMP for the project.

The obsession with GMP may have a serious negative impact on project implementation. The project may have already reached the preliminary working-drawings stage when the guaranteed price is produced. If this price is considerably higher than budgeted funds, changes may have to be made to reduce the size of the building and/or to use substitute building systems, equipment, and finishes. Should the building be completed close to the original budgeted price and considerably lower than the guaranteed price, the state or county would be left with a less desirable building than the original that could have been built with the budgeted funds, and the CM company may have benefited unfairly from being paid the percentage of the difference between the actual price and the project price guaranteed. This monetary benefit to the company could be substantial if the guaranteed price was much higher than the actual cost of the completed building. On the other hand, if the court building were to be completed close to the guaranteed price, then the hiring of the CM company would have been justified. Since it is difficult to evaluate the accuracy of the GMP, the client/owner and project architects may wish to have a third party check all potential subcontractors' cost estimates if the guaranteed price submitted is unusually high or low.

The CM company can perform a variety of services that are essential to the successful and on-time completion of the courthouse project. The CM company can be hired, without risk to the CM company, to provide specific services such as value management workshops, cost estimating, schedule and budget control during construction, and a GMP for the completion of the project as early as possible in the design process. These services can be performed for a fee. In addition, the CM company would assume considerable financial risk if it were to provide or arrange for the financing of the construction of the courthouse. The government would lease the building, upon completion, at a specific amount annually that is adequate to retire the debt over a period of years, or the government could purchase the building earlier by paying a predetermined purchase price. Because of the financial risk involved, and the fee and project involved in the financing and management of the project, the overall cost of project implementation could be significantly higher than if the government had the capital funds available for the design and construction of the courthouse.

Effective Site Selection

The selection of an adequate and appropriate site for a new court building is a major step toward project implementation. Adequate size and dimensions of site are determined by the adopted facility program of the building and the site use restrictions imposed by the local zoning and building codes. Appropriateness of site is dependent on a variety of locational, political, and social factors, the interaction of which may result in the selection of a site that may or may not be appropriate for the efficient operation of the court system.

The site selected for the State Judiciary Building in Denver, Colorado, was not the site most highly recommended in the original site selection and planning study. Its selection was based primarily on the fact that half the site was already owned by the state and that the remaining properties on the site could be purchased by the state at reasonable costs. The recommended site, while more appropriate from locational and functional considerations, had a larger number of commercial property owners to be displaced and the acquisition and displacement costs would have been considerably higher to the state.

The site selected of the Garrahy Judicial Complex in Providence, Rhode Island, while not the most impressive site for the complex, was the preferred site of local business concerns. The site was primarily a large parking lot with two older buildings. The downtown business association lobbied heavily for this site and relied upon it to help generate more business and social activities in the downtown business district.

Ownership of property is an important consideration in the site selection process. For this reason, each county should develop a long-term master plan of the downtown business district, which would also include the judiciary building or complex. Since county boards are involved in accommodating the expansion needs of county departments and the court system, such a master plan would assist in determining which properties the county should purchase over a period of time in order to adequately and suitably accommodate the projected expansion needs of the county. In most instances, other appropriate properties are identified for county use. It may be advantageous for the county to proceed with negotiations to purchase the properties or to acquire them through condemnation procedures. Prime downtown locations with potential increase in value should be purchased early in order to avoid paying for inflated values at a later date.

A wrong decision on site selection may result in costly long-term expenditures and inefficient operation. What differentiates an appropriate from an inappropriate site for a court building? There are evaluation criteria that can be applied to alternative available sites in order to select the site most appropriate for courthouse construction. These criteria may include the following: functional and locational relationships; locational prominence of courthouse; effect on housing supply and private business; proximity to public transportation facilities; impact on traffic and parking; environmental and site conditions; urban design concepts; and land and project costs.

Functional and Locational Relationships

External locational relationships between related functions have a significant impact on site selection. The highest state court, usually the supreme court, generally prefers to be near the state capitol for both functional and symbolic reasons. Close working relationships between judicial budget and program staff of the governor's office, legislative committees, and members of the legislative assembly necessitate reasonably easy access between the judiciary building and the state capitol and its annexes.

Trial court buildings housing courts of general and limited jurisdictions in criminal cases should be near the county jail or city presentence detention facility. In fact, the courthouse and the jail should be close enough together that they could be connected by an overhead bridge, a tunnel, or other secure corridors. The cost of providing secure prisoner transportation between the courthouse and jail becomes prohibitively expensive once prisoners have to be transported between the jail and the courthouse by vehicle. Such recurrent costs normally escalate with time, and will become a long-term financial burden on the community.

Courthouses are usually located in the downtown area mainly because it makes them convenient to business, transportation, and professional service activities. They are conveniently accessible to attorneys, expert witnesses, potential jurors, defendants, and the general public. Because many people involved in court matters have to travel from suburban areas, it is desirable for the courthouse to be located within walking distance from major transportation terminals (bus, train, subway, etc.) and to be provided with adequate public parking on the courthouse site or on adjoining properties. One of the major complaints from court personnel in many locations is the lack of adequate parking. In view of the high cost of parking in downtown metropolitan centers, either an adequate parking structure or an efficient public transportation system should be installed to bring people expeditiously to the downtown area and to the courthouse complex.

Locational Prominence of Courthouse

The judiciary represents the coequal third branch of government, whether it be at the federal, state, county, or city level. Traditionally, the courthouse not only served as the center of judicial activities, it was also the center of community activities. The location of a new addition to an existing courthouse on the same site or the construction of a new courthouse on a remote site should involve an assessment of locational prominence of the courthouse during the site selection process. The character of the surrounding buildings and neighborhood, the visibility of the site from various approaches, the spaciousness and adequacy of the site to accommodate the projected facility needs of the court system, and the architectural quality of the existing courthouse on the same site are important site selection considerations.

The locational prominence of the state supreme court building is especially significant in view of the fact that the facility represents the judicial branch of government at the state level. To incorporate the supreme court facility within the state capitol building, in which the executive and legislative branches are also housed, is not symbolically appropriate in terms of the separation-of-powers doctrine. While construction cost would no doubt be higher, it would be preferable for each of the three branches of government to have its own building, which could be physically connected to the others by overhead bridges or underground tunnels. A large building complex with three wings representing the three separate branches would also be appropriate. However, since the growth rate of the three branches may be significantly different, a building with three wings may find one wing expanding considerably faster than the other two, resulting in a visually unbalanced building complex.

In some states, internal political and financial pressures exist to simply provide additional space within the state capitol building to house the expansion needs of the supreme court. Political jealousies among members of the three branches and the reluctance of the legislative assembly to appropriate sufficient funds for a separate supreme court building have sometimes resulted in the supreme court inheriting vacated space within the state capitol for short-term expansion. Such a short-term, piecemeal approach, if accepted by the supreme court, may have detrimental long-term impact on the functional efficiency and space adequacy of the supreme court. Beyond such practical considerations is the appearance that the financial survival of the judiciary is dependent upon the wishes and whims of the state legislature. For the judiciary to function as a coequal branch of government, in accordance with the intent of the U.S. Constitution, it should be symbolically and in fact separate and distinct from the other two branches of government. Alaska is one of only a few states where the judiciary operates fully as an independent branch of government. The location of court facilities and the specifications for the planning of court facilities are under the direct administration of the Office of the Administrative Director of the Alaska Court System. However, one would be naive to assume that there are no political compromises on what the court system receives in general and capital improvement appropriations. The administrative director and his or her deputies spend considerable time at the state capitol lobbying for their bills and the budget for the following fiscal year. Cooperation and compromise with the other branches of government are necessary for the judiciary to fund building projects that are most appropriate to their needs and objectives.

Effect on Housing Supply and Private Businesses

What exists on a potential courthouse site has a direct impact on the successful acquisition of the site and on the length of time required to acquire the site. While the governmental unit can always condemn properties it needs through the judicial process, widespread objections by residents in the neighborhood may create political and social problems that are difficult to resolve. Interest groups can make site condemnation and acquisition a tedious and costly process. Replacing existing housing with a court building is never popular, regardless of the dilapidated condition of the housing units, and should be avoided. Replacing private businesses can have a greater impact on businesses, which may have been on the property over a long period of time, and the relocation of such businesses may seriously affect the livelihood of owners and employees. Both cases, relocation of residents or businesses, would require the government's assistance in finding suitable housing and commercial site alternatives for residents and businesspeople and employees. This may become a tedious and emotional experience. Acquisition of such a site should be considered only as a final resort or when the particular site is ideally suited to the needs of the court system.

Pressures from interest groups invariably influence the location of the selected site. For example, business owners in the downtown area may prefer to have the courthouse located in a certain site, which they consider would have a beneficial impact on business growth and economic improvement of the downtown area. Over the past decade, many downtown business districts have lost considerable businesses and customers to large shopping centers developed in suburban centers, which are located nearer to residential areas and which do not usually present parking problems normally experienced in the downtown area. There have been considerable efforts in many major cities to rejuvenate the economic and financial climate of their downtown business districts. The location of a major governmental complex in the downtown area can have a favorable impact on employment and on the patronizing of downtown business establishments. The location of the courthouse in marginal neighborhoods would have some impact on improving the land use and environmental quality of the surrounding neighborhood. The placement of a justice complex, involving courts, police, and detention facilities, in such a location may have a positive influence on the reduction of certain types of crimes in that neighborhood.

On the other hand, the location of such a complex in a marginal neighborhood would require a higher level of planning and design for security, especially for employees who, because of their jobs, have to work in the complex after working hours and during weekends. Adequate and suitable employees' parking becomes an important design factor. Employees should not have to walk long distances unescorted at night from the courthouse to where their cars are parked. Judges' and other officials' parking spaces should not be identified by name.

Proximity to Public Transportation Facilities

A major site selection criterion is the walking distance between the site and public transportation system facilities. While many of the professional people and court employees drive to work, the public involved in the judicial process often has to rely on public transportation to get to and from the courthouse complex. Proximity to bus, train, and subway terminals and stations is crucial to the convenient location of the courthouse site.

A notable deficiency in all transportation terminals is a coordinated directory sign system to guide people who are not familiar with the surrounding area to the courthouse site. This is especially crucial when the terminal or station is located some distance away from the courthouse. This sign system should be coordinated with the street and traffic signs between the terminal and the courthouse, and then with the directory sign system around and within the courthouse complex. By using conspicuous logos and directional signs that can be easily identified along the route used by pedestrians requiring direction to the courthouse, as well as along highways and streets to aid drivers requiring parking space near the courthouse site, the confusion of finding out how to get to the courthouse is minimized. Directions to the courthouse and information on the most appropriate route to the transportation station closest to the courthouse can also be printed on the back of parking citations, summonses, and warrants to help offenders find their way to the courthouse.

In metropolitan centers or cities where the presentence detention facility is located some distance away from the courthouse, secure prisoner transportation between the jail and courthouse could be coordinated with and integrated into the public transportation systems of those cities. For example, in cities with an efficient train or subway system, the trains can be carefully compartmentalized so that one of the compartments can be specially designed and equipped to hold prisoners. This is feasible only if the subway trains stop at both the jail and at the courthouse, and if the stations are specially designed and equipped to handle prisoners at an appropriate level of prisoner security. The subway train compartment containing prisoners should at no time be accessible to the public at intermediate subway stations. As security risk increases with the increase in the number of intermediate subway stops, it would be essential to transport prisoners only on express trains with the minimum number of such stops. A better system would be to design a specially equipped subway train consisting of one or more compartments entirely for prisoner transportation. This train would not have any intermediate stops between the jail and the courthouse, and the time that it operates would be varied to avoid any routine schedule that could be detected. At the jail's subway station, prisoners would be brought down to the station by secure elevators remotely controlled and CCTV supervised at the central control station. There would be no access at the train platform to any other spaces. The train platform would be fully enclosed. Boarding of the subway train would involve simultaneous opening of both platform and train doors, with no opportunity for prisoner escape. The train could be remotely controlled and programmed to stop only at the platform in the courthouse location. The security procedure at the courthouse subway station would be the same as that at the jail. Prisoners would be transferred directly from the subway platform into the secure central prisoner-holding facilities from which they are transported by means of prisoner elevators to the individual holding facilities outside the judicial areas of courtrooms. After their court appearance, the procedure of returning prisoners to the jail would be reversed. The level of prisoner security, however, remains the same throughout. The operating and maintenance cost of such a system would be considerably less than the cost of vehicular transportation of prisoners, which would require considerably more security personnel.

Impact on Traffic and Parking

A major courthouse generates considerable traffic and parking requirements. The potential additional traffic created by cars brought to the courthouse site by attorneys, witnesses, jurors, defendants, court personnel, government personnel, and the general public must be considered as a significant site evaluation factor. This additional traffic may necessitate the widening of the surrounding streets, which could substantially reduce the effective width of the proposed site. The proximity and location of the site in relation to highway on-ramps and off-ramps are also important site considerations, and usually determine the approach and location of parking facilities on the site, which, in turn, has an impact on the overall design of the courthouse.

Because of high downtown land costs, parking is invariably accommodated in multilevel parking structures adjoining, below, or near the courthouse structure. Bridge connections between various levels of the parking structure and the courthouse should be determined by both functional and security considerations. In general, there should only be one bridge connection for public use at the first-floor or mezzanine-floor level. This would enable all people from the parking structure to enter at one level and pass through security screening control points located at the main public entrance level. If entry points at upper levels are needed and can be made secure by adequate personnel and/or electronic supervision, they can be provided. However, consideration should be given to the long-term escalated recurring costs normally involved in providing security control points on more than one floor. Related to this, of course, is the need for separating secured prisoner and restrictive judges' and staff circulation patterns and access points. In multilevel courthouses that handle criminal cases involving detained defendants, secure vehicular transportation and loading and unloading of prisoners usually takes place in the basement or on the ground level, separated from the public and private entrances. If the jail adjoins the courthouse, an overhead bridge connecting the jail with the courthouse at the appropriate level can be constructed for the secure transfer of prisoners. Parking for police cars and prisoner-transportation vehicles is located in the vehicular sallyports in the basement. Judges and senior court staff may have secure parking in the basement completely separated from the prisoner sallyports. Transportation to judges' chambers and offices would be via a private judges' elevator, accessible through a private staff lobby in the basement and on the main entry floor.

Secure parking should be provided for staff members who work after regular hours and during weekends so that they would not have to walk long distances outside the building to reach their cars. Parking areas must be adequately lit, handicapped accessible, and free of elements that can be used for hiding.

Environmental and Site Conditions

Existing environmental and site conditions have significant impact on placement and design of the building and on the utilization of the site. Surrounding roads and highways with high traffic volume may generate noise levels that cannot be tolerated during trials, hearings, jury deliberation, and private conferences. This environmental factor alone may dictate the location of quieter areas within the courthouse complex, such as windowless courtrooms and hearing rooms at the center of the complex, separated from high noise transmission by other rooms along the perimeter. Building orientation, physical sound barriers, site landscaping, and design of facade treatment and materials are all important considerations in reducing noise levels within the building. The natural slope of the site and the site location in relation to the transportation system would determine vehicular and pedestrian entrances on the site—for example, using the lower portion of the site for the secure prisoner entrance into a basement level while major public entrances are provided along the higher portion of the site on the first floor level.

Serious consideration should be given to the location and capacity of present utilities on and around the proposed sites. In many cities, the width of a city block is divided into two equal sections by an alley intended for delivery of goods. The alley is also where major overhead power cables are located. If the courthouse is to occupy one half of the city block, the power cables can remain along the alley. On the other hand, if it is to occupy the entire city block, or if the configuration of the building is such that it has to be built over the alley, then the power cables may have to be relocated to an underground utility tunnel. This may become a high-cost item in the project budget.

The location of the central power and utility plant determines the length of the piping and ducting to the selected courthouse site and, therefore, determines the cost of providing adequate power and utility services. When a courthouse, such as the state's supreme court building, is constructed within the state capitol complex, there is usually a central power station or substation on the state property to provide adequate services to government buildings on the capitol site and its surrounding areas. Such government buildings may also enjoy lower rates for their power supply. In addition, it is also possible that the central plant for the complex may include boiler and chiller capacity to heat and cool the new courthouse or addition. This would result in substantial savings in power and equipment costs. Being centrally located, utility services could be provided within the state capitol complex with short pipe runs, thus reducing construction and annual operating and maintenance costs.

Where such a centralized plant and services are not available, a careful analysis would have to be made of the power and utility services on the site, and the cost of providing such services.

Urban Design Concepts

One commodity that is invariably lacking in downtown centers of large metropolitan cities is adequate open space surrounding the major courthouse structure and for the design of a suitable approach to it. A courthouse, and especially the state's supreme court building, symbolically represents the judicial system. Its location and design should not be determined by the same factors that determine the location and design of an office or university building. The prominence of the site, together with the appropriate design of the courthouse, can add significantly to the urban design quality of the downtown area. Being able to see the courthouse while walking down a street, using the courthouse as a visual element in the urban context, can enhance the prominence of the building.

The approach to the courthouse can be made to convey dignity, just as approaches to airports and hospitals may convey the sense of movement and urgency, or approaches to hotels the sense of comfort and luxury. On a limited downtown site a courthouse may need to occupy the entire site in order to provide the necessary floor space, leaving no open space for a suitable approach. By raising the entrance level of the first floor several feet above the ground level, primarily to provide maximum space for basement and subbasement floors, wide steps and carefully designed ramps for handicapped people can be integrated with planting and seating areas as part of the overall approach to this main entrance to the courthouse. A person approaching the courthouse for the first time should be able to feel that he or she is about to enter an important structure that houses the justice system not only of the county or state, but also of the United States.

In many major cities, there is a trend to decentralize judicial services, relocating them to outlying areas of the city as the downtown courthouse structure becomes increasingly inadequate to accommodate the changing and growing needs of the system. This trend is expected to continue and even to accelerate. As medium-size cities grow to become metropolitan centers, the distance of travel from outlying suburbs and anticipated severe traffic problems in the downtown center are likely to influence the decision to provide regional or satellite governmental or judicial centers in outlying areas to handle cases that are minor and local in nature, such as small claims, traffic, preliminary bail hearings, violations, and minor civil disputes. All major jury trials would continue to be heard in the central downtown courthouse, where clerical and jury functions are centralized and consolidated. These regional or satellite judicial centers in outlying areas should also be carefully located in relation to the commercial and business centers within these areas. In view of the importance of the symbolic images of the court system that should be brought forth by the architectural and urban design, standardized facilities for a varying number of courtrooms and ancillary and support facilities should be developed and constructed in designated locations, either in conjunction with other governmental buildings, or in separate judicial structures. Standardized court facilities have been experimented with successfully in many states over the past quarter century.

Land and Project Costs

Ownership of a proposed courthouse site is a very important site evaluation criterion. The construction of a courthouse on state- or county-owned property could be completed one or two years ahead of a courthouse constructed on privately owned property. The ideal situation would be for the existing courthouse to be located on state- or county-owned property large enough to accommodate a new courthouse addition. In view of the need for expansion facilities in most counties throughout the country, it is surprising how inadequate most counties are in the ownership or acquisition of downtown properties adjacent to the existing courthouse and government center. If counties had the foresight years ago to acquire several city blocks of land in appropriate downtown sites for their expansion and construction needs, most would not have the difficulties today of trying to acquire and assemble small lots of land for courthouse and governmental building expansion. Acquisition through condemnation of property is a tedious and unpleasant procedure, especially when the owners do not wish to sell and the residents in surrounding areas do not want the courthouse or jail to be built in their neighborhood.

Ownership by the county or state or properties surrounding the present state capitol, governmental complex, courthouse, and county administration building should be acquired as soon as possible if such properties are privately owned. Accompanying property acquisitions by the state or county should be a master plan of the property showing the detailed recommendations on site and space utilization of the short- and long-term. This would enable the state or county to make the appropriate decisions on what to do with the property today, during the short-term and in the long-term. For example, if a portion of the property will not be needed for the next ten to fifteen years, it could be leased to a private concern for its use until it is needed by the county or state. Through this means the county or state would not be holding vacant property for that period of time with no return on its investment, and at the same time could have the flexibility to utilize the property for county and judicial expansion when the need arises.

If the state or county owns part of the property needed for the construction of a courthouse or an addition, it would be advisable for the state or county to negotiate for the purchase of the remaining part of the property, preferably without having to resort to condemnation proceedings. Once a fair market price for the property is reached though appropriate appraisals, the county or state should proceed with the purchase of the property so that the design and construction of the courthouse can proceed without unnecessary delay. In most government centers, choice downtown real estate properties invariably appreciate in value with time, so that it would be unlikely for the government to lose money in the purchase of a property needed for the construction of a courthouse complex. If there is any reduction in the purchase price of the site as a result of condemnation proceedings, the time and expenses involved in such proceedings are, in the long term, not worth the savings. Condemnation proceedings should be used only as a last resort when the price differential between the buyer and seller is too great and an agreement cannot be reached through negotiation.

Method of Applying Evaluation Criteria

In analyzing the comparative advantages and disadvantages of the various proposed judicial building sites in an integrated manner, the evaluation criteria and the comparative evaluation of sites require quantification and integration. A seven-point scale, with values ranging from 3 to −3, is used for the first step of the analysis. The values represented by the points on the scale are:

3 Very High Impact
2 High Impact
1 Medium Impact
0 No Impact

- −1   Adverse Impact
- −2   High Adverse Impact
- −3   Very High Adverse Impact

Based on the analysis of each criterion as applied to each alternative site, values are assigned according to the evaluation of significance of impact on site evaluation. This system is used primarily to provide an indication of the combined comparative significance of the alternative available sites.

By using the seven-point scale to assign relative weighted values to the various sites according to the degrees to which they satisfy each evaluation criterion, the assumption is that the relative values between all evaluation criteria are of the same weight. In other words, the same seven-point scale is assigned to the evaluation of each criterion without an assessment of the different potential value of the impact of each criterion on other criteria. To refine that analysis process, another weighted scale (five or seven points) is used to assign relative weights to each evaluation criterion. This assumes that the significance of the criterion could be stronger in the site evaluation process than other criteria. For example, the functional and locational relationships criterion could be very highly significant in the evaluation of sites and, therefore, assigned a high value number, whereas the proximity to proposed mass transit criterion could be lower in relative significance and, therefore, be assigned a lower-value number.

Having considered the relative significance of sites in relation to each evaluation criterion, and the relative significance of evaluation criteria in the site selection process, the relative values of the former are multiplied by the weighted values assigned to the corresponding evaluation criteria to yield the combined values which provide the basis for comparing one site with another.

Tables 11.1 and 11.2 show quantitative measurements of relative significance between alternative sites and between evaluation criteria and alternative sites, respectively, for the Supreme Court Building in Denver, Colorado.

Table 11.1. Quantitative Measurement of Relative Significance between Alternative Sites*

Evaluation Criteria	Site A	Site B	Site C	Site D	Site E	Site F	Site G
Functional & Locational Relationships	2	2	-2	2	2	2	3
Locational Prominence	2	2	1	2	2	2	3
Effect on Housing Supply	-3	-2	-1	0	-1	-1	0
Effect on Private Business	-2	-1	-1	-3	0	0	0
Neighborhood Impact	-2	-1	1	2	1	0	0
Proximity to Proposed Mass Transit	1	1	3	1	1	1	1
Traffic Impact	-1	-1	0	-1	-1	-1	-1
Parking Impact	1	1	-1	1	1	-2	-2
Environmental Considerations	1	1	2	-1	-1	0	2
Power & Utilities Supplies	2	2	-3	2	3	3	3
Provision of Open Space	2	1	1	2	1	-1	0
Land Costs	-2	-2	-1	-3	1	-2	0
Relocation Costs	-3	-2	-2	-3	-3	-3	-2
Renovation & Construction Costs	-3	-3	-3	-3	-3	-3	-3
Adequacy of Site/Existing Facility	3	3	2	3	1	-3	-2
Structural & Planning Constraints	3	3	2	3	1	-3	-3
Totals**	2	3	0	7	7	-11	-1

*Step 1 in analysis process: a seven-point scale with values from −3 to +3 is used to assign relative weight to the various sites according to the degree that they satisfy the evaluation criteria considered or investigated. Totals for the various sites assume equal weights between criteria.

**Assuming equal weights between criteria.

Table 11.2. Quantitative Measurement of Relative Significance between Evaluation Criteria and Alternative Sites

Evaluation Criteria	Relative Weight Assigned*	Site A	Site B	Site C	Site D	Site E	Site F	Site G
Functional & Locational Relationships	5	10	10	-10	10	10	10	15
Locational Prominence	3	6	6	3	6	6	6	9
Effect on Housing Supply	4	-12	-8	-4	0	-4	-4	0
Effect on Private Businesses	3	-6	-3	-3	-9	0	0	0
Neighborhood Impact	2	-4	-2	2	4	2	0	0
Proximity to Proposed Mass Transit	1	1	1	3	1	1	1	1
Traffic Impact	1	-1	-1	0	-1	-1	-1	-1
Parking Impact	1	1	1	-1	1	1	-2	-2
Environmental Considerations	1	1	1	2	-1	-1	0	2
Power & Utilities Supplies	3	6	6	-9	6	9	9	9
Provision of Open Space	1	2	1	1	2	1	-1	0
Urban Design Concepts	2	2	-2	4	6	4	0	0
Land Costs	3	-6	-6	-3	-9	3	-6	0
Relocation Costs	3	-9	-6	-6	-9	-9	-9	-6
Renovation & Construction Costs	3	-9	-9	-9	-9	-9	-9	-9
Adequacy of Site/Existing Facility	5	15	15	10	15	5	-15	-10
Structural & Planning Constraints	4	12	12	8	12	4	-12	-12
Totals		9	16	-12	25	22	-33	-4

* Relative Weight Assigned 1 to 5: Relative Significance = Weight x Values in Table 11.1.

Step 2 in analysis process: a five-point weighted scale is used to assign relative weight to evaluation criteria. This assumes that the significance of one criterion could be stronger in the site evaluation process than other criteria.

Step 3 in analysis process: multiply the relative weight assigned to each criterion with the corresponding relative values of the various sites. For example, the relative weight assigned to "functional and locational relationship" is 5 (Table 11.2) and the corresponding values for Site A and Site C (Table 11.1) are 2 and -2, respectively, the combined relative values of Sites A and C on Table 11.2 are 5 x 2 = 10 and 5 x -2 = -10, respectively.

12

Conclusion

In the past forty years, human beings have successfully explored and traveled in space. Space technologies have developed within a short time period through the commitment of this country to its development and the infusion of a tremendous amount of resources and funding. If a similar commitment of resources was to be made over the next quarter century, mankind would witness the development of space and underwater cities, together with tremendous technologies to make their existence and maintenance possible.

Judicial space management and judicial administration were relatively new professions to the late sixties and early seventies. The full potential development of both professions is far from being reached. Our understanding of the potential impact of technologies on judicial administration components and our knowledge of the consequences of decisions on caseflow and other management systems is still in its infancy. The county courthouse has been in existence since the late eighteenth century; its design is for the needs of a past era. Political discord and violence in the late 1960s and early 1970s emphasized the need for greater prisoner security and separation of circulation systems in court buildings. The cruciform plan of the older courthouses has been rendered ineffective and obsolete. Design improvements were made throughout the seventies and eighties in response to the changing needs of state judicial systems. Changes in judicial administration concepts, methodologies, technologies, and solutions have been experimented with and applied with varying degrees of success over the past decade. These changes have been accompanied by experimental space management design concepts applied to both minor renovation and major construction projects. Seldom in the history of our country have two entirely diverse disciplines developed so closely and in such an integral manner as judicial administration and judicial space management. However, complete integration is far from being accomplished, and even closer collaboration among the judiciary, architects, and consultants will be needed if our court facilities are to adequately and suitably accommodate the projected needs of the court system.

Technologies widely used in other government agencies and private industries for several decades have gradually been applied to selected areas of the judiciary. Automated information systems have been developed and operated in most courts. Data-processing systems are widely used for numerous court applications such as calendar control, caseload statistics, case tracking, jury selection and impaneling, statistical analysis, transcription, communications, and security. Systems and equipment have become indispensable components of all court facility planning and design. Technology in the court must achieve parity with that in private industry. To accommodate rapidly changing technologies, court buildings may need to achieve the same flexibility as office buildings, including large open spaces that can be subdivided according to functional and spatial relationships established for the court system at any point in time.

While it is almost certain that court buildings of the twenty-first century will continue to have courtrooms for trials, new methods of settling disputes may require a larger number of hearing rooms and conference rooms that can be easily accommodated within regular office space. Mechanical, electrical, and plumbing ducts and pipes will have to be carefully located within certain areas of the building to enable the greater ceiling heights necessary for judicial areas of trial courtrooms. To accommodate these courtrooms, certain floors will have greater floor-to-ceiling height than others. New methods of construction and assembly in the future will see the development of a system of adding floors to existing buildings without the tremendous noise, vibration, and dirt problems that presently plague such projects. When this occurs, court buildings will only need to be large enough to accommodate the short-term needs of the judicial system. Long-term facility needs would be provided by adding extra floors on an as-needed basis. This would reduce the amount of capital expenditure presently allocated to construct building shells of floors that can be finished when needed by the judiciary. If state or county departments could be housed in finished additional office floors on a temporary basis until the space is needed by the judiciary, then the present approach of constructing more floors than are needed in the short-term will remain valid for many years to come.

Over the next several decades, new methods of controlling case assignment or docket will have been fully tested in all types of courts, and the method most suited to the type of court operation and administration in any state will have been established. It is predictable that more court buildings will be designed with judges' chambers and support offices separated from trial courtrooms so that judges are assigned to courtrooms on the basis of type of case, with the spatial and environmental requirements for the most appropriate disposition of that case. The energy shortage experiences and the limitations thus imposed on all citizens will no doubt condition them to maximize the utilization of available energy resources, and encourage them to conserve energy in governmental and privately owned buildings alike. Assignment of judges to available courtrooms will enable all courtrooms on one floor to be utilized before courtrooms on another floor are assigned. Energy will be used only on fully utilized floors, and energy for floors or parts of floors that are not being used can be switched off. Long-term savings in annual operating and maintenance costs will be realized.

Beyond energy conservation considerations, the groupings of judges' chambers and support offices away from courtrooms present many advantages, among which are the potential of sharing an adequate law library, conference rooms, secretarial and clerical facilities, storage and duplicating equipment spaces, and staff amenities; a higher level of privacy and security; and an opportunity for judges to meet on a more frequent basis if desired. In multilevel courts and courtroom floors, it is possible for judges' chambers and support facilities to be sandwiched between every two floors of courtrooms and ancillary facilities. This would provide the same advantages but would also allow judges' chambers to be near the courtrooms, thus reducing travel time for judges between their chambers and the courtrooms to which they are assigned.

With the trend toward conservative budgeting and financing systems in the foreseeable future, it is likely that judges may need to share courtrooms. This is feasible only if courtrooms and ancillary facilities such as jury deliberation rooms are grouped and separated from courtrooms by a private circulation corridor, if the specific court operation allows any judge to be assigned to any one of a number of available trial courtrooms, and if judges are assigned to specialized court departments. For example, an administrative judge in a very busy court may not have a trial docket, but would be able to use an available courtroom for calendar call and a hearing room for uncontested procedural and administrative matters. Judges or referees in juvenile and probate courts are likely to be assigned to hearing rooms; however, contested hearings or trials may require the use of a courtroom.

The difference in construction costs for a hearing room or nonjury courtroom and a jury courtroom may be significant in the total capital budget for the project. It is essential for state legislators and county commissioners to note, however, that the additional cost of construction, when amortized over the life span of the building, is minute compared to recurring program or personnel costs, which escalate with time. The creation of a judgeship by the state legislature is equivalent to a minimum annual expenditure of $500,000 to $700,000, including salaries and fringe benefits for support staff, operating and travel costs, and the amortization, operation, and maintenance costs of facilities needed by the new judge. Capital expenditures for facilities are one-time costs that can be amortized at a fraction of the total cost over a period of thirty to forty years. Personnel and operating costs are recurring expenses that invariably increase each year. Consequently, it is more critical for legislators and county commissioners to understand and evaluate the financial obligation and impact of creating new judgeships against the cost of providing adequate and suitable facilities at high initial construction costs.

The coming years will see more efficient space utilization in court buildings. Austere budgets will require that all available space be optimally utilized by all court and court-related personnel. Jury assembly spaces will be designed to accommodate the average number of jurors called regularly to serve on jury duty, but part of this space can be subdivided and used for hearings and meetings once jury panels have been escorted to trial courtrooms. Another possibility is to use two rooms to orient potential jurors. One of these rooms can subsequently be used for hearings and meetings while the other remains the jury assembly room.

Imaging and other electronic storage of older court records and the adoption of records retention and destruction schedules will also reduce the amount of inactive court records storage needed, as most inactive records will be either destroyed or relocated to archival storage spaces, while records with historical significance can be moved to historical societies or university libraries. Anticipated increases in technological, communications, and data-processing applications will inevitably demand significant increases in the capacity of power supply and in the flexibility of distribution. To operate and maintain these new applications, more technical and operational personnel knowledgeable in sophisticated and complex computer, data-processing, closed-circuit television, teleconferences, real-time reporting, video technologies, security and communication systems and equipment will be employed by the court system. The facility requirements for this new breed of personnel will be different from the present administrative, secretarial, and clerical personnel.

Despite the inherent power doctrine, closer cooperation and collaboration among the judiciary, legislative, and executive branches of government must occur in the future. The realization that confrontation between governmental agencies usually does not accomplish the desired result, but that cooperation and collaboration does, will bring agency personnel into a closer working relationship with each other in order to achieve the goal of providing more adequate and suitable facilities for the court system, as well as for other state and county departments.

With the increases in county population and the expansion of the boundaries of metropolitan centers beyond business centers, branch or satellite court locations are likely to be created in order to relieve the congestion of downtown court facilities and, at the same time, bring justice closer to the people in the community where the case was generated. Regionalization of court systems and consolidation of judicial facilities, with major trial centers and branch locations to handle local cases, will be experimented with over the next decade; counties facing serious financial difficulties may be forced to share centralized trial court facilities in order to effect some personnel and operational cost savings. These cost savings, however, will be achieved only at the expense of greater costs to the trial participants (attorneys, jurors, witnesses, etc.,) and of even greater social costs (such as loss in symbolic importance of the local courthouse, convenience to local trial and prisoner-holding facilities, and loss of a certain degree of control by the county) to the community.

In spite of predictable advances in judicial administration and space management, political, social, and human relationship problems will continue to plague project implementation. Experience gained from project planning, design, and implementation over the past decades should lead to better cooperation and collaboration between the judiciary and the legislative and executive branches of government. Bridging existing communication gaps between the three branches will result in a better understanding of each other's facility needs. More comprehensive planning of legislative, executive, and judicial facilities will be the trend of the future. Conflicting needs will be resolved more frequently through objective assessment of all the facility needs of the state and the local government. Appropriation, funding, and financing of project implementation will more likely be based on a phased implementation program, developed in accordance with anticipated long-term budget and projected available funds. Implementation of major court facility projects will increase in complexity. Decisions on project implementation will continue to be based on political and social considerations. Interest groups will continue to lobby for or against project proposals, and many eminently worthwhile projects will be abandoned as a result of the judiciary's inability or reluctance to get involved in the political process of obtaining appropriate approvals and adequate funds. Subjective opinions and personal expenditures against the judiciary by decision-making individuals or organization will continue to delay or halt important capital improvement projects of the judiciary. An active and aggressive court will be needed to overcome many of the political and social impediments to successful project implementation.

F. Michael Wong, Ph.D., is recognized nationally as one of the preeminent researchers and consulting architects on judicial facilities projects. He was instrumental in the publication of *The American Courthouse* (1973) and *Space Management and the Courts—Design Handbook* (1973), and the revision of the *U.S. Courts Design Guide* (1991). His firm, Space Management Consultants, Inc., has successfully completed more than 320 judicial facilities projects in 43 states and several foreign countries. Dr. Wong was recently conferred the 2000 National AIA Institute Honor Award for Collaborative Achievement, and the AIA California Council's 2000 Honor Award for Research and Technology. He may be reached via e-mail at: smc.michaelwong@prodigy.net.

www.ingramcontent.com/pod-product-compliance
Lightning Source LLC
Chambersburg PA
CBHW021333230426
43666CB00006B/283